Automated Machine Learning in Action

Automated Machine Learning in Action

QINGQUAN SONG
HAIFENG JIN
XIA HU

MANNING

SHELTER ISLAND

For online information and ordering of this and other Manning books, please visit
www.manning.com. The publisher offers discounts on this book when ordered in quantity.
For more information, please contact

    Special Sales Department
    Manning Publications Co.
    20 Baldwin Road
    PO Box 761
    Shelter Island, NY 11964
    Email: orders@manning.com

Manning Publications Co.
20 Baldwin Road
PO Box 761
Shelter Island, NY 11964

Development editor: Toni Arritola
Technical development editor: Kostas Passadis
Review editor: Aleksandar Dragosavljević
Production editor: Andy Marinkovich
Copy editor: Pamela Hunt
Proofreader: Keri Hales
Technical proofreaders: Karsten Strøbaek, Ninoslav Čerkez
Typesetter: Dennis Dalinnik
Cover designer: Marija Tudor

ISBN: 9781617298059
Printed and bound by CPI Group (UK) Ltd, Croydon, CR0 4YY

brief contents

PART 1 FUNDAMENTALS OF AUTOML 1

    1 ▪ From machine learning to automated
        machine learning 3

    2 ▪ The end-to-end pipeline of an ML project 17

    3 ▪ Deep learning in a nutshell 41

PART 2 AUTOML IN PRACTICE...71

    4 ▪ Automated generation of end-to-end ML solutions 73

    5 ▪ Customizing the search space by creating
        AutoML pipelines 99

    6 ▪ AutoML with a fully customized search space 138

PART 3 ADVANCED TOPICS IN AUTOML 185

    7 ▪ Customizing the search method of AutoML 187

    8 ▪ Scaling up AutoML 223

    9 ▪ Wrapping up 249

contents

preface xiii
acknowledgments xv
about this book xvii
about the authors xx
about the cover illustration xxii

PART 1 FUNDAMENTALS OF AUTOML 1

1 *From machine learning to automated machine learning* 3

1.1 A glimpse of automated machine learning 4

1.2 Getting started with machine learning 6

*What is machine learning? 6 ▪ The machine learning process 7
Hyperparameter tuning 9 ▪ The obstacles to applying machine
learning 11*

1.3 AutoML: The automation of automation 12

*Three key components of AutoML 12 ▪ Are we able to achieve full
automation? 15*

2 *The end-to-end pipeline of an ML project* 17

2.1 An overview of the end-to-end pipeline 18

2.2 Framing the problem and assembling the dataset 19

2.3   Data preprocessing   22

2.4   Feature engineering   25

2.5   ML algorithm selection   28

   Building the linear regression model   29 ▪ Building the decision tree model   31

2.6   Fine-tuning the ML model: Introduction to grid search   34

3   *Deep learning in a nutshell*   *41*

3.1   What is deep learning?   42

3.2   TensorFlow and Keras   43

3.3   California housing price prediction with a multilayer perceptron   43

   Assembling and preparing the data   44 ▪ Building up the multilayer perceptron   45 ▪ Training and testing the neural network   49 ▪ Tuning the number of epochs   52

3.4   Classifying handwritten digits with convolutional neural networks   55

   Assembling and preparing the dataset   55 ▪ Addressing the problem with an MLP   57 ▪ Addressing the problem with a CNN   59

3.5   IMDB review classification with recurrent neural networks   64

   Preparing the data   65 ▪ Building up the RNN   67 Training and validating the RNN   69

PART 2   AUTOML IN PRACTICE..................................71

4   *Automated generation of end-to-end ML solutions*   *73*

4.1   Preparing the AutoML toolkit: AutoKeras   73

4.2   Automated image classification   76

   Attacking the problem with five lines of code   76 ▪ Dealing with different data formats   80 ▪ Configuring the tuning process   81

4.3   End-to-end AutoML solutions for four supervised learning problems   83

   Text classification with the 20 newsgroups dataset   83 ▪ Structured data classification with the Titanic dataset   85 ▪ Structured data regression with the California housing dataset   88 ▪ Multilabel image classification   89

4.4 Addressing tasks with multiple inputs or outputs 91

Automated image classification with the AutoKeras IO API 91
Automated multi-input learning 93 ▪ Automated multi-output
learning 94

5 Customizing the search space by creating AutoML pipelines 99

5.1 Working with sequential AutoML pipelines 100

5.2 Creating a sequential AutoML pipeline for automated
hyperparameter tuning 102

Tuning MLPs for structured data regression 103 ▪ Tuning CNNs
for image classification 109

5.3 Automated pipeline search with hyperblocks 111

Automated model selection for image classification 112
Automated selection of image preprocessing methods 117

5.4 Designing a graph-structured AutoML pipeline 121

5.5 Designing custom AutoML blocks 125

Tuning MLPs with a custom MLP block 125 ▪ Designing a
hyperblock for model selection 132

6 AutoML with a fully customized search space 138

6.1 Customizing the search space in a layerwise fashion 139

Tuning an MLP for regression with KerasTuner 139 ▪ Tuning
an autoencoder model for unsupervised learning 147

6.2 Tuning the autoencoder model 151

6.3 Tuning shallow models with different search
methods 154

Selecting and tuning shallow models 154 ▪ Tuning a shallow
model pipeline 157 ▪ Trying out different search methods 158
Automated feature engineering 159

6.4 Controlling the AutoML process by customizing
tuners 169

Creating a tuner for tuning scikit-learn models 170 ▪ Creating a
tuner for tuning Keras models 174 ▪ Jointly tuning and selection
among deep learning and shallow models 176 ▪ Hyperparameter
tuning beyond Keras and scikit-learn models 179

PART 3 ADVANCED TOPICS IN AUTOML 185

7 *Customizing the search method of AutoML* *187*

   7.1 Sequential search methods 188

   7.2 Getting started with a random search method 189

   7.3 Customizing a Bayesian optimization search method 193

      Vectorizing the hyperparameters 194 ▪ Updating the surrogate function based on historical model evaluations 198 ▪ Designing the acquisition function 201 ▪ Sampling the new hyperparameters via the acquisition function 204 ▪ Tuning the GBDT model with the Bayesian optimization method 206 ▪ Resuming the search process and recovering the search method 208

   7.4 Customizing an evolutionary search method 210

      Selection strategies in the evolutionary search method 210 ▪ The aging evolutionary search method 212 ▪ Implementing a simple mutation operation 215 ▪ Evaluating the aging evolutionary search method 219

8 *Scaling up AutoML* *223*

   8.1 Handling large-scale datasets 224

      Loading an image-classification dataset 225 ▪ Splitting the loaded dataset 226 ▪ Loading a text-classification dataset 229 Handling large datasets in general 231

   8.2 Parallelization on multiple GPUs 234

      Data parallelism 236 ▪ Model parallelism 237 ▪ Parallel tuning 238

   8.3 Search speedup strategies 240

      Model scheduling with Hyperband 241 ▪ Faster convergence with pretrained weights in the search space 244 ▪ Warm-starting the search space 247

9 *Wrapping up* *249*

   9.1 Key concepts in review 250

      The AutoML process and its key components 250 ▪ The machine learning pipeline 251 ▪ The taxonomy of AutoML 252 Applications of AutoML 252 ▪ Automated deep learning with AutoKeras 253 ▪ Fully personalized AutoML with KerasTuner 255 ▪ Implementing search techniques 257 Scaling up the AutoML process 258

9.2   AutoML tools and platforms   259

Open source AutoML tools   259 ▪ *Commercial AutoML platforms   261*

9.3   The challenges and future of AutoML   262

Measuring the performance of AutoML   262 ▪ *Resource complexity   263* ▪ *Interpretability and transparency   263 Reproducibility and robustness   263* ▪ *Generalizability and transferability   264* ▪ *Democratization and productionization   264*

9.4   Staying up-to-date in a fast-moving field   264

appendix A   Setting up an environment for running code   266
appendix B   Three examples: Classification of image, text, and tabular data   278

index   305

preface

The goal of automated machine learning (AutoML) is to make machine learning (ML) accessible to everyone, including physicians, civil engineers, material scientists, and small business owners, as well as statisticians and computer scientists. This long-term vision is very similar to that of Microsoft Office—enabling normal users to easily create documents and prepare reports—and cameras in smartphones, facilitating convenient photos taken from anywhere at any time. Although the ML community has devoted a lot of R&D efforts to pursuing this goal, through our collaboration with domain experts and data scientists, we determined that there is a high demand to reveal the magic behind AutoML, including fundamental concepts, algorithms, and tools.

To begin, we would like to share several steps that got us here. (Okay, now you can skip to our main content if you want, but hey, who doesn't like a good story?)

We started our data science and ML journey many years ago and have been researching and developing ML algorithms and systems from scratch ever since. In the early days, we were tortured, like many of you, by complicated equations, unstable results, and hard-to-understand combinations of hyperparameters. Later, more and more advanced algorithms were developed, and open source implementations became available. Unfortunately, training an effective machine learning/deep learning model is still very much like alchemy, and it takes years of training to become a capable alchemist . . . yes, we are certified alchemists.

Over the years, we were approached by many domain experts who wanted to try out the magical tool called machine learning because of its premier performance on many tasks (or simply because everyone was talking about it). Not surprisingly, it worked well on many datasets and improved traditional rule-based or heuristic-based methods. After working with many people with similar tasks again and again (classification, clustering, and prediction), we were not only tired of applying ML tools but also felt strongly that we could do something to democratize ML for all. AutoML, here we go!

Since then, we have worked on a project called Data-Driven Discovery of Models (D3M), supported by DARPA, and initiated the open source project, AutoKeras. We were happy to see many people interested in our developed software, and they provided copious positive and harsh feedback on the tools we developed. At the same time, we got the chance to know and collaborate with great researchers and engineers working on similar problems. Everything was going in the right direction!

Our vision evolved as we worked with more and more data scientists and ML engineers. Initially, we wanted to just help people quickly make use of ML with a few lines of code, but we gradually realized, as we were facing too many downstream tasks and problems, that we had a long way to go to achieve this goal. What was most urgent was that many practitioners were working on their own AutoML systems, which could run well with their own internal, small-scale problems, such as automated outlier detection, automated recommender systems, and automated feature engineering. Our goal then became making ML accessible to everyone. Oops! This seemed to be the same as our original plan! To better achieve the goal, we decided to spend a big chunk of our time writing this book to help you make better use of, and easily develop, AutoML tools.

We hope you enjoy the book and look forward to your feedback!

acknowledgments

We would like to thank everyone who helped us while we wrote this book, without whom it would not have been possible. The first person on this list is François Chollet. He not only provided valuable guidance and feedback on the content of our book, but also made major contributions to the design and implementation of KerasTuner and AutoKeras, which made these libraries so delightful to use. We also really appreciate his amazing work with Keras, which laid a solid foundation for the hyperparameter tuning and AutoML work to build upon.

Thank you to all the open source contributors to KerasTuner and AutoKeras who provided valuable feedback, and even code contributions, to these open source libraries. Although we have not met all of you, your code became an indispensable part of this large ecosystem, which has helped thousands (or maybe even millions) of people.

We send a heartfelt thank you to our lab mates from DATA Lab at Texas A&M University, who helped us during the writing of this book. We are especially grateful for Yi-Wei Chen, who helped us write the examples in chapter 9, which made this book even better.

To all the reviewers: Alain Couniot, Amaresh Rajasekharan, Andrei Paleyes, David Cronkite, Dewayne Cushman, Didier Garcia, Dimitris Polychronopoulos, Dipkumar Patel, Gaurav Kumar Leekha, Harsh Raval, Howard Bandy, Ignacio Ruiz, Ioannis Atsonios, Lucian Mircea Sasu, Manish Jain, Marco Carnini, Nick Vazquez, Omar El Malak, Pablo Roccatagliata, Richard Tobias, Richard Vaughan, Romit Singhai, Satej Kumar Sahu, Sean Settle, Sergio Govoni, Sheik Uduman Ali M, Shreesha Jagadeesh, Stanley Anozie, Steve D Sussman, Thomas Joseph Heiman, Venkatesh Rajagopal,

Viton Vitanis, Vivek Krishnan, Walter Alexander Mata López, Xiangbo Mao, and Zachery Beyel, your careful reviews and suggestions gave us the incentive to keep polishing the book.

Finally, this book would not be possible without the amazing people at Manning Publications. We send our special thanks to our editors, Toni Arritola and Rachel Head, who provided valuable comments and worked diligently in revising our manuscripts. They made the book so smooth to read and taught us how to write a good book. We also would like to thank Paul Wells, Andy Marinkovich, and Keri Hales on the production staff and our technical proofreaders, Karsten Strøbaek and Ninoslav Čerkez. This book could not have been written without you.

about this book

Automated Machine Learning in Action was written to help you learn the basic concepts of AutoML and adopt AutoML techniques to address machine learning tasks and improve the machine learning pipeline in practice, with the help of advanced AutoML toolkits such as AutoKeras and KerasTuner. It begins by focusing on the elements of AutoML and its connection with machine learning, then gradually leads you to the intangibles of working with AutoML problems—from those that require the least experience with machine learning to the ones that allow the most flexible customization.

Who should read this book

The book aims at providing systematic guidance for learning, using, and designing handy AutoML pipelines to students, instructors, practitioners, and researchers who want to learn AutoML basics and adopt AutoML techniques. It's our intention to avoid onerous mathematical formulations and notations and instead introduce the AutoML concepts and techniques with specific usage examples and code design snippets from both users' and developers' perspectives.

How this book is organized: A road map

The book has three main sections that cover nine chapters. Part 1 introduces the core concepts and some popular models of machine learning to help readers understand the basic machine learning building blocks and gain the knowledge for learning AutoML. Readers who do not have much experience solving ML problems should be sure to read this part of the book so that they can be prepared for learning AutoML.

- Chapter 1 introduces the definition, core ideas, and concepts of automated machine learning.
- Chapter 2 walks through several concrete examples of solving an ML problem to help you understand the machine learning building blocks and gain the knowledge for learning AutoML.
- Chapter 3 presents the basic building blocks of deep learning and serves as a stepping-stone to help you better understand the AutoML methods for generating and tuning deep learning methods, introduced in the second part of the book.

Part 2 explains the ways to adopt AutoML to address ML problems and improve ML solutions in practice.

- Chapter 4 teaches you how to use AutoML to create an end-to-end deep learning solution specifically for supervised learning problems.
- Chapter 5 discusses how to customize the AutoML search space based on your requirements and automatically discover certain kinds of deep learning solutions for different types of tasks.
- Chapter 6 goes deep into the customization of the AutoML search space. A layerwise design gives you more flexibility for tuning unsupervised learning models and optimizing algorithms.

Part 3 explores some advanced AutoML design and setup from the perspectives of search methods and acceleration strategies.

- Chapter 7 discusses how to implement a sequential search method for exploring the AutoML search space.
- Chapter 8 introduces various techniques to accelerate the search process with limited computing resources.
- Chapter 9 reviews the core concepts we've covered and provides you with a short list of resources and strategies for expanding your AutoML horizons and staying up to date with the state of the art.

About the code

This book contains many examples of source code both in numbered listings and in line with normal text. In both cases, source code is formatted in a `fixed-width font` `like this` to separate it from ordinary text. Sometimes code is also **in bold** to highlight code that has changed from previous steps in the chapter, such as when a new feature adds to an existing line of code.

In many cases, the original source code has been reformatted; we've added line breaks and reworked indentation to accommodate the available page space in the book. In rare cases, even this was not enough, and listings include line-continuation markers (➠). Additionally, comments in the source code have often been removed from the listings when the code is described in the text. Code annotations accompany many of the listings, highlighting important concepts.

You can get executable snippets of code from the liveBook (online) version of this book at https://livebook.manning.com/book/automated-machine-learning-in-action. The complete code for the examples in the book is available for download from the Manning website at http://mng.bz/y48p.

As the technologies and the open source libraries used in this book continue to develop and evolve, the source code examples in this book are subject to changes in the future. Please refer to our GitHub repository (http://mng.bz/M2ZQ) as the latest source of truth for the code examples.

liveBook discussion forum

Purchase of *Automated Machine Learning in Action* includes free access to liveBook, Manning's online reading platform. Using liveBook's exclusive discussion features, you can attach comments to the book globally or to specific sections or paragraphs. It's a snap to make notes for yourself, ask and answer technical questions, and receive help from the author and other users. To access the forum, go to https://livebook .manning.com/book/automated-machine-learning-in-action/discussion. You can also learn more about Manning's forums and the rules of conduct at https://livebook .manning.com/discussion.

Manning's commitment to our readers is to provide a venue where a meaningful dialogue between individual readers and between readers and the author can take place. It is not a commitment to any specific amount of participation on the part of the author, whose contribution to the forum remains voluntary (and unpaid). We suggest you try asking the author some challenging questions lest their interest stray! The forum and the archives of previous discussions will be accessible from the publisher's website as long as the book is in print.

Other online resources

Check out these resources for additional help on the topics covered in this book:

- The GitHub page (http://mng.bz/aDEj) provides a great place to submit issues or provide comments related to our books.
- The GitHub discussion of AutoKeras (http://mng.bz/g4ve) is also a great place to both ask questions and help others. Helping someone else is a great way to learn!

about the authors

DR. QINGQUAN SONG is a machine learning and relevance engineer in the AI Foundation team at LinkedIn. He received his PhD in computer science from Texas A&M University. His research interests are automated machine learning, dynamic data analysis, tensor decomposition, and their applications in recommender systems and social networks. He is one of the authors of AutoKeras. His papers have been published at major data mining and machine learning venues, including KDD, NeurIPS, Transactions on Knowledge Discovery from Data (TKDD), and others.

DR. HAIFENG JIN is a software engineer on the Keras team at Google. He is the creator of AutoKeras and the project lead of KerasTuner. He is also a contributor to Keras and TensorFlow. He received his PhD in computer science from Texas A&M University. His research interests focus on machine learning and AutoML.

DR. XIA "BEN" HU is an associate professor at Rice University in the department of computer science. Dr. Hu has published more than 100 papers in several major academic venues, including NeurIPS, ICLR, KDD, WWW, IJCAI, and AAAI. An open source package developed by his group, namely AutoKeras, has become the most-used automated deep learning system on GitHub (with over 8,000 stars and 1,000 forks). Also, his work on deep collaborative filtering, anomaly detection, and knowledge graphs has been included in the TensorFlow package, Apple production system, and Bing production system, respectively. His papers have received several Best Paper (Candidate) awards from venues such as WWW, WSDM, and ICDM. He is the recipient of an NSF CAREER Award and the ACM SIGKDD Rising Star Award. His work has been cited more than 10,000 times with an h-index of 43. He was the conference general co-chair for WSDM 2020.

about the cover illustration

The figure on the cover of *Automated Machine Learning in Action* is "Homme de l' Aragon," or man from Aragon, taken from a book by Jacques Grasset de Saint-Sauveur, published in 1797. Each illustration is finely drawn and colored by hand.

In those days, it was easy to identify where people lived and what their trade or station in life was just by their dress. Manning celebrates the inventiveness and initiative of today's computer business with book covers based on the rich diversity of regional culture centuries ago, brought back to life by pictures from collections such as this one.

Part 1

Fundamentals of AutoML

The first three chapters of the book provide you an introduction of some basic concepts and models of machine learning to help you understand the basic machine learning building blocks and lay the groundwork for learning AutoML. You'll start to get a glimpse of AutoML, its concepts, and its connection with general machine learning in chapter 1. You'll learn the research value and practical benefits of AutoML. Chapter 2 introduces the classic machine learning pipeline for addressing a machine learning problem. Considering the popularity of deep learning models in the AI community and beyond, in chapter 3, we cover the basic knowledge of deep learning with the examples of three popular types of models. We do not touch the complicated deep learning concepts but just introduce the basic building blocks and three classical models applied on different data formats. If you don't have much experience with machine learning, deep learning, and how to apply them with Python, you should definitely begin by reading part 1 in full before moving on to the practical applications of AutoML in part 2. You can also find additional examples in appendix B to become more familiar with the basic machine learning pipeline after reading this part of the book.

From machine learning to automated machine learning

Artificial intelligence (AI), which reaches into many aspects of everyday life, has been extensively explored in recent years. It attempts to use computational devices to automate tasks by allowing them to perceive the environment as humans do. As a branch of AI, *machine learning* (ML) enables a computer to perform a task through self-exploration of data. It allows the computer to learn, so it can do things that go beyond what we know how to order it to do. But the barriers to entry are high: the cost of learning the techniques involved and accumulating the necessary experience with applications means practitioners without much expertise cannot easily use ML. Taking ML techniques from their ivory tower and making them accessible to more people is becoming a key focus of research and industry. Toward this end, *automated machine learning* (AutoML) has emerged as a prevailing research field. Its aim is to simulate how human experts solve ML problems and discover the optimal ML solutions for a given problem automatically, thereby granting practitioners without extensive experience access to off-the-shelf ML techniques. As well as being

3

beneficial for newcomers, AutoML will relieve experts and data scientists of the burden of designing and configuring ML models. Being a cutting-edge topic, it is new to most people, and its current capabilities are often exaggerated by mass media. To give you a glimpse of what AutoML is, this chapter provides some background and an introduction to the fundamental concepts and orients you to its research value and practical benefits. Let's start with a toy example.

1.1   A glimpse of automated machine learning

Suppose you want to design an ML model to recognize handwritten digits in images. The ML model will take the images as inputs and output the corresponding digits in each of the images (see figure 1.1).

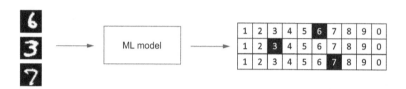

Figure 1.1   Recognizing handwritten digits with an ML model

In case you're not experienced with ML, let's use a programmatic illustration with Pythonic style to show how we usually achieve this goal in practice. We take an ML model as an object instantiated from a class, as shown in listing 1.1. This class corresponds to a specific type of ML algorithm (a set of procedures) that we would like to use in our model.[1] To instantiate a model, besides selecting the algorithm class to be used, we also need to feed the algorithm some historical data and arguments (arg1 and arg2). The historical data used here consists of images of handwritten digits, whose labels (corresponding numbers) are already known. This helps the machine (or the ML algorithm) to conduct the learning process—that is, to learn how to recognize the digits in images, similar to how a child is trained to recognize objects from pictures. (You'll see the details of this process in later sections.) The arguments here are used to control the algorithm, instructing it how to do this process. The resulting ML model will be able to predict the digits in previously unseen images (see figure 1.1) with the second line of code in the next listing.

Listing 1.1   A simplified ML process

```
ml_model = MachineLearningAlgorithm1(                          Creates an ML model
    arg1=..., arg2=..., data=historical_images)
digits=[model.predict_image_digit(image) for image in new_images]

                                        Makes predictions with the ML model
```

---

[1] Many well-known ML packages provide these kinds of classes corresponding to ML algorithms, such as scikit-learn.

As you can see from the code, besides the dataset, which we may need to prepare ourselves, we need to provide the following two things based on our prior knowledge to address the task:

- The ML algorithm (or method) to be used; that is, `MachineLearningAlgorithm1`
- The arguments of the algorithm

Selecting the algorithm and configuring its arguments can be difficult in practice. Let's use algorithm selection as an example. As a beginner, a typical approach is to collect some learning materials, explore the code for some related tasks, and identify a pool of ML algorithms you might be able to use for the task at hand. You can then try them out one by one on your historical data (as we do in listing 1.1) and pick the best one based on their performance at recognizing the digits in the images. This repetitive process is summarized in the next code sample.

Listing 1.2 A naive way of selecting ML algorithms

```
ml_algorithm_pool = [
    MachineLearningAlgorithm1,          A pool of ML
    MachineLearningAlgorithm2,          algorithms to
    ...,                                be tested
    MachineLearningAlgorithmN,
]
for ml_algorithm in ml_algorithm_pool:          Loops over all the
    model = ml_algorithm(                        candidate ML algorithms
        arg1=..., arg2=...,             Instantiates and evaluates the ML
        data=historical_images)         model based on each ML algorithm
    result = evaluate(model)
    push result into the result_pool
    push model into the model_pool
best_ml_model = pick_the_best(result_pool,          Selects the best ML model
                       ml_model_pool)               based on the performance
return best_ml_model
```

The process looks intuitive but may take you hours or days if you do not have much ML knowledge or experience for a few reasons. First, collecting a pool of feasible ML algorithms could be challenging. You may need to explore the literature, identify the state-of-the-art algorithms, and learn how to implement them. Second, the number of feasible ML algorithms could be huge. Trying them out one by one may not be a good choice and may even be prohibitive. Third, each algorithm has its own arguments. Configuring them correctly requires expertise, experience, and even some luck.

Might there be a better way of doing this? Is it possible to let the machine perform automatically for you? If you have faced similar problems and want to adopt ML in a more labor-saving way, AutoML could be the tool you are looking for. Loosely speaking, AutoML mimics the manual process described in the preceding pseudocode. It tries to automate the repetitive and tedious process of selecting and configuring ML algorithms and can allow you access to many advanced algorithms without even knowing they exist. The following two lines of pseudocode illustrate how to use an AutoML algorithm to generate the ML solution:

```
automl_model = AutoMLAlgorithm()
best_ml_model = automl_model.generate_model(data=historical_images)
```

Creating an AutoML model object from an AutoML algorithm means you don't even need to provide the pool of ML algorithms to test, and you can generate the desired model simply by feeding data into it.

But how do you select an AutoML algorithm? What are the ML algorithms it will choose from? How does it evaluate them and choose a model? Before going any further, I'll give you some background on ML so you can better understand what AutoML automates and how to use it in practice to save yourself time and effort. The focus here will be on what you need to know to learn and use AutoML. If you want to learn more about these algorithms, I recommend referring to other ML books, such as *Machine Learning in Action* by Peter Harrington (Manning, 2012) and *Deep Learning with Python*, 2nd ed., by François Chollet (Manning, 2021). For readers who are already familiar with the basics of ML, this next section will serve as a recap, make sure we're all on the same page with some terminology, and better motivate the following introduction to AutoML.

1.2 Getting started with machine learning

This section provides a brief introduction to ML—what it is, the critical components in an ML algorithm, and how an ML model is created based on a selected algorithm and data input. Learning these basics is essential to understanding the concepts of AutoML introduced in the next sections.

1.2.1 What is machine learning?

Before the emergence of ML, the dominant paradigm in AI research was *symbolic AI*, where the computer could process data only based on predefined rules explicitly input by humans. The advent of ML revolutionized the programming paradigm by enabling knowledge to be learned from the data implicitly. For example, suppose you want a machine to recognize images of apples and bananas automatically. With symbolic AI, you would need to provide human-readable rules associated with the reasoning process, perhaps specifying features like color and shape, to the AI method. In contrast, an ML algorithm takes a bunch of images and their corresponding labels ("banana" or "apple") and outputs the learned rules, which can be used to predict unlabeled images (see figure 1.2).

The essential goals of ML are *automation* and *generalization*. Automation means an ML algorithm is trained on the data provided to automatically extract rules (or patterns) from the data. It mimics human thinking and allows the machine to improve itself by interacting with the historical data fed to it, which we call *training* or *learning*. The rules are then used to perform repetitive predictions on new data without human

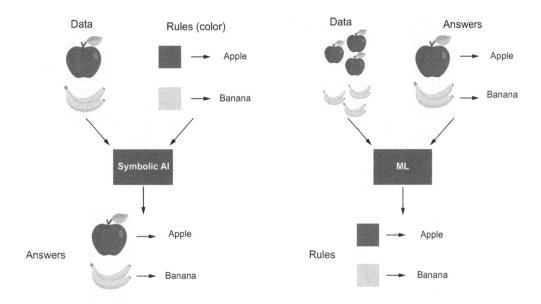

Figure 1.2 Comparison of symbolic AI and ML

intervention. For example, in figure 1.2, the ML algorithm interacts with the apple and banana images provided and extracts a color rule that enables it to recognize them through the training process. These rules can help the machine classify new images without human supervision, which we call *generalizing* to new data. The ability to generalize is an important criterion in evaluating whether an ML algorithm is good. In this case, suppose an image of a yellow apple is fed to the ML algorithm—the color rule will not enable it to correctly discern whether it's an apple or a banana. An ML algorithm that learns and applies a shape feature for prediction may provide better predictions.

1.2.2 *The machine learning process*

An ML algorithm learns rules through exposure to examples with known outputs. The rules are expected to enable it to transform inputs into meaningful outputs, such as transforming images of handwritten digits to the corresponding numbers. So, the goal of learning can also be thought of as enabling *data transformation*. The learning process generally requires the following two components:

- *Data inputs*—Data instances of the target task to be fed into the ML algorithm, for example, in the image recognition problem (see figure 1.2), a set of apple and banana images and their corresponding labels
- *Learning algorithm*—A mathematical procedure to derive a model based on the data inputs, which contains the following four elements:
  - An ML model with a set of *parameters* to be learned from the data

- A *measurement* to measure the model's performance (such as prediction accuracy) with the current parameters
- A way to update the model, which we call an *optimization method*
- A *stop criterion* to determine when the learning process should stop

After the model parameters are intialized,[2] the learning algorithm can update the model iteratively by modifying the parameters based on the measurement until the stop criterion is reached. This measurement is called a *loss function* (or *objective function*) in the training phase; it measures the difference between the model's predictions and the ground-truth targets. This process is illustrated in figure 1.3.

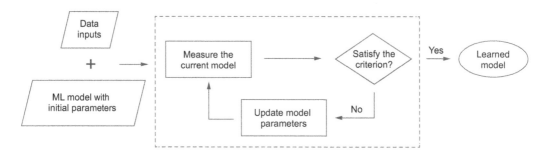

Figure 1.3   The process of training an ML model

Let's look at an example to help you better understand the learning process. Imagine we have a bunch of data points in two-dimensional space (see figure 1.4). Each point is either black or white. We want to build an ML model that, whenever a new point arrives, can decide whether this is a black point or a white point based on the point's position. A straightforward way to achieve this goal is to draw a horizontal line to separate the two-dimensional space into two parts based on the data points in hand. This line could be regarded as an ML model. Its parameter is the horizontal position, which can be updated and learned from the provided data points. Coupled with the learning process introduced in figure 1.3, the required components could be chosen and summarized as follows:

- The data inputs are a bunch of white and black points described by their location in the two-dimensional space.
- The learning algorithm consists of the following four selected components:
  - *ML model*—A horizontal line that can be formulated as $y = a$, where a is the parameter that can be updated by the algorithm.
  - *Accuracy measurement*—The percentage of points that are labeled correctly based on the model.

---

[2] The parameter values may be intialized randomly or assigned following a strategy such as a warm start, where you begin with some existing parameters learned by similar models.

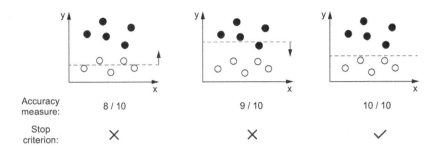

Figure 1.4 An example of the learning process: Learning a horizontal line to split white and black points

- *Optimization method*—Move the line up or down by a certain distance. The distance can be related to the value of the measurement in each iteration. It will not stop until the stop criterion is satisfied.
- *Stop criterion*—Stop when the measurement is 100%, which means all the points in hand are labeled correctly based on the current line.

In the example shown in figure 1.4, the learning algorithm takes two iterations to achieve the desired line, which separates all the input points correctly. But in practice, this criterion may not always be satisfied. It depends on the distribution of the input data, the selected model type, and how the model is measured and updated. We often need to choose different components and try different combinations to adjust the learning process to get the expected ML solution. Also, even if the learned model is able to label all the training inputs correctly, it is not guaranteed to work well on unseen data. In other words, the model's ability to generalize may not be good (we'll discuss this further in the next section). It's important to select the components and adjust the learning process carefully.

1.2.3 Hyperparameter tuning

How do we select the proper components to adjust the learning process so that we can derive the expected model? To answer this question, we need to introduce a concept called *hyperparameters* and clarify the relationship between these and the parameters we've been discussing as follows:

- *Parameters* are variables that can be updated by the ML algorithm during the learning process. They are used to capture the rules from the data. For example, the position of the horizontal line is the only parameter in our previous example (figure 1.4) to help classify the points. It is adjusted during the training process by the optimization method to capture the position rule for splitting the points with different colors. By adjusting the parameters, we can derive an ML model that can accurately predict the outputs of the given input data.

- *Hyperparameters* are also parameters, but they're ones we predefine for the algorithm before the learning process begins, and their values remain fixed during the learning process. These include the measurement, the optimization method, the speed of learning, the stop criterion, and so on. An ML algorithm usually has multiple hyperparameters. Different combinations of them have different effects on the learning process, resulting in ML models with different performances. We can also consider the algorithm type (or the ML model type) as a hyperparameter, because we select it ourselves, and it is fixed during the learning process.

The selection of an optimal combination of hyperparameters for an ML algorithm is called *hyperparameter tuning* and is often done through an iterative process. In each iteration, we select a set of hyperparameters to use to learn an ML model with the training dataset. The ML algorithm block in figure 1.5 denotes the learning process described in figure 1.3. By evaluating each learned model on a separate dataset called the *validation set*, we can then pick the best one as the final model. We can evaluate the generalizability of that model using another dataset called the *test set*, which concludes the whole ML workflow.

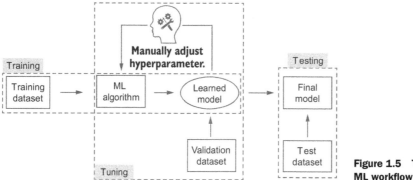

Figure 1.5   The classic ML workflow

In general, we will have three datasets in the ML workflow. Each dataset is distinct from the other two, as described next:

- The training set is used during the learning process to train a model given a fixed combination of hyperparameters.
- The validation set is used during the tuning process to evaluate the trained models to select the best hyperparameters.
- The test set is used for the final testing, after the tuning process. It is used only once, after the final model is selected, and should not be used for training or tuning the ML algorithm.

The training and test sets are straightforward to understand. The reason we want to have an additional validation dataset is to avoid exposing the algorithm to all the training data during the tuning stages—this enhances the generalizability of the final model to unseen data. If we don't have a validation set, the best model selected in the tuning stage would be the one that focuses on extracting any subtle features in the training data to ceaselessly increase the training accuracy without caring about any unseen dataset. This situation will likely lead to bad performance on the final test set, which contains different data. When the model performs worse on the test set (or validation set) than the training set, this is called *overfitting*. It's a well-known problem in ML and often happens when the model's learning capacity is too strong and the size of the training dataset is limited. For example, suppose you want to predict the fourth number of a series, given the first three numbers as training data: $a_1 = 1$, $a_2 = 2$, $a_3 = 3$, $a_4 = ?$ (a_4 is the validation set here; a_5 onward are the test sets.) If the right solution is $a_4 = 4$, a naive model, $a_i = i$, would provide the correct answer. If you use a third-degree polynomial to fit the series, a perfect solution for the training data would be $a_i = i^3 - 6i^2 + 12i - 6$, which will predict a_4 as 10. The validation process enables a model's generalization ability to be better reflected during evaluation so that better models can be selected.

> **NOTE** Overfitting is one of the most important problems studied in ML. Besides doing validation during the tuning process, we have many other ways to address the problem, such as augmenting the dataset, adding regularization to the model to constrain its learning capacity during training, and so on. We won't go into this in more depth here. To learn more about this topic, see Chollet's *Deep Learning with Python*.

1.2.4 *The obstacles to applying machine learning*

At this point, you should have a basic understanding of what ML is and how it proceeds. Although you can make use of many mature ML toolkits, you may still face difficulties in practice. This section describes some of these challenges—the aim is not to scare you off, but to provide context for the AutoML techniques that are described afterward. Obstacles you may meet include the following:

- *The cost of learning ML techniques*—We've covered the basics, but more knowledge is required when applying ML to a real problem. For example, you'll need to think about how to formulate your problem as an ML problem, which ML algorithms you could use for your problem and how they work, how to clean and preprocess the data into the expected format to input into your ML algorithm, which evaluation criteria should be selected for model training and hyperparameter tuning, and so on. All these questions need to be answered in advance, and doing so may require a large time commitment.
- *Implementation complexity*—Even with the necessary knowledge and experience, implementing the workflow after selecting an ML algorithm is a complex task. The time required for implementation and debugging will grow as more advanced algorithms are adopted.

- *The gap between theory and practice*—The learning process can be hard to interpret, and the performance is highly data driven. Furthermore, the datasets used in ML are often complex and noisy and can be difficult to interpret, clean, and control. This means the tuning process is often more empirical than analytical. Even ML experts sometimes cannot achieve the desired results.

These difficulties significantly impede the democratization of ML to people with limited experience and correspondingly increase the burden on ML experts. This has motivated ML researchers and practitioners to pursue a solution to lower the barriers, circumvent the unnecessary procedures, and alleviate the burden of manual algorithm design and tuning—AutoML.

1.3   *AutoML: The automation of automation*

The goal of AutoML is to allow a machine to mimic how humans design, tune, and apply ML algorithms so that we can adopt ML more easily (see figure 1.6). Because a key property of ML is automation, AutoML can be regarded as automating automation.

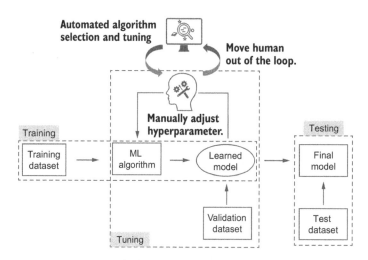

Figure 1.6   **The main goal of AutoML: taking humans out of the loop of ML algorithm design and tuning**

To help you understand how AutoML works, let's first go over the key components.

1.3.1   *Three key components of AutoML*

Here's a recap of the pseudocode introduced in section 1.1:

```
ml_algorithm_pool = [
    MachineLearningAlgorithm1,
    MachineLearningAlgorithm2,
    ...,
```

```
        MachineLearningAlgorithmN,
]
for ml_algorithm in ml_algorithm_pool:
    model = ml_algorithm(arg1=..., arg2=..., data=historical_images)
    result = evaluate(model)
    push result into the result_pool
    push model into the model_pool
best_ml_model = pick_the_best(result_pool, ml_model_pool)
return best_ml_model
```

This pseudocode can be regarded as a simple AutoML algorithm that takes a pool of ML algorithms as input, evaluates them one by one, and outputs a model learned from the best algorithm. Each AutoML algorithm consists of the following three core components (see figure 1.7):

- *Search space*—A set of hyperparameters, and the ranges of each hyperparameter from which to select. The range of each hyperparameter can be defined based on the user's requirements and knowledge. For example, the search space can be a pool of ML algorithms, as shown in the pseudocode. In this case, we treat the type of ML algorithm as a hyperparameter to be selected. The search space can also be the hyperparameters of a specific ML algorithm, such as the structure of the ML model. The design of the search space is highly task-dependent, because we may need to adopt different ML algorithms for various tasks. It is also quite personalized and ad hoc, depending on the user's interests, expertise, and level of experience. There is always a tradeoff between the convenience you'll enjoy by defining a large search space and the time you'll spend identifying a good model (or the performance of the model you can achieve in a limited amount of time). For beginners, it can be tempting to define a broad search space that is general enough to apply to any task or situation, such as a search space containing all the ML algorithms—but the time and computational cost involved make this a poor solution. We'll discuss these consider-

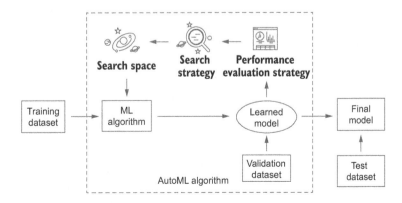

Figure 1.7   The AutoML process

ations more in the second part of the book, where you'll learn how to customize your search space in different scenarios based on additional requirements.

- *Search strategy*—A strategy to select the optimal set of hyperparameters from the search space. Because AutoML is often an iterative trial-and-error process, the strategy often sequentially selects the hyperparameters in the search space and evaluates their performance. It may loop through all the hyperparameters in the search space (as in the pseudocode), or the search strategy may be adapted based on the hyperparameters that have been evaluated so far to increase the efficiency of the later trials. A better search strategy can help you achieve a better ML solution within the same amount of time. It may also allow you to use a larger search space by reducing the search time and computational cost. How to adopt, compare, and implement different search algorithms will be introduced in the third part of the book.

- *Performance evaluation strategy*—A way to evaluate the performance of a specific ML algorithm instantiated by the selected hyperparameters. The evaluation criteria are often the same as the ones used in manual tuning, such as the validation performance of the model learned from the selected ML algorithm. In this book, we discuss different evaluation strategies in the context of adopting AutoML to solve different types of ML tasks.

To facilitate the adoption of AutoML algorithms, an AutoML toolkit often wraps up these three components and provides some general application programming interfaces (APIs) with a default search space and search algorithm so that you don't need to worry about selecting them yourself. For end users, in the simplest case, all you need to do to obtain the final model is provide the data, as shown here—you don't even need to split the data into training and validation sets:

```
automl_model = AutoMLAlgorithm()
best_ml_model = automl_model.generate_model(data=...)
```

But because different users may have different use cases and levels of ML expertise, they may need to design their own search spaces, evaluation strategies, and even search strategies. Existing AutoML systems, therefore, often also provide APIs with configurable arguments to allow you to customize different components. A broad spectrum of solutions are available, from the simplest to the most configurable (figure 1.8).

Simple   Configurable

Less ML   More ML   **Figure 1.8   The spectrum**
experience   experience   **of AutoML APIs**

The range of APIs available allows you to pick the most suitable one for your use case. This book will teach you how to select the right API in an advanced AutoML toolkit, *AutoKeras*, for different AutoML applications. You'll also learn how to create your own AutoML algorithm with the help of KerasTuner.

1.3.2 Are we able to achieve full automation?

The field of AutoML has been evolving for three decades, with the involvement of industry and the open source community. Many successful implementations and promising developments have been seen, as described here:

- Many company internal tools and open source platforms have been developed to help with hyperparameter tuning of ML models and model selection (Google Vizier, Facebook Ax, and so on).
- AutoML solutions performing at near human levels have been observed in many Kaggle data science competitions.
- Vast open source ML packages for improved hyperparameter tuning and ML pipeline creation have been developed, such as Auto-sklearn, AutoKeras, and so on.
- Commercial AutoML products are helping many companies, big and small, to adopt ML in production. For example, Disney has successfully used Google Cloud AutoML to develop ML solutions for its online store without hiring a team of ML engineers (https://blog.google/products/google-cloud/cloud-automl-making-ai-accessible-every-business/).
- Researchers in fields other than computer science, such as medicine, neurobiology, and economics, are also leveraging the power of AutoML. They can now bring new ML solutions to domain-specific problems such as medical image segmentation,[3] genomic research,[4] and animal recognition and protection,[5] without going through the long learning curve of ML and programming.

We are still exploring the full capabilities of AutoML to democratize ML techniques and make them accessible to more people in different domains. Despite the many successful applications of AutoML that have been seen so far, we still have a lot of challenges and limitations to further explore and address, including the following:

- *The difficulty of building AutoML systems*—Compared to building an ML system, building an AutoML system from scratch is a more complex and involved process.
- *The automation of collecting and cleaning data*—AutoML still requires people to collect, clean, and label data. These processes are often more complicated in practice than the design of ML algorithms, and, for now at least, they cannot be automated by AutoML. For AutoML to work today, it has to be given a clear task and objective with a high-quality dataset.
- *The costs of selecting and tuning the AutoML algorithm*—The "no free lunch" theorem tells us that there is no omnipotent AutoML algorithm that fits any hyperparameter tuning problem. The effort you save on selecting and tuning an ML

---

[3] Weng, Yu, et al., "NAS-Unet: Neural Architecture Search for Medical Image Segmentation," *IEEE Access* 7 (2019): 44247–44257.

[4] Liu, Denghui, et al., "AutoGenome: An AutoML Tool for Genomic Research," bioRxiv (2019): 842526.

[5] Liu, Yao, and Ze Luo, "Species Recognition of Protected Area Based on AutoML," *Computer Systems and Applications* 28 (2019): 147–153.

algorithm may be amortized or even outweighed by the effort you need to put into selecting and tuning the AutoML algorthm.

- *Resource costs*—AutoML is a relatively costly process, in terms of both time and computational resources. Existing AutoML systems often need to try more hyperparameters than human experts to achieve comparable results.
- *The cost of human–computer interaction*—Interpreting the solution and the tuning process of AutoML may not be easy. As these systems become more complex, it will become harder and harder for humans to get involved in the tuning process and understand how the final model is achieved.

AutoML is still in its early stages of development, and its continuing progress will rely heavily on the participation of researchers, developers, and practitioners from different domains. Although you may contribute to that effort one day, the goal of this book is more modest. It mainly targets practitioners who have limited expertise in machine learning, or who have some experience but want to save themselves some effort in creating ML solutions. The book will teach you how to address an ML problem automatically with as few as five lines of code. It will gradually approach more sophisticated AutoML solutions for more complicated scenarios and data types, such as images, text, and so on. To get you started, in the next chapter, we'll dig more deeply into the fundamentals of ML and explore the end-to-end pipeline of an ML project. It will help you better understand and make use of AutoML techniques in the later chapters.

Summary

- Machine learning refers to the capacity of a computer to modify its processing by interacting with data automatically, without being explicitly programmed.
- The ML process can be described as an iterative algorithmic process to adjust the parameters of an ML model based on the data inputs and certain measurements. It stops when the model is able to provide the expected outputs, or when some particular criterion defined by the user is reached.
- Tuning the hyperparameters in an ML algorithm allows you to adjust the learning process and select components tailored to the ML problem at hand.
- AutoML aims to learn from the experience of designing and applying ML models and automate the tuning process, thereby relieving data scientists of this burden and making off-the-shelf ML techniques accessible to practitioners without extensive experience.
- An AutoML algorithm consists of three key components: the search space, search strategy, and evaluation strategy. Different AutoML systems provide different levels of APIs that either configure these for you or allow you to customize them based on your use case.
- AutoML contains many unaddressed challenges, preventing it from living up to the highest expectations. Achieving true automatic machine learning will be difficult. We should be optimistic but also take care to avoid exaggerating AutoML's current capabilities.

The end-to-end pipeline of an ML project

2

This chapter covers

- Getting familiar with the end-to-end pipeline for conducting an ML project
- Preparing data for ML models (data collection and preprocessing)
- Generating and selecting features to enhance the performance of the ML algorithm
- Building up linear regression and decision tree models
- Fine-tuning an ML model with grid search

Now that the first chapter has set the scene, it's time to get familiar with the basic concepts of ML and AutoML. Because AutoML is grounded in ML, learning the fundamentals of ML will help you better understand and make use of AutoML techniques. This is especially the case when it comes to designing the search space in an AutoML algorithm, which characterizes the ML components to be used and the ranges of their hyperparameters. In this chapter, we will walk through a concrete example of solving an ML problem. This will help you gain a deeper understanding of the overall process of building up an ML pipeline, especially if you have little experience working on ML projects. You will also learn a naive way of tuning

17

the hyperparameters of an ML model. This can be thought of as one of the simplest applications of AutoML, showing how it can help you find a better ML solution. More advanced AutoML tasks and solutions will be introduced in the second part of the book.

> **NOTE**   All of the code snippets included in this and later chapters are written in Python, in the form of Jupyter notebooks. They are all generated by Jupyter Notebook (https://jupyter.org), an open source web application that offers features such as interactive code design, data processing and visualization, narrative text, and so on. It is widely popular in the machine learning and data science communities. If you're not familiar with the environmental setup or do not have sufficient hardware resources, you can also run the code in Google Colaboratory (http://colab.research.google.com/), a free Jupyter notebook environment where anyone can run ML experiments. Detailed instructions for setting up the environment in Google Colaboratory, or Colab for short, are provided in appendix A. The notebooks are available at https://github.com/datamllab/automl-in-action-notebooks.

2.1   *An overview of the end-to-end pipeline*

An *ML pipeline* is a sequence of steps for conducting an ML project. Those steps follow:

- *Problem framing and data collection*—Frame the problem as an ML problem and collect the data you need.
- *Data preprocessing and feature engineering*—Process the data into a suitable format that can be input into the ML algorithms. Select or generate features that are related to the target output to improve the performance of the algorithms. This step is usually done by first exploring the dataset to get a sense of its characteristics. The operations should accommodate the specific ML algorithms you are considering.
- *ML algorithm selection*—Select ML algorithms appropriate for the task that you would like to test, based on your prior knowledge of the problem and your experience.
- *Model training and evaluation*—Apply the selected ML algorithm (or algorithms) to train an ML model with your training data, and evaluate its performance on the validation dataset.
- *Hyperparameter tuning*—Attempt to achieve better performance by iteratively tuning the model's hyperparameters.
- *Service deployment and model monitoring*—Deploy the final ML solution, and monitor its performance so you can maintain and improve the pipeline continuously.

As you can see, an ML project is a human-in-the-loop process. Starting from problem framing and data collection, the pipeline involves multiple data processing steps, which typically happen asynchronously (see figure 2.1). We will focus on the steps before service deployment and monitoring in the rest of the book. To learn more about deploying and serving models, please refer to a reference such as *Machine Learning Systems* by Jeff Smith (Manning, 2018) or *Machine Learning for Business* by Doug Hudgeon and Richard Nichol (Manning, 2019).

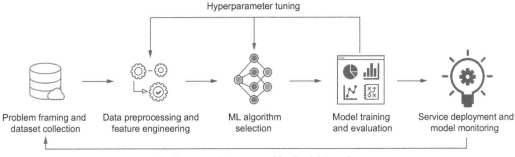

Figure 2.1 The end-to-end ML project pipeline

Let's start working on a real problem to get you familiar with each component in the pipeline. The problem we explore here is predicting the average house price in a housing block, given features of the houses such as their locations and number of rooms. The data we use is the California housing dataset featured in R. Kelley Pace and Ronald Barry's 1997 article "Sparse Spatial Autoregressions," collected via the 1990 census. This is a representative problem used in many practical ML books as a starter, due to the small scale of the data and the simplicity of the data preparation.

NOTE Selecting the right problem to work on can be difficult. It depends on multiple factors, such as your business need and research objectives. Before really engaging in a problem, ask yourself what solutions you expect to achieve and how they will benefit your downstream applications and whether any existing work has already fulfilled the need. This will help you decide whether the problem is worth investing in.

2.2 *Framing the problem and assembling the dataset*

The first thing you need to do in any ML project is frame the problem and collect the corresponding data. Framing the problem requires you to specify the inputs and outputs of the ML model. In the California housing problem, the inputs are the set of features describing the housing blocks.

In this dataset, a housing block is a group of, on average, 1,425 individuals living in a geographically compact area. The features are the average number of rooms per house in the housing block, the latitude and longitude of the center of the block, and so on. The outputs should be the average housing prices of the blocks. We are trying to train an ML model given housing blocks with known median prices and predict the unknown prices of housing blocks based on their features. The returned predicted values are also called the *targets* (or *annotations*) of the model. Generally, any problem aiming to learn the relationship between data inputs and targets based on existing annotated examples is called a *supervised learning problem*. This is the most widely studied branch of ML and will be our main focus in the rest of this book.

We can further classify supervised learning problems into different categories based on the type of target value. For example, any supervised learning problem with continuous targets can be categorized as a *regression problem*. Because price is a continuous variable, predicting California housing prices is, therefore, essentially a regression problem. If instead the target values in a supervised learning problem are discrete values with limited categories, we call the problem a *classification* problem. You can find some examples of classification problems in appendix B, and we will also explore them in the next chapter.

After framing the problem, the next step is to collect the data. Because the California housing dataset is one of the most-used ML datasets, you can easily access it with scikit-learn, a popular ML library. It should be noted, however, that in real life, discovering and acquiring datasets is a nontrivial activity and might require additional skills, such as knowledge of *Structured Query Language* (SQL), which is beyond the scope of this book. (To learn more about this, see Jeff Smith's book *Machine Learning Systems.*) The following code will load the dataset for our problem.

Listing 2.1   Loading the California housing dataset

```
from sklearn.datasets import fetch_california_housing     ◁─┐ Imports the dataset-
                                                             loading function from
                                                             the scikit-learn library

house_dataset = fetch_california_housing()     ◁─┐ Loads the California
                                                   housing dataset
```

The original data is a dictionary containing the data points formatted as an instance-feature matrix. Each data point is a housing block described by the features in a row of the matrix. Their targets are formatted as a vector. The dictionary also contains the feature names and descriptions indicating the features' meanings and creation information for the dataset, as shown next:

```
>>> house_dataset.keys()
dict_keys(['data', 'target', 'feature_names', 'DESCR'])
```

After loading the original dataset, we extract the data points and convert them into a *DataFrame*, which is a primary structure of the pandas library. pandas is a potent tool for data analysis and manipulation in Python. As shown in listing 2.2, the targets are formatted as a *Series* object; it's a vector with the label "MedPrice," standing for the median price of the housing block in millions of dollars.

Listing 2.2   Extracting the data samples and the targets

```
                      Imports the pandas package        Extracts the features with
import pandas as pd  ◁─┘                                 their names into a DataFrame
data = pd.DataFrame(house_dataset.data, columns=house_dataset.feature_names)  ◁─┘

target = pd.Series(house_dataset.target, name = 'MedPrice')   ◁─┐
                      Extracts the targets into a Series
                      object with the name "MedPrice"
```

Let's print out the first five samples of the data (shown in figure 2.2). The first row indicates the feature names, details of which can be found at https://scikit-learn.org/stable/datasets.html. For example, the "AveRooms" feature indicates the average number of rooms within a housing block. We can also check the values of the target data the same way, shown here:

```
>>> data.head(5)
```

	MedInc	HouseAge	AveRooms	AveBedrms	Population	AveOccup	Latitude	Longitude
0	8.3252	41.0	6.984127	1.023810	322.0	2.555556	37.88	-122.23
1	8.3014	21.0	6.238137	0.971880	2401.0	2.109842	37.86	-122.22
2	7.2574	52.0	8.288136	1.073446	496.0	2.802260	37.85	-122.24
3	5.6431	52.0	5.817352	1.073059	558.0	2.547945	37.85	-122.25
4	3.8462	52.0	6.281853	1.081081	565.0	2.181467	37.85	-122.25

Figure 2.2　**Features of the first five samples in the California housing dataset**

Before moving on to the data-preprocessing step, let's first do a data split to separate the training data and test set. As you learned in the previous chapter, the primary purpose of doing this is to avoid testing your model on the same data that you use to conduct your analysis and train your model. The code for splitting the data into training and test sets is shown in the following listing.

Listing 2.3　Splitting the data into training and test sets

```
from sklearn.model_selection import train_test_split          ◁─┐ Imports the data
                                                                 │ split function from
X_train, X_test, y_train, y_test = train_test_split(           ─┘ scikit-learn
    data, target,
    test_size=0.2,              │ Randomly splits 20% of
    random_state=42)         ◁─┘ the data into the test set
```

We split a random 20% of the data into the test set. Now let's do a quick check of the split. Looking at the full dataset, you'll see that it contains 20,640 data points. The number of features for each housing block is eight. The training set contains 16,512 samples, and the test set contains 4,128 samples, as depicted in the next code snippet:

```
>>> (data.shape, target.shape), (X_train.shape, y_train.shape), (X_test.shape,
    y_test.shape)
(((20640, 8), (20640,)), ((16512, 8), (16512,)), ((4128, 8), (4128,)))
```

You should not touch the target data in the test set until you have your final ML solution. Otherwise, all your analysis, including the data preparation and model training, may overfit to the test data, resulting in the final solution performing badly on unseen data when it is deployed. It is feasible to combine the features in the test set with the training features in data preprocessing and feature engineering, however, as we will do in the following sections. It can be helpful to aggregate the feature information, especially when the dataset size is small.

2.3   Data preprocessing

Our next step is to do some preprocessing to transform the data into a suitable format for feeding into the ML algorithms. The procedure usually involves some *exploratory data analysis* (EDA) based on prior assumptions or questions about the data. EDA can help us get familiar with the dataset and gain more insights into it, to enable better data preparation. Some commonly asked questions include the following:

- What are the data types of the values in each feature? Are they strings or other objects that can be used in later steps in the pipeline, or do they need to be transformed?
- How many distinct values does each feature have? Are they numerical values, categorical values, or something else?
- What are the scales and basic statistics of each feature? Can we gain some insights by visualizing the distribution of the values or correlations between them?
- Are there missing values in the data? If so, do we have to remove them or fill them in?

In practice, different data usually requires tailored data preprocessing techniques depending on its format and features, the problems we are concerned with, the selected ML models, and so on. This is generally a heuristic, empirical process, resulting in various ad hoc operations being proposed.

We'll use the four previously mentioned questions as the basis for some preliminary data preprocessing in this example. You can find more examples in appendix B. The first question we're concerned about is the data types of the feature values. In this example, all the features and their targets are floating-point values, which can be directly fed into the ML algorithms without further manipulation, as shown next:

```
>>> data.dtypes
MedInc        float64
HouseAge      float64
AveRooms      float64
AveBedrms     float64
Population    float64
AveOccup      float64
Latitude      float64
Longitude     float64
dtype: object

>>> target.dtypes
dtype('float64')
```

The second thing we're concerned about is the number of distinct values in the features. Counting the distinct values can be helpful for distinguishing the feature types so that we can design tailored strategies to process them. This may also help us remove any redundant features. For example, if all the data samples have the same value for a feature, that feature cannot provide any useful information for prediction. It's also possible that every data point has a unique value for a feature, but we're confident that these values will not be helpful for classification. This is often the case for the ID feature of the data points, if it indicates only the order of the data samples. In listing 2.4, we can see that in this dataset, there is no feature whose value is identical for all the points, and there are no features where each data point has a unique value. Although some of them have large numbers of distinct values, such as "MedInc," "AveRooms," and "AveBedrms," because these are numerical features whose values are useful for comparing the housing blocks and predicting the price, we should not remove them.

> **Listing 2.4   Checking the number of unique values in each feature**

```
>>> data.nunique()
MedInc         12928
HouseAge          52
AveRooms       19392
AveBedrms      14233
Population      3888
AveOccup       18841
Latitude         862
Longitude        844
dtype: int64
```

We can further display some basic statistics of the features to gain more insights (as shown in figure 2.3). For example, the average population in a housing block is 1,425, but the most densely populated block in this dataset has over 35,000 inhabitants and the most sparsely populated block has just 3.

	MedInc	HouseAge	AveRooms	AveBedrms	Population	AveOccup	Latitude	Longitude
count	20,640.00	20,640.00	20,640.00	20,640.00	20,640.00	20,640.00	20,640.00	20,640.00
mean	3.87	28.64	5.43	1.10	1,425.48	3.07	35.63	-119.57
std	1.90	12.59	2.47	0.47	1,132.46	10.39	2.14	2.00
min	0.50	1.00	0.85	0.33	3.00	0.69	32.54	-124.35
25%	2.56	18.00	4.44	1.01	787.00	2.43	33.93	-121.80
50%	3.53	29.00	5.23	1.05	1,166.00	2.82	34.26	-118.49
75%	4.74	37.00	6.05	1.10	1,725.00	3.28	37.71	-118.01
max	15.00	52.00	141.91	34.07	35,682.00	1,243.33	41.95	-114.31

Figure 2.3   Feature statistics of the California housing data

One of the key challenges in real-world applications is missing values in the data. This problem can be introduced during the collection or transmission of the data, or it can be caused by corruption, failure to correctly load the data, and so on. If not handled properly, missing values can affect the performance of the ML solution, or even cause the program to crash. The process of replacing missing and invalid values in the data with substitute values is called *imputation*.

The following listing checks for the existence of missing values in our training and test datasets.

> **Listing 2.5   Checking for missing values in the training and test sets**

```
train_data = X_train.copy()                  ◄───┤  Copies the training data to
                                                    avoid changing it in place

train_data['MedPrice'] = y_train             ◄──────────────────┐
                                                                 Combines the features and
                                                                 the target by adding a column
print(f'-- check for missing values in training data --        'MedPrice' for the target
     {training_data.isnull().any()}')        ◄───────┐
                                                     Checks whether
                                                     the training set
print(f'-- check for missing values in training data --  has missing values
     {Xtest.isnull().any()}')                ◄────┐
     Checks whether the test set has missing values │
```

The following results show that the dataset has no missing values, so we can proceed with our analysis without considering this problem further (you will see an example of dealing with missing values in chapter 3):

```
-- check for missing values in training data --
MedInc        False
HouseAge      False
AveRooms      False
AveBedrms     False
Population    False
AveOccup      False
Latitude      False
Longitude     False
MedPrice      False
dtype: bool

-- check for missing values in test data --
MedInc        False
HouseAge      False
AveRooms      False
AveBedrms     False
Population    False
AveOccup      False
Latitude      False
Longitude     False
dtype: bool
```

For simplicity, we won't do any additional data preprocessing here. You will often want to take some other common steps, such as checking for *outliers*, which are distant points that can affect the training of ML models, and removing them if they exist in your data. Also, real-world datasets are often not formatted quite as well as the one used in this example. More examples of data-preprocessing techniques dealing with different data types are provided in appendix B; I recommend you go over those examples before going on to the next chapter if you're not familiar with this topic. Next we'll move on to the feature-engineering step, which is often carried out concurrently with data preprocessing.

2.4   Feature engineering

Different from data preprocessing, which focuses on getting the raw data into a useful or efficient format, feature engineering aims to generate and select a set of good features to boost the performance of ML algorithms. It often relies on specific domain knowledge and proceeds iteratively with the following two steps:

- *Feature generation* aims at generating new features by transforming existing ones. It can be done on a single feature, such as by substituting a categorical feature with the frequency count in each category to obtain a measurable numerical feature, or on multiple features. For example, by counting the number of male and female employees with different occupations, we may arrive at a more instructive feature for analyzing the fairness of recruiting across different industries.
- *Feature selection* aims at selecting the most useful subset of the existing features, to improve the efficiency and accuracy of the ML algorithms.

Feature selection and generation are often done in an iterative manner, leveraging immediate feedback from certain measures, such as the correlation of the generated features and the targets, or delayed feedback based on the performance of the trained ML model on the evaluation dataset.

In listing 2.6, we perform a simple feature selection by measuring the correlation between each feature and the target using *Pearson's correlation coefficient.* Pearson's correlation coefficient measures the linear correlation between two variables (feature and target). The value can range from –1 to 1, where –1 and 1 indicate a perfect negative and a perfect positive linear relationship, respectively. A coefficient of 0 indicates no relationship exists.

Listing 2.6   Plotting the Pearson's correlation coefficient matrix

Imports the library for general plotting configuration

Imports the seaborn library to plot the heatmap

Pretties the figure display in Jupyter notebooks

Sets the figure size

Calculates the Pearson's correlation coefficient matrix

Plots the correlations between all the features and the target

```
import matplotlib.pyplot as plt
import seaborn as sns
%matplotlib inline

plt.figure(figsize=(30,10))

correlation_matrix = train_data.corr().round(2)
sns.heatmap(data=correlation_matrix, square= True,
        annot=True, cmap='Blues')
```

We'll focus on the last row of the matrix (see figure 2.4), which shows the pairwise correlation between the target housing price and each feature. We'll then discuss the two features we've chosen.

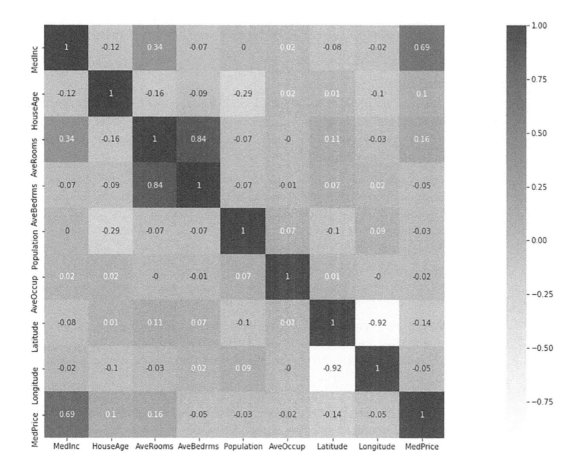

Figure 2.4   Pearson's correlation coefficient matrix among all the features and the target

Based on the coefficient matrix and the following assumptions, we select the top two correlated features:

- *MedInc*—This feature, which indicates the median income for households within a block of houses, shows a high positive linear correlation with the target values. This is aligned with the intuition that people with higher incomes are more likely to live in the blocks with higher housing prices (positive correlation).
- *AveRooms*—This feature indicates the average number of rooms in each house in a block. Houses with more rooms are more likely to have higher prices (positive correlation).

We select only two features here as examples for simplicity. The feature selection is implemented in listing 2.7. It is also possible to automate the selection of features, instead of basing it on a visual inspection, by choosing a threshold for the calculated Pearson's correlation coefficients (such as 0.5). The number of features to select is a hyperparameter that we need to carefully decide. We can try different feature combinations to train our ML model and select the best one by trial and error.

Listing 2.7 Feature selection

```
selected_feature_set = ['MedInc', 'AveRooms',]        ◁──┐  The selected feature set
sub_train_data = train_data[
    selected_feature_set + ['MedPrice']]      ◁──┐  Extracts the new
                                                  training features

X_train = sub_train_data.drop(['MedPrice'], axis=1)   ◁──┐
X_test = X_test[selected_feature_set]   ◁──┐              Drops the target and
                                                          keeps only the training
      Selects the same feature set for the test data      features in X_train
```

After selecting the two features, we can draw scatterplots to display the pairwise correlations between them and the target. Their distributions can be jointly shown via histogram plots using the following code:

```
sns.pairplot(sub_train_data, height=3.5, plot_kws={'alpha': 0.4})
```

The scatterplots show a strong positive correlation between the "MedInc" feature and the target, "MedPrice." The correlation between the "AveRooms" feature and "MedPrice" is comparably less conspicuous, due to the scale differences between the features and the outliers (see figure 2.5).

Using Pearson's correlation coefficient to select features is easy, but it may not always be effective in practice. It ignores nonlinear relationships between the features and the target, as well as the correlations among the features. Moreover, the correlation between feature and target may not be meaningful for categorical features, whose values are not ordinal. As more and more feature engineering techniques have been proposed, deciding how to select the best one has become a pain point. That brings up an important topic in AutoML—automated feature selection and transformation—but we'll leave discussion of that to the second part of the book, and for now continue solving the problem at hand.

Now that we have prepared the training data and selected our features, we're ready to choose the algorithms to use to train an ML model with the preprocessed data. (In practice, you can also select the ML algorithms before the data-preprocessing and feature-engineering steps to pursue a more tailored data-preparation process.)

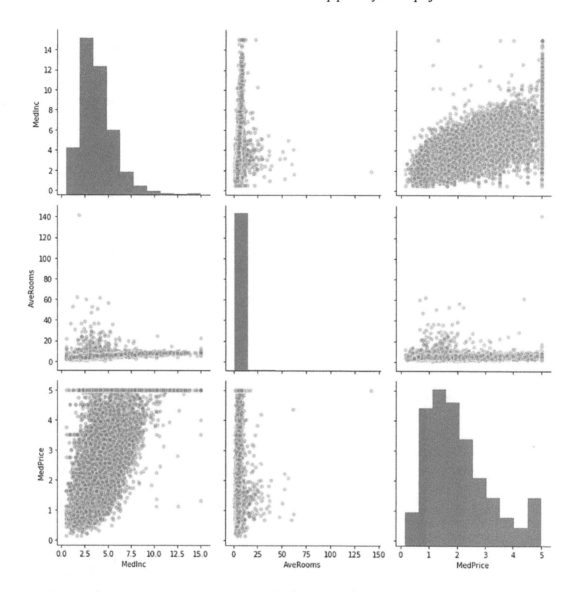

Figure 2.5   Pairwise relationships between the selected features and the target

2.5   *ML algorithm selection*

Remember that for each ML algorithm, we have four core components to select: an ML model to be trained, a metric to measure the model's efficacy, an optimization method to update the model's parameters based on that metric, and a stop criterion to terminate the updating process. Because our main focus here is not optimization, we will talk only briefly about the optimization method and stop criterion for each selected model.

For this example we will use two simple, classic models. The first one is the *linear regression model*, and the second is the *decision tree model*. We'll start by recapping the core idea behind the linear regression model and the process of creating, training, and evaluating it. We will train the model using the whole training set and evaluate it on the test set, without further splitting the training data into training and validation sets for hyperparameter tuning. We will discuss the hyperparameter tuning step after the introduction of the decision tree model.

2.5.1 *Building the linear regression model*

Linear regression is one of the simplest models in supervised ML, and probably the first ML model you learned about. It tries to predict the target value of a data point by computing the weighted sum of its features: $\hat{y} = w_0 + \sum_{i=1}^{m} w_i x_i$, where the m is the number of features. In the current example m is 2 because we selected only two features: "MedInc" and "AveRooms." w_i are the parameters (or *weights*) to be learned from the data, where w_0 is called the *intercept* and $w_i (i \geq 1)$ is called a *coefficient* for feature x_i. The parameters are learned based on the training data to capture the linear relationship between the features and the target. The code to build a linear regression model with scikit-learn follows:

```
from sklearn.linear_model import LinearRegression

linear_regressor = LinearRegression()
```

To learn the weights, we need to select an optimization method and a metric to measure their performance. *Mean squared error* (MSE) is a widely used loss function and evaluation metric for regression problems—it measures the average squared difference between the model's predictions and the targets. We'll use MSE as the loss function in the training stage to learn the model, and we'll use the evaluation metric in the testing phase to measure the model's predictive power on the test set. To help you understand how it's calculated, a code illustration is provided in listing 2.8. In the training stage, `true_target_values` is a list of all the target values (actual prices of the houses) in the training dataset, and `predictions` is all the housing prices predicted by the model.

Listing 2.8 Computing the MSE

```
def mean_squared_error(predictions, true_target_values):      Initializes the
    mse = 0                                                    sum to zero
    for prediction, target_value in zip(predictions, true_target_values):
        mse += (prediction - target_value) ** 2               Sums up the
    mse /= len(predictions)        Averages the sum           squared errors
    return mse                     of squared errors
```

Figure 2.6 is a simple illustration of a linear regression model with a single variable (or feature). The learning process aims to find the best slope and intercept to minimize

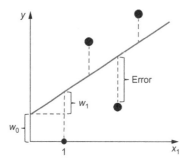

Figure 2.6   Illustration of linear regression with only one feature

the mean of the squared errors, indicated by the dashed lines between the data points and the regression line.

With the help of scikit-learn, we can easily optimize the weights by calling the `fit` function and feeding in the training data. MSE is used as the loss function by default, as shown here:

```
linear_regressor.fit(X_train, y_train)
```

We can print the learned weights with the following code.

Listing 2.9   Displaying the learned parameters

```
>>> coeffcients = pd.DataFrame(
>>> coefficients = pd.DataFrame(
...     linear_regression.conf_,            Converts the
...     X_train.coluns,                     coefficient values
...     columns=['Coefficient'])            to a DataFrame
>>> print(f'Intercept: {linear_regressor.intercept_:.2f}\n')     Prints the
>>> print(coeffcients)        Prints the                         intercept value
                              coefficients
Learned intercept: 0.60

--The coefficient value learned by the linear regression model--
        Coefficient
MedInc          0.44
AveRooms       -0.04
```

The learned coefficients show that the "MedInc" feature and the target do have a positive linear correlation. The "AveRooms" feature has a negative correlation, contrary to our expectations. This could be due to the following two possible factors:

- The outliers in the training data (some high-priced housing blocks have fewer rooms) are affecting the training process.
- The two features we have selected are positively linearly correlated. This is because they share some common information that is useful for predicting the target. Because "MedInc" already covers some of the information provided by

"AveRooms," the effect of "AveRooms" is reduced, resulting in a slight negative correlation.

Ideally, a good set of features for linear regression should be only weakly correlated with one another but highly correlated with the target. At this stage, we could iteratively proceed with feature selection and model training to try different sets of features and select a good combination. I'll leave that process for you to try as an exercise, and we'll go directly to the test phase. The MSE of the learned model on the test set can be calculated and printed with the following code.

Listing 2.10 Testing the linear regression model

```
>>> from sklearn.metrics import mean_squared_error                    ◁─────────
>>> y_pred_test = linear_regressor.predict(X_test)                    ◁──
>>> print(f'Test MSE: {mean_squared_error(y_test, y_pred_test):.2f}')

Test MSE: 0.70                          Predicts the targets of the test data

                                        Imports the evaluation metric
```

The test MSE is 0.70, which means on average, the squared difference between the model's predictions and the ground-truth targets of the test data is 0.70. A lower value for the MSE is better; ideally, you want this to be as close to 0 as possible. Next we'll try out a decision tree model and compare the performance of the two.

2.5.2 Building the decision tree model

The key idea of a decision tree is to split the data into different groups based on a series of (usually binary) conditions, as shown in figure 2.7. Each of the non-leaf nodes in a decision tree is a condition that causes each data sample to be placed in one of the child nodes. Each leaf node has a specific value as the prediction. Each data sample will navigate from the root (top) of the tree to one of the leaf nodes, giving us the prediction for that sample. For example, suppose we have a house with MedInc=5 and AveRooms=3. We'll start from the root node and go through the No path and the Yes path until we reach a leaf node with the value $260,000, which is the predicted price for this house.

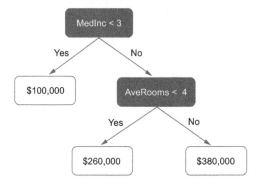

Figure 2.7 Predicting values with a decision tree model

Both the splits of the tree and the predictions in each leaf are learned based on the training data. A typical process for constructing a decision tree is shown in listing 2.11. The tree is constructed recursively. In each recursion, we find the optimal split for the dataset in the current node. In each split node, the prediction given by the node equals the mean value of all the training samples that fall into this node. The optimal split is defined as the one that minimizes the MSE between the predicted value and the target values of all the samples in the two child nodes. The recursion will stop when an exit condition is met. We have multiple ways to define this condition. For example, we can predefine the maximum depth of the tree, so that when that depth is reached, the recursion stops. We can also base it on the stop criterion of the algorithm. For example, we can define the exit condition of the recursion as "stop if the number of training samples that fall into the current node is less than five."

Listing 2.11   Constructing a decision tree model

```
decision_tree_root = construct_subtree(training_data)

def construct_subtree(data):
    if exit_condition(data):
        return LeafNode(get_predicted_value(data))
    condition = get_split_condition(data)
    node = Node(condition)
    left_data, right_data = condition.split_data(data)
    node.left = construct_subtree(left_data)
    node.right = construct_subtree(right_data)
    return node
```

If the exit condition is met, computes the predicted value

Gets the optimal split condition from the data

Makes a new node with the condition

Splits the data into two parts with the condition

Constructs the left subtree recursively

Constructs the right subtree recursively

It's easy to build a decision tree with scikit-learn. Code for training and testing is shown in listing 2.12. The max_depth argument is a hyperparameter constraining the maximum depth of the tree model during training. It will stop growing either when a node of this max_depth is achieved or when the current node contains less than two samples (a default stop criterion).

Listing 2.12   Building a decision tree model with scikit-learn

```
from sklearn.tree import DecisionTreeRegressor

tree_regressor = DecisionTreeRegressor(max_depth=3,
                                       random_state=42)
tree_regressor.fit(X_train, y_train)

y_pred_train = tree_regressor.predict(X_train)
y_pred_test = tree_regressor.predict(X_test)
```

Creates a decision tree regressor

Let's print the MSE results for both the training and test sets, as shown next. The difference between them indicates a small amount of overfitting:

```
>>> print(f'Train MSE: {mean_squared_error(y_train, y_pred_train):.2f}')

>>> print(f'Test MSE: {mean_squared_error(y_test, y_pred_test):.2f}')

Train MSE: 0.68
Test MSE: 0.71
```

Compared to the linear regression model, the current decision tree model performs slightly worse on the test set. But it's worth pointing out that we should not select our model based only on these test results. The right way of doing model selection and hyperparameter tuning is to try out different models on a separate validation set through the validation process. The reason we directly evaluate the test set here is to get you familiar with the training and testing procedure. We can also visualize the learned tree model to gain a more intuitive understanding, using the following code.

Listing 2.13 Visualizing the decision tree

```
from sklearn.externals.six import StringIO
import sklearn.tree as tree
import pydotplus

from IPython.display import Image
dot_data = StringIO()
tree.export_graphviz(tree_regressor,
                     out_file=dot_data,
                     class_names=['MedPrice'],          ◁—   The target's name
                     feature_names=selected_feature_set,
   Whether to fill in the  ↳  filled=True,
   boxes with colors          rounded=True)              ◁—   Whether to round
graph = pydotplus.graph_from_dot_data(dot_data.getvalue())   the corners of
Image(graph.create_png())                                    the boxes
```

The learned tree is a balanced binary tree with a depth of three, as shown in figure 2.8. Except for the leaf nodes, which do not have a split condition, each node conveys four messages: the split condition, which decides which child node a sample should fall into based on a feature; the number of training samples that fall into the current node; the mean value of their targets; and the MSE of all the samples that fall into the current node. The MSE of each node is calculated based on the ground-truth targets and the prediction given by the tree, which is the mean value of the targets.

We have now created two ML models and know that the decision tree model performs a bit worse than the regression model on our test dataset. The question now is whether, without touching the test set, we will be able to improve the decision tree model to make it perform better than our linear regression model in final testing. This introduces an important step in the ML pipeline: hyperparameter tuning and model selection.

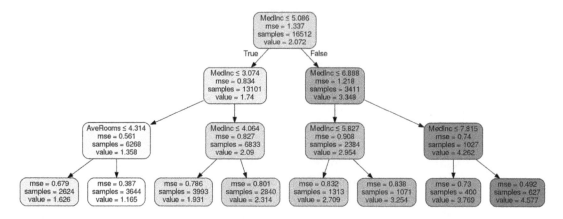

Figure 2.8   Visualization of the learned decision tree

2.6   *Fine-tuning the ML model: Introduction to grid search*

Knowing the optimal hyperparameters for an ML algorithm, such as the `max_depth` of the decision tree model, before you get started is usually impossible. So, hyperparameter tuning is a very important step—it allows you to select the best components to form your ML algorithm and improve the performance of the algorithm you create. Tuning is generally a trial-and-error process. You predefine a set of candidate combinations of hyperparameters and select the best combination by applying them to the training data with the validation process and evaluating the results. To help you better understand the tuning process, let's try to improve the decision tree model by tuning its `max_depth` hyperparameter.

The first thing we should do is construct a validation set so we can compare our different models based on their validation performance. Always remember that you should not touch the test set during the hyperparameter-tuning process. The model should be exposed to this data only once tuning is complete. There are many ways to partition the training data and conduct model validation. We'll use *cross-validation* here; it's a technique that is widely used for model validation, especially when the dataset size is small. Cross-validation averages the results of multiple rounds of model training and evaluation. In each round, the dataset is randomly partitioned into two complementary subsets (the training and validation sets). Every data point has an equal chance of being in either the training set or the validation set across different rounds. The two main groups of cross-validation methods follow:

- With *exhaustive* cross-validation methods, you train and evaluate a model on all the possible ways to make up the two sets into which you partition the data. For example, suppose you decide to use 80% of the dataset for training and 20% for validation. In that case, you'll need to exhaust every possible combination of data points in those two sets and average the training and testing results of the model on all these partitions. A representative example of exhaustive cross-validation is *leave-one-out cross-validation,* in which each example is an individual test set whereas all the rest form the corresponding training set. Given *N* samples, you'll have *N* partitions for *N*-time training and evaluation of your candidate models.

- With *nonexhaustive* cross-validation methods, as the name implies, you don't have to exhaust all the possibilities for each partition. Two representative examples are the *holdout method* and *k-fold cross-validation.* The holdout method simply involves randomly partitioning the original training data into two sets. One is the new training set, and the other is the validation set. People often treat this method as simple validation rather than cross-validation because it typically involves a single run and the individual data points are not used for both training and validation. *k*-fold cross-validation divides the original training data into *k* equally partitioned subsets. Each subset in turn is used as the validation set, whereas the rest are the corresponding training set at that time (see figure 2.9). Given *N* samples, *N*-fold cross-validation is equivalent to leave-one-out cross-validation.

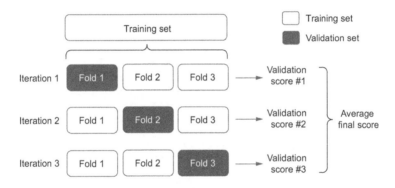

Figure 2.9 Three-fold cross-validation

Let's try using five-fold cross-validation to tune the `max_depth` hyperparameter. In listing 2.14, we use the `KFold` cross-validator in the scikit-learn library to generate the cross-validation sets and loop through all the candidate values of the `max_depth` hyperparameter to generate the tree model and conduct cross-validation. This search strategy is called *grid search,* and it's one of the most naive AutoML approaches for searching for the best hyperparameters. The main idea is to traverse all the combinations of the values in the candidate hyperparameter sets and select the best combination based on the evaluation results. Because we have only one candidate hyperparameter to tune, it becomes a simple loop over all the possible values.

Listing 2.14 Generating cross-validation sets, tuning `max_depth`

```
import numpy as np
from sklearn.model_selection import KFold
```

```
kf = KFold(n_splits = 5)          ◄─┐ Creates a five-fold cross-validation
                                    │ object for data partitioning
cv_sets = []
for train_index, test_index in kf.split(X_train):
    cv_sets.append(((X_train.iloc[train_index],
                    y_train.iloc[train_index],
                    X_train.iloc[test_index],
                    y_train.iloc[test_index]))

max_depths = list(range(1, 11))    ◄─┐ Constructs the candidate
                                     │ value list for the max_depth
for max_depth in max_depths:         │ hyperparameter
    cv_results = []
    regressor = DecisionTreeRegressor(max_depth=max_depth, random_state=42)

                                                    ┌─ Loops through all the cross-
    for x_tr, y_tr, x_te, y_te in cv_sets:   ◄──────┤ validation sets and averages
        regressor.fit(x_tr, y_tr)                   └─ the validation results
        cv_results.append(mean_squared_error(regressor.predict(x_te) , y_te))
    print(f'Tree depth: {max_depth}, Avg. MSE: {np.mean(cv_results)}')
```

From the evaluation results that follow, we can observe that `max_depth=6` gives the lowest MSE, as shown next:

```
Tree depth: 1, Avg. MSE: 0.9167053334390705
Tree depth: 2, Avg. MSE: 0.7383634845663015
Tree depth: 3, Avg. MSE: 0.68854467373395
Tree depth: 4, Avg. MSE: 0.6388802215441052
Tree depth: 5, Avg. MSE: 0.6229559075742178
Tree depth: 6, Avg. MSE: 0.6181574550660847
Tree depth: 7, Avg. MSE: 0.6315191091236836
Tree depth: 8, Avg. MSE: 0.6531981343523263
Tree depth: 9, Avg. MSE: 0.6782896327438639
Tree depth: 10, Avg. MSE: 0.7025407934796457
```

We can use the same technique to select the values for other hyperparameters, and even the model type. For example, we can do cross-validation for both the linear regression and decision tree models with the same validation set and select the one with the better cross-validation results.

Sometimes you may have more hyperparameters to tune, which makes it hard to use a simple `for` loop for this task. scikit-learn provides a built-in class called `GridSearchCV` that makes this task more convenient. You provide it the search space of the hyperparameters as a dictionary, the model you want to tune, and a scoring function to measure the performance of the model. For example, in this problem, the search space is a dictionary with only one key, `max_depth`, whose value is a list containing its candidate values. The scoring function can be transformed from the performance metric using the `make_scorer` function. For example, we can transform the MSE into a scoring function as shown in listing 2.15. It should be noted that `GridSearchCV` in scikit-learn assumes by default that higher scores are better. Because we want to find the model with the smallest MSE, we should set `greater_is_better` to `False` in the `make_scorer` function when defining the scoring function for the grid search.

Listing 2.15   Grid search for the `max_depth` hyperparameter

```
from sklearn.model_selection import GridSearchCV
from sklearn.metrics import make_scorer              Builds the
                                                     decision tree
                                                     regressor
regressor = DecisionTreeRegressor(random_state=42)  ◄─┘

                                                      Creates a dictionary as
hps = {'max_depth':list(range(1, 11))}          ◄──┤  the search space for the
                                                      hyperparameter max_depth
scoring_fnc = make_scorer(mean_squared_error,
                     greater_is_better=False)  ◄─┐ Defines a scoring
                                                 │ function

grid_search = GridSearchCV(estimator=regressor, param_grid=hps,
                    scoring=scoring_fnc,              Creates the grid search
                    cv=5)                  ◄──────┤   cross-validation object with
                                                      five-fold cross-validation
grid_search = grid_search.fit(X_train, y_train)  ◄─┐

               Fits the grid search object to the training
                    data to find the optimal model
```

We can retrieve the cross-validation results and plot the MSE against `max_depth` using the following code.

Listing 2.16   Plotting the grid search cross-validation results

```
cvres = grid_search.cv_results_    ◄──┘ Retrieves the cross-validation results
for mean_score, params in zip(cvres['mean_test_score'], cvres['params']):
    print(-mean_score, params)

plt.plot(hps['max_depth'], -cvres['mean_test_score'])
plt.title('MSE change with hyperparameter tree max depth')   Plots the MSE
plt.xlabel('max_depth')                                       curve by increasing
plt.ylabel('MSE')                                             max_depth
plt.show()
```

In figure 2.10, we can see that the MSE first decreases and then increases as `max_depth` increases. This is because as the depth of the tree grows, the model gains more flexibility and better capacity to refine the partitions. This will help the model better fit the training data, but eventually it will start to overfit. In our case this happens when `max_depth>6`. The model achieves the best performance when `max_depth=6`.

You may be wondering whether cross-validation will accurately reflect the models' generalization ability on unseen examples. We can verify this by plotting both the

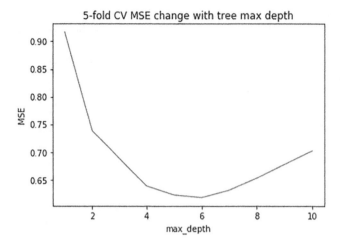

**Figure 2.10   Variation of five-fold cross-validation results with
increasing** `max_depth`

cross-validation MSE curve and the test MSE curve of the 10 models with different values of `max_depth`, as shown here:

```
>>> test_results = []
>>> for max_depth in hps['max_depth']:
...     tmp_results = []
...     regressor = DecisionTreeRegressor(max_depth=max_depth,
...                                       random_state=42)
...     regressor.fit(X_train, y_train)
...     test_results.append(mean_squared_error(
...                         regressor.predict(X_test) , y_test))
...     print(f'Tree depth: {max_depth}, Test MSE: {test_results[-1]}')

>>> plt.plot(hps['max_depth'], -cvres['mean_test_score'])
>>> plt.plot(hps['max_depth'], test_results)
>>> plt.title('Comparison of the changing curve of the CV results
➥ and real test results')
>>> plt.legend(['CV', 'Test'])
>>> plt.xlabel('max_depth')
>>> plt.ylabel('MSE')
>>> plt.show()

Tree depth: 1, Test MSE: 0.9441349708215667
Tree depth: 2, Test MSE: 0.7542635096031615
Tree depth: 3, Test MSE: 0.7063353387614023
Tree depth: 4, Test MSE: 0.6624543803195595
Tree depth: 5, Test MSE: 0.6455716785858321
Tree depth: 6, Test MSE: 0.6422136569733781
Tree depth: 7, Test MSE: 0.6423777285754818
Tree depth: 8, Test MSE: 0.6528185531960586
Tree depth: 9, Test MSE: 0.6751884166016034
Tree depth: 10, Test MSE: 0.7124031319320459
```

Based on the test MSE values and figure 2.11, we can observe that the validation results perfectly select the max_depth corresponding to the best test results, and the two curves roughly align. Note that this is done only to illustrate the effectiveness of cross-validation—you should never use the test curve to select the model in practice!

Comparison of the changing curve of the CV results and real test results

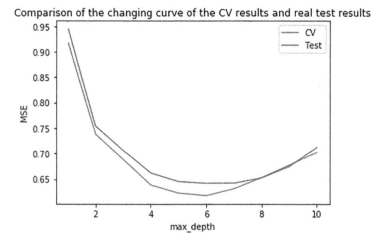

Figure 2.11   Comparison of the cross-validation result curve and the test result curve with increasing max_depth

Up to now, we've been using the California housing price-prediction problem to demonstrate the general steps in an ML pipeline before deploying the ML solution. The data we've used is structured in a table format, with rows representing the instances and columns indicating their features. This type of data is usually called *tabular data* or *structured data*. Besides tabular data, you might encounter many other types of data in different ML applications that require different treatment by selecting tailored components in the ML pipeline. Appendix B provides three more examples showing how to deal with image, text, and tabular data for classification tasks. All of them use classic data preparation methods and ML models. I recommend that you take a look at them before going on to the next chapter if you're not familiar with these problems. These examples also show how to tune multiple hyperparameters jointly in an ML pipeline using the grid search method in scikit-learn. More advanced options for hyperparameter tuning will be discussed in the second part of the book.

Summary

- In an ML project, the first task is to frame the problem as an ML problem and assemble the dataset to be used.
- Exploring and preparing the dataset is important. Extracting useful patterns from the data can improve the performance of the final ML solution.

- During the process of selecting an ML model, one should try out different models and evaluate their relative performance.
- Using the right hyperparameters for your model is critical to the final performance of the ML solution. Grid search is a naive AutoML approach that can be used for hyperparameter tuning and model selection.

Deep learning in a nutshell

3

This chapter covers

- The basics of building and training deep learning models
- Using a multilayer perceptron for regression on tabular data
- Classifying image data with a multilayer perceptron and a convolutional neural network
- Classifying text data with a recurrent neural network

Deep learning, a subfield of ML, has become a scorching topic in the AI community and beyond. It drives numerous applications across various fields and has achieved superior performance compared with many of the more traditional models introduced earlier. This chapter will present the basic building blocks of deep learning and show you how to apply three popular types of models to solve supervised learning tasks on different data types. The chapter will also serve as a stepping stone to help you better understand the AutoML methods for generating and tuning deep learning methods introduced in the second part of the book.

3.1 *What is deep learning?*

The "deep" in "deep learning" refers to the successively added *layers*, as shown in figure 3.1. The number of layers stacked together is called the *depth* of the deep learning model. For example, the depth of the model in figure 3.1 is four. You can think of the layers as sets of operations to transform features, such as multiplying the features with a matrix. The layers are jointly trained to perform the transformation for us instead of us performing them one by one. We call the output of each layer a *representation* (or *embedding*) of the original input. For example, the cat image on the left side of figure 3.1 is the model's input. The pixel values of the image can be treated as the original representation of the image. The first layer of the model takes the image as input and outputs five different images, which are transformed representations of the original image. Finally, the output of layer 4 is a vector indicating that the predicted label of the image is "cat."

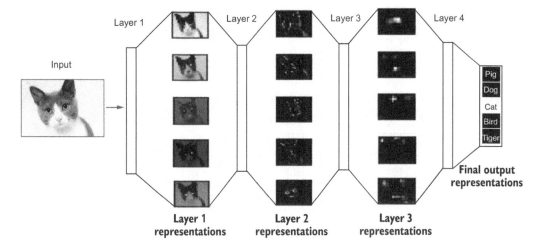

Figure 3.1 A deep learning model for animal classification

Deep learning models are often collectively called *neural networks* because they are mainly based on *artificial neural networks* (ANNs), a type of model loosely inspired by the biological architecture of the brain.

Applying deep learning in practice follows the same ML pipeline introduced in chapter 2. But the following two properties of deep learning models distinguish them from the models introduced before:

- The model structure reduces the effort of feature engineering, such as doing principal component analysis (PCA) for dimensionality reduction in images. The feature transformations learned with the layers can bring about similar effects, as you will see.

- Deeper models introduce more parameters to be learned and hyperparameters to be tuned than "shallower" models like the traditional models introduced in the previous chapters (such as decision trees and linear regression models) or neural networks with no more than two layers.

Deep learning models offer high performance on a broad range of problems, especially problems with large amounts of data. This chapter will walk through three typical deep learning applications with code examples to help you understand these distinctions and the way to apply deep learning in practice. Before we get to the examples, though, let's take a quick look at the tools you'll use to implement deep learning.

3.2 TensorFlow and Keras

TensorFlow is an open source platform for machine learning. It has a comprehensive, flexible ecosystem of tools and libraries that researchers and developers can use to build and deploy ML-powered applications. TensorFlow implements a comprehensive set of math operations to run on different hardware, including CPUs, GPUs, and *tensor processing units* (TPUs) for deep model training. The training can scale up to multiple GPUs on multiple machines, and the trained model can be deployed in a variety of environments, like web pages and embedded systems.

> **NOTE** TPUs are dedicated hardware specially designed for *tensor* computations. GPUs and TPUs are heavily used in deep learning to facilitate the model training and inference speed.

A *tensor*, the most commonly used data type in deep learning, is an *n*-dimensional array. Tensors are a generalization of vectors and matrices that can have more than two dimensions: a vector is a one-dimensional tensor, and a matrix is a two-dimensional tensor. In practical terms, an RGB image can be treated as a three-dimensional tensor (color channel × height × width), and a video can be viewed as a four-dimensional tensor, where the extra dimension is the time (or frame) dimension.

Keras is a Python library that provides a simpler set of APIs for building and training ML models by encapsulating the functionality of TensorFlow. It vastly reduces the effort required to build up deep learning algorithms and is well received by the community. Keras originated as a separate Python package but has been integrated into the TensorFlow package as a high-level API, facilitating customization, scaling, and deployment of deep learning models. From now on, we will mainly use the Keras API in TensorFlow to implement all our deep learning workflows.

3.3 California housing price prediction with a multilayer perceptron

The first problem we will target is one we worked on in chapter 2: the California housing price-prediction problem. It's a regression problem where the aim is to predict the average price of a housing block based on eight features, such as the average number of rooms in the houses in the block. We will follow the typical process for creating an ML pipeline to proceed with the analysis, but I'll skate over the duplicate parts and emphasize the distinct parts in the context of deep learning.

3.3.1 Assembling and preparing the data

We follow the same process we used earlier to collect the data using the scikit-learn library and prepare it for the deep learning model. The first step is to load the California housing dataset and split out 20% of the data for testing, as shown in the next listing.

> **Listing 3.1   Loading and splitting the California housing dataset**

```
from sklearn.datasets import fetch_california_housing

house_dataset = fetch_california_housing()          ◁————  Loads the
                                                            dataset

from sklearn.model_selection import train_test_split
train_data, test_data, train_targets, test_targets = train_test_split(
    data, target,
    test_size=0.2,              Splits out 20% of the
    random_state=42)     ◁——    data for testing
```

As we've seen before, the shapes of the feature matrices in the training and test sets are (16512, 8) and (4128, 8), respectively, as shown next:

```
>>> train_data.shape, test_data.shape
((16512, 8), (4128, 8))
```

Because all the dataset features are numerical features without missing values, as we learned in section 2.3, the data is already suitable for feeding into a neural network. However, different features have different scales. This could be a problem in practice, causing the training process to be much slower. At worst, training may not *converge*, which means the optimization loss or the weights of the network does not settle to within an error range around the optimal value. Typically, the training of a neural network will stop when the weights converge. Otherwise, we consider the training to have failed, and the produced model often will not be able to work well. To deal with the different feature scales, *feature-wise normalization* is a good idea. We do this by subtracting the means of the features and dividing by their standard deviations, as shown in the following listing.

> **Listing 3.2   Performing feature-wise normalization on the training and test data**

```
def norm(x, mean, std):       ◁——┐ Defines a function to do the
    return (x - mean) / std        feature-wise normalization

mean = train_data.mean(axis=0)      Calculates the mean and standard
std = train_data.std(axis=0)        deviation for each feature

normed_train_data = norm(train_data, mean, std)     Normalizes the training
normed_test_data = norm(test_data, mean, std)       and test data
```

Notice that we use the `mean` and `std` calculated for the training data to normalize the test data for the following two reasons:

- We assume the training and test data follow the same distribution.
- The test data may not always have enough instances for calculating trustworthy `mean` and `std` values.

This normalization will be the only feature engineering done in this example. It can also be done with shallow models, but we didn't do it in chapter 2 because the optimization algorithms for linear regression and decision tree models would not benefit much from it. To learn more about this, see Joel Grus's *Data Science from Scratch*, 2nd edition (O'Reilly, 2019).

We're now ready to create the deep learning algorithm.

3.3.2 Building up the multilayer perceptron

To implement the deep learning algorithm, let's first import Keras in TensorFlow as follows:

```
from tensorflow import keras
```

As a quick recap, building an ML algorithm requires you to specify four components: the model type, the measurement to measure the quality of the current model, the optimization method for updating the model weights, and the stopping criterion to terminate the updating process. We'll begin with the first component and instantiate a three-layer neural network. We use the following code to build up the network, and the network structure is shown in figure 3.2.

Listing 3.3 Creating a three-layer neural network

```
from tensorflow import keras
from tensorflow.keras import layers

model = keras.Sequential([
    layers.Dense(64, activation='relu', input_shape=[8]),
    layers.Dense(64, activation='relu'),
    layers.Dense(1)              Creates a multilayer perceptron
])                               model with the Keras API
```

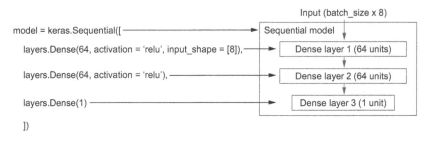

Figure 3.2 A three-layer network

The three layers are of the same type, known as *fully connected* or *dense*. The first two, which are closer to the input, are also called *hidden layers*. The last layer, for generating the predicted housing price, is called the *output layer*. The inputs and outputs of a dense layer are all tensors (*n*-dimensional arrays). The keras.Sequential indicates that the model we chose is a Keras model constructed by stacking multiple layers sequentially. A sequential model constituting multiple dense layers is called a *multi-layer perceptron* (MLP).

To better understand the code, let's dig in and see how a dense layer works. A dense layer can be formulated as *output = activation(dot(input, weight_matrix) + bias)*. It is composed of the following three operations:

- *Tensor-matrix dot product*—This is a generalization of matrix–matrix multiplication. The tensor-matrix dot product will multiply the input tensor with a matrix (often called the *kernel matrix*) to convert it into a new tensor, whose last dimension is different from the original tensor's. When defining the layer, we should explicitly define this last dimension's shape, or the number of *units* of this layer. For example, in this problem each input housing block instance is a one-dimensional vector with eight elements. The first dense layer has 64 units. It will create an 8×64–weight matrix (that can be learned) to transform each input vector to a new vector (tensor) of length 64. If each input sample is a three-dimensional tensor of size 3×10×10, by defining the dense layer with the same code, we will create a 20×64–weight matrix to transform the input tensor to a 3×10×64 tensor. The specific calculation is done in a matrix–matrix multiplication fashion, which means the input will be split into multiple matrices and multiplied by the weight matrix. We use a toy example to illustrate the calculation in figure 3.3.

- *Bias addition operation*—After doing the dot product, we add a bias weight to each instance. The bias weight is a tensor of the same shape as the instance representation after the dot product. For example, in this problem, the first dense layer will create a learnable bias vector of shape 64.

- *Activation operation*—The selected activation function defines an activation operation. Because the concept of the neural network was originally inspired by neurobiology, each element in the representation (tensor) output by a layer is called a *neuron*. An activation function is introduced to approximate the influence of an extracellular field on the neuron. Equipped with the view of a neural network, we often choose the activation function as a nonlinear mapping function applied on each neuron to introduce nonlinearities in the transformation defined by each layer. If we use linear activations, stacking multiple linear layers will result in a constrained representation space with only linear transformations. Thus, the produced neural network would not be a universal approximator transformation. Some commonly used activation functions include ReLU (rectified linear unit), sigmoid, and tanh (hyperbolic tangent). Their shapes are shown in figure 3.4.

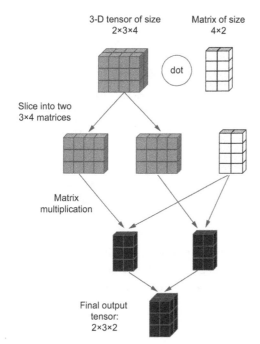

3-D tensor of size
2×3×4

Matrix of size
4×2

dot

Slice into two
3×4 matrices

Matrix
multiplication

Final output
tensor:
2×3×2

Figure 3.3 Tensor dot product: A 3-D
tensor multiplied by a 2-D matrix

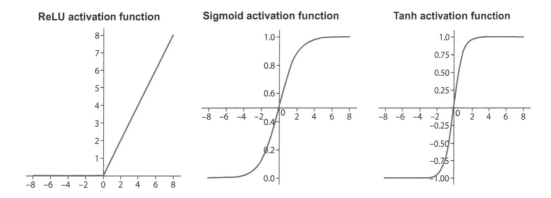

ReLU activation function

Sigmoid activation function

Tanh activation function

Figure 3.4 Three common activation functions: From left to right, ReLU, sigmoid, and tanh

When instantiating a dense layer, you need to specify the shape of its output (number of units). If it's the first layer, you also need to provide the shape of the input. This is not needed for the rest of the layers, because their input shape can be automatically determined from the output of the previous layers.

When applying the MLP model to the dataset, we can feed the data points in one at a time or provide a batch of instances at a time. The number of data points fed into the network at any one time is called the *batch size*. It does not need to be specified for the model until the data is fed into the network. The flow of passing inputs through a neural network to achieve outputs is called a *forward pass*. Let's try out the created model now, slicing an example batch of five data points from the training data and doing a forward pass as shown in the next code listing.

Listing 3.4 Trying out the model with an example batch of data

```
>>> example_batch = normed_train_data[:5]
>>> example_result = model.predict(example_batch)
>>> example_result
array([[-0.06166808],
       [-0.12472008],
       [-0.01898661],
       [-0.1598819 ],
       [ 0.17510001]], dtype=float32)
```

Slices a batch of the first five normalized data points

Feeds the data batch into the model for predictions

Because we haven't trained the weights in the network, the predictions are calculated based on randomly initialized weights in each layer. The Keras API provides a convenient way to visualize the output shape and weights of each layer in the defined model using the summary function, as shown here:

```
>>> model.summary()
Model: "sequential"
```

Layer (type)	Output Shape	Param #
dense (Dense)	(None, 64)	576
dense_1 (Dense)	(None, 64)	4160
dense_2 (Dense)	(None, 1)	65

```
Total params: 4,801
Trainable params: 4,801
Nontrainable params: 0
```

The model can accept data batches of any size. The first dimension of the output shape is None in each layer because we do not predefine the number of data points in each batch. The model will identify the number of data points in each batch after they've been fed in. The parameters include the weight matrix in the tensor-matrix dot product and the bias vector. For example, the first layer has 8 * 64 + 64 = 576 parameters. Again, these parameters are all randomly initialized before training, so they can not transform the features into correct predictions. But the exercise of checking the weight and output shape can help us debug the model structure. Now let's begin to train the network and test its performance.

3.3.3 *Training and testing the neural network*

Training the network requires a complete deep learning algorithm with the folowing three remaining components selected:

- *Optimizer*—The optimization method used to update the weights of a neural network.

- *Loss function*—A function to measure the performance of the neural network and guide the optimizer during training. It usually measures the difference between the ground-truth values and the predicted values. For example, mean squared error (introduced in section 2.5) is an acceptable loss function for regression tasks. During training, the optimizer will try to update the weights to achieve minimum loss.

- *Metrics*—Statistics to monitor during the training and testing process, such as the accuracy of a classification task. These will not affect the training process but will be calculated and recorded for both the training and the validation set. These values are used as auxiliary information to analyze and adjust the designed algorithm.

What is the most commonly used optimizer in deep learning, and how does it work?

The most widely used optimization method for training neural networks is called *stochastic gradient descent* (SGD). The following figure illustrates how a naive SGD optimizer works. In this figure, the *y*-axis is the loss value of a neural network, and the *x*-axis represents the weights of the network to be updated. We consider only one weight here for the purposes of illustration. The goal of applying SGD is to update this singular to find the *global optimum point* in the curve, whose *y*-value corresponds to the minimum value of the loss function. This goal may not always be reached, depending on the hyperparameters and the complexity of the network. We may end up identifying an inferior point instead, such as the *local optimum point* in the figure.

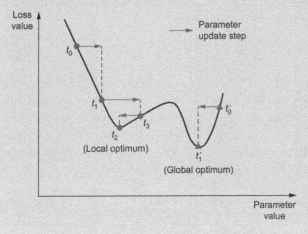

Illustration of stochastic gradient descent down a 1-D loss curve (one learnable parameter)

(continued)

At every iteration, SGD uses a subset of the training data to calculate the gradients of the parameters by taking derivative of the loss function. The weights are then updated by adding the gradients to them. Usually, the gradients are not directly added to the weights but instead are multiplied by a value called the *learning rate*, which is a hyperparameter controlling the rate of updating. The pseudocode for this process is shown in the following listing.

Listing 3.5   Pseudocode of stochastic gradient descent

```
for i in range(num_iterations):
    gradients = calculate_gradients(loss, data_subset)
    weights = weights - gradients * learning_rate
```

Each arrow in the figure indicates the changing direction of the weight at an iteration. Its length is the value of gradients * learning_rate. If the weight starts at t_0, it will end up at t_2, which is a local optimum. However, the weight initialized at t'_0 reaches the global optimum on the right side. As this example shows, the initialization values and the learning rate selected can lead to different optimization results. Variants of the naive SGD optimizer such as RMSprop and Adam try to increase the optimization effectiveness and efficiency, which is why you will see them introduced in our code implementations.

In this example, we have only one weight to update. But because neural networks often have multiple layers with multiple weights in each layer, computing the gradients can become very complicated. The most common way of calculating the gradients for all the weights is called *backpropagation*. It treats the layers as a chain of composed functions (tensor operations) and applies the chain rule to calculate the gradients for the weights in each layer. The gradients of a later layer can be used to calculate the gradients of the previous layer, so that they are eventually passed back from the last layer to the first layer of the neural network.

Setting the loss function, optimizer, and metrics of the deep learning algorithm can be done with the following one line of code:

```
model.compile(loss='mse', optimizer='rmsprop', metrics=['mae', 'mse'])
```

The `compile` method configures the model for training. We use the mean squared error (MSE) as the loss function to measure the performance of the neural network during training, as we did for the linear regression model in chapter 2. The optimizer selected is RMSprop, which is a variant of SGD. We apply two metrics, mean absolute error (MAE) and MSE, to evaluate the model. We can also customize the configuration of the optimizer, such as the learning rate, as follows:

```
optimizer = tf.keras.optimizers.RMSprop(0.01)
model.compile(loss='mse', optimizer=optimizer, metrics=['mae', 'mse'])
```

After preparing the network for training, we can feed the data to it with the `fit` method like so:

```
model.fit(normed_train_data,
          train_targets,
          epochs=300,
          batch_size=1024,
          verbose=1)
```

The training process will terminate based on predefined stopping criteria, such as the number of *epochs* to train for. Because the inputs are split into batches (1,024 per batch here), an epoch in this case means feeding all the batches into the neural network and updating its weights once. For example, if we have 100 examples for training and the batch size is 1, an epoch equals 100 iterations of model update.

Recapping the general learning process of ML introduced in chapter 1, a counterpart workflow for training a neural network is depicted in figure 3.5. Given a batch of input data, the loss function will measure the accuracy of the current network's predictions by comparing them to the targets. The optimizer will take the feedback from the loss function and use it to update the network's weights in each layer.

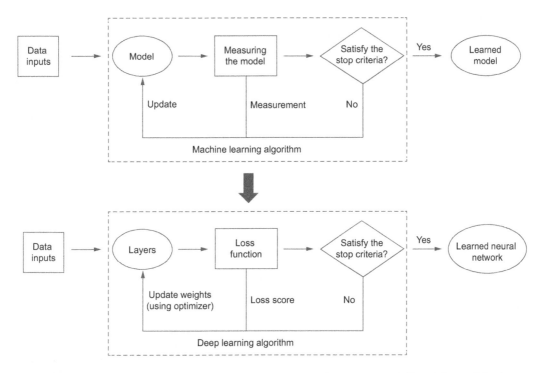

Figure 3.5 The workflow of training a neural network (converted from the general ML training workflow)

To test the trained network, we can call the evaluate function. Our model trained for 300 epochs reaches an MSE of 0.34 on the test set, as shown in the following code snippet:

```
>>> loss, mae, mse = model.evaluate(normed_test_data, test_targets, verbose=0)
>>> mse
0.34268078
```

We have successfully trained and tested our first deep learning model. The next step is to tune the hyperparameters to see if we can improve its performance.

3.3.4   Tuning the number of epochs

Tuning a deep learning algorithm is crucial to improving its performance, but it is often a time-consuming and expensive process because a deep neural network contains many hyperparameters (number of layers, layer types, number of units, and so on). The learning process is often treated as a black box, without many theoretical guarantees being discovered in the existing literature. Here, we take the simple example of tuning the number of epochs using a holdout validation set. The tuning of more complex hyperparameters, such as the number of layers and the number of units in the layers, will be introduced in later chapters using advanced AutoML tools.

As shown in listing 3.6, we split off 20% of the data to use as the validation set and use holdout cross-validation to decide the number of epochs. We train the neural network for a high number of epochs, save the training history into a pandas DataFrame, and plot the MSE curves by epoch for both the training and validation sets.

> **Listing 3.6   Validating the MLP model with holdout cross-validation**

```
def build_model():
    model = keras.Sequential([                          ◁──┐ Creates a function to help repeatedly
        layers.Dense(64, activation='relu',                │ build fresh compiled models
                     input_shape=[normed_train_data.shape[1]]),
        layers.Dense(64, activation='relu'),
        layers.Dense(1)
    ])
    model.compile(loss='mse', optimizer='rmsprop', metrics=['mae', 'mse'])
    return model

model = build_model()          ◁──┤ Creates a new
                                  │ compiled model

EPOCHS=500
history = model.fit(normed_train_data, train_targets,
                    validation_split=0.2,
                    epochs=EPOCHS, batch_size=1024,
                    verbose=1)

    import pandas as pd
    hist = pd.DataFrame(history.history)    ◁──┤

    hist['epoch'] = history.epoch    ◁──┐
```

Holds out 20% of the data for validation during training ⌐────▷ (points to `verbose=1`)

Retrieves the history into a DataFrame— history.history is a dictionary containing the loss, MAE, and MSE results at each epoch on both training and validation sets.

Appends an epoch column to the DataFrame for plotting purposes

```
import matplotlib.pyplot as plt
plt.plot(hist['epoch'], hist['mse'], label='train mse')
plt.plot(hist['epoch'], hist['val_mse'], label='val mse')
plt.xlabel('Epochs')
plt.ylabel('MSE')
plt.title('Training and Validation MSE by Epoch')
plt.legend()
plt.show()
```

Plots the training and validation MSE curves

The training and validation MSE curves are shown in figure 3.6.

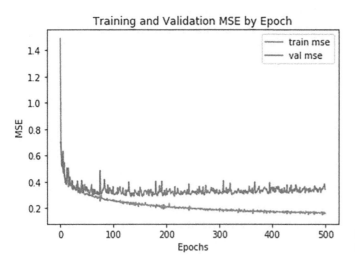

Figure 3.6   Training and validation MSE by epoch

It's not easy to interpret these curves due to the scale variation and the fluctuation between epochs, especially when the number of epochs is large. Using the code in listing 3.7, we can limit the *y*-axis to values below 0.5 to zoom in and smooth the training and validation curves with Gaussian smoothing (see Shapiro and Stockman, *Computer Vision*, Prentice Hall, 2001, pp. 137, 150).

Listing 3.7   Smoothing the accuracy curves

```
import numpy as np
def smooth_curve(values, std=5):
    width = std * 4
    x = np.linspace(-width, width, 2 * width + 1)
    kernel = np.exp(-(x / 5) ** 2)

    values = np.array(values)
    weights = np.ones_like(values)

    smoothed_values = np.convolve(values, kernel, mode='same')
    smoothed_weights = np.convolve(weights, kernel, mode='same')

    return smoothed_values / smoothed_weights
```

Smoothes a list of values with a Gaussian smoothing function

```
plt.plot(hist['epoch'], smooth_curve(hist['mse']), label = 'train mse')
plt.plot(hist['epoch'], smooth_curve(hist['val_mse']), label = 'val mse')
plt.xlabel('Epochs')
plt.ylabel('MSE')
plt.ylim((0, 0.5))
plt.title('Training and Validation MSE by Epoch (smoothed)')
plt.legend()
plt.show()
```

The adjusted plot is shown in figure 3.7. It shows that the training MSE continues decreasing during the 500 epochs. In comparison, the validation MSE displays an increased tendency to fluctuate after around 150 epochs. This means that the network tends to overfit the training data after about 150 epochs.

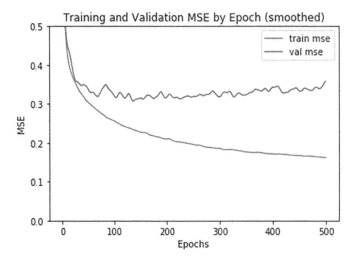

Figure 3.7 Training and validation MSE by epoch (smoothed), with the y-axis limited to values below 0.5

With the optimal number of epochs selected, we can now retrain the model on the full dataset (training and validation sets) and do the testing, as shown in the next code listing.

Listing 3.8 Retraining the final model on the full training set

```
model = build_model()
model.fit(normed_train_data, train_targets, epochs=150, batch_size=1024, verbose=1)
```

The final MSE for the test set is 0.31, which is better than we achieved with the model trained for 300 epochs, as shown here:

```
>>> loss, mae, mse = model.evaluate(normed_test_data, test_targets, verbose=0)
>>> mse
0.30648965
```

In this example, we trained the model only once to select the best number of epochs. Tuning other hyperparameters may require some trial and error. For example, you can use the grid search method to tune the depth of the network—that is, build up multiple MLPs with different numbers of layers and try them on the same split of training and validation sets to select the optimal network depth. We'll introduce more convenient ways to implement this in the second part of the book.

We have now built our first deep neural network, an MLP, to address a tabular data regression problem. In the next two sections, you will learn about two more deep learning models that you can use to address classification problems with image data and text data, respectively.

3.4 Classifying handwritten digits with convolutional neural networks

In this section, we will explore a new model, the *convolutional neural network* (CNN), which is the dominant deep learning model in computer vision applications. We'll use handwritten digit classification to explain how it works and build an MLP network for comparison.

3.4.1 Assembling and preparing the dataset

Let's first collect the dataset and make a few preparations. In chapter 1, we used a dataset that comes with scikit-learn containing 1,797 8×8-pixel images of handwritten digits. In this example, we'll use a similar but larger dataset called *MNIST*, which is commonly used as a starter kit for deep learning. It contains 60,000 training images and 10,000 testing images collected by the National Institute of Standards and Technology (NIST). Each image is of size 28×28 and is labeled with a number from 0 to 9. The dataset can be assembled with the Keras API, as shown in the following listing.

Listing 3.9 Loading the MNIST dataset with TensorFlow Keras API

```
from tensorflow.keras.datasets import mnist

(train_images, train_labels), (test_images, test_labels) =
➥ mnist.load_data()
```

The loaded data is already split into training and test sets. The images and labels are in the form of NumPy arrays. Let's take a look at the training and test data in the next listing.

Listing 3.10 Exploring the shape of the training and test data

```
>>> train_images.shape, test_images.shape
((60000, 28, 28), (10000, 28, 28))
>>> len(train_labels), len(test_labels)
(60000, 10000)
>>> train_labels, test_labels
(array([5, 0, 4, ..., 5, 6, 8], dtype=uint8),
 array([7, 2, 1, ..., 4, 5, 6], dtype=uint8))
```

We can also visualize a sample image using the following code.

Listing 3.11   **Visualizing a training image**

```
import matplotlib.pyplot as plt

plt.figure()
plt.imshow(train_images[0])
plt.colorbar()
plt.title('Label is {label}'.format(label=train_labels[0]))
plt.show()
```

In figure 3.8, we can see that the values of each pixel in the image range from 0 to 255, and the label of the image is 5.

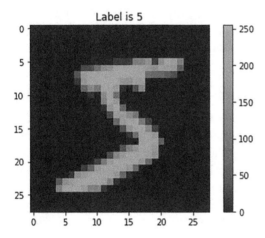

Figure 3.8   **A training sample in MNIST**

Similar to the normalization we did in the previous problem, we can normalize the image by rescaling the values of the pixels to the range of 0 to 1. We use a normalization method called *min-max rescaling* in listing 3.12. It rescales the pixel values by dividing them by the difference between the maximum possible value (255) and the minimum possible value (0). The normalization methods we use here and in the previous example are quite common in deep learning to improve the effectiveness of the learning algorithm.

Listing 3.12   **Rescaling the image**

```
train_images = train_images / 255.0
test_images = test_images / 255.0
```

After preparing the data, we can start to build the network. Before we create our first CNN, let's build an MLP that we can use as a baseline model for comparison.

3.4.2 Addressing the problem with an MLP

We know that an MLP model is composed of multiple dense (fully connected) layers, where the dot product in each layer is applied between the last axis of the input tensor and the kernel matrix. To make sure the first layer computes the dot product using all the features of an image, we can first convert each 28×28 image to a 1×784 vector with a Keras layer called `Flatten`. We'll stack it with two `Dense` layers to create a joint pipeline. Figure 3.9 provides a visual illustration of the `Flatten` layer.

Figure 3.9 Reshape the 2-D image to a 1-D vector (with a Keras `Flatten` layer)

The code for building the MLP is shown in the following listing.

Listing 3.13 Building an MLP for MNIST handwritten digit classification

```
from tensorflow import keras
from tensorflow.keras import layers

mlp_model = keras.Sequential([
    keras.layers.Flatten(input_shape=train_images.shape[1:]),
    keras.layers.Dense(128, activation='relu'),
    keras.layers.Dense(10),
    keras.layers.Softmax()
])
```

The flattening layer takes the shape of an image as input, and it does not have any weights to be learned. You may have noticed the following main differences by comparing this MLP to the one we built up in the previous regression task:

- In the previous model, we set the units in the output layer to 1, to output a predicted housing price. In this multiclass classification problem, the number of units of the last dense layer is 10, to align with the number of classes for classification purposes (0–9). The 10 values output by the last dense layer are called *logits.*
- We do not apply the activation function in the last dense layer but add a layer called `Softmax` layer at the end, which applies a *softmax function* to transform the 10 logits into the probabilities of the input belonging to each class to perform the final prediction. The image will be assigned to the class with the highest transformed probability. The softmax function can be written as $S(y_i) = \frac{e^{y_i}}{\sum_{j=1}^{c} e^{y_j}}$, where c is the number of classes. y_i indicates the logits. There is no parameter to be learned in the `Softmax` layer, and the shapes of its input and output are the same. The `Softmax` layer can also be treated as the activation function of the last

dense layer, which allows us to write the model specification more concisely, as shown next.

Listing 3.14   The same MLP structure with a softmax activation for the output dense layer

```
mlp_model = keras.Sequential([
    keras.layers.Flatten(input_shape=train_images.shape[1:]),
    keras.layers.Dense(128, activation='relu'),
    keras.layers.Dense(10, activation='softmax')
])
```

We can now compile the model for training by specifying the loss function, optimizer, and some evaluation metrics to be retrieved, as shown here.

Listing 3.15   Compiling the MLP model

```
mlp_model.compile(optimizer='adam',
                  loss=tf.keras.losses.SparseCategoricalCrossentropy(),
                  metrics=['accuracy'])
```

We use classification accuracy as the evaluation metric. The adam optimizer is selected, which is a variant of the sgd optimizer. Both adam and rmsprop are commonly used optimization schemes, and you can try out different schemes to select the most suitable one based on its performance. The loss function is a type of cross-entropy loss, which measures the distance between two discrete probability distributions. Here it measures the difference between the predicted probabilities of images belonging to each of the 10 classes and the ground-truth probabilities. The ground-truth probabilities will be 1 for the correct label of the image and 0 for all the other labels. Note that we use SparseCategoricalCrossentropy in listing 3.15, which requires the input labels to be integers (0–9 in this example). If you want to use a *one-hot* representation of the ground-truth labels—for example, [0, 1, 0, 0, 0, 0, 0, 0, 0, 0] for the label 2—you should use tf.keras.losses.CategoricalCrossentropy.

Let's fit the network and check its performance. Here, we train the network for five epochs with 64 images fed into the network in each training batch (the number of epochs and batch size can be tuned):

```
>>> mlp_model.fit(train_images, train_labels,
...     epochs=5, batch_size=64, verbose=0)
>>> test_loss, test_acc = mlp_model.evaluate(
...     test_images, test_labels, verbose=0)
>>> test_acc
0.9757
```

The test accuracy is 97.57%, meaning that the MLP network could classify approximately 98 of 100 images correctly, which is not bad.

3.4.3 Addressing the problem with a CNN

In this section, we introduce a CNN model to solve the problem. The core idea of CNNs is to extract some local patterns, such as the edges, arcs, and textures in an image, and gradually condense them into more complex patterns layer by layer, such as *arcs, edges* → *tire* and *headlight* → *car*.

To achieve this goal, in addition to dense layers, a simple CNN often contains two more types of layers: the *convolutional layer* and the *pooling layer*. Let's first build the CNN and then examine the two layers by looking at the shapes of their input and output tensors. The code for creating a simple CNN is shown next.

Listing 3.16 Building a simple CNN model

```
def build_cnn():
    model = keras.Sequential([
        keras.layers.Conv2D(32, (3, 3), activation='relu',
                            input_shape=(28, 28, 1)),
        keras.layers.MaxPooling2D((2, 2)),
        keras.layers.Conv2D(64, (3, 3), activation='relu'),
        keras.layers.MaxPooling2D((2, 2)),
        keras.layers.Conv2D(64, (3, 3), activation='relu'),
        keras.layers.Flatten(),
        keras.layers.Dense(64, activation='relu'),
        keras.layers.Dense(10, activation='softmax')
    ])

    model.compile(optimizer='adam',
        loss=tf.keras.losses.SparseCategoricalCrossentropy(),
        metrics=['accuracy'])
    return model

cnn_model = build_cnn()
```

Builds up the CNN model structure → applies to the `keras.Sequential([ ... ])` block

Compiles the model for training → applies to the `model.compile(...)` block

After the `Flatten` layer, the network structure is the same as with a simple MLP, apart from the difference in the number of units. The first five layers consist of three convolutional layers interleaved with two pooling layers. They're all two-dimensional layers aiming to extract the spatial characteristics of an image. Before introducing the specific operations, let's display the shapes of the inputs and outputs for each layer here:

```
>>> cnn_model.summary()
Model: "sequential_1"
```

Layer (type)	Output Shape	Param #
conv2d (Conv2D)	(None, 26, 26, 32)	320
max_pooling2d (MaxPooling2D)	(None, 13, 13, 32)	0
conv2d_1 (Conv2D)	(None, 11, 11, 64)	18496
max_pooling2d_1 (MaxPooling2	(None, 5, 5, 64)	0

conv2d_2 (Conv2D)	(None, 3, 3, 64)	36928
flatten_1 (Flatten)	(None, 576)	0
dense_2 (Dense)	(None, 64)	36928
dense_3 (Dense)	(None, 10)	650

```
=================================================================
Total params: 93,322
Trainable params: 93,322
Nontrainable params: 0
```

Regardless of the first batch-size dimension, a convolutional layer takes inputs of three dimensions (height, width, channels) and outputs a three-dimensional tensor, which we often call a *feature map*. The first two dimensions are the spatial dimensions indicating the size of the image (28×28 for MNIST images). The last dimension denotes the number of channels in the feature map. For the original input image, the channel dimension is the number of color channels. For example, an RGB image has three channels: red, blue, and green. A grayscale image, like those in the MNIST dataset, has only one channel.

HOW THE CONVOLUTIONAL LAYER WORKS

When instantiating a convolutional layer, we need to specify two main arguments. The first is the number of filters (or kernels), which determines the number of channels (size of the last dimension) in the output feature map. The second argument is the size of each filter. A *filter* is a trainable tensor that tries to discover a certain pattern in the input feature map. It scans through the input feature map and outputs a matrix indicating where in the inputs the target feature appears. By aggregating the output matrices of different filters, we get the output feature map of the convolutional layer. Each channel in the output feature map is generated from a unique filter. Using the first convolutional layer in listing 3.16 as an example, we set its channel to 32, and the size of each filter is 3×3×1. Each of the filters will generate a 26×26 matrix (I'll explain why later). Because we have 32 filters, they will generate 32 26×26 matrices, which together compose the output feature map of shape (26, 26, 32). The number of trainable weights in a convolutional layer is equal to the sum of the number of elements in the filters plus the channel number (the length of the bias vector). For example, in the first convolutional layer, there are 3 * 3 * 32 + 32 = 320 parameters to be learned.

Now let's see how a three-dimensional filter transforms a three-dimensional input feature map into another three-dimensional feature map and how to calculate the shape of the output feature map. We'll use a 4×4×1 input feature map with filter size 3×3 as an example (see figure 3.10). The filter walks step-by-step through the feature map. We can also specify the step size, called the *stride*. Here we assume the step size is one, which means a 3×3×1 filter has to take two steps to go either horizontally or vertically through the 4×4×1 feature map. At each step, it will cover a region in the input

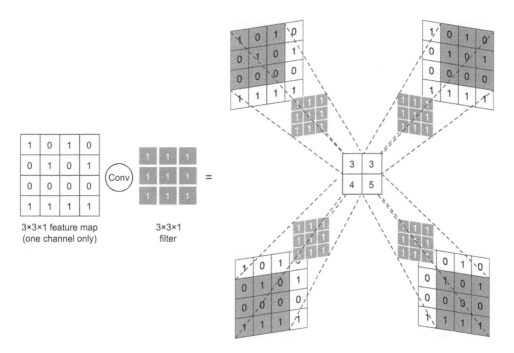

Figure 3.10   Convolution operation between one 4×4×1 feature map and one 3×3×1 filter with stride 1 to produce a 2×2×1 feature map

feature map of the same size as itself and do a convolution operation (this is where the name of the convolutional layer comes from).

Mathematically, at each step, it first does an element-wise multiplication between the covered feature map and the filter. This will result in a three-dimensional tensor of the same size as the filter. Then it sums up all the elements in the tensor into a single value. By walking through the input feature map, we will achieve a matrix (or a three-dimensional tensor if we take the channel axis into account). The size of this matrix is decided by both the filter size and the stride. Generally, the size of the output feature map is equal to the number of valid steps that the stride can take. For example, in figure 3.11, we will achieve a matrix of 2×2 because the stride can take two valid steps along both the height and width dimensions. Similarly, in the MNIST example, each 3×3 filter can take 26 steps along each dimension, transforming a 28×28 image into a 26×26 feature map.

If we set `stride=(2,2)` when defining the `Conv2D` layer, each filter will take two steps along each dimension. Suppose we define the filter size as (3, 3) and have a 4×4 input feature map. There is no room for the filter to take two steps vertically and horizontally, and some pixels along the borders cannot be covered and considered, as shown in figure 3.11. If we set the stride to be (1, 1), the filter will be able to take two steps along each dimension. However, the pixels on the boundaries will be considered in fewer steps than the ones in the middle. This is called the *border effect.*

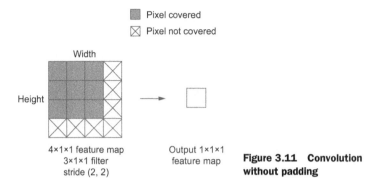

4×1×1 feature map
3×1×1 filter
stride (2, 2)

Output 1×1×1
feature map

Figure 3.11   Convolution without padding

To help the filter achieve full coverage of the feature map, we can extend the boundaries of the input feature by adding zeros around its edges. This *padding* will add rows and columns as appropriate to ensure the pixels are considered equally (in both convolutional and pooling layers). For example, as shown in figure 3.12, adding one column or row along each edge allows a 3×3 filter to keep the shape of the 4×4 input feature map when the stride is (1, 1). Each pixel in the padded feature map will be considered in the same number of steps in the convolution operation.

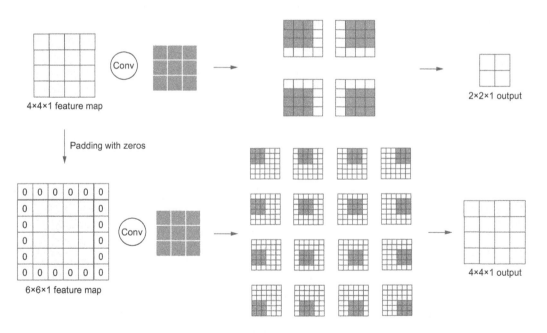

Figure 3.12   Comparison of output dimensions without and with padding of the input feature maps with zeros

HOW THE POOLING LAYER WORKS

Now let's talk about pooling. Figure 3.13 shows how a pooling layer works. This kind of layer is used to reduce the size of a feature map along the spatial dimension for the following two purposes:

- To reduce the computational complexity and the number of parameters to be learned in the later layers (especially the fully connected layers whose weight sizes correspond to the input sizes).
- To maintain scale, rotation, and translation invariance while reducing the size of the feature map. In figure 3.13, each small piece of the image is not scaled or rotated after passing the pooling layer. They are aggregated into a coarse image that keeps the meaning of the original one.

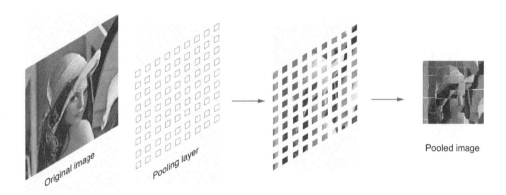

Pooled image

Original image   Pooling layer

Figure 3.13   Pooling can keep the image properties invariant to a certain extent.

Pooling layers conduct similar operations to convolutional layers but do not have any filters (kernels) to learn. The convolution operation is replaced by a particular hard-coded operation such as the `max` operation in the `MaxPooling2D` layers we defined in our first CNN. When instantiating a pooling layer, we need to specify which type we want to use, such as `MaxPooling2D` in our example, and define a pooling size (similar to the kernel size) to identify the regions of the feature map, to which to apply the pooling operation. The stride of a pooling layer is required to be the same as the pooling size, which means the pooling size for each dimension should be a factor of the size of that dimension. If it's not, a padding operation must be applied beforehand; this is done by specifying the `padding='valid'` argument when instantiating a pooling layer with the Keras API.

Applying a pooling layer will divide the input feature map into a set of patches of the same size as the user-specified pooling size. In each patch, it will apply a pooling operation. For example, the `MaxPooling2D` layer will select the maximum value in each patch of the feature map (see figure 3.14).

Practically, pooling layers are often interleaved with convolutional or dense layers to gradually reduce the size of the feature map.

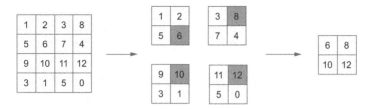

Figure 3.14   Max pooling on a 4×4 feature map with pooling size (2, 2)

TRAINING AND TESTING THE CNN

Before feeding the MNIST data into our CNN, we need to add an extra channel dimension for the original images, as shown here:

```
>>> train_images_4d = train_images[..., tf.newaxis]
>>> test_images_4d = test_images[..., tf.newaxis]
>>> train_images_4d.shape, test_images_4d.shape
((60000, 28, 28, 1), (10000, 28, 28, 1))
```

Compiling and training a CNN model is no different from an MLP. By checking the performance, as shown here, we can see that the simple CNN model achieves 99.02% accuracy, decreasing the error rate by over 40%:

```
>>> cnn_model.fit(train_images_4d, train_labels,
...               epochs=5, batch_size=64, verbose=1)
>>> test_loss, test_acc = cnn_model.evaluate(
...     test_images_4d, test_labels, verbose=0)
>>> test_acc
0.9902
```

Also, although the CNN has more layers than the MLP we designed, the total number of parameters is less than in the MLP thanks to the pooling layer for reducing the size of the feature map.

Again, we could tune the CNN model by tuning hyperparameters such as filter size, stride size, pooling size, number and combination of convolutional and pooling layers, learning rate, optimizer, and so on. There are too many options to cover here, but you should be able to tune them manually by writing a simple loop function, trying different values of the concerned hyperparameters, and comparing their performance with cross-validation. I'll introduce AutoML methods to help you do this more conveniently in the second part of the book.

3.5   *IMDB review classification with recurrent neural networks*

In this last example of the chapter, I'll show you how to solve a text classification problem with a classic deep learning model for sequential data called the *recurrent neural network* (RNN). The dataset we will use is the IMDB movie reviews dataset. The goal is to predict whether the reviews written by the users are positive or negative.

3.5.1   Preparing the data

Similar to the MNIST dataset, the IMDB dataset can be loaded with Keras, as shown next.

Listing 3.17   Loading the IMDB data

```
from tensorflow.keras.datasets import imdb

max_words = 10000

(train_data, train_labels), (test_data, test_labels) = imdb.load_data(
    num_words=max_words)
```

**Loads the data and keeps only the
num_words most frequent words**

This code loads the reviews into `train_data` and `test_data` and the labels (positive or negative) into `train_labels` and `test_labels`. The dataset has already been converted from raw text reviews to lists of integers via tokenization. The tokenization process first splits each review into a list of words and then assigns an integer to each of the words based on a word-integer mapping dictionary. The integers don't have special meaning but provide a numerical representation for words that can be fed into the network. The labels are Boolean values of whether each review is positive or negative. Let's inspect the data, shown next:

```
>>> train_data.shape
(25000,)
>>> train_labels.shape
(25000,)
>>> train_data[0]
[1, 14, 22, 16, 43, 530, 973, 1622, 1385, 65, 458, 4468, 66, 3941, 4,
 173, 36, 256, 5, 25, 100, 43, 838, 112, 50, 670, 2, 9, 35, ...]
>>> len(train_data[0])
218
>>> len(train_data[1])
189
>>> train_labels[:2]
[1 0]
```

Because reviews may be of different lengths, as this output shows, we pad the sequences to be the same length to format them into a matrix. The padding operation is illustrated in figure 3.15. We first select a maximum length (`max_len`) to which all the sequences will be converted. If the sequence is shorter than `max_len`, we add zeros at the end; if it's longer, we cut off the excess.

We select a maximum length of 100 in this example and implement this with Keras as shown in listing 3.18.

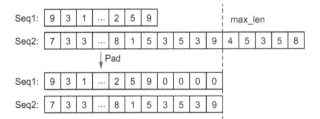

Figure 3.15   Pad the sequences to the same length.

```
from tensorflow.keras.preprocessing import sequence

max_len = 100

train_data = sequence.pad_sequences(train_data, maxlen=max_len)
test_data = sequence.pad_sequences(test_data, maxlen=max_len)
```

The returned padded training data is grouped into a matrix, which is of shape (25000, 100), as shown next:

```
>>> train_data.shape
(25000, 100)
```

Each integer in the matrix is only a numerical representation of a word, so they do not have specific meanings for the network to learn. To provide meaningful input to the network, we use a technique called *word embedding* to create a learnable vector for each word, which we call the *embedding vector*. The method will randomly initialize an embedding vector for each word. These vectors serve as inputs for the network and are jointly learned with the weights of the network. Word embeddings provide a flexible way to map human language into a geometric space, which is very powerful when you have enough learning data. If you don't have a large dataset, you can use embedding vectors learned for other datasets (*pretrained* word embeddings) as an initialization to help the algorithm learn the task-specific embeddings better and faster.

Because the embedding vectors are learnable parameters, the word-embedding method is encapsulated as a layer in Keras named Embedding. It can be stacked together with the RNN. We can implement the whole pipeline by creating a Keras sequential model and adding an embedding layer as the first layer, as shown here.

```
from tensorflow.keras.layers import Embedding
from tensorflow.keras import Sequential

max_words = 10000
embedding_dim = 32
```

```
model = Sequential()                                          ←──────    Creates a Keras
model.add(Embedding(max_words, embedding_dim))     ←──┐               sequential model
                                                       │               object
            Adds an embedding layer into the sequential model
```

The `max_words` parameter defines the vocabulary size, or the maximum possible number of words contained in the input data. The embedding dimension here (`32`) indicates the length of each word-embedding vector. The output tensor of the embedding layer is of shape (`batch_size, max_len, embedding_dim`), where `max_len` is the length of the padded sequences we used before. Each review sequence is now a matrix composed of a set of word-embedding vectors.

3.5.2   *Building up the RNN*

After the embedding layer, we build an RNN for classification. An RNN handles sequential inputs, which are formatted as vectors. It takes one embedding vector at a time along with a *state vector* and generates a new state vector for the next step to use (see figure 3.16). You can think of the state vector as the memory of the RNN: it extracts and memorizes the information in the previous words of the sequence to take the sequential correlation among words in the same sequence into account. In fact, each RNN cell in the figure is a copy of the same cell that contains certain transformations defined by some learnable weight matrices. In the first step, the RNN has no previous words to remember. It takes the first word-embedding vector and an initial state, which is usually empty (a zero vector), as input. The output of the first step is the state to be input to the second step. For the rest of the steps, the RNN will take the previous output and the current input as input and output the state for the next step. For the last step, the output state is the final output we will use for the classification.

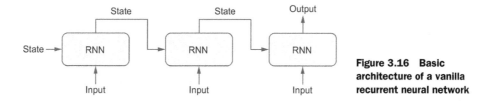

Figure 3.16   **Basic architecture of a vanilla recurrent neural network**

We can use the Python code in the following listing to illustrate the process. The returned state is the final output of the RNN.

Listing 3.20   Pseudocode of the RNN

```
                          ┌── Sets the number of
                          │    recurrent states
state = [0] * 32    ←─────┘
for i in range(100):
    state = rnn(embedding[i], state)    │ Recurrently generates
return state                            │ new state
```

Sometimes, we may also need to collect the output of each step as shown in figure 3.17. We can collect not only the last state vector as output but also all the state vectors. Because the output now is a sequence of vectors, we can make the RNN deeper by stacking multiple RNN layers and use the outputs of one layer as the inputs for the next. It is worth pointing out that the dimensions of each output vector do not have to be the same as those of the input vectors.

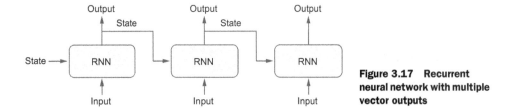

Figure 3.17   Recurrent neural network with multiple vector outputs

We can also stack multiple RNN chains into a multilayer RNN model (see figure 3.18). The output states of each RNN layer will be collected as inputs for the subsequent layer.

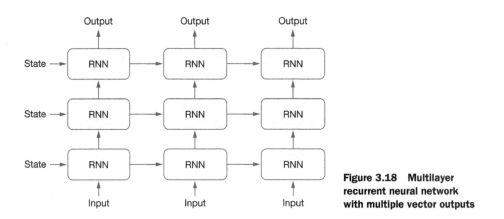

Figure 3.18   Multilayer recurrent neural network with multiple vector outputs

To implement the RNN, we can use the `SimpleRNN` class in Keras. In listing 3.21, we stack four RNN layers to form a multilayer RNN. Each `SimpleRNN` creates an RNN chain (not a single RNN cell). The output states in each of the first three RNN layers are collected as inputs for the subsequent layer. The output state of the fourth RNN layer is fed into the dense layer for final classification.

Listing 3.21   Creating the RNN model

```
from tensorflow.keras.layers import SimpleRNN
from tensorflow.keras.layers import Dense
```

```
model.add(SimpleRNN(units=embedding_dim,
                    return_sequences=True))
model.add(SimpleRNN(units=embedding_dim,
                    return_sequences=True))
model.add(SimpleRNN(units=embedding_dim,
                    return_sequences=True))
model.add(SimpleRNN(units=embedding_dim))
model.add(Dense(1, activation='sigmoid'))
```

Stacks four RNN layers

Adds a dense layer to generate the final classification probability

The units argument defines the length of each output vector (or state vector), which is the same as the length of the input vectors here. The return_sequences argument controls whether to collect all the output vectors of an RNN or only the final output. It is set to False by default. The last layer is a dense layer with a sigmoid activation function to map the state vector of length 32 to a single value (unit), indicating the probability of a review belonging to the positive class.

3.5.3 Training and validating the RNN

We can compile and train the model using a similar process to the MNIST example. We choose binary_crossentropy as the loss function, as shown in the next listing, which is a special case of cross-entropy loss for binary classification.

Listing 3.22 Adding a classification layer

```
model.compile(optimizer='adam', metrics=['acc'], loss='binary_crossentropy')
model.fit(train_data,
          train_labels,
          epochs=2,
          batch_size=128)
```

For illustration purposes, we train for just two epochs with a batch size of 128. The trained RNN model can then be evaluated on the test set like so:

```
>>> model.evaluate(test_data, test_labels)
782/782 [==============================] - 28s 35ms/step -
   loss: 0.3684 - acc: 0.8402
[0.36835795640945435, 0.8402000069618225]
```

Again, we'll skip the tuning of RNNs here and leave that for the next part of the book, with the help of AutoML toolkits.

Summary

- Deep learning models are composed of multiple layers stacked together to distill the input data and generate hierarchical representations. They can be jointly trained in an iterative process via feeding the data forward, determining the loss (error) in the output, and updating the parameters in each layer through the selected optimization method using backpropagation.

- TensorFlow and Keras help us easily implement deep learning models. You should now be able to implement three classic deep learning models, including MLPs for tabular data classification, CNNs for image classification, and RNNs for text classification.
- Compiling and training a deep learning model requires the specification of a loss function, an optimizer, metrics to retrieve, and a stopping criterion (such as the number of epochs to train for).
- Deep learning models usually require less data preprocessing and feature engineering than classic ML models. However, the algorithms often have multiple hyperparameters to be tuned, such as the number of layers, the type of layers, the specific configurations in each layer, and the hyperparameters of the optimization method.

Part 2

AutoML in practice

The previous chapters provided a basic introduction to machine learning, different kinds of ML models, and the workflow of handling ML problems. You've also seen one of the most intuitive AutoML methods for hyperparameter tuning: using grid search to tune an ML pipeline with the help of the scikit-learn toolkit.

Starting with chapter 4, you learn how to address ML problems and improve ML solutions with AutoML. We focus mainly on generating deep learning solutions in the next two chapters, considering the prominence of deep learning models and how complicated it is to design and tune them. You will be able to create deep learning solutions for different ML tasks with the help of advanced AutoML toolkits: AutoKeras and KerasTuner. Chapter 6 introduces a general solution to customize the entire AutoML search space, giving you more flexibility in designing the search space for tuning unsupervised learning models and optimizing algorithms.

Automated generation of end-to-end ML solutions

This chapter covers

- A brief introduction to AutoKeras
- Automated classification and regression
- Addressing multi-input and multi-output problems with AutoML

This chapter begins by teaching you how to create an end-to-end deep learning solution without selecting or tuning any deep learning algorithms. This can be done with as few as five lines of code, which is much simpler than the process introduced in chapter 3 for implementing a deep learning pipeline. Then you'll learn how to perform classification and regression on image, text, and tabular data, as we did in the previous chapters, but with AutoML. We'll also explore several more complex scenarios, including tasks with multiple types of inputs, such as both images and text, and tasks with multiple targets, such as a joint prediction of regression responses and classification labels.

4.1 Preparing the AutoML toolkit: AutoKeras

Before starting to work on the real problems, let's first explore our primary tool for AutoML, AutoKeras. AutoKeras is a Python library focused on the automated generation of deep learning solutions. To install AutoKeras, you can simply run pip install autokeras at your command line or !pip install autokeras in a Jupyter notebook. A more detailed discussion of the package installation is given in appendix A.

AutoKeras is built on the TensorFlow backend (https://tensorflow.org), the TensorFlow Keras API (https://keras.io), and the KerasTuner library (https://keras.io/keras_tuner/). These four components illustrate a complete spectrum of deep learning software. From the user's perspective, as illustrated in figure 4.1, TensorFlow is the most configurable but is also the most complicated; AutoKeras, at the other end of the spectrum, is the simplest. The components on the right were developed based on those on the left, and they offer more advanced and encapsulated automation but less customizability.

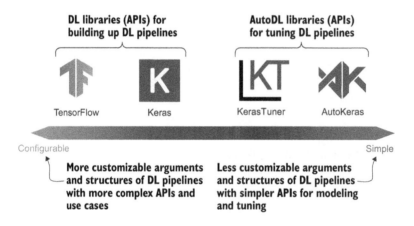

Figure 4.1   The Keras ecosystem

NOTE   "More configurable" here means more arguments for users to specify in the APIs, which allows greater flexibility to customize the ML pipeline and the AutoML algorithm (mainly the search space). Users with more ML expertise can achieve more personalized solutions to meet their requirements using lower-level libraries such as TensorFlow and the Keras API. These allow users to customize their deep learning models layer by layer. On the other hand, users with less knowledge of ML who want to save themselves some effort in modeling and tuning and don't mind sacrificing some flexibility may want to use the higher-level libraries, such as KerasTuner and AutoKeras.

In this book, we'll focus on using AutoKeras to address deep learning problems, with a brief look at KerasTuner in chapter 7. Compared with AutoKeras, KerasTuner can be applied to a wider array of ML problems (beyond the scope of deep learning) and is more flexible in terms of search space design and search algorithm selection. Correspondingly, it requires more knowledge about the ML pipelines to be tuned and about AutoML algorithms. If you're interested in exploring conventional deep learning and the lower-level functionality of TensorFlow and Keras, François Chollet's book *Deep Learning with Python*, 2nd edition (Manning, 2021), provides a more detailed introduction.

AutoKeras is positioned as the highest-level library of all the libraries in the Keras ecosystem. It offers the highest level of automation. As illustrated in figure 4.2, it provides the following three levels of APIs—namely, a set of task APIs, an input/output (IO) API, and a functional API—to cover different scenarios when applying AutoML in real-world applications:

- The task APIs help you generate an end-to-end deep learning solution for a target ML task, such as image classification. These are the most straightforward AutoKeras APIs because they enable you to achieve the desired ML solution with only one step: feeding in the data. Six different task APIs support six different tasks in the latest release of AutoKeras, including classification and regression for image, text, and structured data.

- Real-world problems can have multiple inputs or outputs. For example, we can use both visual and acoustic information to detect actions in a video. We may also want to predict multiple outputs, such as using the consumption records of customers to predict their shopping interests and income levels. To address these tasks, we can use AutoKeras's IO API. You'll see two examples in section 4.4.

- The functional API is mainly for advanced users who want to tailor the search space to their needs. It resembles the TensorFlow Keras functional API, which we used in chapter 3 to create deep neural networks, and allows us to build a deep learning pipeline by wiring some AutoKeras building blocks. A building block often represents a specific deep learning model composed of multiple Keras layers such as a CNN, meaning that we don't have to specify these models layer by layer. The search space of the hyperparameters for each block is also designed and set up for us so that we can focus on the hyperparameters that concern us without worrying about the rest.

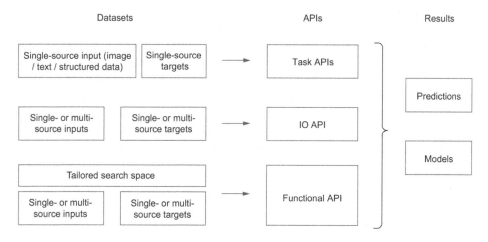

Figure 4.2 Different levels of AutoKeras APIs

This chapter will focus on the task APIs and the IO API. Both of these allow you to generate end-to-end solutions without customizing the search space. The functional API will be discussed in the next chapter.

4.2   *Automated image classification*

Ideally, given an ML problem and the corresponding data, we expect an AutoML algorithm to be able to provide a satisfactory ML solution with minimal human effort or configuration. In this section, we use the image classification problem with the MNIST dataset as an example to introduce how to achieve this goal with only the following two steps:

- Select the AutoKeras task API that is suited to the problem at hand.
- Feed the data to the selected API.

You'll be able to create the image classifier without creating any deep learning models or touching the AutoML algorithm. We will discuss more examples related to different tasks and data types in the next section.

4.2.1   *Attacking the problem with five lines of code*

Remember that we addressed the image classification problem in the previous chapter by building up a CNN with TensorFlow and its Keras API. The following five steps were in the deep learning workflow:

1. Load the training and test datasets with TensorFlow.
2. Preprocess the images via normalization.
3. Build a neural network.
4. Compile and train the neural network.
5. Evaluate the pipeline on the test data.

Implementing this process requires the selection of each component in the deep learning algorithm. You need to define the hyperparameters for the whole pipeline and construct the network layer by layer. Even with this process, it's not always easy to obtain the desired result, because there's no guarantee that you will set all the hyperparameters suitably on your first attempt. Tuning the hyperparameters on a separate validation set requires extra effort during the implementation phase and is a trial-and-error process. With the help of AutoML, you can settle all the matters in one go. Let's automatically generate a deep learning model for classifying MNIST digits using Auto-Keras. The whole problem can be addressed with as few as five lines of code, as you can see in the following listing.

Listing 4.1   **Multiclass image classification with AutoKeras task API**

```
from tensorflow.keras.datasets import mnist

(x_train, y_train), (x_test, y_test) =
    mnist.load_data()                              Loads the data
```

```
import autokeras as ak

clf = ak.ImageClassifier(max_trials=2)

clf.fit(x_train, y_train, epochs=3, verbose=2)
```

**Initializes an AutoKeras
ImageClassifier**

**Feeds the ImageClassifier
with training data**

After loading the datasets, the only thing you need to do to get the final solution is to initialize the API and feed the training data into the initialized `ImageClassifier` object. Fitting is an iterative process using the following three steps:

1 Select a deep learning pipeline (composed of the preprocessing methods, a CNN model, and the training algorithm implemented with Keras) from the search space based on the AutoML search algorithm. For each ML task, Auto-Keras integrates a tailored search space and a task-specific search algorithm in the corresponding task API. You don't need to specify them when using the API. In this example, because we're tackling an image classification problem, the `ImageClassifier` in AutoKeras will automatically populate the search space with a set of deep learning pipelines composed of different data preprocessing methods for images and CNNs.

2 Train the selected pipeline and evaluate it to get its classification accuracy. By default, 20% of the training data will be split off as the validation set. The validation loss or accuracy will be used to compare the performance of all the selected pipelines.

3 Update the AutoML search algorithm. Some AutoML algorithms can learn from the performance of the previously explored pipelines to make their later explorations more efficient. This step may not be required because some AutoML algorithms, such as grid search, do not need to be updated.

This iterative process imitates manual tuning but removes the human element, letting the AutoML algorithm do the selection. The number of tuning iterations is decided by the number of trials you want to conduct—that is, how many pipelines you want the AutoML algorithm to explore in the search space. When initializing the `Image-Classifier`, you can set this in the `max_trials` argument. After all the trials are completed, the best pipeline found so far will be trained again using the full training dataset to achieve the final solution (see figure 4.3).

Calling the `fit()` method of `ImageClassifier` is the same as calling the `fit()` method of a Keras model. All the arguments for fitting a single Keras model can be seamlessly adopted here to control the training process of each selected pipeline, such as the number of epochs. All the trials and the model weights of the best pipeline will be saved to disk, so they are preserved for evaluation and later use.

The evaluation of the final solution is also similar to evaluating a Keras model. After the fitting is done, we can test the best pipeline by calling the `evaluate()` method. It will first preprocess the test images using the preprocessing methods contained in the best pipeline and then feed the processed data into the model. As shown

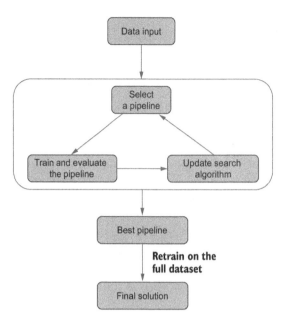

Figure 4.3   The AutoML process of the AutoKeras task API

in the next code sample, the evaluation accuracy of the best pipeline in this example is 98.74%, which is not bad considering that we conducted only two trials (explored two pipelines):

```
>>> test_loss, test_acc = clf.evaluate(x_test, y_test, verbose=0)
>>> print('Test accuracy: ', test_acc)
Test accuracy:  0.9873999953269958
```

You can also get the predicted labels of the test images by calling the predict() function like so:

```
>>> predicted_y = clf.predict(x_test)
>>> print(predicted_y)
[[7]
 [2]
 [1]
 ...
 [4]
 [5]
 [6]]
```

The best found pipeline can be exported as a Keras model. The best model achieved in this example can be exported and printed out as follows:

```
>>> best_model = clf.export_model()
>>> best_model.summary()
```

```
Model: 'model'

_____
Layer (type)                 Output Shape              Param #
=================================================================
input_1 (InputLayer)         [(None, 28, 28, 1)]       0

normalization (Normalization (None, 28, 28, 1)         3

conv2d (Conv2D)              (None, 26, 26, 32)        320

conv2d_1 (Conv2D)            (None, 24, 24, 64)        18496

max_pooling2d (MaxPooling2D) (None, 12, 12, 64)        0

dropout (Dropout)            (None, 12, 12, 64)        0

flatten (Flatten)            (None, 9216)              0

dropout_1 (Dropout)          (None, 9216)              0

dense (Dense)                (None, 10)                92170

classification_head_1 (Softm (None, 10)                0
=================================================================
Total params: 110,989
Trainable params: 110,986
Nontrainable params: 3
_____
```

The model stacks a normalization layer, two convolutional layers, and a pooling layer after the input layer. The *dropout* layer is used to randomly set partial input tensor elements to zero during each training iteration (batch of data), effectively dropping them out of consideration. It is applied only during the training process to help overcome the overfitting issue of the network.

Why a dropout layer can mitigate overfitting

A dropout layer can mitigate overfitting when training a neural network for three reasons:

- It reduces the complexity of the correlations between the neurons. The dropout layer masks some neurons during the training; only the unmasked neurons are interacted with and updated during each forward pass and backpropagation iteration.
- It averages the effects of subnetworks. To some extent, dropout can be regarded as an ensemble strategy to average the predictions of multiple subnetworks randomly selected from the whole network during the training process.
- It introduces extra randomness into the training process, which can help the network layers adapt to different input conditions. This will improve its generalizability to unseen cases during testing.

To learn the details of the dropout layer, see François Chollet's book *Deep Learning with Python*, 2nd edition (Manning, 2021).

The exported Keras model can be saved to disk and loaded for further use by providing the saved path. As mentioned previously, the exported model does not contain the reshaping layer at the beginning to preprocess the input images. We need to first expand the input images into 3-D images before making predictions with the loaded model, as shown in the following listing.

> **Listing 4.2   Saving and loading the best model**

```
from tensorflow.keras.models import load_model        Saves the model in the
                                                       model_autokeras folder
best_model.save('model_autokeras')          ⤶

loaded_model = load_model('model_autokeras')     ⤶  Loads the model

predicted_y = loaded_model.predict(          Predicts with the
    tf.expand_dims(x_test, -1))       ⤶      loaded model
```

As this example shows, compared to the conventional deep learning solution we created with the TensorFlow Keras API, using AutoML with the AutoKeras task APIs allows us to address ML tasks with much less effort spent on data preparation, algorithm configuration, and knowledge acquisition. To conclude this example and further showcase the flexibility of AutoML, let's take a look at some additional use cases.

4.2.2   *Dealing with different data formats*

In practice, we may have data in different formats. AutoML should be able to accommodate and process the different formats automatically without extra manual preprocessing. Some examples follow:

- Images may or may not have an explicitly specified channel dimension. We expect the AutoML API can directly handle both situations, whereas (as we saw in the previous chapter) to feed the MNIST images to a Keras model, we need to manually add an extra channel dimension for each image to convert their shapes when the channel dimension is not presented.
- Labels of images could be strings, integers, or even be prepared into a one-hot-encoded format (vectors of 0s and 1s).
- The data structure of images and labels may vary, depending on the packages used for loading and preparing the datasets. They might be formatted as NumPy arrays (np.ndarray), pandas DataFrames (pd.DataFrame), or TensorFlow Datasets (tf.data.Dataset).

To reduce the burden of data preparation, AutoML libraries often provide the flexibility to handle different data formats. For example, all the cases that were just described can be handled by the ImageClassifier. Testing that is left to the reader as an exercise.

4.2.3 Configuring the tuning process

As well as the data format, you may want to configure the search process by specifying how much data you want to use as the validation set, the evaluation metric you want to collect for the explored pipelines, how you want to compare the pipelines (such as by comparing the accuracy or loss on the validation set), and so on.

Listing 4.3 provides an example. The loss function for training a pipeline is defined as categorical cross-entropy loss. The selected evaluation metric is accuracy. The search objective is set to validation accuracy, so the best pipeline will be the one with the highest classification accuracy on the validation set. Finally, we set aside 15% of the training data to use as the validation set for the tuning process.

Listing 4.3 Customizing the configuration for the tuning process

```
from tensorflow.keras.datasets import mnist
(x_train, y_train), (x_test, y_test) = mnist.load_data()

import autokeras as ak

clf = ak.ImageClassifier(max_trials=2,

                 loss='categorical_crossentropy',

                 metrics=['accuracy'],

                 objective='val_accuracy')

clf.fit(x_train, y_train,
        validation_split=0.15,
        epochs=3, verbose=2)
```

Uses categorical cross-entropy loss for classification

Uses accuracy as the evaluation metric

Sets validation accuracy as the tuning objective

Splits out 15% of the data for validation

We may want to use a custom evaluation metric rather than the default one to compare the performance of the pipelines. For example, we can create our own metric function and wrap it up as an evaluation objective in the AutoML process. As we're tuning deep learning models constructed with TensorFlow Keras, the creation of the objective metric should follow the creation of a Keras metric function, which takes the ground-truth responses (labels in the classification problem) and the model predictions for a batch of data points as inputs and outputs the metric value, as shown next.

Listing 4.4 Creating a customized Keras metric function

```
def my_metric(y_true, y_pred):
    correct_labels = tf.cast(y_true == y_pred, tf.float32)
    return tf.reduce_mean(correct_labels, axis=-1)
```

Compares the model predictions with the ground-truth labels

Computes the prediction accuracy in this batch of data

> **NOTE** Multiple metrics may be added to an `ImageClassifier`, which will all be computed during the evaluation. However, only one objective is set for an `ImageClassifier`—the metric used to select the best model. It is true for the rest of the task APIs as well.

To set the customized metric as the metric and objective in the AutoML process, we should first pass the function as one of the metrics so that it will be calculated during the evaluation process for each selected pipeline. Then we can wrap it up as a search objective, which is used by the search algorithm to compare the performance of the pipelines. Wrapping the objective requires the `Objective` class in the KerasTuner library (see listing 4.5). Two arguments should be provided to instantiate an objective. The first one specifies the name of the metric to be used as the search objective (val_my_metric in this example). Because we want to use the validation accuracy of the pipelines as the objective, we should add a val_ prefix to the function (or metric) name. The second argument (`direction`) indicates whether larger values for the metric (direction='max') or smaller values (direction='min') are better. In this example, we want to find a pipeline to maximize the customized accuracy, so we set the direction to 'max'.

Listing 4.5   Passing the customized metric to the AutoML process

```
import keras_tuner

clf = ak.ImageClassifier(
    seed=42,
    max_trials=2,
    loss='categorical_crossentropy',
    objective=keras_tuner.Objective(
        'val_my_metric', direction='max'),    ⟵  Wraps the customized metric function in a KerasTuner Objective and passes it to AutoKeras
    metrics=[my_metric],    ⟵  Includes the customized metric as one of the metrics
)

clf.fit(x_train, y_train,
        validation_split=0.15,
        epochs=3)
```

It's worth pointing out that the task APIs do not directly provide arguments for selecting the search algorithm and configuring the search space, because their goal is to simplify the whole ML workflow and reduce your burden as much as possible. Let's look at a few more examples of using the AutoKeras task APIs. You'll learn a more general AutoML solution to deal with tasks with multiple inputs and outputs in the last section of this chapter.

4.3   *End-to-end AutoML solutions for four supervised learning problems*

In this section, we'll use AutoML to generate end-to-end solutions for four more supervised ML problems with the help of different AutoKeras task APIs. The problems we will solve follow:

- Text classification with the 20 newsgroups dataset
- Structured data classification with the Titanic dataset
- Structured data regression with the California housing dataset
- Multilabel image classification with a synthetic dataset

We've already solved the first three problems with traditional ML methods in the previous chapters; here, we reapproach them with AutoML to get you familiar with the use of AutoKeras's task APIs.

Before going into the problem, let's quickly recap the differences between the traditional ML methods and the AutoML methods. Traditional ML methods create one model for a problem. Therefore, you have to specify the details of the model. AutoML methods search for different types of models so that you don't specify all the details but leave some part of the model for the search. This difference results in the API of AutoML being different from traditional methods. The AutoML APIs are more concise because they leave the detailed configurations to the search.

The final problem is a more sophisticated image classification scenario, in which each image is related to multiple labels (such as an image containing both a cat and a dog). You may not know how to address it with conventional ML, but with the help of AutoML and the AutoKeras task API, you need to change only one argument in `ImageClassifier`, and everything will be done in one go.

4.3.1   *Text classification with the 20 newsgroups dataset*

The first example is a text classification problem using the 20 newsgroups dataset, fetched with the scikit-learn library. The goal is to classify each document into one of the 20 newsgroups, based on its topic. If you're not familiar with the basic ML process of text classification, we recommend you check out appendix B. We provide more details there related to the preprocessing of text data and two probabilistic classification models. Here we use AutoML to address the problem with the `TextClassifier` task API in AutoKeras.

We first download the data with the built-in data loader `fetch_20newsgroups` in scikit-learn. It has already been split into training and test sets for ease of use. As shown in the following listing, we load only two of the 20 newsgroup categories (`rec.autos` and `rec.motorcycles`), to make running the search process faster.

> **Listing 4.6   Loading the 20 newsgroups dataset**

```
import numpy as np
from sklearn.datasets import fetch_20newsgroups
```

```
categories = ['rec.autos', 'rec.motorcycles']

news_train = fetch_20newsgroups(subset='train',
                                shuffle=True,
                                random_state=42,
                                categories=categories)       ◄─┐  Loads the
news_test = fetch_20newsgroups(subset='test',                  │  training and
                               shuffle=True,                   │  test datasets
                               random_state=42,
                               categories=categories)        ◄─┘

doc_train, label_train = \
    np.array(news_train.data), np.array(news_train.target)   ◄─┐  Formats the
doc_test, label_test =  \                                       │  datasets into
    np.array(news_test.data), np.array(news_test.target)     ◄─┘  NumPy arrays
```

Let's explore the training and test datasets. Each document has been formatted as a string of terms as shown here:

```
>>> print('The number of documents for training: {}.'.format(len(doc_train)))
>>> print('The number of documents for testing: {}.'.format(len(doc_test)))
>>> type(doc_train[0]), doc_train[0]

The number of documents for training: 1192.
The number of documents for testing: 794.


(numpy.str_,
 'From: gregl@zimmer.CSUFresno.EDU (Greg Lewis)\nSubject: Re:
 WARNING.....(please read)...\nKeywords: BRICK, TRUCK, DANGER\
 nNntp-Posting-Host: zimmer.csufresno.edu\nOrganization: CSU
 Fresno\nLines: 33\n\nIn article <1qh336INNfl5@CS.UTK.EDU>
 larose@austin.cs.utk.edu (Brian LaRose) writes:\n>This just a
 warning to EVERYBODY on the net.  Watch out for\n>folks standing
 NEXT to the road or on overpasses. They can\n>cause
 SERIOUS HARM to you and your car. \n>\n>(just a cliff-notes version
 of my story follows)\n>\n>10pm last night, I was
 travelling on the interstate here in\n>knoxville, I was taking an
 offramp exit to another interstate\n>and my wife suddenly
 screamed and something LARGE hit the side\n>of my truck.  We slowed
 down, but after looking back to see the\n>vandals standing
 there, we drove on to the police station.\n>\n>She did get a
 good look at the guy and saw him 'cock his arm' with\n>something
 the size of a cinderblock, BUT I never saw him.
 We are \n>VERY lucky the truck sits up high on the road; if it
 would have hit\n>her window, it would have killed her.
 \n>\n>The police are looking for the guy, but in all likelyhood he is
 gone. \nStuff deleted...\n\nI am sorry to report that in
 Southern California it was a sick sport\nfor a while to drop concrete
 blocks from the overpasses onto the\nfreeway. Several persons
 were killed when said blocks came through\ntheir
 windshields. Many overpass bridges are now fenced, and they\nhave
 made it illegal to loiter on such bridges (as if that
 would stop\nsuch people). Yet many bridges are NOT fenced.
 I always look up at a\nbridge while I still have time to take
```

```
➥ evasive action even though this\n*sport* has not reached us
➥ here in Fresno.\n_____
➥ _____\nGreg_Lewis@csufresno.edu\nPhotojournalism sequence,
➥ Department of Journalism\nCSU Fresno, Fresno, CA 93740\n')
```

After loading the data, we can directly input these raw documents into the API without any further preprocessing, such as transforming the documents into numerical vectors. In listing 4.7, we set the number of pipelines to be searched and compared as three. We do not specify the number of epochs to train each of them. The TextClassifier API will, by default, train each pipeline for, at most, 1,000 epochs and stop training whenever the validation loss does not improve in 10 consecutive epochs to minimize the training time and avoid overfitting.

Listing 4.7 Classifying text with AutoKeras task API

```
import autokeras as ak                          Initializes an
                                                AutoKeras
                                                TextClassifier
clf = ak.TextClassifier(max_trials=3)    ◄────┘

clf.fit(doc_train, label_train, verbose=2)   ◄──┤ Feeds the TextClassifier
                                                  with training data
```

The best pipeline found in the three trials achieves 96.1% accuracy on the final test set, as shown here:

```
>>> test_loss, test_acc = clf.evaluate(doc_test, label_test, verbose=0)
>>> print('Test accuracy: ', test_acc)
 0.9609571695327759
```

We can get the predicted labels of the documents by feeding them into the predict() function and export the best model by calling the export_model() method. Because the procedure is the same as in the previous example, it's not repeated here.

4.3.2 Structured data classification with the Titanic dataset

In this example, we'll use the Titanic dataset to automatically generate an ML solution for a structured data classification task. This dataset contains both categorical features, or string types, and numerical features. Some features also have missing values, so they require extra preprocessing before they are input into a neural network. More details of the dataset and the classical way of preprocessing it are introduced in appendix B. When using AutoML to address the classification problem, as we do here, you don't need to worry about these manual preprocessing steps.

Structured data is often formatted and saved as tables in CSV files. You can also feed in these raw CSV files as inputs without loading them into NumPy arrays or pandas DataFrames.

We use a real structured dataset, the Titanic dataset. The features of the dataset are the profiles of the passengers of the Titanic. The prediction target is whether the passenger survived the accident.

We can download the dataset using the code shown in listing 4.8. We have two files to download—the training data and the testing data. We use the get_file(…) function from tf.keras.utils, which downloads the CSV files from the URLs. The first argument is the filename to use for saving the file locally. The second argument is the URL to download the file. The function returns the path to the location that the file is saved locally.

Listing 4.8   Downloading the Titanic dataset

```
import tensorflow as tf

TRAIN_DATA_URL = 'https://storage.googleapis.com/tf-
    datasets/titanic/train.csv'
TEST_DATA_URL = 'https://storage.googleapis.com/tf-datasets/titanic/eval.csv'

train_file_path = tf.keras.utils.get_file('train.csv',
                                  TRAIN_DATA_URL)
test_file_path = tf.keras.utils.get_file('eval.csv',
                                  TEST_DATA_URL)
```

The first five lines in the training CSV file are shown in figure 4.4. The first line gives the names of the target response (survived) and the nine features. The next four lines denote four passengers and their corresponding features. The missing values are marked as "unknown," such as the deck feature of the first passenger. A total of 627 passengers are in the training set. The testing CSV file is in the same format and contains data on 264 passengers.

	A	B	C	D	E	F	G	H	I	J
1	survived	sex	age	n_siblings_s	parch	fare	class	deck	embark_tow	alone
2	0	male	22	1	0	7.25	Third	unknown	Southamptor	n
3	1	female	38	1	0	71.2833	First	C	Cherbourg	n
4	1	female	26	0	0	7.925	Third	unknown	Southamptor	y
5	1	female	35	1	0	53.1	First	C	Southamptor	n

Figure 4.4   The first five lines of the Titanic training CSV file

To solve structured data classification problems, we can use the StructuredData-Classifier API in AutoKeras. We fit an initialized StructuredDataClassifier object with the path of the training CSV file. It will load and preprocess the data automatically. The name of the target label column (survived) should be provided as an argument, as shown in the next listing.

Listing 4.9   Structured data classification with AutoKeras task API

```
import autokeras as ak

clf = ak.StructuredDataClassifier(max_trials=10)
```

```
clf.fit(x=train_file_path,          ←——┐  Path to the training CSV file
        y='survived',               ←—┐
        verbose=2)                    └──  Name of the target label column
```

The `StructuredDataClassifier` will load the names of each feature from the header of the training CSV file and infer the types of the features (categorical or numerical) automatically. You can also explicitly specify them when initializing the `Structured-DataClassifier`, as shown in the following listing.

Listing 4.10 Providing feature information to the AutoKeras API

```
clf = ak.StructuredDataClassifier(
    column_names=[                    ←——┐  Specifies the
        'sex',                            │  feature names
        'age',
        'n_siblings_spouses',
        'parch',
        'fare',
        'class',
        'deck',
        'embark_town',
        'alone'],
    column_types={'sex': 'categorical',   ←——┐  Specifies the data
                  'fare': 'numerical'},       │  types of the two
    max_trials=10,                            │  features
)
clf.fit(x=train_file_path,
        y='survived',
        verbose=2)
```

To make predictions using the best discovered pipeline, we can feed the path of the testing CSV file to the `predict()` method. All the feature columns adopted from the training file should be provided in the testing file. Similarly, we can evaluate the best pipeline using the `evaluate()` method by providing the path of the testing CSV file, as shown next.

Listing 4.11 Testing the structured data classifier

```
>>> predicted_y = clf.predict(test_file_path)        ←——┐  Gets predictions for
>>> print(predicted_y[:5])                               │  the testing data from
                                                         │  the CSV file
[[0]
 [0]
 [1]
 [0]
 [0]]

>>> test_loss, test_acc = clf.evaluate(test_file_path,
...                                    'survived',
...                                    verbose=0)         ←——┐  Evaluates the
>>> print('Test accuracy: ', test_acc)                       │  classifier

Test accuracy:  0.780303
```

We've now solved three classification tasks on different types of data with the help of AutoKeras's task APIs. Next, we'll explore a regression problem.

4.3.3   *Structured data regression with the California housing dataset*

In this example, we will use AutoML to address a structured data regression problem. The only difference compared with a structured data classification problem lies in selecting the task API in AutoKeras. We first fetch the dataset from scikit-learn and split off 20% of the data to use as the test set, as shown in the next listing.

Listing 4.12   Loading and splitting the California housing dataset

```
from sklearn.datasets import fetch_california_housing          Fetches the
house_dataset = fetch_california_housing()                     dataset

import pandas as pd
data = pd.DataFrame(house_dataset.data, columns=house_dataset.feature_names)
target = pd.Series(house_dataset.target, name = 'MEDV')
                                                              Packs the features into
from sklearn.model_selection import train_test_split          a pandas DataFrame
train_data, test_data, train_targets, test_targets = \
    train_test_split(data, target,
                     test_size=0.2,              Splits off 20% of the
                     random_state=42)            data for testing
```

Then we use AutoKeras's `StructuredDataRegressor` API to perform the regression task, as shown in listing 4.13. We use a larger batch size here (1024) to increase the training speed of each pipeline. The final testing MSE of the best pipeline discovered in the 10 trials is 0.31. Compared to the result we got in chapter 3 using traditional ML methods, which was 0.34, the result from AutoML is significantly better.

NOTE   This code example may take a long time to run.

Listing 4.13   Structured data regression with AutoKeras task API

```
>>> import autokeras as ak

>>> regressor = ak.StructuredDataRegressor(max_trials=10)
                                                              Fits the API with
>>> regressor.fit(x=train_data, y=train_targets,             training data
...               batch_size=1024, verbose=2)

>>> test_loss, test_mse = regressor.evaluate(
...     test_data, test_targets, verbose=0)          Tests
                                                     the final
>>> print('Test MSE: ', test_mse)                    regressor

Test MSE:  0.31036660075187683
```

Besides the `StructuredDataRegressor`, AutoKeras also provides `ImageRegressor` and `TextRegressor` APIs for image and text data regression tasks, respectively. They are used in the same way, which allows you to draw inferences about other cases from this example.

4.3.4 *Multilabel image classification*

Our last example is a *multilabel classification problem.* We have already explored some examples of multiclass classification, such as classifying handwritten digits in the MNIST dataset and assigning newsgroups to the related topic. In those cases, each instance can belong to only one of the classes, which means all the classes are mutually exclusive. But in real-world situations, a sample may have multiple labels. For example, an image of a scene may contain both a mountain and a river, and a news document may cover both political and economic topics. In multilabel classification, a sample can be associated with multiple labels, as indicated via a set of Boolean variables (whether or not the instance belongs to a label). The goal is to assign the sample to all its possible labels.

This may not seem like a trivial extension of multiclass classification. But with the help of AutoML, and specifically the task APIs in AutoKeras, you don't have to learn, select, and implement a tailored pipeline by yourself. You need to change only one argument to settle the matter in one go. We'll use the image classification API (Image-Classifier) as an example and construct a synthetic multilabel image classification dataset with the scikit-learn library. In the next listing, we create 100 samples with 64 features. There are three classes in total. Each sample should belong to at least one class and at most three classes. The average number of labels per sample is set to be two (n_labels=2).

> **Listing 4.14 Creating a synthetic multilabel image classification dataset**

```
from sklearn.datasets import make_multilabel_classification

X, Y = make_multilabel_classification(n_samples=100,
                                      n_features=64,
                                      n_classes=3,
                                      n_labels=2,
                                      allow_unlabeled=False,
                                      random_state=1)

X = X.reshape((100, 8, 8))

x_train, x_test, y_train, y_test = \
          X[:80], X[80:], Y[:80], Y[80:]
```

Creates the synthetic dataset

Formats the features into 100 8×8 synthetic images

Splits off 20% of the data as a test set

Next, we use the ImageClassifier as before—but this time we set the argument multi_label to True, as shown in listing 4.15. Similar methods can be used to retrieve the prediction results and test accuracy.

```
 Listing 4.15   Multilabel classification with AutoKeras task API
>>> clf = ak.ImageClassifier(max_trials=10, multi_label=True)
>>> clf.fit(x_train, y_train, epochs=3, verbose=2)         ◄──┐  Fits the AutoML
>>> test_loss, test_acc = clf.evaluate(x_test,                │  algorithm
                                        y_test,
            Tests the final model  ────►  verbose=0)
                                                   ┌─  Gets the
                                                   │   predicted labels
>>> predicted_y = clf.predict(x_test)            ◄─┘
>>> print(f'The prediction shape is : {predicted_y.shape}')
>>> print(f'The predicted labels of the first five instances are:\n
    {predicted_y[:5, :]}')

The prediction shape is: (20, 3)
```

As shown in the previous code, the prediction for each instance is a vector, whose length is the same as the number of classes. The values in the vector can only be 1s or 0s representing whether or not the instance belongs to the corresponding class. It is similar to the one-hot encoding vectors but with multiple 1s in the vector. Therefore, it is named *multi-hot encoding*.

You can also use `StructuredDataClassifier` and `TextClassifier` with the `multi_label` argument.

For regression problems, if the target response of an instance is a vector rather than a single value, you don't have to explicitly change any argument; the APIs will automatically infer whether we have single or multiple regression responses from the data.

You've now seen how to use AutoKeras's task APIs to address classification and regression problems with different data types. They're quite friendly for users with limited ML knowledge and convenient for deriving end-to-end deep learning solutions. But this method has the following two limitations:

- You're not able to change the search space and the search algorithm with the provided arguments. You trade a certain amount of flexibility, customizability, and extensibility for convenience.
- The running time can be very slow when the dataset size or the number of trials is large.

Mitigating these problems and accommodating more complicated scenarios requires greater knowledge of the ML models and AutoML algorithms you want to use. You'll learn about designing your own search space in the next two chapters, and the topics of customizing search algorithms and accelerating the AutoML process will be discussed in the third part of the book. But before we get to that, let's first work on two scenarios that are a little more complex than the previous examples. They don't require you to have knowledge of the models you want to use, but they do require a bit more customization of the search space. The aim of the next section is to introduce a more general solution that accommodates different data types and supervised learning tasks without switching across different APIs in AutoKeras.

4.4 Addressing tasks with multiple inputs or outputs

An ML task could involve multiple inputs collected from different resources, which we call different data *modalities*. For example, images could be associated with tags and other text descriptions, and videos could contain both visual and acoustic information (as well as metadata) that is useful for classification. Multiple inputs augment information resources. They could benefit and compensate with each other to help train a better ML model. This approach is called *multi-input learning* or *multimodal learning*. Similarly, we might want to have multiple outputs corresponding to different tasks (regression or classification) that we address simultaneously. This is called *multi-output learning* or *multitask learning*.

This section looks at how we can use the AutoKeras IO API to handle tasks with multiple inputs or outputs. Unlike the task APIs, where we have multiple variants targeting different specific data types and tasks, the IO API provides a fairly general solution—there's only one API class, named `AutoModel`—but requires extra configuration to specify the types of inputs and outputs. In fact, all the classes of the task APIs inherit from the `AutoModel` class, so you can use the IO API to address all the previous tasks. Here we'll explore examples focusing on three scenarios: multiclass classification, multi-input learning, and multi-output learning.

4.4.1 Automated image classification with the AutoKeras IO API

We'll begin by using the IO API to address a simple image classification task with the MNIST dataset. The goal is to introduce the basic configuration of the IO API so that we can examine more advanced scenarios.

We load the data as usual with TensorFlow and construct an `AutoModel` object to address the problem (see listing 4.16). The main difference between using the IO API (`AutoModel`) and the image classification task API (`ImageClassifier`) is in the initialization. When using the task APIs, because each API is tailored to a specific problem (classification or regression) and data type (image, text, or structured data), we don't need to specify anything except the number of trials (pipelines) to explore in the search space. However, the IO API can generalize to all types of data and tasks, so we need to provide information about the data types and task types during initialization, so it can select the appropriate loss function, metrics, search space, and search objective. In this example, our inputs are images and the task is a classification task. Thus, when initializing the `AutoModel`, we feed its `inputs` argument with ak.`Image-Input()`, an AutoKeras placeholder for image data, and we set its `outputs` argument to ak.`ClassificationHead()`, indicating the task is a classification task. We also specify the loss function and evaluation metrics for the training of each pipeline. If this were a multilabel classification task, we would set the `multi_label` argument to `True`.

NOTE This code example may take a long time to run.

Listing 4.16   MNIST image classification with AutoKeras IO API

```
from tensorflow.keras.datasets import mnist
(x_train, y_train), (x_test, y_test) = mnist.load_data()

io_model = ak.AutoModel(                          Specifies the
    inputs = ak.ImageInput(),                     input data type
    outputs = ak.ClassificationHead(
        loss='categorical_crossentropy',          Specifies the task
        metrics=['accuracy']),                    type and training
        multi_label=False),                       configurations
    objective='val_loss',
    tuner='random',                    Selects the
    max_trials=3)                      search objective
io_model.fit(x_train, y_train, epochs=10, verbose=2)

Selects the search                              Fits the model with
algorithm                                       the prepared data
```

To control the search process, we can set the search objective used to compare the performance of different pipelines (validation loss, in this example). As with the task APIs, you can create custom evaluation metrics and objectives to compare the performance of the pipelines and select the best candidate (we do not elaborate it again here). The IO API also provides an extra argument named `tuner` that you can set during initialization. A *tuner* defines a search algorithm to explore and select different pipelines in the search space. For example, the `'random'` tuner used in this example selects pipelines in the search space randomly: it constructs a pipeline at each trial by randomly selecting a value for each of the hyperparameters. The tuner also controls the training and evaluation process for each constructed pipeline so that the search process can proceed smoothly. AutoKeras provides tuners corresponding to several of the most popular search algorithms in the current AutoML field. You'll learn more about tuners in chapter 7.

We can use the other methods of the IO API the same way as the task APIs, as illustrated in the following listing. You should be able to use them as long as you know how to use one of the task APIs.

Listing 4.17   Exporting, testing, and evaluating using the IO API

```
best_model = io_model.export_model()              Exports the best
                                                  model found by
predicted_y = io_model.predict(x_test)            AutoKeras

test_loss, test_acc = io_model.evaluate(x_test,   Makes predictions
        Evaluates the model's performance    y_test,   on the test data
                                             verbose=0)
```

This example showed how to use the IO API for a multiclass image classification task, but it's easy to draw inferences about other use cases from it. For example, if the data type is structured data or text data, you can change `ak.ImageInput()` to ak.StructuredDataInput() or ak.TextInput(). If the task is a regression task, you can change ak.ClassificationHead() to ak.RegressionHead(), and the loss and metrics can also be changed accordingly. Next, we'll look at a more complicated case.

4.4.2 Automated multi-input learning

A typical pipeline structure to handle multiple inputs in conventional ML is shown in figure 4.5. The pipeline first applies data-specific operations to each input source, such as normalization and convolutional layers for images, numerical embedding for text, and so on. Then it merges all the processed data to generate the classification or regression outputs. This structure can also be adopted for all the pipelines in the search space to conduct AutoML, and we can leverage the IO API of AutoKeras to specify the inputs and the output head.

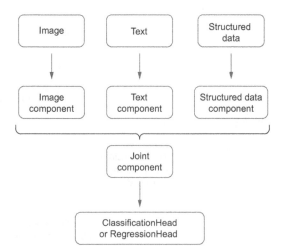

Figure 4.5   Multi-input learning pipeline structure

In listing 4.18, we create a synthetic multi-input classification dataset with both images and structured data. The images are of three dimensions, with shape (32, 32, 3). Each 3-D image is associated with a row vector in the structured data representing its attributes (a synthetic description of the image). The target labels have five classes, and we split out 20% of the data as a validation set.

Listing 4.18   Creating a synthetic multi-input classification dataset

```
import numpy as np
num_instances = 100

image_data = np.random.rand(num_instances, 32, 32, 3).astype(np.float32)
image_train, image_test = image_data[:80], image_data[80:]
```

Generates the image data

```
structured_data = np.random.rand(
    num_instances, 20). astype(np.float32)      ◁─┐  Generates the
structured_train = structured_data[:80]            │  structured data
structured_test = structured_data[80:]      ◁──────┘

classification_target = np.random.randint(
    5, size=num_instances)                    ◁─┐  Generates the classification
target_train, target_test = classification_target[:80],  │  labels of five classes
    classification_target[80:]               ◁──┘
```

It is quite intuitive to configure the IO API to accommodate multiple inputs—we need to input a list of placeholders only during the initialization of an AutoModel object, as shown in listing 4.19. The placeholders can have the same type, such as two structured data placeholders, or different types. Their number aligns with the number of inputs (modalities). During the fitting and evaluation phase, we need to feed the data in the same order as the corresponding placeholders.

Listing 4.19 Performing multi-input classification with AutoKeras IO API

```
import autokeras as ak

multi_input_clf = ak.AutoModel(                          ┐  Defines
    inputs=[ak.ImageInput(), ak.StructuredDataInput()],  ◁─┘  multiple inputs
    outputs=ak.ClassificationHead(),
    max_trials=3,
)
                                              ┐  Feeds multiple
                                              │  inputs to the
multi_input_clf.fit(                          │  AutoModel
    [image_train, structured_train],   ◁──────┘
    target_train,
    epochs=10,
)                                             ┐  Evaluates the best
                                              │  found pipeline with
test_loss, test_acc = multi_input_clf.evaluate(  ◁──┘  the test set
    [image_test, structured_test],
    target_test,
)
```

The training process and search algorithms are configured the same way as in the previous example.

4.4.3 Automated multi-output learning

We can also use the IO API to deal with multiple outputs. This situation usually happens when we want to jointly address multiple tasks, such as predicting a person's age and gender. A common pipeline structure for multi-output learning (or multitask learning) is shown in figure 4.6. We use different heads here to represent different output targets, but the heads could also have the same type. For example, if we treat multilabel classification with N labels as a combination of N binary classification tasks,

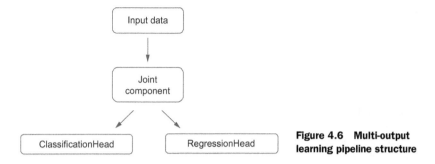

Figure 4.6   Multi-output learning pipeline structure

we can form a multi-output learning problem with *N* ClassificationHeads. The data input could also contain multiple inputs, as discussed in the previous example.

In listing 4.20, we generate a synthetic dataset with multiple inputs and multiple outputs to serve as a general example of multitask learning with multiple inputs. The inputs include both images and structured data, and the outputs cover classification and regression responses. When initializing the AutoModel, we input a list of input placeholders corresponding to the data types we're providing and a list of heads corresponding to the different output targets. The full implementation is shown here.

Listing 4.20   Multi-output learning with AutoKeras IO API

```
import numpy as np
import autokeras as ak

num_instances = 100

image_data = np.random.rand(
    num_instances, 32, 32, 3).astype(np.float32)      Generates two
image_train, image_test = image_data[:80], image_data[80:]    input sources
structured_data = np.random.rand(
    num_instances, 20).astype(np.float32)
structured_train, structured_test =
    structured_data[:80], structured_data[80:]


classification_target = np.random.randint(
    5, size=num_instances)
clf_target_train, clf_target_test =
    classification_target[:80], classification_target[80:]    Generates
regression_target = np.random.rand(                           two target
    num_instances, 1).astype(np.float32)                      responses
reg_target_train, reg_target_test =
    regression_target[:80], regression_target[80:]


multi_output_learner = ak.AutoModel(
    inputs=[ak.ImageInput(), ak.StructuredDataInput()],       Specifies
    outputs=[ak.ClassificationHead(), ak.RegressionHead()],   multiple
    max_trials=3,                                             output targets
)
```

```
multi_output_learner.fit(
    [image_train, structured_train],
    [clf_target_train, reg_target_train],
    epochs=10,
    verbose=2
)
```

Let's display the best model to see what it looks like, as shown next.

Listing 4.21 Displaying the best model

```
best_model = multi_modal_clf.export_model()
tf.keras.utils.plot_model(best_model, show_shapes=True, expand_nested=True)
```

In figure 4.7, we can see that the model has a crossing structure connecting the two input sources and generating the two output targets from top to bottom. The image input is processed by a CNN branch, and an MLP branch processes the structured data input. We use the categorical encoding layer to transform the categorical features in the structured data into numerical vectors to feed into the MLP. For each instance, the output representations from the two branches are two vectors of length 800 and 32, respectively. They are concatenated to generate both classification and regression predictions.

As these three examples show, unlike the task APIs (which trade off convenience for customizability), the IO API provides the flexibility to define the inputs and the outputs of the pipelines in the search space. It also enables the selection of search algorithms. However, at this point we don't know much about the search space or how to customize it. We will explore the topic of search space design in the next two chapters.

So far we have learned how to use AutoKeras to solve problems with AutoML techniques. However, AutoKeras does have some limitations. First, it is hard to automatically select models by their inferencing time and model size, which may be important for the final deployment of the machine learning model. Second, another limitation of AutoKeras, which is also the limitation of AutoML, is that it cannot take into account any knowledge of the dataset content. For example, it cannot understand the meaning of each column in the Titanic dataset. Therefore, it may not be able to design a better model than the human experts who have a deeper understanding of the problem. Third, AutoKeras is more about providing concise and easy-to-learn APIs to the users and producing a model with good performance, rather than producing the best model that beats all the state-of-the-art solutions.

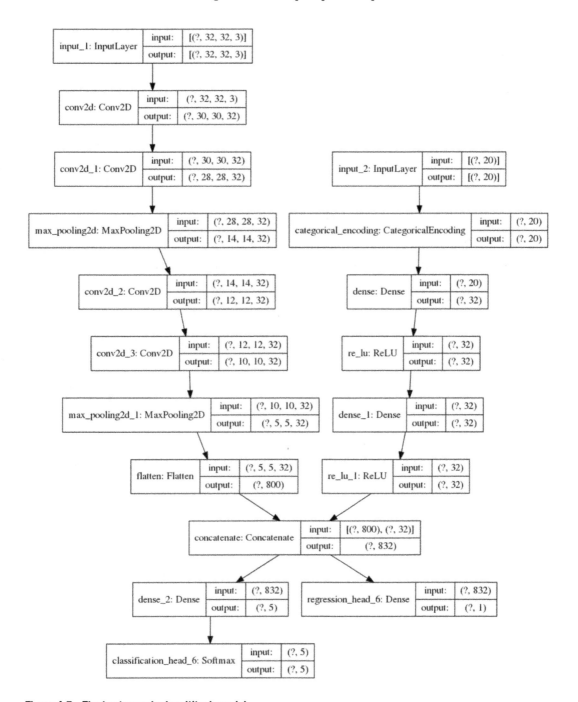

Figure 4.7   The best searched multitask model

Summary

- AutoML allows you to create end-to-end ML solutions for different ML tasks by feeding in the dataset directly. You can achieve this in Python with the help of AutoKeras's task APIs.
- To apply AutoML to different tasks with AutoKeras, you need to clarify the data type and learning paradigm of the task at hand, such as multiclass or multilabel classification, so you can select the corresponding task API and settings.
- With AutoKeras's IO API, you can address tasks with multiple inputs and data types. You can also define different heads to generate multiple outputs for multitask learning.
- The search space is usually tailored to different tasks. AutoKeras provides a default search space for each task to save you effort on search space design. To customize the search space for personalized use cases, you need to use the functional API, which will be introduced in the next chapter.

5

Customizing the search space by creating AutoML pipelines

This chapter covers

- Understanding an AutoML pipeline
- Customizing sequential and graph-structured AutoML pipelines
- Automated hyperparameter tuning and model selection with customized AutoML pipelines
- Customizing the AutoML blocks in the AutoML pipeline

In chapter 4, we solved a variety of problems with AutoKeras without customizing the search space. To recap, in AutoML, a search space is a pool of models with specific hyperparameter values that potentially can be built and selected by the tuning algorithm. In practice, you may want to use a specific ML algorithm or data preprocessing method to solve a problem, such as an MLP for a regression task. Designing and tuning a particular ML component requires tailoring the search space, tuning only the relevant hyperparameters while fixing some others.

This chapter introduces how to customize the search space based on your requirements and automatically discover certain kinds of deep learning solutions for different types of tasks. Constraining the search space can also reduce your search time, allowing you to achieve better results with fewer trials. You will learn how to customize the search space by creating both sequential and graph-structured AutoML pipelines. I'll show you how to implement an AutoML pipeline with the AutoKeras functional API and how to use the built-in blocks in AutoKeras to conduct automated hyperparameter tuning and model selection for different tasks. You'll also learn how to customize your own building blocks when the pre-existing blocks do not satisfy your need.

5.1   *Working with sequential AutoML pipelines*

An ML pipeline comprises a sequence of ML components, such as the data preprocessing methods, the ML algorithm used for conducting the ML task, and so on. A sequential AutoML pipeline characterizes a search space of sequential ML pipelines. It's composed of a sequence of *blocks*, each of which represents one or more ML components, as well as the search space of their hyperparameters. By selecting a component in each block and fixing its hyperparameters, the AutoML pipeline will instantiate an ML pipeline to be trained and evaluated on the dataset. An illustrative example of selecting a deep learning pipeline from the search space created by a sequential AutoML pipeline is shown in figure 5.1.

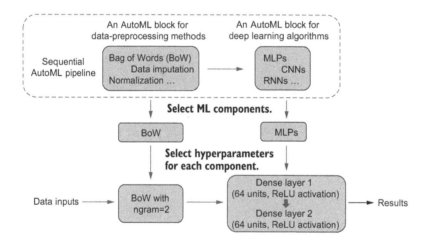

Figure 5.1   Instantiating a deep learning pipeline with a sequential AutoML pipeline

This can be thought of as a two-level search space, because in each iteration the search algorithm first selects the type of model and preprocessing methods to use and then selects their appropriate hyperparameters. If we have only one concerned model and processing method in the pipeline, we need to perform only a single-step selection of the appropriate hyperparameters. So, we can separate the AutoML problems that we mainly target in practice into the following two categories:

- *Automated hyperparameter tuning (a general definition)*—The model type and preprocessing methods are fixed. We want to tune only the hyperparameters of each specified ML component in the pipeline. In this case, the AutoML blocks in the AutoML pipeline will each contain only one ML model or preprocessing method. The search space will include only the relevant hyperparameters for each fixed component. For example, suppose we want to apply an MLP to solve a regression problem and want to tune the model's hyperparameters, such as the number of layers and units. In that case, we can constrain the search space by creating the AutoML algorithm block with only MLPs in it. The search space will be the feasible number of layers and units in the MLP model.

- *Automated pipeline search*—In some situations, we may not know which model or data preparation method to adopt ahead of time. We want to search not only the suitable models and preprocessing methods but also their hyperparameters. In this case, one or more of the AutoML blocks will contain multiple components. For example, we might want to explore both the CNN and MLP models to see which is more suitable for our task and find the best hyperparameters for each. To do this, we can include blocks for each model architecture. The preprocessing method can be either fixed or selected and tuned along with the model.

Another category of AutoML problems, which is especially useful for serving shallow models, is *automated feature engineering*. It aims to automatically discover informative and discriminative features for learning the ML models based on certain feature selection criteria, such as Pearson correlations introduced in chapter 2. Automated feature engineering often involves an iterative feature-generation and feature selection process that mimics the way of manual feature engineering. Because a deep learning algorithm enjoys the natural talent of extracting and learning condensed data representations without much feature engineering operation, let's first focus on the tuning of the deep learning algorithm and its data preparation methods in this chapter and then touch on the automated feature engineering and the tuning of shallow models in chapter 6.

In the next two sections, we'll explore how to create a sequential AutoML pipeline with the AutoKeras functional API to solve the automated hyperparameter tuning and automated pipeline search in the context of deep learning. An extension of the sequential AutoML pipeline to a more general graph-structured pipeline will be introduced afterward. Beyond using the built-in AutoML blocks of AutoKeras, you'll also learn how to customize your own block in the last section of this chapter.

> **NOTE** The taxonomy of AutoML tasks can be more complex than we describe here and could be categorized differently. The most widely used categorization methods are automated data preprocessing, automated feature engineering, automated model selection, and automated hyperparameter tuning.

In this book, we are considering a more general definition of automated hyperparameter tuning, where we take the ML model type and data preprocessing methods as special hyperparameters. This will unify the automated data preprocessing, automated model selection, and automated hyperparameter tuning into one category: automated hyperparameter tuning, as we've described in the previous sections. Of course, we can also have automated pipeline tuning to tune the entire ML workflow as we've introduced earlier. In particular, some work also explicitly separates the subfield of selecting and tuning of deep learning algorithms as *automated deep learning*, considering the complexity of designing the neural network architectures (or we call it *neural architecture search*).

5.2   Creating a sequential AutoML pipeline for automated hyperparameter tuning

In this section, I'll show you how to create an AutoML pipeline to do automated hyperparameter tuning. Creating an AutoML pipeline with the AutoKeras functional API is quite similar to building up a neural network with the Keras functional API, as introduced in chapter 3. The only difference is that the Keras layers are replaced with AutoKeras's built-in AutoML blocks. Each block contains one or more deep learning models (or preprocessing methods) and a default search space for their hyperparameters. You can also modify the search space for each hyperparameter. To build up a network, we stack multiple Keras layers by wiring together their inputs and outputs sequentially. Comparably, to form a sequential AutoML pipeline, we select AutoKeras blocks and wire them together one by one, as shown in figure 5.2.

Figure 5.2   A sequential AutoML pipeline created with the AutoKeras functional API

The pipeline should start with an input placeholder indicating the data type, such as images or text, and end with an output head corresponding to the task we want to solve, such as classification or regression. The two intermediate blocks are AutoML blocks characterizing the search space of the preprocessing methods and deep learning models. Let's take a closer look at the components (blocks) in the pipeline, described next:

- The *input node* is a placeholder for the tensor input of the pipeline, such as ImageInput, TextInput, or StructuredDataInput (as introduced in chapter 4). You can also define a general tensor input with the Input class in AutoKeras. The input node accepts data in multiple formats, such as NumPy arrays, pandas DataFrames, and TensorFlow Datasets. It will also conduct certain preprocessing operations automatically, such as extending the dimensions of images if they do not have a channel dimension. The input node does not have any hyperparameters that can be set or tuned.
- The *preprocessor block* defines additional preprocessing operations (i.e., if certain operations have already been conducted by the input node, as mentioned

previously) to perform on the inputs, such as image normalization, text embedding, and so on. Depending on the operation, we may have hyperparameters to tune, such as the maximum size of the vocabulary table to use to convert text documents to their vector representations if text embedding is performed. In this block, there are no weights to be trained through backpropagation.

- The *network block* is the most important type of AutoML block in AutoKeras. Each block represents a set of neural network models of the same structure. For example, a ConvBlock, which you'll see in this section, encompasses a set of convolutional neural networks (CNNs). Each CNN is composed of convolutional layers and pooling layers. The number and types of layers are treated as hyperparameters. You can select one or more network blocks to create the pipelines based on the task at hand and specify the search space of their hyperparameters based on your requirements. Unlike the preprocessor block, there are weights to be trained through backpropagation after specifying the hyperparameters in the network block.

- The *output head* is a task-specific component used to generate the final outputs, such as the ClassificationHead and RegressionHead introduced in the discussion of the IO API in chapter 4. It reshapes each instance's representation to a vector and applies a dense layer to transform it to the size of the target output. For example, if the head is a ClassificationHead and the problem is a multiclass classification problem, the output of each instance from the dense layer will be a vector of length 10 corresponding to the ten labels. Each head also specifies the loss function and metrics to help compile each deep learning pipeline selected from the search space for training.

In the rest of this section, we will walk through two hyperparameter tuning examples using a sequential AutoML pipeline. The examples will also introduce several built-in AutoML blocks in AutoKeras that can be used to create an AutoML pipeline.

5.2.1 Tuning MLPs for structured data regression

Our first task will be to tune the network structure of an MLP to solve a structured data regression problem. In chapter 3, we solved the California housing price-prediction problem by creating an MLP with Keras. We tuned the number of training epochs by observing the MSE curves for the training and validation sets during the training process. Here, we'll use AutoML to tune the structural hyperparameters of the MLP: the number of layers and the number of units in each layer. An intuitive way of doing this is to create multiple MLPs with different numbers of layers and units, train them, and select the best one based on the validation MSE. This process can be done by creating a sequential AutoML pipeline without manually creating and exploring multiple MLPs.

To create the AutoML pipeline, we can leverage two of AutoKeras's built-in AutoML blocks as follows:

- Normalization is a preprocessor block that performs featurewise normalization by subtracting the means of the features and dividing by their standard deviations. We used this operation in chapter 3 to normalize the features for the California housing price data. This block helps preprocess the data for the MLPs. It does not contain any hyperparameters to be tuned.

- DenseBlock is a network block forming a search space of models with the MLP structure. Unlike the simplest MLP, which only stacks dense layers with certain activation functions, each "layer" (or *cell*) in the DenseBlock is a combination of three Keras layers: a dense layer, a dropout layer to help mitigate the overfitting issue, and a *batch normalization layer*, which normalizes the input tensor of a batch of instances to a mean of 0 and a standard deviation of 1. The batch normalization layer is added between a dense layer without an activation and a ReLU activation layer. Whether to use the batch normalization layer is a hyperparameter to be tuned. The dropout layer is added at the end (as shown in figure 5.3). The number of dense layers, the number of units in each dense layer, and the dropout rate (ranging from 0 to 1) are also hyperparameters to be tuned in this block, if not fixed. The default choices for the number of layers are in the range 1 to 3, and the default choices for the number of units are in the list [16, 32, 64, 128, 256, 512, 1024].

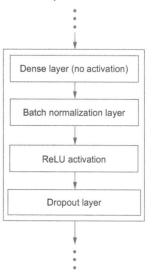

Figure 5.3   A cell in the DenseBlock

As you can see in listing 5.1, we stack the two blocks to form a structured data regression pipeline with the structure shown in figure 5.2. We'll use this pipeline to find a good MLP structure for the California housing price-prediction problem. The output head is defined as a RegressionHead, which generates the final prediction by applying a linear transformation to its input. By default, a dropout layer exists before the final linear transformation in the output head. We remove it by fixing the dropout rate at 0 for simplicity. We also remove the batch normalization layer by setting the use_batchnorm argument to False. Besides the two hyperparameters (number of layers and number of units) in the DenseBlock, the search space also contains two hyperparameters for the optimization algorithm, which are the algorithm's type and the learning rate. By tuning them jointly with the MLP structure, we can achieve more accurate performance for different pipelines, making it easier for us to compare and select among them. The number of trials is set to 10 in the last line, which means we select 10 different pipelines from the search space in total and choose the best one among them.

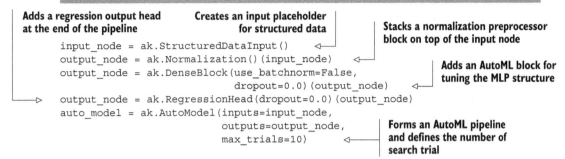

Listing 5.1 Creating an AutoML pipeline with MLPs for structured data regression

Adds a regression output head at the end of the pipeline · **Creates an input placeholder for structured data** · **Stacks a normalization preprocessor block on top of the input node** · **Adds an AutoML block for tuning the MLP structure** · **Forms an AutoML pipeline and defines the number of search trial**

```
input_node = ak.StructuredDataInput()
output_node = ak.Normalization()(input_node)
output_node = ak.DenseBlock(use_batchnorm=False,
                dropout=0.0)(output_node)
output_node = ak.RegressionHead(dropout=0.0)(output_node)
auto_model = ak.AutoModel(inputs=input_node,
                outputs=output_node,
                max_trials=10)
```

Now we load the data with scikit-learn and conduct the search process by feeding the data to it (as shown in listing 5.2). The batch size and maximum number of epochs to train for are fixed at 1,024 and 150, respectively, to help reduce the search time. Generally, a larger batch size and fewer epochs will reduce the time it takes to train a network. This is a naive way of accelerating the search speed in AutoML work—it is not guaranteed that each pipeline explored will be able to converge within 150 epochs—but we'll assume this is long enough to give an indication of how they perform and allow us to discriminate among them. More ways of accelerating the speed, even without harnessing the evaluation performance of each pipeline, will be introduced in chapter 8.

Listing 5.2 Tuning the MLP for structured data regression

```
import pandas as pd
from sklearn.datasets import fetch_california_housing
from sklearn.model_selection import train_test_split

house_dataset = fetch_california_housing()

data = pd.DataFrame(house_dataset.data,
                columns=house_dataset.feature_names)
target = pd.Series(house_dataset.target, name='MEDV')

train_data, test_data, train_targets, test_targets =
    train_test_split(data, target, test_size=0.2, random_state=42)

auto_model.fit(train_data, train_targets,
            batch_size=1024, epochs=150)
```

Fits the AutoML pipeline with the data · **Loads the dataset, packs it into a pandas DataFrame, and splits off 20% for testing**

As shown in listing 5.3, the final testing MSE of the best MLP is 0.28—better than that of the one we designed in chapter 3 (MSE = 0.31). We can display the hyperparameters of the MLP with the `results_summary()` method; it has two layers with 32 and 512 units, respectively. Its validation MSE during the search process is 0.29.

Listing 5.3   Evaluating the best deep learning pipeline

```
>>> test_loss, test_acc = auto_model.evaluate(test_data,
...                                            test_targets,          Evaluates the
...                                            verbose=0)       ◁─┤  best MLP
>>> print('Test accuracy: ', test_acc)
Test accuracy:   0.2801434397697449
>>> auto_model.tuner.results_summary(num_trials=1)      ◁─┐
Results summary                                            │  Summarizes
Results in ./auto_model                                    │  the best trial
Showing 1 best trials                                      │  during search
Objective(name='val_loss', direction='min')
Trial summary
Hyperparameters:
dense_block_1/num_layers: 2
dense_block_1/units_0: 32
dense_block_1/dropout: 0.0
dense_block_1/units_1: 512
regression_head_1/dropout: 0.0
optimizer: adam
learning_rate: 0.001                                 │  Exports the
Score: 0.2891707420349121                            │  best MLP
>>> best_model = auto_model.export_model()      ◁───┘
>>> tf.keras.utils.plot_model(best_model,                 Visualizes the
...                           show_shapes=True,        │  best MLP
...                           expand_nested=True)   ◁──┘
```

Because the exported best model is a Keras model, you can easily save and load your best model as shown here:

```
from tensorflow import keras
best_model.save('saved_model')
best_model = keras.models.load_model('saved_model')
```

We export the best MLP and visualize its structure, shown in figure 5.4. Each of its layers can be associated with the corresponding component in the sequential AutoML pipeline. For example, the two dense layers with ReLU activation are selected from the search space characterized in the DenseBlock.

Because we use the default search space for the number of layers ([1, 2, 3]) and units ([16, 32, 64, 128, 256, 512, 1024]) in the DenseBlock, the total number of different MLP structures is $7 + 7^2 + 7^3 = 399$. This is a fairly large search space compared to the 10 trials we performed, indicating that we won't have tested many of the possibilities. The search space is even larger if we take the optimization algorithms (three choices by default) and learning rates (six choices by default) into account. And by extension, by testing only 10 options, we're relatively unlikely to have hit upon the top ones out of all the possibilities. To help constrain the search space, we can fix some of the hyperparameters or constrain their scope manually. For example, we can draw on

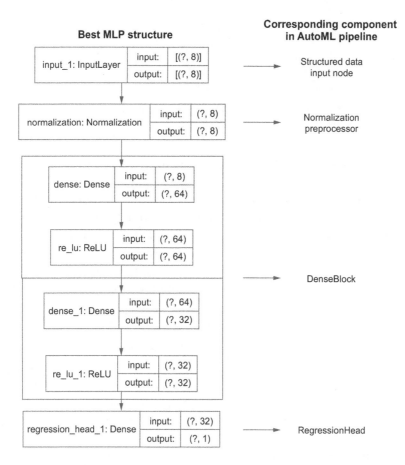

Figure 5.4   The best discovered MLP structure and the corresponding component in the AutoML pipeline

past experience in tuning MLPs to constrain the number of layers and units. Here are a few assumptions we can base our changes on:

- Because the dataset in this example is small, an MLP with fewer layers should be likely to have enough capacity to learn the data and avoid overfitting.
- MLPs with triangular or diamond structures often perform better than ones with rectangular structures. Using a three-layer MLP as an example, the units in an MLP with a triangular structure could be [32, 64, 128] or [128, 64, 32]. Two MLPs with diamond and rectangular structures could have units [32, 64, 32] and [32, 32, 32], respectively. An illustration of these three types of structures is shown in figure 5.5.

We can fix the number of layers to be two in this example and constrain the numbers of units in the two layers to be selected from [128, 256, 512, 1024] and [16, 32,

Diamond MLP structure

Rectangular MLP structure

Triangular MLP structure

Figure 5.5   Three types of MLP structures

64], respectively. This will help form a search space of inverted triangular MLP structures. The constraints can be implemented by connecting two DenseBlocks and defining the choices for the units in each layer, as shown in listing 5.4. KerasTuner provides a hyperparameters module (hp for short) to help create the search space for both continuous and discrete hyperparameters. For example, because the number of units is a discrete hyperparameter, we can use the hyperparameters.Choice class in the module to specify a list of possible values for that hyperparameter. You'll see more uses of this class in chapter 6 when designing your own AutoML block.

Listing 5.4   Customizing the search space for tuning the MLP

```
>>> from keras_tuner.engine import hyperparameters as hp     Customizes the search
                                                             space of the units
                                                             hyperparameter in
>>> input_node = ak.StructuredDataInput()                    the dense layers
>>> output_node = ak.Normalization()(input_node)
>>> output_node = ak.DenseBlock(
...     num_layers=1, num_units=hp.Choice('num_units', 512, 1024]),   ◁────────┐
...     use_batchnorm=False,                                                    │
...     dropout=0.0)(output_node)                                               │
>>> output_node = ak.DenseBlock(                                               │
...     num_layers=1, num_units=hp.Choice('num_units', [16, 32, 64]),   ◁──────┘
...     use_batchnorm=False,
...     dropout=0.0)(output_node)
>>> output_node = ak.RegressionHead()(output_node)
>>> auto_model = ak.AutoModel(inputs=input_node, outputs=output_node,
...                           max_trials=10, overwrite=True, seed=42)

>>> auto_model.fit(train_data, train_targets, batch_size=1024, epochs=150)

>>> test_loss, test_acc = auto_model.evaluate(
...     test_data, test_targets, verbose=0)
>>> print('Test accuracy: ', test_acc)
Test accuracy:  0.2712092995643616
```

The new search space only has 12 different MLP structures. We use a similar method to search for, retrieve, and evaluate the best MLP; this time, the best MLP discovered in 10 trials achieves a testing MSE of 0.27, which beats the previous MLP discovered in the larger search space.

NOTE   The construction of the search space often plays a vital role in the success of AutoML. A good search space can help you discover a promising pipeline with less search time. Designing a good search space can be even more important than designing a good search algorithm, because it provides cheap constraints to accelerate the search process. However, it often requires prior knowledge and understanding of the models as well as the coupled search algorithm, which runs counter to the ultimate goal of AutoML (saving human effort). If you don't have prior knowledge to build on, you can start with a large search space and gradually decrease its size with a trial-and-error approach. This idea also motivates some advanced AutoML algorithms that aim to gradually tailor the search space or narrow it down to a finer region. We will introduce some representative examples in chapter 7.

Now that you've seen how to tune MLPs for a structured data regression task, let's take a look at another example: tuning CNNs for an image classification task.

5.2.2 *Tuning CNNs for image classification*

In this example, we'll tune a CNN with a sequential AutoML pipeline to solve an image classification problem using the MNIST dataset. In chapter 3, we created a CNN and showed that it achieved better performance on this task than an MLP network. But we didn't explore how we set up and tuned the hyperparameters in the CNN, such as the number of filters in the convolutional layers. Let's now build up an AutoML pipeline to improve the CNN structure and achieve better classification accuracy.

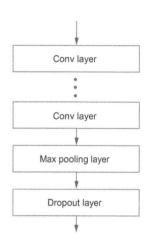

Figure 5.6   The structure of each convolutional block in a `ConvBlock`

We use a `ConvBlock` in AutoKeras to tune the three main hyperparameters of the CNN: the number of filters, the number of convolutional layers, and the kernel size of the convolutional layers. A `ConvBlock` sequentially stacks multiple *convolutional blocks* (or *convolutional cells*). Each convolutional block sequentially stacks multiple convolutional layers, a max pooling layer, and a dropout layer (see figure 5.6).

All the convolutional blocks have the same number of convolutional layers, but each layer can contain a different number of filters. The search space of a `ConvBlock` has the following seven hyperparameters:

- *Number of convolutional blocks*
- *Number of convolutional layers in each block*—This is the same in all the convolutional blocks.
- *Type of the convolutional layer*—Each convolutional layer can be one of two types: it can be a regular 2-D convolutional layer, as introduced in chapter 3, or a *separable convolutional layer*, which contains fewer weights than a normal convolutional

layer but may achieve comparable performance. A more detailed explanation of this layer type will be provided when we discuss the XceptionBlock in the next section.

- *Number of filters in the convolutional layer*—This can be different for each layer of each block.
- *Kernel size of the convolutional layer*—The kernel size of the max pooling layers is set to be the kernel size minus one. Once the kernel size is selected by the tuning algorithm for a ConvBlock in a trial, it will be applied for every pooling layer and convolutional layer in all the cells of that ConvBlock.
- *Whether to apply the max pooling layer in each cell*—Once this is selected for a trial, it's applied for every cell in the ConvBlock.
- *Whether to apply the dropout layer in each cell*—Once this is selected for a trial, it's applied for every cell in the ConvBlock.

To keep this example simple, we'll constrain the search space by fixing the number of blocks at two, as shown in listing 5.5. We do not apply the dropout layer or use separable convolutional layers. The hyperparameters to be tuned are the number of layers, the kernel size, and the number of filters in each layer in the blocks. By default, they are selected from the lists [1, 2], [3, 5, 7], and [16, 32, 64, 128, 256, 512], respectively. Without considering the optimizer and learning rate, we have 3 * (6 + 6 * 6) * (6 + 6 * 6) = 5,292 different CNN structures in this search space.

NOTE   This code example may take a long time to run.

Listing 5.5   MNIST classification with the AutoKeras functional API

```
>>> import autokeras as ak
>>> from tensorflow.keras.datasets import mnist

>>> (x_train, y_train), (x_test, y_test) =
    mnist.load_data()

>>> input_node = ak.ImageInput()
>>> output_node = ak.Normalization()(input_node)
>>> output_node = ak.ConvBlock(
...     num_blocks=2,
...     max_pooling=True,
...     separable=False,
...     dropout=0.0)(output_node)
>>> output_node = ak.ClassificationHead(dropout=0.0)(output_node)

>>> auto_model = ak.AutoModel(
...     inputs=input_node,
...     outputs=output_node,
...     max_trials=10,
...     overwrite=True,
...     seed=42)

>>> auto_model.fit(x_train, y_train, epochs=3)
```

Loads the MNIST data

Creates the input node

Adds a Normalization preprocessor block

Stacks a ConvBlock to create a search space for CNNs

Finalizes the pipeline with a classification head

Wraps up the pipeline into an AutoModel

Executes the search process by fitting the training data to the pipeline

```
>>> test_loss, test_acc = auto_model.evaluate(x_test, y_test, verbose=0)    ◄──────┐
>>> print('Test accuracy: ', test_acc)                                      Evaluates the
Test accuracy:  0.9937999844551086                                          best CNN on
                                                                            the test set
>>> best_model = auto_model.export_model()    │ Exports the best CNN and
>>> best_model.summary()                      │ prints out its structure
Model: 'functional_1'
```

Layer (type)	Output Shape	Param #
input_1 (InputLayer)	[(None, 28, 28)]	0
cast_to_float32 (CastToFloat	(None, 28, 28)	0
expand_last_dim (ExpandLastD	(None, 28, 28, 1)	0
normalization (Normalization	(None, 28, 28, 1)	3
conv2d (Conv2D)	(None, 24, 24, 128)	3328
conv2d_1 (Conv2D)	(None, 20, 20, 16)	51216
max_pooling2d (MaxPooling2D)	(None, 5, 5, 16)	0
conv2d_2 (Conv2D)	(None, 5, 5, 16)	6416
conv2d_3 (Conv2D)	(None, 5, 5, 512)	205312
max_pooling2d_1 (MaxPooling2	(None, 2, 2, 512)	0
flatten (Flatten)	(None, 2048)	0
dense (Dense)	(None, 10)	20490
classification_head_1 (Softm	(None, 10)	0

```
Total params: 286,765
Trainable params: 286,762
Nontrainable params: 3
```

The best CNN achieves 99.38% accuracy on the test set, which decreases the error rate of the CNN we manually designed in chapter 3 by over 30%. However, the size of the network is larger, mainly due to the large number of filters. To discover smaller architectures, we can limit the number of layers and filters in the search space. It is possible to find a smaller architecture with comparable performance to the CNN we constructed here; I'll leave that as an exercise for you to try out.

5.3 *Automated pipeline search with hyperblocks*

In this section, we'll talk about another commonly faced scenario in AutoML applications: selecting the best types of components (models or preprocessors) to use in the deep learning pipeline. This is a more complex scenario than tuning only the hyperparameters of a specific type of model, as introduced in the previous section, because different models and preprocessors may comprise different operations and have unique hyperparameters. It requires us to jointly select the combination of preprocessors and models and their coupled hyperparameters. For example, in image classification, a lot of advanced models are proposed beyond the naive CNN we used previously, such as ResNet, Xception, and so on. Even if you have heard of these models, you may not know how they work, which tasks they are best used for, or how to tune them. You'll also need to decide on suitable preprocessing methods, such as choosing whether to use normalization. We'll work through some image classification examples here to show you how to automatically select models and preprocessing methods.

5.3.1   Automated model selection for image classification

The CNN model introduced in chapter 3, which stacks convolutional and pooling layers recursively, is the simplest CNN architecture, often called a *vanilla CNN*. Existing work has proposed multiple advanced variations that try to improve the runtime performance and accuracy of the CNN. Two of the most powerful are the ResNet (residual network)[1] and Xception[2] architectures. Because no model performs the best in all situations, selecting the model and its hyperparameters based on the task and the dataset at hand is very important. We'll begin by looking at these two models and how to tune their hyperparameters separately, and then I'll show you how to do joint model selection and hyperparameter tuning with the AutoML pipeline.

RESNET

In a ResNet, multiple small neural network blocks (or cells) are stacked together to build a complete neural network. The block structure is similar to the convolutional block in AutoKeras's `ConvBlock`, but with a special connection called a *skip connection* that adds the input tensor of a block to its output tensor in an elementwise fashion (see figure 5.7). The sizes of the input and output of a cell should be the same to ensure a valid skip connection. The result of the addition will serve as the input tensor for the next cell. This is helpful for building up a deeper network because it avoids the problem of *gradient vanishing*, where the gradients for updating the weights of the first layers become smaller and smaller during the backpropagation process due to the use of the chain rule for calculating the derivative of composite layer transformations. The "vanished" gradients are

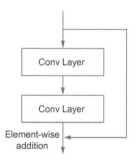

Figure 5.7   Substructure of ResNet

---

[1] See Kaiming He et al., "Deep Residual Learning for Image Recognition," available at https://arxiv.org/pdf/1512.03385.pdf.

[2] See "Xception: Deep Learning with Depthwise Separable Convolutions" by François Chollet, available at https://arxiv.org/pdf/1610.02357.pdf.

unable to update the weights in the early layers, which prevents the creation of a deeper network. You can learn more about this in Chollet's book *Deep Learning with Python*.

We can create various ResNets with different cell structures or different numbers of cells. Some traditional architectures include ResNet-18 and ResNet-50, where the number in the name indicates the total number of layers accumulated from all its stacked cells. To implement a ResNet and tune its structure, we can build up a sequential AutoML pipeline with AutoKeras using the built-in `ResNetBlock`, as shown in the following listing. The `ResNetBlock` contains a search space of classical ResNet structures, which are predefined and included in the Keras API (https://keras.io/api/applications/resnet/).

Listing 5.6   Creating a ResNet AutoML pipeline for image classification

```
input_node = ak.ImageInput()
output_node = ak.Normalization()(input_node)
output_node = ak.ResNetBlock()(output_node)
output_node = ak.ClassificationHead()(output_node)
```

XCEPTION

Xception is a CNN architecture that uses separable convolutional layers to improve the network's performance. As briefly mentioned in the earlier discussion of the `ConvBlock`, a separable convolutional layer contains fewer weights than a normal convolutional layer but is able to achieve comparable performance on many tasks. It produces the filters (weights) of a normal convolutional layer using the weights from two separable layers, and then uses its generated filters in the same way as the standard convolutional layer. The following listing shows how this works. We use a 2-D squared weight matrix of size 3×3 and a vector of length 16 to generate a regular 3-D convolutional filter of size 3×3×16 via tensor product.

Listing 5.7   Producing the weights with a separable convolutional layer

```
import numpy as np
kernel_size = 3
num_filters = 16                                          Initialize a variable
                                                          for what we are
sep_conv_weight_1 = np.random.rand(kernel_size,           bringing.
                                   kernel_size)   ◁─┘

                                                          The weight vector
sep_conv_weight_2 = np.random.rand(num_filters)   ◁─      of a separable
                                                          convolutional layer

sep_conv_filters = np.zeros(shape=(kernel_size,
                                   kernel_size,
                                   num_filters))  ◁─      Initializes an array
                                                          with the convolutional
for i in range(kernel_size):                              layer weights
    for j in range(kernel_size):
        for k in range(num_filters):
```

```
            sep_conv_filters[i][j][k] = sep_conv_weight_1[i][j]
⇨ * sep_conv_weight_2[k]          ◁┐
                                     │  Computes the convolutional
                                     │  weights with the tensor product
```

As shown in figure 5.8, Xception uses two types of neural network cells. They are similar to ResNet cells but with separable convolutional layers. The first type of cell uses a convolutional layer with the kernel size equal to 1 to process the input before adding it to the output of the separable convolutional layers.

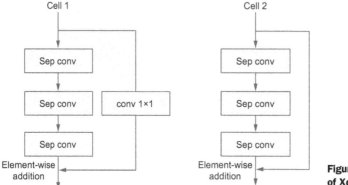

Figure 5.8   Two types of Xception cells

The original Xception architecture is shown in figure 5.9. It contains normal convolutional layers at the beginning, different types of cells in the middle, and some separable convolutional layers at the end. Different variations of the Xception architecture can be generated by stacking a different number of cells or selecting different hyperparameters, such as the number of filters or kernel size for the layers.

Figure 5.9   Xception architecture

We can build up an AutoML pipeline to search for a good Xception structure with the help of the XceptionBlock in AutoKeras, as shown in the next listing. It covers the original Xception architecture as described by Chollet (https://arxiv.org/abs/1610.02357) as well as a bunch of variations included in the TensorFlow Keras API (https://keras.io/api/applications/xception/).

Listing 5.8   Creating an Xception AutoML pipeline for image classification

```
input_node = ak.ImageInput()
output_node = ak.Normalization()(input_node)
```

```
output_node = ak.XceptionBlock()(output_node)
output_node = ak.ClassificationHead()(output_node)
```

Besides ResNet and Xception, many other popular variations on vanilla CNNs exist. I recommend that you explore the available models based on your interests. For practical use, you can directly apply the AutoML pipeline to save you effort in learning how they work and tuning them.

JOINT MODEL SELECTION AND HYPERPARAMETER TUNING FOR IMAGE CLASSIFICATION

The "no free lunch" theorem[3] tells us that no single model works best in any situation. "Which ML model should I use for my task?" is a commonly asked question. Because we know how to design an AutoML pipeline to tune a specific type of model, such as a vanilla CNN, a straightforward option is to tune different types of models one by one, find the optimal set of hyperparameters for each, and select the best-performing one among them. This is a feasible solution, but it's not an elegant one because it requires us to create multiple AutoML pipelines. We expect to be able to create a single AutoML pipeline to address the problem in one step. This requires the AutoML pipeline to cover all the relevant types of models as well as their unique hyperparameters. In each search trial, the search algorithm can first select a model and then select its hyperparameters to generate a pipeline. We can implement such an AutoML pipeline with an `ImageBlock` in AutoKeras (see figure 5.10), which is a sort of "hyperblock" that groups together several lower-level AutoML blocks: the `ConvBlock`, `ResNetBlock`, and `XceptionBlock`. You can use the `block_type` hyperparameter to choose which type of block to use, or if left unspecified, it will be tuned automatically. It also includes normalization and image augmentation preprocessor blocks (we'll talk more about preprocessing methods in the next section).

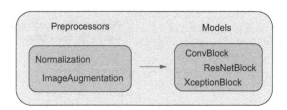

Figure 5.10 An `ImageBlock`
in AutoKeras

The number of models in the search space is quite large, because it encompasses all of the included block types. It often requires many search trials to find a good model. In addition, some of the models, such as ResNet-152, are much larger than the vanilla CNN we designed previously. These models may require a larger number of training epochs to achieve good accuracy and ensure a fair comparison and selection. Both of these factors result in a longer search process. Moreover, large model sizes lead to

---

[3] Described by David Wolpert in "The Lack of A Priori Distinctions between Learning Algorithms," available at http://mng.bz/xvde.

increased memory consumption during the search process, which may prevent us from using large datasets or batch sizes (in an effort to reduce the search cost). These are the crucial barriers in the study and application of AutoML. We will not explore these issues in more depth here, but instead, we will use a small number of search trials and training epochs as a workaround to help you get a sense of the model selection process. We'll talk more about how to accelerate the search process and reduce memory consumption in chapter 8.

In listing 5.9, we implement an AutoML pipeline for selecting a suitable model (vanilla CNN, ResNet, or Xception) to use for image classification on the MNIST dataset. We search for 10 trials. Each model is trained for three epochs with a batch size of 32 (the default batch size of AutoKeras). If the batch size is too large, AutoKeras will automatically reduce it to avoid memory overflow.

> **Listing 5.9   Selecting an image classification model using `ImageBlock`**

```
>>> import timeit
>>> import autokeras as ak

>>> input_node = ak.ImageInput()
>>> output_node = ak.ImageBlock(
...      normalize=True,              Fixes the two preprocessor blocks
...      augment=False,              contained in the ImageBlock
...      )(input_node)
>>> output_node = ak.ClassificationHead(dropout=0.0)(output_node)
>>> auto_model = ak.AutoModel(
...      inputs=input_node,
...      outputs=output_node,
...      max_trials=10,
...      overwrite=True,
...      seed=42)

>>> start_time = timeit.default_timer()
>>> auto_model.fit(x_train, y_train, epochs=3,      Performs the search and
...                batch_size=32)                    marks the total time
>>> stop_time = timeit.default_timer()
>>> print(f'total time: {round(stop_time - start_time, 2)} seconds.')
Total time: 4008.61 seconds.

>>> auto_model.tuner.results_summary(num_trials=1)      Summarizes the
Results summary                                          best found pipeline
Results in ./auto_model
Showing 1 best trials
Objective(name='val_loss', direction='min')
Trial summary
Hyperparameters:
image_block_1/block_type: xception
classification_head_1/spatial_reduction_1/reduction_type: global_avg
optimizer: adam
learning_rate: 0.001
image_block_1/xception_block_1/pretrained: False
image_block_1/xception_block_1/imagenet_size: False
Score: 0.06062331795692444
```

```
>>> test_loss, test_acc = auto_model.evaluate(x_test,
...     y_test,
...     verbose=0)
>>> print('Accuracy: {accuracy}%'.format(accuracy=round(test_acc*100,2)))
Accuracy: 98.57%
```

**Evaluates the
best model**

From the search results, we can see that it takes more than an hour on a single GPU (NVIDIA 2080 Titan) to finish the 10 trials, which is super long. The best model is an Xception model, but its performance is not as good as a vanilla CNN we found earlier with a `ConvBlock` using the same number of search trials and the same settings for model training. This shows that although enlarging the search space enables selection from different models, it may cost you more resources, such as more search time using more trials or more computing resources, to find a good architecture. Although it can save you effort on tuning, the tradeoff between the convenience of AutoML and its cost should never be ignored and remains an active area of study in the AutoML field.

5.3.2 *Automated selection of image preprocessing methods*

Besides model selection, we may also want to select suitable data-preprocessing methods to better prepare the data for our models and improve their performance. For example, working with a small dataset is a common situation in deep learning applications. Learning from insufficient training data can introduce a high risk of overfitting, especially when we have a larger model, causing the model to not generalize well to new data. This problem can be mitigated through the following two main approaches:

- On the model or learning algorithm side, we can use a technique called *regularization*. We've already seen some examples of this, such as using dropout layers, limiting the model size by reducing the number of layers or neurons, and using fewer training epochs.
- On the data side, we may be able to collect more data or use *data augmentation* methods to tweak the instances in the existing dataset to generate new instances. Data augmentation gives the ML models a larger pool of instances to learn from, which can improve their performance. For example, for an image dataset, each image might be flipped horizontally or rotated by a certain degree before passing it into the neural network. We can use many such operations to tweak the images, and we can apply different operations to different images randomly to achieve more diversified training data. In different epochs, we may also apply different operations on the same image. In figure 5.11, you can see some images generated this way. The first image is the original, and the other nine images were all generated with data augmentation techniques. As you can see, the content is always the same, but the size, position, and so on have been changed.

Figure 5.11   Image augmentation

Because many regularization techniques are related to the selection of model structures, the AutoML method introduced in previous sections is already able to discover some of them to mitigate the issue of overfitting. In fact, it is also straightforward to extend the AutoML pipeline to tune and select a suitable data augmentation method—that is, to use an AutoML block to select and evaluate various data augmentation methods. The `ImageBlock` also allows us to select among multiple data preprocessing methods, such as deciding whether to use normalization and/or data augmentation methods to prepare the data.

Let's use an image classification example to illustrate how to automatically select preprocessing methods for a ResNet model. We decide whether to use data augmentation and normalization methods. The dataset we use in listing 5.10 is a subset of the CIFAR-10 dataset, which contains 60,000 RGB images of size 32×32×3. The 50,000 images in the training set belong to 10 classes, such as "bird," "cat," "dog," and so on (5,000 images per class). To make things easier, we'll use images from only two classes, "airplane" and "automobile." The first nine images from the subsampled dataset are visualized in figure 5.12.

Listing 5.10   Loading and visualizing a subset of the CIFAR-10 dataset

```
>>> from tensorflow.keras.datasets import cifar10          Loads the
>>> (x_train, y_train), (x_test, y_test) =                 CIFAR-10
⮑ cifar10.load_data()                              ◁        dataset

>>> airplane_automobile_indices_train = \
...     (y_train[:, 0]==0) | (y_train[:, 0]==1)
>>> airplane_automobile_indices_test = \                    Picks the images
...     (y_test[:, 0]==0) | (y_test[:, 0]==1)               belonging to the
>>> x_train = x_train[airplane_automobile_indices_train]    "airplane" and
>>> y_train = y_train[airplane_automobile_indices_train]    "automobile"
>>> x_test = x_test[airplane_automobile_indices_test]       classes
>>> y_test = y_test[airplane_automobile_indices_test]
```

```
>>> print('Training image shape:', x_train.shape)
>>> print('Training label shape:', y_train.shape)
>>> print('First five training labels:', y_train[:5])
Training image shape: (10000, 32, 32, 3)
Training label shape: (10000, 1)
First five training labels: [[1]
 [1]
 [0]
 [0]
 [1]]

>>> from matplotlib import pyplot as plt
>>> for i in range(9):
...     plt.subplot(330 + 1 + i)
...     plt.imshow(x_train[i])
>>> plt.show()
```

Plots the first nine images

Figure 5.12   The first nine images from the "airplane" and "automobile" classes in the CIFAR-10 dataset

Let's first create an AutoML pipeline to select the data augmentation method for the ResNet models. The pipeline has the same structure as the sequential AutoML pipelines we built in the previous section for tuning a single ResNet model. The only difference is that we add an ImageAugmentation AutoML block between the normalization preprocessor and the network block, as shown in listing 5.11. The ImageAugmentation block in AutoKeras does not have parameters to be updated via backpropagation but contains multiple image transformation operations that can be jointly selected with other hyperparameters in the pipeline. We fix the type of ResNet to narrow down the search space. 'v2' here means the version 2 search space, covering three ResNet structures.[4] The augmentation methods are selected

---

[4] See "Identity Mappings in Deep Residual Networks" by Kaiming He et al., available at https://arxiv.org/abs/1603.05027.

along with the structure and other hyperparameters, such as the optimization method and learning rate.

NOTE   This code example may take a long time to run.

Listing 5.11   Selecting image preprocessing methods for a ResNet model

```
input_node = ak.ImageInput()
output_node = ak.Normalization()(input_node)
output_node = ak.ImageAugmentation()(output_node)
output_node = ak.ResNetBlock(version='v2')(output_node)
output_node = ak.ClassificationHead(dropout=0.0)(output_node)
auto_model = ak.AutoModel(
    inputs=input_node,
    outputs=output_node,
    overwrite=True,
    max_trials=10)
auto_model.fit(x_train, y_train, epochs=10)
```

As mentioned in the previous section, the image hyperblock (ImageBlock) in Auto-Keras also contains preprocessing methods, so we can use it to select the data augmentation method as well. It can also decide whether to use normalization if we set the normalize argument to None, as in the following listing. Setting normalize to True (or False) will fix that we want to use (or not use) the normalization method.

NOTE   This code example may take a long time to run.

Listing 5.12   Selecting augmentation and normalization methods for ResNet models

```
input_node = ak.ImageInput()
output_node = ak.ImageBlock(          Does not specify whether we want to use
                                      normalization and data augmentation methods;
    normalize=None,                   lets them be searched automatically
    augment=None,

    block_type='resnet',             Searches only the
    )(input_node)                    ResNet architectures
output_node = ak.ClassificationHead(dropout=0.0)(output_node)
auto_model = ak.AutoModel(
    inputs=input_node,
    outputs=output_node,
    overwrite=True,
    max_trials=10)
auto_model.fit(x_train, y_train, epochs=10)
```

Because the search and model evaluation process is the same as in all the examples introduced earlier, we do not repeat it again here.

You now know how to use an AutoML pipeline to do hyperparameter tuning for a single type of model and how to use an ImageBlock for model selection. Although we used an image classification task as an example, this process can be generalized to text and structured data use cases. For example, to jointly select models and preprocessors for text or structured data classification or regression tasks, you can use `TextBlock` or `StructuredDataBlock` in AutoKeras to create the AutoML pipeline and change the input node from `ImageInput` to `TextInput` or `StructuredDataInput`. `TextBlock` and `StructuredDataBlock` both cover some representative models and preprocessors for the corresponding data types. For more details on these and the other AutoML blocks, check out https://autokeras.com/tutorial/overview/. For practical use, you can pick the one that is related to the type of neural network you want to tune or select and use it to create your AutoML pipeline using the default search space for the hyperparameters, or you can customize the hyperparameters based on your requirements. In the next section, we'll turn to a slightly more complicated use case: designing graph-structured AutoML pipeline beyond just sequentially stacking blocks.

5.4 Designing a graph-structured AutoML pipeline

In many applications, our requirements go beyond a sequential deep learning model (stacking layers sequentially). For example, for multi-input and multi-output classification problems, we may need to use different layers and preprocessing components for different inputs and create different heads to generate different outputs. We may need to preprocess images with the normalization method before feeding them into ResNet models and encode structured data with categorical features into numerical values before feeding them into MLPs. We can then merge the outputs from the models to generate the outputs for different targets. In other situations, we may want to leverage the combined power of multiple deep learning models, such as using ResNet and Xception networks together to do image classification. Different models can learn different feature representations from the data, and combining these representations can potentially enhance their predictive power. Tuning the models in these scenarios requires going beyond a sequential pipeline to a *graph-structured pipeline*, where each block can take input from multiple blocks (see figure 5.13). The pipeline is a *directed acyclic graph* (DAG) in which the nodes are the AutoML blocks introduced in the previous sections. Their order indicates the input/output connections among the blocks, which also denotes the flow of data.

In this section, we will take a quick look at how to tune models with multiple inputs and outputs by creating a graph-structured pipeline. The models we want to tune have a cross structure, as shown on the left side of figure 5.13. We'll begin by creating a synthetic dataset similar to the one we used in chapter 4, with both synthetic images and structured data. We have two targets: a classification target and a regression response. Code for creating the dataset is shown in listing 5.13. We generate 1,000 synthetic instances, of which 800 are used for training and validation and 200 are reserved for testing. Each instance comprises an image with size 32×32×3 and three categorical features. The output consists of a classification label (one of five classes) and a regression response.

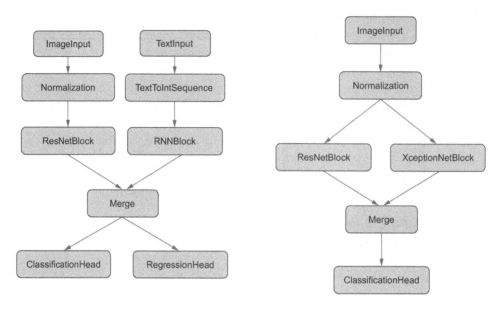

Figure 5.13   Graph-structured AutoML pipelines

Listing 5.13   Creating a synthetic dataset with multiple inputs and outputs

```
>>> import numpy as np

>>> num_instances = 1000
                                                              Generates image data
>>> image_data = np.random.rand(num_instances, 32, 32, 3).astype(np.float32)
>>> image_train, image_test = image_data[:800],
⇒ image_data[800:]

>>> structured_data = np.random.choice(
...     ['a', 'b', 'c', 'd', 'e'], size=(num_instances, 3))      Generates structured
>>> structured_train, structured_test =                          data with three
⇒ structured_data[:800], structured_data[800:]                  categorical features

>>> classification_target = np.random.randint(
...     5, size=num_instances)                                  Generates
>>> clf_target_train, clf_target_test =                         classification labels
⇒ classification_target[:800], classification_target[800:]      for five classes

>>> regression_target = np.random.rand(
...     num_instances, 1).astype(np.float32)                    Generates
>>> reg_target_train, reg_target_test =                         regression targets
⇒ regression_target[:800], regression_target[800:]

>>> structured_train[:5]                    Displays the categorical
array([['b', 'b', 'e'],                     features of the first five
       ['e', 'e', 'b'],                     instances
```

```
    ['c', 'c', 'c'],
    ['c', 'b', 'd'],
    ['c', 'c', 'a']], dtype='<U1')
```

The creation of the pipeline should follow the topological order of the nodes in the graph, which means we should follow the flow of the data—we begin by creating the AutoML blocks that appear at the front of the pipeline, so that their outputs can be fed into the blocks that appear later. You can imagine how a data instance will go from input to output in order to set up the blocks of the AutoML pipeline one by one. The code for creating the AutoML pipeline shown on the left in figure 5.13 is presented in listing 5.14. After stacking the AutoML blocks to process each type of data, the outputs from the two branches are combined to generate the two responses via a `Merge` block. This block will add the two outputs elementwise if their dimensions are the same. Otherwise, it will reshape the input tensors into vectors and then concatenate them. The specific merge operations to be used are tuned during the search process if not specified during initialization.

Listing 5.14 Tuning a model with a graph-structured AutoML pipeline

```
import autokeras as ak

input_node1 = ak.ImageInput()
branch1 = ak.Normalization()(input_node1)          Stacks two blocks in the
branch1 = ak.ConvBlock()(branch1)                  image branch

input_node2 = ak.StructuredDataInput()
branch2 = ak.CategoricalToNumerical()(input_node2)  Stacks two blocks in the
branch2 = ak.DenseBlock()(branch2)                  structured data branch

merge_node = ak.Merge()([branch1, branch2])
output_node1 = ak.ClassificationHead()(merge_node)  Merges the two blocks
output_node2 = ak.RegressionHead()(merge_node)

auto_model = ak.AutoModel(
    inputs=[input_node1, input_node2],
    outputs=[output_node1, output_node2],
    max_trials=3,
    overwrite=True,        Generates the graph-structured
    seed=42)          ◁─── AutoML pipeline with multiple
                           inputs and outputs
auto_model.fit(
    [image_train, structured_train],
    [clf_target_train, reg_target_train],
    epochs=3,
)                   ◁───   Feeds the data into
                           the AutoML pipeline

best_model = auto_model.export_model()              ◁───────────┐
tf.keras.utils.plot_model(                                      Plots the best model
    best_model,show_shapes=True, expand_nested=True) ◁──────────┘
```

The best architecture found in three trials is visualized in figure 5.14. I've annotated each component in the discovered deep network with the corresponding element in the AutoML pipeline. Their hyperparameters are selected to form the search space of the AutoML block. For example, two dense layers are used to process structured data, and there are two convolutional cells, each of which contains two convolutional layers with a max pooling layer to encode the images.

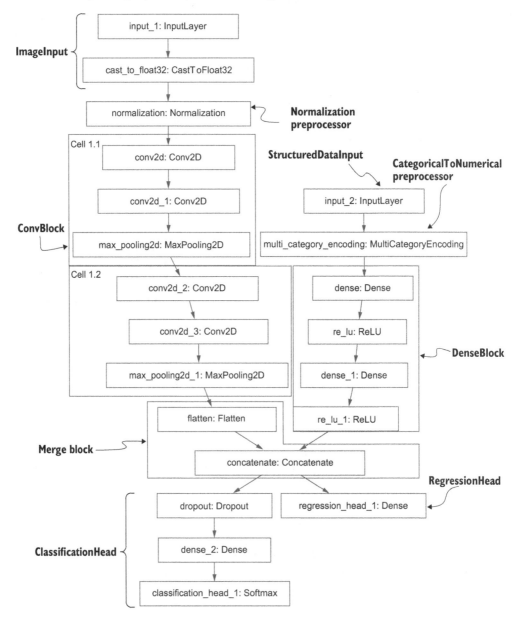

Figure 5.14   The best model identified for the task with multiple inputs and outputs

We can create more complicated graph-structured pipelines to tune more complex architectures, and we can use a hyperblock to help us select among different models.

Though it is convenient to use the built-in blocks of AutoKeras to create these pipelines, you may find that they don't cover all the models you know about or are not able to support all the hyperparameters you want to tune. This introduces a question: is it possible to create our own AutoML blocks to select and tune our concerned neural networks or preprocessing methods? The aim of the last section is to introduce how to customize your own AutoML blocks to build up the AutoML pipeline.

5.5 *Designing custom AutoML blocks*

Using AutoKeras's built-in blocks may not always fulfill your hyperparameter tuning and model selection needs. Hundreds, if not thousands, of neural networks might exist beyond the scope of the search space the blocks define. For example, suppose you want to tune a CNN that you've created yourself or found in the literature for image classification. It is not contained in the search space of any of the built-in AutoKeras blocks, including the `ConvBlock`, `ResNetBlock`, and so on. You need a new AutoML block, whose search space consists of models with the same structure as this new CNN model but with different hyperparameters (such as different numbers of units or layers). With this new AutoML block, you can tune the hyperparameters of the new neural network and compare it with other models covered by the pre-existing AutoKeras blocks.

This section teaches you how to create your own AutoML block to do hyperparameter tuning and model selection. We'll start by creating a custom block to tune MLPs without using the built-in MLP block (`DenseBlock`). Then we'll explore how to customize a hyperblock to perform model selection. The aim of this section is not to teach you how to design advanced neural networks but to show you a general way of creating the search space (the AutoML block) that can be used to tune and select from different types of neural networks if you already know how to create them with TensorFlow and Keras.

5.5.1 *Tuning MLPs with a custom MLP block*

In section 5.2, we used a built-in AutoKeras block (`DenseBlock`) to select a good MLP structure for regression tasks. This section will show you how to implement an MLP block yourself to achieve the same goal. It will familiarize you with the basic operations to create an AutoML block that defines the search space for deep learning models and can be generalized to create AutoML blocks for tuning more complex architectures.

CUSTOMIZING A BLOCK FOR TUNING THE NUMBER OF UNITS

Chapter 3 showed you how to create an MLP with TensorFlow and Keras. We start with an input node to specify the shape of the inputs. Then we create multiple dense layers and stack them sequentially, layer by layer. Finally, the layers are grouped into an MLP model for training and testing via the `tensorflow.keras.Model` class (or the `tensorflow.keras.Sequential` class we've used before). Listing 5.15 creates a three-layer

MLP, whose two hidden layers have 32 units each. We ignore the model-compiling part and implement only the creation of the model structure. Calling the build function will return an MLP model with the structure defined here.

Listing 5.15   MLP implementation in Keras

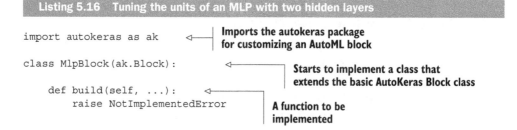

```
from tensorflow import keras            Defines the input      Stacks two hidden dense
from tensorflow.keras import layers     dimensions of          layers with 32 units each
                                        the network            and ReLU activation
def build_mlp():
    input_node = keras.Input(shape=(20,))

    output_node = layers.Dense(units=32, activation='relu')(input_node)
    output_node = layers.Dense(units=32, activation='relu')(output_node)
    output_node = layers.Dense(units=1, activation='sigmoid')(output_node)

    model = keras.Model(input_node, output_node)
    return model

mlp_model = build_mlp()
```

Groups the layers into a Keras model

Adds a dense classification layer with sigmoid activation

Suppose we want to tune the number of units in the two hidden layers. The `units` hyperparameter should be an integer, so to create a finite search space, we'll assume its value to be a multiple of 32 and smaller than 512. This gives us the following search space of values to choose from: [32, 64, ..., 512]. To create an AutoML block that defines this search space, we need to do three things. First, in listing 5.16, we create a class that extends the basic AutoKeras `Block` class (`ak.Block`). We'll use this for tuning our MLP, so we'll name it `MlpBlock`. Extending the basic `Block` class guarantees we can use the customized block to create an AutoML pipeline by connecting it with other AutoKeras components. It contains a `build()` function, to be overridden, that can help us define the search space and instantiate MLP models during the search process.

Listing 5.16   Tuning the units of an MLP with two hidden layers

```
import autokeras as ak              Imports the autokeras package
                                    for customizing an AutoML block

class MlpBlock(ak.Block):          Starts to implement a class that
                                   extends the basic AutoKeras Block class

    def build(self, ...):          A function to be
        raise NotImplementedError  implemented
```

Next, we implement the `build` function. This function is the core part of the AutoML block. It has two roles: defining the search space for the hyperparameters we want to tune and building an MLP in each trial during the search process whenever it is called by the search algorithm. Implementing it is very similar to writing a function to build an MLP model (see listing 5.15), but with the following main changes:

- Because this AutoML block will connect with other blocks to form an AutoML pipeline, it should take the outputs from one or more previous blocks as its input and output a tensor that can be fed as input into other blocks, rather than a complete Keras model to be trained and evaluated.

- Because an AutoML block is used to define the search space of the relevant hyperparameters, we should define a search space for each hyperparameter we want to tune. These hyperparameters will not be assigned fixed values in advance, like the units=32 in listing 5.15, but will be dynamically assigned a value sampled from the search space (by the search algorithm) in each search trial.

To reflect the first change, in listing 5.17, we remove the Keras input initializer (keras.Input()) and directly feed a list of the output nodes (or tensors) of the previous AutoML blocks to the build() function. Because the inputs can be a list of tensors, we use a flatten operation (tf.nest.flatten()) to combine them into a single tensor that can be directly fed into the dense layers. We leave only the two hidden layers to be tuned in the block and return the outputs without adding a classification layer or wrapping them into a Keras model.

Listing 5.17 Tuning the two hidden layers with the same number of units

```
import autokeras as ak
import tensorflow as tf
from tensorflow.keras import layers          Implements a
                                             class extending
                                             the Block class
class MlpBlock(ak.Block):                 ◄
                                             Overrides the
  def build(self, hp, inputs):         ◄   build function
                                                     Gets the input node from
                                                     the inputs, which may be
    input_node = tf.nest.flatten(inputs)[0]   ◄     either a list of nodes or a
                                                     single node
    units = hp.Int(name='units', min_value=32,
                   max_value=512, step=32)   ◄       Declares the number of units
                                                     as an integer hyperparameter
    output_node = layers.Dense(
        units=units, activation='relu')(input_node)   ◄   Uses the same
    output_node = layers.Dense(                            number of units for
        units=units, activation='relu')(output_node)  ◄   both of the layers

    return output_node   ◄   The return value of the build
                             function should be the output node.
```

To define the search space of the units hyperparameter and assign it a value dynamically, we use a module in KerasTuner called keras_tuner.engine.hyperparameters. It contains different classes to create the search spaces for different types of hyperparameters (integer, float, Boolean) and a container named HyperParameters (hp for short) that contains information about the search spaces for all the relevant hyperparameters. The hp container has different methods corresponding to the different search-space-creation classes. For example, the hp.Choice method corresponds to the keras_tuner.engine.hyperparameters.Choice class we used in chapter 5. Here, we use hp.Int to define a search space of integer values for the units hyperparameter (see the fourth annotation in listing 5.17). It creates a list of values ([32, 64, …, 512]), similar to the hp.Choice method, but more conveniently: you don't have to list every value in the search space one by one but can define a *step value* to generate them automatically (step=32 in this example, because the values are multiples of 32). The max_value and min_value arguments limit the scope of the search space. The name argument provides a reference to the hyperparameter in the search space.

In listing 5.18, we assume the two hidden layers have the same number of units. We can also separately tune the number of units in each of the hidden layers, as shown in the following listing. In this case, we assign a different name to each hyperparameter and assign them to the corresponding layers.

Listing 5.18   Separately tuning the number of units in the two hidden layers

```
import autokeras as ak
import tensorflow as tf
from tensorflow.keras import layers

class MlpBlock(ak.Block):

  def build(self, hp, inputs):
    input_node = tf.nest.flatten(inputs)[0]
    units_1 = hp.Int(name='units_1', min_value=32,
                    max_value=512, step=32)          ◁┐ Creates separate search
    units_2 = hp.Int(name='units_2', min_value=32,      │ spaces for the number of
                    max_value=512, step=32)          ◁┘ units in each layer
    output_node = layers.Dense(units=units_1,
        activation='relu')(input_node)    ◁┐ Assigns the units to the
    output_node = layers.Dense(units=units_2,   │ corresponding layers
        activation='relu')(output_node)   ◁┘
    return output_node
```

We do not create the hp container in the build() function but rather feed it to the build() function as input. The container is a global container for all the AutoML blocks. It plays the following two roles:

- *Search space container*—The hp container holds information on all the hyperparameter search spaces created in each AutoML block. Thus, once the complete AutoML pipeline has been created, it will hold details on the complete search space for the entire pipeline.
- *Current hyperparameter value container*—During the search process, in each trial, the container will keep track of the hyperparameter values given by the search algorithm and assign them to the corresponding hyperparameters in each block based on their names. In this example, the hp container will provide fixed units values selected by the search algorithm to help build the two hidden layers in our MlpBlock.

Although it looks like we are assigning a search space for each hyperparameter (such as units=hp.Int(…)) in the build() function, during the search process, the function will always create the layers with fixed hyperparameter values. These are set by default or selected by the search algorithm. This means the hp.Int() method will always return a fixed value when it is called, and the search space's definition is saved in the hp container. This also illustrates why the names of hyperparameters should be different: so that the container can distinguish between them when saving their search spaces and assign the correct values to them when building the models in each trial.

CUSTOMIZING A BLOCK FOR TUNING DIFFERENT TYPES OF HYPERPARAMETERS

We tuned an integer hyperparameter in the previous example, but many different types of hyperparameters can exist in an MLP. For example, whether we should use a dropout layer (to help avoid overfitting, as discussed in chapter 4) can be treated as a hyperparameter with a Boolean (true/false) value. The dropout rate in the dropout layer is a floating-point value. The key point in tuning different types of hyperparameters is selecting the correct search-space-creation method. We list several examples in table 5.1. Intuitively, the methods for creating the search space accord with the value types of the hyperparameters. Keep in mind that although the hp container methods, such as hp.Choice() and hp.Int(), define a search space, they will always return a value.

Table 5.1 Different hyperparameter types in an MLP mode

Hyperparameter	Type	Search space example	Search-space-creation method
Number of units in a layer	Integer	[10, 30, 100, 200] / [10, 20, 30, 40]	hp.Choice, hp.Int
Number of layers	Integer	[1, 2, 3, 4]	hp.Choice, hp.Int
Whether to use a dropout layer	Boolean	[True, False]	hp.Boolean
Dropout rate	Float	Any real value between 0.1 and 0.2	hp.Float

Tuning a single hyperparameter is straightforward. But what if we want to jointly search the number of layers as well as the number of units in each layer? These two hyperparameters are dependent on each other, because the number of layers determines how many "units" hyperparameters we want to tune if we assume the hidden layers can have different numbers of units. We can create a search space for the number of layers using the hp.Choice() method as usual, as shown in listing 5.19. The returned value will determine how many layers we will have in the MlpBlock and can be used in a for loop to help create the layers and set up the search space for the number of units in each layer. Note that we use different names for the units hyperparameter in each layer to distinguish between them for the search algorithm.

```
import autokeras as ak
import tensorflow as tf
from tensorflow.keras import layers

class MlpBlock(ak.Block):
    def build(self, hp, inputs):
        output_node = tf.nest.flatten(inputs)[0]
        for i in range(hp.Choice('num_layers', [1, 2, 3])):
            output_node = layers.Dense(units=hp.Int(
                'units_' + str(i),
                min_value=32,
                max_value=512,
                step=32),
                activation='relu')(output_node)
        return output_node
```

Defines the number of layers as a hyperparameter

Dynamically generates one new hyperparameter for each layer, while ensuring the hyperparameter names are not the same

We can flesh out our MlpBlock by adding more hyperparameters, as shown listing 5.20. For example, whether to use a dropout layer is worth exploring in practice. Because it's a choice between true and false, we can use hp.Boolean() to tune this hyperparameter. As mentioned earlier, we can also tune the dropout rate, which determines the percentage of neurons to ignore during the training process. This is a floating-point value, so we'll use hp.Float() to tune this hyperparameter.

```
import autokeras as ak
import tensorflow as tf
from tensorflow.keras import layers

class MlpBlock(ak.Block):
    def build(self, hp, inputs):
        output_node = tf.nest.flatten(inputs)[0]
        for i in range(hp.Choice('num_layers', [1, 2, 3])):
            output_node = layers.Dense(units=hp.Int('units_' + str(i),
                min_value=32,
                max_value=512,
                step=32),
                activation='relu')(output_node)
            if hp.Boolean('dropout'):
                output_node = layers.Dropout(rate=hp.Float('dropout_rate',
                    min_value=0,
                    max_value=1))
        return output_node
```

Uses hp.Boolean to decide whether to use a dropout layer

Uses hp.Float to decide on the dropout rate

When using hp.Float(), note that we did not specify the step argument like in hp.Int(). The search algorithm will select a floating-point value in the continuous range.

USING THE CUSTOM BLOCK TO CREATE AN AUTOML PIPELINE

Now you know how to write a neural network block to define a customized search space. The next step is to connect it with other components (input node, output head, and other blocks) to create a full AutoML pipeline for tuning the relevant hyperparameters.

To make sure the block does not contain implementation bugs before the connection, you can write a simple test to see if it builds correctly, as shown in the next listing. The inputs can be a single Keras input node or a list of nodes. An `hp` container is created for testing purposes. You may also insert some print statements (or assertions) in the `build()` function to print out (or assert) some intermediate outputs to better test the block.

Listing 5.21 Testing the neural network block

```
import keras_tuner as kt
hp = kt.HyperParameters()
inputs = tf.keras.Input(shape=(20,))
MlpBlock().build(hp, inputs)
```

If the `build()` function of the block runs smoothly without errors, we can use this block just as we would use any of the built-in blocks in AutoKeras introduced in chapter 4. Let's use it to tune an MLP for a structured data regression task with a synthetic dataset. In the following listing, we first randomly generate a tabular dataset with 20 features, 100 training instances, and 100 test instances. We then connect the `MlpBlock` with the input node and the output regression head to create a full AutoML pipeline and initialize the `AutoModel` to conduct the search process on the training dataset.

Listing 5.22 Building and fitting a model with the custom block

```
>>> import numpy as np
>>> x_train = np.random.rand(100, 20)     Generates the
>>> y_train = np.random.rand(100, 1)      synthetic structured
>>> x_test = np.random.rand(100, 20)      data for regression

>>> input_node = ak.StructuredDataInput()           Passes the input node
>>> output_node = MlpBlock()(input_node)     ◁──     to the custom block
>>> output_node = ak.RegressionHead()(output_node)  ◁─┐ Passes the output node
>>> auto_model = ak.AutoModel(input_node, output_node,  │ of the custom block to
...       max_trials=3, overwrite=True)                 │ the regression head
>>> auto_model.fit(x_train, y_train, epochs=1)
```

We can also print out the search space of the created AutoML pipeline, as shown in listing 5.23. As you can see, it contains seven hyperparameters. Four of them are the ones we designed in the `MlpBlock`: number of layers, number of units, whether to use a dropout layer, and the dropout rate (`mlp_block_1/dropout_rate`). The other three are the dropout rate in the regression head, the optimization algorithm, and the learning rate of the optimization algorithm.

Listing 5.23 Printing out a summary of the search space

```
>>> auto_model.tuner.search_space_summary()
Search space summary
Default search space size: 7
mlp_block_1/num_layers (Choice)
{'default': 1, 'conditions': [], 'values': [1, 2, 3], 'ordered': True}
mlp_block_1/units_0 (Int)
{'default': None, 'conditions': [], 'min_value': 32,
  'max_value': 512, 'step': 32, 'sampling': None}
mlp_block_1/dropout (Boolean)
{'default': False, 'conditions': []}
regression_head_1/dropout (Choice)
{'default': 0, 'conditions': [], 'values': [0.0, 0.25, 0.5],
  'ordered': True}
optimizer (Choice)
{'default': 'adam', 'conditions': [], 'values': ['adam', 'sgd',
  'adam_weight_decay'], 'ordered': False}
learning_rate (Choice)
{'default': 0.001, 'conditions': [], 'values': [0.1, 0.01, 0.001,
  0.0001, 2e-05, 1e-05], 'ordered': True}
mlp_block_1/dropout_rate (Float)
{'default': 0.0, 'conditions': [], 'min_value': 0.0, 'max_value': 1.0,
  'step': None, 'sampling': None}
```

The process for designing an MLP block is generalizable to designing an AutoML block for tuning any kind of neural network architecture that can be directly built up with Keras layers. You may want to create a custom block for tuning your architectures if the following two conditions are satisfied:

- There is no built-in block in AutoKeras that you can use to build up your AutoML pipeline.
- You know how to create the network architecture by stacking the Keras layers.

5.5.2 Designing a hyperblock for model selection

Beyond tuning the hyperparameters of a single model, you may want to implement an AutoML block for model selection. In this section, you'll learn how to implement your own hyperblock like the ones we used in chapter 4 for selecting among different models. Because different models can also have different hyperparameters, this is in fact a joint hyperparameter tuning and model selection task, which requires a hierarchical search space to show the relations between each model and its unique hyperparameters. We will first look at a simple case of model selection, where each model does not have hyperparameters to tune, and then learn to how to deal with the joint hyperparameter tuning and model selection.

SELECTING AMONG DIFFERENT DENSENET MODELS

DenseNet is a widely used type of CNN. It stacks multiple DenseNet cells together to build a complete neural network. The basic cell of a DenseNet is shown in figure 5.15. In the cell, the input for each convolutional layer is the concatenation of all the output tensors of the previous convolutional layers within the same cell as well as the input tensor to the cell. The tensors are concatenated on their last dimension. For example, a tensor with shape (32, 32, 3) and a tensor with shape (32, 32, 16) can be concatenated to become (32, 32, 19). Extra pooling layers can be applied to reduce the size of the first two dimensions of the resulting tensor. Stacking different numbers of cells or different cell structures (e.g., with different numbers of convolutional layers in each cell or a different number of filters in the convolutional layers) can result in different versions of the DenseNet. For more details on DenseNet, check out Ferlitsch's book, *Deep Learning Design Patterns*.

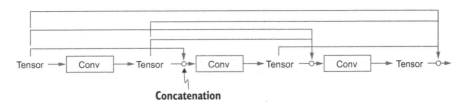

Figure 5.15   A DenseNet cell

Because DenseNets are quite popular in image-related applications, several representative ones are implemented in Keras Applications, a TensorFlow Keras module that collects various widely used deep learning models. It contains functions for instantiating three versions of DenseNet: DenseNet121, DenseNet169, and DenseNet201, which are created by stacking different numbers of DenseNet cells (each of which has two convolutional layers). The numbers in the names indicate how many layers the final model contains. We can directly call these functions to use these models without implementing them by ourselves layer by layer. For example, to create a DenseNet121, we can call the function tf.keras.applications.DenseNet121, as shown in listing 5.24. The function returns a Keras model. We can pass a NumPy array to it to see its output shape or directly call model.summary() to see the details of the model. For example, the model can take 100 synthetic images of shape 32×32×3. The output is a tensor with shape (100, 1, 1, 1024) (see listing 5.24). If we want the network to not include the classification head but only the convolutional layers of the neural network, we can use include_top=False in the arguments. By default, the weights in the network layers are initialized with weights that have been pretrained on larger datasets to improve the training speed and accuracy on the dataset at hand.

Listing 5.24   Building up a DenseNet model using a function in Keras Applications

```
import tensorflow as tf
import numpy as np

model = tf.keras.applications.DenseNet121(
    include_top=False,
    weights=None)
print(model(np.random.rand(100, 32, 32, 3)).shape)
```

A function to create a DenseNet model

This argument says to use only the convolution part of the network without the classification head.

Feeds a synthetic input to the created DenseNet121 model and prints out the output shape

This argument says to not use any pretrained weights.

Considering the different versions of DenseNet available in Keras Applications, you may be wondering how you determine which version is best for the task at hand. You can implement a custom AutoML block to select the best model with the help of the `hp.Choice()` function. In listing 5.25, we implement a `DenseNetBlock` to select among the three versions of DenseNet models. Note that we should not directly pass the models in Keras Applications to the `hp.Choice()` function because they are not serializable; we should always use the basic data types in Python, such as strings, Booleans, and numeric types, in the list we pass to `Choice()`. So, we use strings here to represent the three versions of DenseNet models, and we use an `if` statement to judge the selection and create the model. Feeding the input tensor to the created model results in an output tensor that can be fed into other AutoML blocks or classification/regression heads.

Listing 5.25   Implementing a DenseNet block

```
import autokeras as ak
import tensorflow as tf

class DenseNet(ak.Block):
    def build(self, hp, inputs):
        version = hp.Choice(
            'version', ['DenseNet121', 'DenseNet169', 'DenseNet201'])
        if version == 'DenseNet121':
            dense_net_func = tf.keras.applications.DenseNet121
        elif version == 'DenseNet169':
            dense_net_func = tf.keras.applications.DenseNet169
        elif version == 'DenseNet201':
            dense_net_func = tf.keras.applications.DenseNet201
        return dense_net_func(include_top=False,
            weights=None)(inputs)
```

Uses strings as the hyperparameter values for model selection because the functions are not serializable

Gets the model and calls it with the input tensor

Because the architectures included in Keras Applications are fixed, we cannot directly tune their hyperparameters (e.g., tuning the cell structure of the DenseNet121). But suppose that in addition to selecting the best model architecture, we want to tune the cell structure. In that case, we will need to define each DenseNet model ourselves, layer by layer, and specify the search space of the relevant hyperparameters, as we did for the `MlpBlock`. It's feasible to create multiple AutoML blocks, each of which defines the search space for one type of DenseNet model. In this case, we can create a hyperblock to select among the different AutoML blocks and tune the hyperparameters in the selected block. The next section will show how to create a hyperblock to do joint model selection and hyperparameter tuning, leveraging the existing AutoML blocks.

SELECTING BETWEEN DENSENET AND RESNET

We've created a `DenseNetBlock` to search among different DenseNet architectures. We also know that we have some built-in blocks in AutoKeras that can be used for image classification, such as the `ResNetBlock` we used in the section 5.3 for tuning a ResNet. Suppose we would like to select the best model, choosing between DenseNet and ResNet architectures. As listing 5.26 shows, we can take advantage of these existing blocks and create a hyperblock to select between the two model types, similar to how we created a normal AutoML block. The names of each block can be fed into the `hp.Choice` function as strings to define the search space for model selection. However, because the hyperblock is also an AutoML block, it should not directly return a selected AutoML block but instead return output tensors processed by Keras layers that can be used for other AutoML blocks. This requires us to call the `build()` function of each selected AutoML block to return its outputs. In other words, our hyperblock (`SelectionBlock`) should call the methods to create the other blocks as subroutines when building a search space. This also helps the `hp` container to collect all the search spaces defined in each block during the search process.

> **Listing 5.26   Creating a model-selection block**

```
class SelectionBlock(ak.Block):
    def build(self, hp, inputs):
        if hp.Choice('model_type',
                    ['densenet', 'resnet']) == 'densenet':    ◁─┐  Defines the
            outputs = DenseNetBlock().build(hp, inputs)            model_type
        else:                                                      hyperparameter
            outputs = ak.ResNetBlock().build(hp, inputs)           for model
        return outputs                                             selection
```

The `model_type` hyperparameter used here is called a *conditional hyperparameter*, which means selecting the hyperparameters in the subroutine is conditioned on which model we select. For example, the hyperparameters in the `DenseNetBlock` will be selected only when the value of the `model_type` hyperparameter in the `Selection-Block` is `'densenet'`.

A problem with conditional hyperparameters is that they can cause problems with the tuning algorithm. If we do not tell the tuning algorithm explicitly about conditional hyperparameters, it will lead to redundancy in searching wrong things and may affect the search performance. For example, the tuning algorithm may want to find an optimal value for the DenseNet version while `'resnet'` is selected as the value for the `model_type`, even though changing the DenseNet version will not affect the model. To declare such an affiliation between the hyperparameters, we use the `hp.conditional_scope()` method to inform the tuning algorithm of the dependency.

Any hyperparameter defined under the conditional scope will then be considered active only when the condition is met. For example, in listing 5.27, hp.conditional_ scope('model_type', ['densenet']) sets the condition that the model_type hyper-parameter's value should be 'densenet' to activate the scope.

Listing 5.27   Creating a model-selection block with conditional scope

```
class SelectionBlock(ak.Block):
    def build(self, hp, inputs):
        if hp.Choice('model_type', ['densenet', 'resnet']) == 'densenet':
            with hp.conditional_scope('model_type', ['densenet']):    ⬅—————
                outputs = DenseNetBlock().build(hp, inputs)
        else:
            with hp.conditional_scope('model_type', ['resnet']):
                outputs = ak.ResNetBlock().build(hp, inputs)
        return outputs
```

All hyperparameters in the build function of DenseNet are under this scope.

Activates the scope only if the value of the model hyperparameter is 'densenet'

Now that we've created our hyperblock, we can build up a complete AutoML pipeline for joint model selection and hyperparameter tuning. In listing 5.28, we pass an ImageInput node to our SelectionBlock and connect it with a ClassificationHead to select the best model from the search space for the image classification task on the CIFAR-10 dataset. We can also check out the entire search space by printing a summary by calling the function search_space_summary().

Listing 5.28   Building the model and conducting the search

```
input_node = ak.ImageInput()
output_node = SelectionBlock()(input_node)
output_node = ak.ClassificationHead()(output_node)
auto_model = ak.AutoModel(input_node, output_node,
                          max_trials=5, overwrite=True)

from tensorflow.keras.datasets import cifar10

(x_train, y_train), (x_test, y_test) = cifar10.load_data()
auto_model.fit(x_train[:100], y_train[:100], epochs=1)    ⬅—————

auto_model.tuner.search_space_summary()    ⬅—————
```

Prints out the search space of the created AutoML pipeline

Sets the number of epochs to 1 to run faster for illustrative purposes

Now that you know how to create your own custom AutoML blocks and hyperblocks for tuning deep learning models on classification and regression tasks, in the next chapter, we'll shift gears and look at defining the search space without connecting a series of these blocks. This will give you a more flexible way of designing the search space for a broader range of AutoML tasks, such as tuning unsupervised learning models, tuning the optimization algorithm or the loss function, and jointly selecting deep learning and shallow models.

Summary

- An AutoML pipeline can be regarded as a search space of ML pipelines. You can create pipelines with the AutoKeras functional API by stacking four components: input nodes, preprocessor blocks, network blocks, and output heads.

- AutoKeras has multiple built-in preprocessor blocks and network blocks. Each preprocessor block represents a specific preprocessing method and the search space of its hyperparameters. Each network block represents a particular type of model, such as MLPs or CNNs, and the default search space of the model's hyperparameters, such as the number of layers and units in an MLP. You can use these blocks to build the AutoML pipeline and tune the relevant hyperparameters by customizing their search spaces while fixing others.

- A hyperblock is a type of AutoML block that enables selection among different kinds of models and preprocessing methods. AutoKeras contains three hyperblocks, for image, text, and structured data, to help you create AutoML pipelines for joint model selection and hyperparameter tuning.

- The AutoML pipeline can be generalized from a sequential structure to a graph structure to tune models with multiple inputs and outputs or pipelines containing an ensemble of preprocessing methods or models. You can follow the data flow to create the pipeline with the AutoKeras functional API, setting up each AutoML block in turn, based on the order in which they appear in the graph.

- You can create a custom AutoML block containing the search space of your own model and connect it with the built-in blocks in AutoKeras. You can also set up a conditional search space in an AutoML block for model selection.

AutoML with a fully customized search space

This chapter covers

- Customizing the entire AutoML search space without connecting AutoML blocks
- Tuning autoencoder models for unsupervised learning tasks
- Tuning shallow models with preprocessing pipelines
- Controlling the AutoML process by customizing tuners
- Joint tuning and selection among deep learning and shallow models
- Hyperparameter tuning beyond Keras and scikit-learn models

This chapter introduces customization of the entire AutoML search space in a layerwise fashion without wiring up AutoML blocks, giving you more flexibility in designing the search space for tuning unsupervised learning models and optimization algorithms. We introduce how to tune a shallow model with its preprocessing pipeline, including feature engineering steps. You will also learn how to control the model-training and evaluation process to conduct the joint tuning and selection of deep learning models and shallow models. This allows you to tune models with different training and evaluation procedures implemented with different ML libraries.

6.1 Customizing the search space in a layerwise fashion

In chapter 5, you learned how to perform hyperparameter tuning and model selection by specifying the search space with AutoML blocks. You also know how to create your own AutoML blocks if the built-in blocks do not fit your needs. However, you may encounter some scenarios that are hard to address by wiring together AutoML blocks or where this simply isn't the best approach, such as the following:

- *Tuning models for tasks beyond classification and regression*—Although these are probably the most widely studied problems in ML, you may face tasks that lie outside these areas. They may not even be supervised learning tasks, where there are pre-existing responses for you to learn from.
- *Customizing the search space of the optimization algorithm (e.g., tuning the learning rate or batch size) and the loss function*

Besides these scenarios, you may find it superfluous to create an AutoML pipeline by wiring together AutoML blocks if you need to customize all the blocks in the pipeline. Why not directly create the pipeline in one `build()` function, like you implement a neural network with TensorFlow Keras, rather than doing a two-step job (wrapping them up into different AutoKeras AutoML blocks and connecting them)?

In this section, you'll see how to fully customize a search space in a layerwise fashion without wiring up AutoML blocks. This method may require more code, but it provides extra flexibility in customizing the search space for tuning tasks beyond supervised learning. If there are no suitable built-in AutoML blocks for you to use, this method can also reduce the burden of creating and wiring multiple custom blocks to define the search space. To achieve this, we'll use KerasTuner, an AutoML library originally proposed for selecting and tuning TensorFlow Keras models and beyond. We used its `hyperparameters` module earlier in the previous two chapters to customize partial search space, and here we'll use it to build a search space from scratch. We'll start by tuning an MLP model for a regression task, which involves the tuning of optimization algorithms and data preprocessing method with custom search space. Then we'll use KerasTuner to tune an autoencoder model for unsupervised learning tasks.

6.1.1 Tuning an MLP for regression with KerasTuner

Let's first work on the problem of tuning an MLP for regression. We'll tune the number of units in the hidden layers first and gradually add more hyperparameters in the search space.

Implementing the search space for tuning an MLP model with KerasTuner is almost the same as building an MLP model with Keras. We need a `build()` function that can generate an MLP model and define the search space for the hyperparameters we're concerned with, such as the number of units. You've seen how to define the search space with the hp container when customizing the AutoML blocks, and the process here is the same. However, because our purpose in this case is not to create an AutoML block and wire it together with other blocks to form the search space, we should create every component of the deep learning pipeline in one build() function. In other words, besides the network architecture, we also need to create the input node, set up the output regression layer, select the optimization algorithm, and compile the model for training. Listing 6.1 shows how to implement the build() function for tuning the number of units with KerasTuner. Except for the use of the hp container for defining the search space of the units hyperparameter, the rest is identical to building up a Keras model for regression, which you learned to do in chapter 3.

Listing 6.1   Implementing the search space for tuning MLP units with KerasTuner

```
import tensorflow as tf
from tensorflow import keras
from tensorflow.keras import layers

def build_model(hp):
    input_node = keras.Input(shape=(20,))
    units = hp.Int('units', min_value=32,
                   max_value=512, step=32)
    output_node = layers.Dense(units=units, activation='relu')(input_node)
    output_node = layers.Dense(units=units, activation='relu')(output_node)
    output_node = layers.Dense(units=1, activation='sigmoid')(output_node)
    model = keras.Model(input_node, output_node)

    optimizer = tf.keras.optimizers.Adam(learning_rate=1e-3)
    model.compile(
        optimizer=optimizer,
        loss='mse',
        metrics=['mae'])
    return model
```

Creates the build function, whose input is an hp container instance

Defines the search space for the number of units in the two hidden layers

Compiles the model with the Adam optimization algorithm and MSE loss, and calculates the MAE metric for the model

The returned model is a Keras model.

After defining the search space, we still need a search method to help conduct the search process. Recall from chapter 5 that when creating an AutoML pipeline, we wrap the blocks in an AutoModel object and then set its tuner argument (or use the default value, 'greedy') to select a search method for tuning. Here, because we do not have an AutoModel object, we directly choose a *tuner* from KerasTuner to do this. A tuner not only specifies a search method but also helps schedule the training and evaluation of the selected models in each search trial to ensure the sequential search process can proceed smoothly. We will discuss more about this later in this chapter. The name of the tuner accords with the search method we want to use. For example, we can use the random search method by choosing the RandomSearch tuner, as shown in listing 6.2.

We provide the search space (the build() function) to it during the initialization and set the number of models we want to explore during the search process (max_trial=5). The objective argument specifies the metric (or loss function) we want to use to compare the models and optimize the search method (for the random search method, there's nothing to optimize). In this example, in each trial, the random tuner will build a model based on the randomly selected units value, train the model, and evaluate it. It will return the best model based on the objective we set, which is the mean absolute error (MAE) of the validation set (indicated by the val_ prefix). This validation set, if not specified, will be split out at random from the training set. We can specify how many times we want each model to be trained and evaluated, to reduce randomness in the evaluation process, by setting the executions_ per_trial argument.

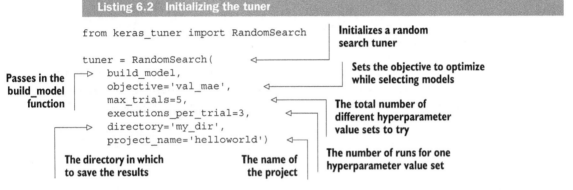

Listing 6.2   Initializing the tuner

```
from keras_tuner import RandomSearch          Initializes a random
                                              search tuner
tuner = RandomSearch(
    build_model,                              Sets the objective to optimize
    objective='val_mae',                      while selecting models
    max_trials=5,
    executions_per_trial=3,                   The total number of
    directory='my_dir',                       different hyperparameter
    project_name='helloworld')                value sets to try
```

Passes in the build_model function

The directory in which to save the results

The name of the project

The number of runs for one hyperparameter value set

Before we start the search process, let's print a summary of the search space using the summarize_search_space() method to make sure the tuner has received it as expected.

Listing 6.3   Printing the search space summary

```
>>> tuner.search_space_summary()          Prints a summary
                                          of the search
Search space summary                      space
Default search space size: 1
units (Int)
{'default': None, 'conditions': [], 'min_value': 32, 'max_value':
  512, 'step': 32, 'sampling': None}
```

We can see that the created search space contains one hyperparameter (units). It is an integer that should be selected from the range 32 to 512, with a step size of 32.

Now let's create a synthetic regression dataset and call the search() method of the tuner to start the search process. The search results are shown in listing 6.4. The arguments to the search() function control the training and evaluation of each model, corresponding to the arguments supported in the fit() method of a Keras model (tf.keras.Model.fit()). For example, in this case each selected MLP will be trained for one epoch.

Listing 6.4   Running the search

```
>>> import numpy as np
>>> x_train = np.random.rand(100, 20)
>>> y_train = np.random.rand(100, 1)
>>> x_val = np.random.rand(20, 20)
>>> y_val = np.random.rand(20, 1)
```

Randomly creates a
synthetic regression
dataset with 20 features
in each instance

```
>> tuner.search(x_train, y_train, epochs=1,
...     validation_data=(x_val, y_val))
```

Runs the search,
which may take
a while

```
Trial 5 Complete [00h 00m 02s]
val_mae: 0.2220905969540278

Best val_mae So Far: 0.2120091120402018
Total elapsed time: 00h 00m 11s
INFO:tensorflow:Oracle triggered exit
```

We can use the results_summary() function to print the five best models and their evaluation results, as shown in the next listing. The best model here has 218 units in each dense layer. Its MAE on the validation set during the search process is 0.212.

Listing 6.5   Printing the five best models and the MAE of each

```
>> tuner.results_summary(5)

Results summary
Results in my_dir/helloworld
Showing 10 best trials
Objective(name='val_mae', direction='min')
Trial summary
Hyperparameters:
units: 288
Score: 0.2120091120402018
Trial summary
Hyperparameters:
units: 128
Score: 0.2220905969540278
Trial summary
Hyperparameters:
units: 320
Score: 0.22237977385520935
Trial summary
Hyperparameters:
units: 256
Score: 0.22893168032169342
Trial summary
Hyperparameters:
units: 192
Score: 0.23000877102216086
```

After the search, we may want to export the best model to save it for future use. Doing this is straightforward, as listing 6.6 shows. The exported model is a Keras model, and we can print the architecture by calling the summary() function.

Listing 6.6 Summarizing and exporting the model

Loads the model from disk   Specifies that the function should
return a list of two models   Gets the best
model in the
returned list

```python
from tensorflow import keras
best_models = tuner.get_best_models(num_models=2)
best_model = best_models[0]
best_model.save('path_to_best_model')
best_model = keras.models.load_model(
    'path_to_best_model')
print(best_model.predict(x_val))
best_model.summary()
```

Saves the
model to disk

Uses the model
for predictions

Prints a summary of the
architecture of the model

JOINTLY TUNING THE OPTIMIZATION FUNCTION

One benefit of customizing the whole pipeline in the `build()` function is that we can
tune the optimization function. Because we need to compile the network ourselves to
make sure it can be trained, we can take full control of which optimization method
to use, as well as its hyperparameters, such as the learning rate. For example, we can
choose from two widely used optimizers in deep learning, Adam and Adadelta, with
the help of the `hp.Choice()` method. The learning rate of the selected optimization
method can be sampled between 1e-5 and 0.1. And because, practically, we often
choose the learning rate on a logarithmic magnitude, such as 0.1 or 0.01, we can set
the `sampling` argument to `'log'` to assign equal probabilities to each order of magnitude range, as shown in the next code listing.

Listing 6.7 Jointly tuning the units and optimization method

Uniformly
random
sample
on the
logarithmic
magnitude

The
function
should
return a
Keras
model.

```python
def build_model(hp):
    input_node = keras.Input(shape=(20,))
    units = hp.Int('units', min_value=32, max_value=512, step=32)
    output_node = layers.Dense(units=units, activation='relu')(input_node)
    output_node = layers.Dense(units=units, activation='relu')(output_node)
    output_node = layers.Dense(units=1, activation='sigmoid')(output_node)
    model = keras.Model(input_node, output_node)
    optimizer_name = hp.Choice('optimizer', ['adam', 'adadelta'])
    learning_rate = hp.Float('learning_rate', min_value=1e-5, max_value=0.1,
                             sampling='log')
    if optimizer_name == 'adam':
        optimizer = tf.keras.optimizers.Adam(learning_rate=learning_rate)
    else:
        optimizer = tf.keras.optimizers.Adadelta(learning_rate=learning_rate)
    model.compile(
        optimizer=optimizer,
        loss='mse',
        metrics=['mae'])
    return model

tuner = RandomSearch(
    build_model,
    objective='val_mae',
```

Defines the search
space for the optimizer

Compiles the model
to set the loss

The metric we're
using is MAE.

```
    max_trials=5,
    executions_per_trial=3,
    directory='my_dir',
    project_name='helloworld')
```

The search process is the same as in the previous example and will not be repeated here. Not surprisingly, we can tune the loss function in the same way, so we won't elaborate on that further here.

TUNING THE MODEL-TRAINING PROCESS

Besides the model-building process, you may also have some hyperparameters to tune in the model-training process. For example, you may want to tune the batch size of the data and whether to shuffle the data. You can specify these in the arguments of model.fit() of a Keras model. However, in the previous code examples, we define the search space only for building and compiling the model, not training the model.

To tune the model-training process, we can use the HyperModel class, which provides an object-oriented style for defining the search space. You can override Hyper-Model.build(hp), which is the same as the build_model() function shown earlier. You need to override HyperModel.fit() to tune the model training. In the arguments of the method, you can access hp, the model we just built, and all the arguments passed to Tuner.search() in **kwargs. It should return the training history, which is the return value of model.fit(). The next listing is an example of defining a search space for tuning whether to shuffle the dataset and tuning the batch size in addition to the rest of the hyperparameters.

Listing 6.8 **Tuning the model-training process**

```
import keras_tuner as kt

class Regressor(kt.HyperModel):

    def build(self, hp):
        input_node = keras.Input(shape=(20,))
        units = hp.Int('units', min_value=32, max_value=512, step=32)
        output_node = layers.Dense(units=units, activation='relu')(input_node)
        output_node = layers.Dense(units=units, activation='relu')(output_node)
        output_node = layers.Dense(units=1, activation='sigmoid')(output_node)
        model = keras.Model(input_node, output_node)
        optimizer_name = hp.Choice('optimizer', ['adam', 'adadelta'])
        learning_rate = hp.Float('learning_rate', min_value=1e-5, max_value=0.1,
                                 sampling='log')
        if optimizer_name == 'adam':
            optimizer = tf.keras.optimizers.Adam(learning_rate=learning_rate)
        else:
            optimizer = tf.keras.optimizers.Adadelta(learning_rate=learning_rate)
        model.compile(
            optimizer=optimizer,
            loss='mse',
            metrics=['mae'])
        return model
```

Tunes the model training →

```
def fit(self, hp, model, **kwargs):
    return model.fit(                          ← Returns the return
        batch_size=hp.Int('batch_size'),        value of model.fit()
        shuffle=hp.Boolean('shuffle'),         ← Tunes the batch size
        **kwargs)
                                               Tunes whether to
tuner = RandomSearch(                          shuffle the dataset
    build_model,
    objective='val_mae',
    max_trials=5,
    executions_per_trial=3,
    directory='my_dir',
    project_name='helloworld')
```

Note that we did not tune the number of epochs in `fit()`—the model will be saved at its best epoch in terms of the objective value, which is the `'val_mae'` here.

So far we have learned how to define and tune the hyperparameters in the model-building, -compiling, and -fitting process.

TUNING THE DATA PREPROCESSING METHOD

Sometimes you may want to include some preprocessing steps in the workflow—for example, normalizing the features before feeding them into the neural network. In this section, we will first see how we can easily include the preprocessing steps in your model. Then, we will see how to tune the hyperparameters involved in these steps.

Instead of creating a normalization function the way you learned in chapter 3, you can use the Keras preprocessing layer to do this. For example, you can stack a normalization layer before the dense layers, as shown in listing 6.9. Note that there is special treatment for the preprocessing layer here: you call a layer adaptation function (`layer.adapt()`) on the full dataset. Neural networks are trained and evaluated on data batches, but the preprocessing method usually needs some statistics from the entire dataset, such as the means and variances of the features, to preprocess the batches. Calling the adaptation function will help the preprocessing layer gather these statistics.

> **Listing 6.9 Using a Keras normalization preprocessing layer**

```
from tensorflow.keras.layers.experimental.preprocessing import Normalization
```

Initializes the normalization layer →

```
layer = Normalization(input_shape=(20,))        Adapts the normalization
layer.adapt(x_train)                        ←   layer to get the mean and
                                                variance of the data
model = tf.keras.Sequential([layer, tf.keras.layers.Dense(1)])
model.compile(optimizer='adam', loss='mse')
model.fit(x_train, y_train)
```

We have multiple ways of using the preprocessing layers. In the previous example, we put it into the `Sequential` model. You may also use it as a standalone step. You can use it to preprocess NumPy arrays. For NumPy arrays, you can just call the layers to get the processed data as shown in the following code sample:

```
normalized_x_train = layer(x_train)
```

However, your data may not always be in the format of NumPy arrays. It could be in the format of `tf.data.Dataset`, which is more generalized. It can be created from a small NumPy array or even large dataset streamed from a local or remote storage. The next code listing shows how to convert a NumPy array to `tf.data.Dataset` and normalize it with the layer we created by calling `Dataset.map(layer)`.

Listing 6.10 Normalizing `tf.data.Dataset`

```
dataset_x_train = tf.data.Dataset.from_tensor_slices(x_train).batch(32)
normalized_dataset = dataset_x_train.map(layer)
```

Now we have learned how to use preprocessing layers for data preprocessing. Let's see if we can have a Boolean hyperparameter to tune whether to use this normalization step.

   Because data preprocessing requires accessing the dataset, we will tune this step in `HyperModel.fit()`, which has the dataset in the arguments passed from `Tuner.search()`, as shown in the next listing. Instead of leaving these useful arguments in `**kwargs`, we will explicitly put x and y in the method signature this time.

Listing 6.11 Using a preprocessing layer in the search space

```
from keras_tuner import HyperModel

class Regressor(HyperModel):

    def build(self, hp):
        model = tf.keras.Sequential()
        model.add(tf.keras.layers.Dense(1))
        model.compile(optimizer='adam', loss='mse')
        return model

    def fit(self, hp, model, x, y, **kwargs):        Specifies whether to
        if hp.Boolean('normalize'):      ◁─────      use a normalization
            layer = Normalization(input_shape=(20,))              layer
            layer.adapt(x)
            x = layer(x)              ◁────    Replaces x with the
        return model.fit(x=x, y=y, **kwargs)      normalized data
```

After implementing the search space, we can feed it to a tuner as we did with the `build_model()` function to search for a good model, as shown next.

Listing 6.12 Searching in a space with a preprocessing layer

```
tuner = RandomSearch(hypermodel,                         Passes the
                  objective='val_loss', max_trials=2)  ◁─  class instance
tuner.search(x_train, y_train, validation_data=(x_val, y_val))   to the tuner
```

Having worked through this example, you may be wondering why, because the layer-wise search space design can resolve all the problems that the blockwise search space design can with even more flexibility, we might ever want to build up an AutoML pipeline by wiring together AutoML blocks. The reason is, compared to layerwise search space design, using the built-in blocks of AutoKeras makes search space creation less laborious (especially if you aren't well practiced in creating the search space in a layerwise fashion). The tradeoff between the implementation difficulty and flexibility will determine which search-space-creation method is best for you and the task at hand.

6.1.2 *Tuning an autoencoder model for unsupervised learning*

All the examples we've worked on so far have been supervised learning tasks, but ML applications aren't all about predicting pre-existing responses. In contrast to supervised learning, an ML paradigm called *unsupervised learning* aims to find hidden or undetected patterns in features without human supervision or involvement. A typical unsupervised learning task is *dimensionality reduction.* The goal is to learn a condensed representation (such as a vector with few elements) for the data instances, to remove the noisy or unimportant information in the data.

An *autoencoder* is a classic type of neural network to use for dimensionality reduction. It is often applied to images to learn a low-dimensional vector representation of each image. The architecture of an autoencoder is shown in figure 6.1.

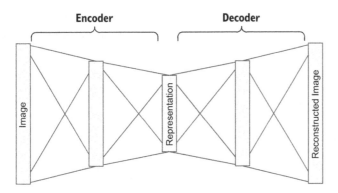

Figure 6.1   The architecture of an autoencoder

As you can see, the input and the output of the autoencoder are both images. The network consists of two parts, the *encoder* and the *decoder.* The encoder is used to condense the images to the low-dimensional vector representation, and the decoder tries to reconstruct the original image based on the encoded vector. The encoder and decoder often have an asymmetric structure. They both can use classic networks, such as MLPs or CNNs. For example, if each input instance is a vector of length 64, a simple encoder could be a single-layer MLP with 32 units in each dense layer. The decoder could also be a single-layer MLP with 64 units in the dense layer to decode each input to the original size.

In this task, because we do not have pre-existing responses to guide the learning process, we use the original images themselves as the responses. During training, the difference between the reconstructed images and the original images will be the loss metric to help update the weights of the network. We can use a regression loss function like mean squared error (MSE) to measure the difference.

In regression tasks, MSE measures the difference between the predicted value and the ground-truth value. In this image reconstruction task, the predicted value is the reconstructed image, whereas the ground-truth is the original image. If the neural network can successfully reconstruct the image, it means all the important information about the image is stored in the vector representation.

The learned vector representations have many potential uses: for example, they could be used to visualize the distribution of the images in 2-D or 3-D space, or we can use them to reconstruct the images to remove noise from the original versions.

IMPLEMENTING AN AUTOENCODER WITH KERAS

Let's walk through an example to show how an autoencoder works. Then we'll explore how to create the search space to tune it. The task we'll work on here is to learn an autoencoder that can compress an image to a low-dimensional vector and then reconstruct the image.

We'll use a benchmark deep learning dataset called Fashion MNIST, which consists of 60,000 images in the training dataset and 10,000 images in the testing dataset. All the images are grayscale, of size 28×28, and the contents of the images are all items of clothing. We can load the data via the Keras dataset API and normalize the pixel values of the images to the range 0 to 1 for ease of network optimization, as shown in the following listing.

Listing 6.13   Loading the Fashion MNIST data

```
from tensorflow.keras.datasets import fashion_mnist

(x_train, _), (x_test, _) = fashion_mnist.load_data()

x_train = x_train.astype('float32') / 255.     │ Normalizes the values in the
x_test = x_test.astype('float32') / 255.       │ images to the range [0, 1]
```

You should already know how to implement the encoder and decoder separately, because they're both conventional networks (CNNs or MLPs). The question is how to combine the two networks and compile them for the training and prediction. A common way to implement such a composite model is to override the `tf.keras.Model` class. When we subclass the `Model` class, we should define all the autoencoder layers in the `__init__()` function so that they can be created when an autoencoder instance is initialized. The next step is to implement the forward pass in a function named `call`. This function will take a batch of input images and output the reconstructed images. We often want to call the encoder individually to extract the representations it provides, so it's a good idea to implement the forward passes of the encoder and decoder networks separately, in two methods. This is also the reason we want to implement the autoencoder by subclassing the `Model` class rather than grouping the layers in a `tf.keras.Model` or `tf.keras.Sequential` object.

Listing 6.14 shows the implementation of the autoencoder we use in this example. Both the encoder and decoder networks are single-layer MLP networks with the number of units specified by a customizable hyperparameter, `latent_dim`. The `latent_dim` hyperparameter also indicates the length of the encoded representation vector. During the forward pass, each image will be flattened into a vector of length 784 and then encoded into a representation vector of length `latent_dim`. The decoder network will decode the representation to a vector of size 784 and reshape the image to the original size (28×28).

Listing 6.14 Subclassing the Keras `Model` class to implement an autoencoder

```
import tensorflow as tf
from tensorflow.keras.models import Model
from tensorflow.keras import layers, losses
```
> **Overrides the Model class**

```
class AutoencoderModel(Model):
    def __init__(self, latent_dim):
        super().__init__()
        self.latent_dim = latent_dim
        self.encoder_layer = layers.Dense(latent_dim,
                                        activation='relu')
        self.decoder_layer = layers.Dense(784, activation='sigmoid')
```
> **The initializer should create all the layer instances.**

The encoding layer should output the representation vector.

```
    def encode(self, encoder_input):
        encoder_output = layers.Flatten()(encoder_input)
        encoder_output = self.encoder_layer(encoder_output)
        return encoder_output
```
Encodes the images with a fully connected layer

> **The 28×28 images are flattened into a vector of length 784.**

```
    def decode(self, decoder_input):
        decoder_output = decoder_input
        decoder_output = self.decoder_layer(decoder_output)
        decoder_output = layers.Reshape(
        (28, 28))(decoder_output)
        return decoder_output
```
Reshapes the images back to 28×28

> **Decodes the representation vector with a fully connected layer**

```
    def call(self, x):
        return self.decode(self.encode(x))
```
> **The call function defines that the neural network should first encode the input and then decode it.**

Next, we'll create an autoencoder model to encode the images to vectors of length 64. The model-compiling, -training, and -fitting process is the same as that for regression with an MLP. The only difference is that we use the images as both features and responses, as you can see here.

Listing 6.15 Fitting the autoencoder model with Fashion MNIST

Fixes the TensorFlow random seed

```
tf.random.set_seed(5)
np.random.seed(5)
```
> **Fixes the NumPy random seed**

```
autoencoder = AutoencoderModel(64)
autoencoder.compile(optimizer='adam', loss='mse')
autoencoder.fit(x_train, x_train,
                epochs=10,
                shuffle=True,
                validation_data=(x_test, x_test))

autoencoder.evaluate(x_test, x_test)
```

Creates the autoencoder

Compiles and fits the autoencoder—images serve as both features and target responses.

Evaluates the autoencoder on the test images

After the autoencoder is trained, we can use it to encode images as vectors by calling the encode() function we've implemented. As you can see in the following listing, the encoded vector of a test image is of length 64, as expected.

Listing 6.16   Encoding the images with the autoencoder

```
>>> autoencoder.encode(x_test[:1])
<tf.Tensor: shape=(1, 64), dtype=float32, numpy=
array([[3.931118  , 1.0182608 , 6.5596466 , 2.8951719 , 1.5840771 ,
        2.3559608 , 2.0955124 , 4.485343  , 1.34939   , 3.600976  ,
        3.5480025 , 1.0803885 , 3.5926101 , 2.34089   , 0.        ,
        1.3521026 , 1.5423647 , 3.7132359 , 2.2019305 , 1.3938735 ,
        0.9601332 , 2.3903034 , 1.4392244 , 2.155833  , 4.196291  ,
        3.8109841 , 3.2413573 , 1.1022317 , 2.7478027 , 0.        ,
        6.3407483 , 2.5890563 , 1.905628  , 0.61499554, 1.7429417 ,
        0.59232974, 2.5122235 , 1.4705787 , 1.5797877 , 2.3179786 ,
        0.19336838, 1.6040547 , 1.8269951 , 2.1929228 , 3.5982947 ,
        2.1040354 , 3.4453387 , 3.405629  , 3.6934092 , 2.5358922 ,
        2.8133378 , 4.46262   , 2.0303524 , 3.7909238 , 2.4032137 ,
        2.2115898 , 2.5821419 , 1.4490023 , 2.3869803 , 0.        ,
        3.246771  , 1.1970178 , 0.5150778 , 0.7152041 ]], dtype=float32)>
```

We can also visualize the original and reconstructed images with the following code.

Listing 6.17   Visualizing the reconstructed images

```
import matplotlib.pyplot as plt


def show_images(model, images):
    encoded_imgs = model.encode(images).numpy()
    decoded_imgs = model.decode(encoded_imgs).numpy()


    n = 10
    plt.figure(figsize=(20, 4))
    for i in range(n):
        ax = plt.subplot(2, n, i + 1)
        plt.imshow(images[i])
        plt.title('original')
        plt.gray()
        ax.get_xaxis().set_visible(False)
        ax.get_yaxis().set_visible(False)

        ax = plt.subplot(2, n, i + 1 + n)
        plt.imshow(decoded_imgs[i])
        plt.title('reconstructed')
```

Gets the encoded and decoded test images— we could also call the call function to make it a one-step process.

Controls the number and size of the displayed images

Displays the first 10 original images in the first row

Displays the first 10 reconstructed images in the second row

```
        plt.gray()
        ax.get_xaxis().set_visible(False)
        ax.get_yaxis().set_visible(False)
    plt.show()

show_images(autoencoder, x_test)
```

As figure 6.2 shows, the reconstructed images look very close to the original images, except for some minor blurring and a few missing details (e.g., the patterns on the shirts look blurry). This means that the 64-dimensional representations preserve almost all the information we need to reconstruct the original images. We can use this autoencoder to compress a large image dataset to save the memory.

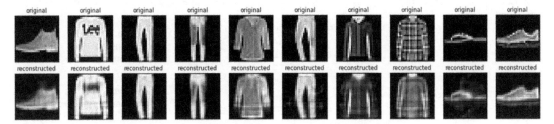

Figure 6.2 Autoencoder reconstructed images

The next step is to create a search space to fine-tune the autoencoder with the help of KerasTuner.

6.2   *Tuning the autoencoder model*

You already know how to define the search space of an MLP in a layerwise fashion by creating a model-building function. Because the autoencoder model is created in a class and the layers are initialized in the __init__() function of the class, we can directly set the search space for these layers when initializing them. To create the search space, we pass an instance of the hp container into the __init__() function. Its methods can be used to define the search space. For example, we can use hp.Int() to define a space for selecting the number of layers in the encoder (or decoder) and use hp.Choice() to tune how many units are in each layer, as shown in the next listing. Because the number of layers is undetermined before we create the autoencoder, we should loop through all the layers when implementing the forward pass through the encoding and decoding networks.

> **Listing 6.18 Building a class to define the search space of the autoencoder model**

```
import keras_tuner
from tensorflow import keras
from keras_tuner import RandomSearch
```

```
class AutoencoderBlock(keras.Model):
    def __init__(self, latent_dim, hp):        ◄─── Adds hp to the
        super().__init__()                           initializer's arguments
        self.latent_dim = latent_dim
        self.encoder_layers = []
        for i in range(hp.Int('encoder_layers',    ◄─┐ Uses hp to decide
                              min_value=0,            │ on the number of
                              max_value=2,            │ encoding layers
                              step=1,
                              default=0)):
            self.encoder_layers.append(             ┐ Uses hp to choose the
                layers.Dense(units=hp.Choice(       │ number of units for each
                    'encoder_layers_{i}'.format(i=i), ◄─┘ encoding layer
                    [64, 128, 256]),
                    activation='relu'))
        self.encoder_layers.append(layers.Dense(latent_dim, activation='relu'))
        self.decoder_layers = []
        for i in range(hp.Int('decoder_layers',    ◄─┐ Uses hp to decide
                              min_value=0,            │ on the number of
                              max_value=2,            │ decoding layers
                              step=1,
                              default=0)):
            self.decoder_layers.append(             ┐ Uses hp to choose the
                layers.Dense(units=hp.Choice(       │ number of units for each
                    'decoder_layers_{i}'.format(i=i), ◄─┘ decoding layer
                    [64, 128, 256]),
                    activation='relu'))
        self.decoder_layers.append(layers.Dense(784, activation='sigmoid'))

    def encode(self, encoder_input):
        encoder_output = layers.Flatten()(encoder_input)
        for layer in self.encoder_layers:          ◄─┐ Takes a forward
            encoder_output = layer(encoder_output)    │ loop through the
        return encoder_output                         │ encoding layers

    def decode(self, decoder_input):                 ┐ Takes a forward loop through
        decoder_output = decoder_input               │ the decoding layers
        for layer in self.decoder_layers:          ◄─┘
            decoder_output = layer(decoder_output)
        decoder_output = layers.Reshape((28, 28))(decoder_output)
        return decoder_output

    def call(self, x):
        return self.decode(self.encode(x))
```

A list of
encoding
layers ⊢→

A list of
decoding
layers ⊢→

To follow the best practice for implementing Keras models, again, we should initialize all the layers in the __init__() function and use them in the call() function. With the hp container, we can get the values of all the hyperparameters needed to build the model and record them.

The next steps follow the normal usage of KerasTuner. In listing 6.19, we create a build_model() function to return the autoencoder model we defined and then feed it into an initialized tuner to proceed with the search process. It's worth noting that the initialization of the autoencoder requires an extra input (an `hp` container instance). We can also tune the optimization function jointly with the same `hp` container, as we did in the MLP example.

Listing 6.19 Running the search for the autoencoder

```
def build_model(hp):                       Initializes the model and
    latent_dim = 20                        passes in the hp instance
    autoencoder = AutoencoderBlock(latent_dim, hp)         Compiles
    autoencoder.compile(optimizer='adam', loss='mse')      the model
    return autoencoder        Returns
                              the model
tuner = RandomSearch(
    build_model,
    objective='val_loss',     Clears the working directory
    max_trials=10,            before starting to remove
    overwrite=True,           any previous results
    directory='my_dir',       The working
    project_name='helloworld')  directory

tuner.search(x_train, x_train,           validation_data is
            epochs=10,                   required for evaluating
            validation_data=(x_test, x_test))   the model.
```

The tuner conducts 10 trials, each of which trains an autoencoder for 10 epochs. We can select the best model and visualize the first 10 reconstructed images with the following code.

Listing 6.20 Evaluating the results

```
autoencoder = tuner.get_best_models(num_models=1)[0]
tuner.results_summary(1)
autoencoder.evaluate(x_test, x_test)

show_images(autoencoder, x_test)
```

By tuning the hyperparameters in the autoencoder, we've made some of the reconstructed images perceptibly clearer, like the flip-flop shown in the ninth picture (see figure 6.3).

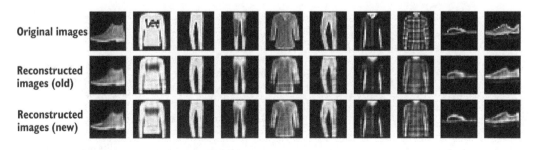

Original images

Reconstructed images (old)

Reconstructed images (new)

Figure 6.3 The reconstructed images from the tuned autoencoder

6.3 *Tuning shallow models with different search methods*

In chapter 2, you learned how to tune a traditional (or shallow) ML model with grid search. Appendix B also covers several more complex examples of tuning multiple components in an ML pipeline. All of the examples leverage the built-in tuner (Grid-SearchCV) in the scikit-learn library. Now that you've seen the power of KerasTuner for selecting and tuning deep learning models, you may be wondering whether you can also tune shallow models with KerasTuner. Compared to tuning using Grid-SearchCV, doing this with KerasTuner has the following two key benefits:

- It gives you a more straightforward way to perform model selection without tuning each model separately and comparing them manually. With the help of the conditional scope defined by the hyperparameter class, you can select between different shallow models the same way you did with deep learning models. We'll introduce how to do this in the next example.

- It gives you more search methods to select from. KerasTuner contains several advanced search methods. Selecting different ones can result in different tuning results, as you'll see in the next example.

In fact, it is also feasible to select from a pool of both deep learning models and shallow models. However, because deep learning models are often created and trained in a different way than shallow models (partly because of implementation differences in the various libraries, considering their diverse model architectures), training and evaluating them during the search process requires different treatment. You'll learn how to create your own tuner with a personalized training and evaluation strategy to accommodate a broader search space in the next section. For now, we'll start with an example that shows how we can select between different shallow models.

6.3.1 *Selecting and tuning shallow models*

In this section, we'll work on an image classification problem, using the digits dataset that comes with the scikit-learn library. The dataset contains 1,797 8×8 grayscale images of handwritten digits, from 0 to 9. We can load the dataset with the built-in function load_digits() in the scikit-learn library and split out 20% of it to use as the test set, as shown in the following listing.

Listing 6.21 Loading the digits data

```
from sklearn.datasets import load_digits
from sklearn.model_selection import train_test_split

digits = load_digits()        ◁──── Loads the digits dataset

images, labels = digits.images, digits.target        ◁─┐ Separately stores the images and corresponding target digits

X = images.reshape((n_samples, -1))        ◁─┤ Reshapes images to vectors

X_train, X_test, y_train, y_test = train_test_split(        ┤ Splits out 20% of the data to use as the final test set
    X, labels, test_size=0.2, shuffle=False)        ◁─┘
```

In appendix B, we introduce how to create an SVM model to classify images and tune its hyperparameters with grid search. You may also want to try out some different shallow classification models, such as decision trees, and select the best one among them. Similar to the selection of deep learning models, introduced in section 6.1.2, you can use KerasTuner to select among different shallow models by setting a conditional hyperparameter for the model type. In listing 6.22, we create a search space to select between two models: SVM and random forest (see appendix B if you're not familiar with the random forest model). The model selection is done by a hyperparameter named `'model_type'`. In each trial of the search process, by choosing a specific `'model_type'` such as svm, narrow the search space down to the conditional scope of the selected model and create the corresponding model. The model selection can be conducted jointly with the hyperparameter tuning of each model.

> ### Listing 6.22 Creating a search space for shallow model selection

```
from sklearn.svm import SVC
from sklearn.ensemble import RandomForestClassifier
from keras_tuner.engine import hyperparameters as hp

def build_model(hp):
    model_type = hp.Choice('model_type',                        Selects the
                           ['svm', 'random_forest'])     ◁────  classifier type
    if model_type == 'svm':
        with hp.conditional_scope('model_type', 'svm'):
            model = SVC(
                C=hp.Float('C', 1e-3, 10, sampling='linear', default=1),
                kernel=hp.Choice('kernel_type',
                                 ['linear', 'rbf'],
                                 default='linear'),
                random_state=42)
    elif model_type == 'random_forest':
        with hp.conditional_scope('model_type',                 Tunes the random
                                  'random_forest'):     ◁────   forest classifier,
            model = RandomForestClassifier(                     if selected
                n_estimators=hp.Int('n_estimators', 10, 200, step=10),
                max_depth=hp.Int('max_depth', 3, 10))
    else:
        raise ValueError('Unrecognized model_type')
    return model
```

Tunes the SVM classifier, if selected (annotation pointing to the `if model_type == 'svm':` block)

As we did in the previous section, we use random search for model selection and hyperparameter tuning. However, an important difference here is that we do not directly use the `RandomSearch` class but instead use a tuner class named `SklearnTuner` specifically designed for tuning scikit-learn models. The reason is that a tuner in KerasTuner controls the training and evaluation of the instantiated models during the search process. Because the scikit-learn models are trained and tested differently than the deep learning models implemented with TensorFlow Keras, we can use different tuners to accommodate the differences in model training. We will introduce how to build a general tuner capable of dealing with both cases in the next section.

Despite the differences in model training and evaluation, the method for selecting the hyperparameters is applicable for all the cases. It's called an *oracle* in KerasTuner. It will decide on the hyperparameters to try out in each trial and take the evaluation results of the previously selected hyperparameters as inputs for its update if needed (see figure 6.4). Because the tuner touches only the hyperparameters and evaluation results, the differences in the evaluation process for different models (deep or shallow) do not affect it.

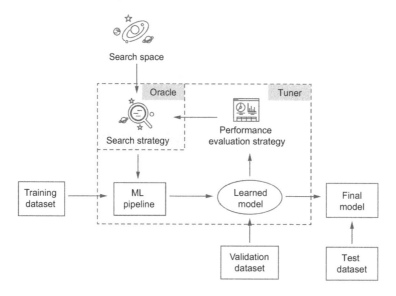

Figure 6.4   The structure of a tuner and its oracle in KerasTuner

To use the random search method to tune the models created with the scikit-learn library, we can create a `SklearnTuner` and set its oracle (search method) to `Random-Search` (see listing 6.23). We can set the number of trials we want to perform during the search process with `max_trials` and set the objective of the search method, which is used to compare different models, using `kt.Objective`. The `score` objective we use here represents the evaluation accuracy score for each model. The `max` argument means the larger the score is, the better the model is. If the objective were the MSE, we would instead use `'min'`, because in that case, smaller scores are better. The evaluation strategy of the tuner, which is defined by the `KFold` module in scikit-learn, is set to three-fold evaluation.

Listing 6.23   Using random search to select and tune scikit-learn models

```
from sklearn.model_selection import KFold
import sklearn.pipeline

random_tuner = kt.tuners.SklearnTuner(
```

> Creates a tuner for
> tuning scikit-learn
> models

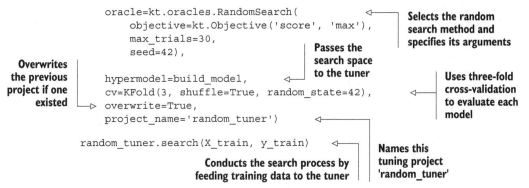

```
oracle=kt.oracles.RandomSearch(
    objective=kt.Objective('score', 'max'),
    max_trials=30,
    seed=42),

hypermodel=build_model,
cv=KFold(3, shuffle=True, random_state=42),
overwrite=True,
project_name='random_tuner')

random_tuner.search(X_train, y_train)
```

Selects the random search method and specifies its arguments

Passes the search space to the tuner

Overwrites the previous project if one existed

Uses three-fold cross-validation to evaluate each model

Conducts the search process by feeding training data to the tuner

Names this tuning project 'random_tuner'

Now let's retrieve the best discovered model and evaluate it on the test data, as shown here.

Listing 6.24   Viewing the results of using random search

```
>>> random_tuner.results_summary(1)
Results summary
Results in ./random_tuner
Showing 1 best trials
Objective(name='score', direction='max')
Trial summary
Hyperparameters:
model_type: svm
C: 2.242630562998417
kernel_type: rbf
Score: 0.9693806541405707

>>> from sklearn.metrics import accuracy_score
>>> best_model = random_tuner.get_best_models(1)[0]
>>> best_model.fit(X_train, y_train)
>>> y_pred_test = best_model.predict(X_test)
>>> test_acc = accuracy_score(y_test, y_pred_test)
>>> print(f'Prediction accuracy on test set: {test_acc * 100:.2f}. %')

Prediction accuracy on test set: 95.83 %
```

Displays the random search results

Retrieves the best model

Retrains the best model on the whole training dataset

Evaluates the best discovered model

The best model found in 30 trials is an SVM model using the RBF kernel with a regularization parameter of $C = 2.24$. By retraining the best model on the whole training set, we arrive at a final testing accuracy of 95.83%.

6.3.2   *Tuning a shallow model pipeline*

You may have multiple components in a pipeline and want to select and tune them jointly. For example, suppose you want to create a pipeline with two components: a PCA component to reduce the images' dimensions and an SVM classifier to classify the preprocessed images. This can be done by stacking the components to form a sequential scikit-learn pipeline (see appendix B). You can then select a model and tune the other component in the pipeline at the same time, as shown in listing 6.25.

Listing 6.25   Selecting and tuning a scikit-learn pipeline

```
from keras_tuner.engine import hyperparameters as hp
from sklearn.decomposition import PCA
from sklearn.svm import SVC
from sklearn.ensemble import RandomForestClassifier
from sklearn.pipeline import Pipeline

def build_pipeline(hp):

    n_components=hp.Choice('n_components', [2, 5, 10], default=5)
    pca = PCA(n_components=n_components)

    model_type = hp.Choice('model_type',
                           ['svm', 'random_forest'])
    if model_type == 'svm':
        with hp.conditional_scope('model_type', 'svm'):
            model = SVC(
                C=hp.Float('C', 1e-3, 10, sampling='linear', default=1),
                kernel=hp.Choice('kernel_type',
                                 ['linear', 'rbf'],
                                 default='linear'),
                random_state=42)
    elif model_type == 'random_forest':
        with hp.conditional_scope('model_type', 'random_forest'):
            model = RandomForestClassifier(
                n_estimators=hp.Int('n_estimators', 10, 200, step=10),
                max_depth=hp.Int('max_depth', 3, 10))
    else:
        raise ValueError('Unrecognized model_type')

    pipeline = Pipeline([
        ('pca', pca),
        ('clf', model)
    ])

    return pipeline

tuner = kt.tuners.SklearnTuner(
        oracle=kt.oracles.RandomSearch(
            objective=kt.Objective('score', 'max'),
            max_trials=30),
        hypermodel=build_pipeline,
        overwrite=True)

tuner.search(X_train, y_train)
```

Selects the **hyperparameters of PCA**

Selects the **model type**

Instantiates a scikit-learn **pipeline with the selected hyperparameters**

Searches with **the random search method**

We evaluate the pipelines and retrieve the best one the same way we did in listing 6.24, so we won't elaborate on that further here.

6.3.3   *Trying out different search methods*

As mentioned at the beginning of this section, a key benefit of using KerasTuner for tuning is that it enables you to easily switch between (or implement) different search methods for tuning shallow models. This can be done by changing the oracle to the one you prefer. For example, we can change the random search method to some more advanced methods, such as the *Bayesian optimization method*, as shown in the following listing. If you're not familiar with this method, don't worry about it for now; we'll talk more about it in chapter 7.

Listing 6.26 Using Bayesian optimization to tune scikit-learn models

```
bo_tuner = kt.tuners.SklearnTuner(
    oracle=kt.oracles.BayesianOptimization(          ◁──┐  Sets the oracle to
        objective=kt.Objective('score', 'max'),         │  BayesianOptimization
        max_trials=30,
        seed=42),
    hypermodel=build_model,
    cv=KFold(3, shuffle=True, random_state=42),
    overwrite=True,
    project_name='bo_tuner')                    ┐  Searches with the
                                                │  Bayesian optimization
bo_tuner.search(X_train, y_train)    ◁──────────┘  method
```

Different search methods often fit different search spaces. For example, the Bayesian optimization method is often more suitable for searching hyperparameters with continuous values. In practice, you can try out different methods and select the best discovered model.

6.3.4　*Automated feature engineering*

In this section, we will introduce how to do automated feature engineering. Before introducing automated feature engineering, we will first see what feature engineering is. It is an important step in machine learning, which may boost the model's performance, and it is especially effective for structured data.

For example, we may have a structured dataset, which is a table consisting of several columns as features and one column as the prediction target. Before directly inputting these features into a machine learning model, we could perform feature engineering, which consists of *feature generation* and *feature selection*. We could create more feature columns based on existing feature columns, which is called feature generation. We could also delete some unuseful features, which is called feature selection.

To show how feature engineering exactly works, we again use the Titanic dataset, which we used in chapter 4. The features of the dataset are the profiles of the passengers of the *Titanic*, and the prediction target is whether the passenger survived the accident. Download the dataset using the following code.

Listing 6.27 Downloading the Titanic dataset

```
import tensorflow as tf

TRAIN_DATA_URL = 'https://storage.googleapis.com/tf-
    datasets/titanic/train.csv'
TEST_DATA_URL = 'https://storage.googleapis.com/tf-datasets/titanic/eval.csv'
```

```
train_file_path = tf.keras.utils.get_file(
    'train.csv', TRAIN_DATA_URL)
test_file_path = tf.keras.utils.get_file(
    'eval.csv', TEST_DATA_URL)
```

After downloading the CSV files, we can load them into pandas DataFrames with the read_csv() function as shown in the next code listing. We will pop out the target column from the DataFrame to use it separately.

Listing 6.28   Loading the downloaded CSV files with Pandas

```
import pandas as pd                                    Loads the CSV
                                                       file into a pandas
x_train = pd.read_csv(train_file_path)                 DataFrame
y_train = x_train.pop('survived')
y_train = pd.DataFrame(y_train)                         Pops the target column
                                                       as the y_train
x_test = pd.read_csv(test_file_path)           Converts the popped column
y_test = x_test.pop('survived')                from Series to DataFrame

x_train.head()            Prints the first few
                          lines of the data
```

The printed content of the training data is shown in figure 6.5.

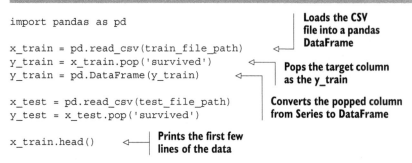

	sex	age	n_siblings_spouses	parch	fare	class	deck	embark_town	alone
0	male	22.0	1	0	7.2500	Third	unknown	Southampton	n
1	female	38.0	1	0	71.2833	First	C	Cherbourg	n
2	female	26.0	0	0	7.9250	Third	unknown	Southampton	y
3	female	35.0	1	0	53.1000	First	C	Southampton	n
4	male	28.0	0	0	8.4583	Third	unknown	Queenstown	y

Figure 6.5   The first few lines of the Titanic dataset

As you can see, some of the features are categorical, and others are numerical. We will need to put them into different groups and use different encoding methods for them.

We set the age and fare they paid as numerical data. We will replace the missing values or NaN values with their median values. Then, we will normalize them to the range of 0 to 1.

We put the number of siblings and spouses and the classes of the passengers as categorical features. Because they don't have many different categories, we will use one-hot encoding to encode them. One-hot encoding is usually not used for categorical features with too many different values because it would create too many columns after the encoding.

The rest of the features, like the gender of the passenger and whether they are on the deck, are also categorical features, but we will use ordinal encoding for them, which encodes the different string values to different integer values.

For these two types of categorical features, before encoding, we will also need to replace the missing values with a constant value. We just use the string of "None" for convenience.

Here we use `sklearn.pipeline.Pipeline` to build a pipeline for each type of the columns for these transformations, the code of which is shown next.

Listing 6.29 Building pipelines for cleaning and encoding the columns

```
from sklearn.preprocessing import OrdinalEncoder, OneHotEncoder, StandardScaler
from sklearn.impute import SimpleImputer
from sklearn.pipeline import Pipeline

numerical_columns = ['age', 'fare']
one_hot_columns = ['n_siblings_spouses', 'class']
int_columns = [
    'sex', 'parch', 'deck', 'embark_town', 'alone']

numerical_transformer = Pipeline(steps=[
    ('imputer', SimpleImputer(strategy='median')),
    ('normalizer', StandardScaler())
])

one_hot_transformer = Pipeline(steps=[
    ('imputer', SimpleImputer(
        strategy='constant', fill_value='None')),
    ('one_hot_encoder', OneHotEncoder(
        handle_unknown='ignore'))
])

int_transformer = Pipeline(steps=[
    ('imputer', SimpleImputer(
        strategy='constant', fill_value='None')),
    ('label_encoder', OrdinalEncoder(
        handle_unknown='use_encoded_value', unknown_value=-1))
])
```

The pipeline for numerical columns

The lists of names of the different types of columns

Replaces the missing values with the median

Scales the values to the range of 0 to 1

Replaces the missing values with 'None'

The pipeline for one-hot encoding columns

One-hot encodes the column. With handle_unknow='ignore', it would not raise an error during inference if it encountered any unknown values, whose encoding would be all zeros.

The pipeline for ordinal encoding columns

Replaces the missing values with 'None'

Encodes the values to integers. For unknown values, it will use –1.

So far, we have finished cleaning the data. After these pipelines, all the columns are numerical, either float or integer. The next step is feature generation.

The first feature generation technique we will introduce is combining different categorical columns. You can think of it as simply concatenating the strings of two selected categorical columns. The concatenated string is the value for the new column generated. This technique may help the machine learning model discover some correlations between the two selected columns.

For example, for the table shown in listing 6.30, the first column of the table contains only the values of A and B, whereas the second column of the table contains only values of 0 and 1. A new column generated using the technique described earlier would contain four different values: A0, A1, B0, B1. We can use an ordinal encoder to encode them to 0, 1, 2, 3.

Listing 6.30 Generating a new column by combining existing columns

```
A   1   A1   1
A   0   A0   0
A   1   A1   1
B   0   B0   2
B   1   B1   3
B   1   B1   3
```

We implemented this technique as a SklearnTransformer, which can be part of a pipeline, as shown in listing 6.31. The fit() function should learn the information from the training data for the feature generation. Our fit() function generates the new column and fits the OrdinalEncoder. The transform() function should transform the data and return the transformed data. Our transform() function generates the new column and encodes it with the OrdinalEncoder.

Listing 6.31 Combining categorical features to generate a new feature

```
from sklearn.base import BaseEstimator, TransformerMixin

class CategoricalCombination(
    BaseEstimator, TransformerMixin):          ◁————  Extends the two classes
    def __init__(self, name_a, name_b):     ◁——       as required to implement
        self.name_a = name_a                          a SklearnTransformer
        self.name_b = name_b                    The initializer takes
        self.encoder = OrdinalEncoder(          two column names.
            handle_unknown='use_encoded_value', unknown_value=-1)

    def fit(self, x, y=None, **kwargs):
        temp_column = x[self.name_a].astype(str) +
            x[self.name_b].astype(str)          ◁—┐  Concatenates
        self.encoder.fit(temp_column.to_frame())     the columns
        return self                                  to build a new
                                                     column

    def transform(self, x, **kwargs):
        temp_column = x[self.name_a].astype(str) +
            x[self.name_b].astype(str)          ◁—┐  Concatenates the columns
        temp_column = self.encoder.transform(        to build a new column
            temp_column.to_frame())         ◁—
        return temp_column                       Uses the encoder to encode
                                                 the new column
```

Prepares an OrdinalEncoder to encode the newly generated feature

Fits the encoder with the new column

With this CategoricalCombination, we can now easily generate a new column that combines the categorical data of two existing columns, as shown in listing 6.32.

Listing 6.32 Generating a new feature with `CategoricalCombination`

```
>>> temp_data = pd.DataFrame({
...     '1': ['A', 'A', 'A', 'B', 'B', 'B'],
...     '2': [1, 0, 1, 0, 1, 1]
... })
>>> print(temp_data.head(6))          ◁──┐  Prints the original
   1  2                                   │  columns
0  A  1
1  A  0
2  A  1
3  B  0
4  B  1                                        ──┐  Initializes the
5  B  1                                          │  transformer
>>> transformer = CategoricalCombination('1', '2')   ◁──┘
>>> print(transformer.fit_transform(temp_data))   ◁──┐  Prints the newly
[[1.]                                                 │  generated column
 [0.]
 [1.]
 [2.]
 [3.]
 [3.]]
```

As shown in the outputs, the data we use and the values in the newly generated column are the same as what we used in the previous example.

The next technique to generate a new feature is using a numerical feature and a categorical feature to generate a new numerical feature. For example, given the table shown in listing 6.33, we first will need to divide the rows of the data into different groups. In this example, the data is divided into three groups, (A 1, A 1), (B 1, B 0), and (C 1, C -1). The rows in the same group have the same values for the first column. Second, we need to calculate the mean value of the numerical values in different groups. In this example, the three values we will get are 1 for group A, 0.5 for group B, and 0 for group C. The last step is to generate a new column identical to the categorical column and replace the categorical values with the corresponding mean value. It is like using the mean values as the encoding for the categorical values. A is replaced by 0.5, B is replaced by 0.5, and C is replaced by 0. You can also see it as using the numerical feature to encode the categorical feature.

Listing 6.33 Generating a new column using numerical and categorical columns

```
A   1   1
A   1   1
B   1   0.5
B   0   0.5
C   1   0
C  -1   0
```

To implement this techinque, we implemented another `SklearnTransformer` as shown in listing 6.34. The initializer also takes two column names, which are the column names of the categorical column and the numerical column. In the `fit()` function, we calculate the mean values of different groups divided according to the different categorical values. In the `transform()` function, we need to replace the categorical values with a numerical column and return the value.

Listing 6.34 Using numerical and categorical features to generate a new feature

```
class MeanEncoder(BaseEstimator, TransformerMixin):
    def __init__(
        self, categorical_name, numerical_name):
        self.categorical_name = categorical_name
        self.numerical_name = numerical_name
        self.means = None

    def fit(self, x, y=None, **kwargs):
        self.mean = x.groupby(self.categorical_name)[self.numerical_name].mean()
        return self

    def transform(self, x, **kwargs):
        return x[self.categorical_name].map(
            self.mean).to_frame()
```

Extends the required classes of a Transformer

The initializer takes two column names.

The fit function groups the rows by the values in the categorical column and calculates the mean value of the numerical values in each group.

Replaces the categorical values with the mean values

With the `MeanEncoder` implemented, we can do another quick test to see if it works correctly as shown in the following listing. The data we use is the same as the example in listing 6.33.

Listing 6.35 Using numerical and categorical features to generate a new feature

```
>>> temp_data = pd.DataFrame({
...     'a': ['A', 'A', 'B', 'B', 'C', 'C'],
...     'b': [1, 1, 1, 0, 1, -1]
... })
>>> print(temp_data.head(6))
   a  b
0  A  1
1  A  1
2  B  1
3  B  0
4  C  1
5  C -1
>>> encoder = MeanEncoder('a', 'b')
>>> print(encoder.fit_transform(temp_data).head(6))
     a
0  1.0
1  1.0
2  0.5
3  0.5
4  0.0
5  0.0
```

Prepares some example data

Initializes the MeanEncoder

Transforms the data

As shown in the printed results, the newly generated column is the same as we expected in the previous example.

Now we have all the modules we need for feature engineering. We will need to put them together into a single pipeline, including the feature encoding pipelines and the transformers for feature generation. We will use the `SklearnColumnTransformer`, which is just for transforming the features before input into the machine learning model. The code is shown in the next code listing. The `ColumnTransformer` accepts the argument of `transformers` as a list of tuples of three, a string as the name of the step, a `Transformer` or `Pipeline` instance, and a list of column names of the columns that will be used by the transformer.

Listing 6.36 Putting the feature encoding and generation together into a pipeline

```
from sklearn.compose import ColumnTransformer

column_transformer = ColumnTransformer(transformers=[
    ('numerical', numerical_transformer, numerical_columns),       The preprocessing
    ('one_hot', one_hot_transformer, one_hot_columns),             steps for different
    ('int', int_transformer, int_columns),                         types of columns
    ('categorical_combination', CategoricalCombination(
        'sex', 'class'), ['sex', 'class']),        ◀──────────     Combines the
    ('mean', MeanEncoder(                                          two categorical
        'embark_town', 'age'), ['embark_town', 'age'])  ◀──┐      columns to
])                                                          │      generate a new
                        Uses the age column to compute      │      column
                        the mean values to encode the       │
                        embark town column                  │
```

So far, we have done the feature generation part. The next step is the feature selection. Feature selection is usually using some metrics to evaluate each of the features, selecting the most useful ones for the task, and discarding the rest of the columns. A typical metric used for feature selection is called *mutual information,* which is an important concept in information theory. It measures the dependency between two variables. Each feature can be seen as a variable, and the values in the corresponding column can be seen as the samples of the variable. If the target column is highly dependent on a feature, the mutual information between these two columns would be high, which means it is a good column to keep. If two variables are independent of each other, the mutual information would be close to zero.

We implement this feature selection step using `sklearn.feature_selection` `.SelectKBest`, which can help us select the k best features base on a given metric. For example, to select the top eight features that have the highest mutual information with the target column, we can use `SelectKBest(mutual_info_classif, k=8)`. It can also be one of the steps of a pipeline.

With all these feature preprocessing, feature generation, and feature selection steps ready, we build a complete end-to-end pipeline as shown in listing 6.37, which uses a support vector machine as the final classification model implemented using `sklearn.svm.SVC`.

Listing 6.37 Building the overall pipeline

Initializes the final
end-to-end pipeline

```
from sklearn.svm import SVC
from sklearn.feature_selection import SelectKBest
from sklearn.feature_selection import mutual_info_classif

pipeline = Pipeline(steps=[
    ('preprocessing', column_transformer),
    ('feature_selection', SelectKBest(mutual_info_classif, k=8)),
    ('model', SVC()),
])
pipeline.fit(x_train, y_train)
```

The preprocessing
and feature
generation
transformer

The feature selection step
to select the top eight
features with the highest
mutual information with
the target column

The support
vector machine
classification model

Fits the model
using the
training data

With the pipeline trained with the training data, we can evaluate it using the testing data as shown in the following code.

Listing 6.38 Evaluating the pipeline using testing data

```
from sklearn.metrics import accuracy_score

y_pred = pipeline.predict(x_test)
print('Accuracy: ', accuracy_score(y_test, y_pred))
```

Predicts the testing
data targets

Prints the
accuracy score

It shows the accuracy score as 0.74.

We have shown an example of feature engineering. In this process, we could perform many parts differently, for example, the categorical columns we choose to combine, the numerical and categorical columns we choose to encode, or the number of columns to keep during the feature selection. If we define these decisions as hyperparameters, tuning these hyperparameters would be the process of automated feature engineering.

We can define the hyperparameters in the following way. First, we generate all the possible combinations of two categorical columns and all the possible combinations of a numerical column and a categorical column. The code is shown here.

Listing 6.39 Generating all possible combinations of the columns

The list for all possible numerical
and categorical column pairs

Iterates through the ordinal
encoded categorical columns

```
import numpy as np

mean_column_pairs = []
for int_col in int_columns:
    for num_col in numerical_columns:
        mean_column_pairs.append((int_col, num_col))
```

Iterates through the
numerical columns

Adds the categorical
and numerical column
pairs to the list

```
cat_column_pairs = []                                    ◄──┐  The list for all possible
┌─► for index1 in range(len(int_columns)):                   │  categorical column pairs
│       for index2 in range(index1 + 1, len(int_columns)):           ◄──────┐
│           cat_column_pairs.append((int_columns[index1], int_columns[index2]))  ◄──┤
│
│   mean_column_pairs = np.array(mean_column_pairs)
│   cat_column_pairs = np.array(cat_column_pairs)
```

Adds the categorical column pairs to the list

Iterates through all the ordinal encoded categorical columns

Iterates through the rest of the ordinal encoded categorical columns

Second, we will use a Boolean hyperparameter for each pair to control whether we generate a new feature using the two columns. The code for defining these hyperparameters would look like the following.

Listing 6.40 Using a Boolean hyperparameter for each of the pairs

```
transformers = []                          Enumerates all the pairs with their indices
for index, (col1, col2) in enumerate(cat_column_pairs):   ◄──┘
    if not hp.Boolean('combine_{i}'.format(i=index)):     ◄──
        continue                  Uses a Boolean hyperparameter for each pair to
    col1 = str(col1)              control whether to generate the new feature
    col2 = str(col2)
    transformers.append((
        col1 + col2,                               Adds the transformer tuple of
        CategoricalCombination(col1, col2),        three to the list, which will be
        [col1, col2]))                             used by a ColumnTransformer
```

Now we are ready to put everything together to build the entire search space. The code is shown in listing 6.41. First, as in the feature engineering example shown earlier, we build three pipelines to preprocess and encode the three types of features. Second, as in listing 6.40, we define the Boolean hyperparameters for each pair of categorical features for generating new features. We also do the same for each numerical and categorical feature pair. Finally, we define a hyperparameter for the number of columns to keep. Then, we put all these steps into a single overall pipeline and return it.

Listing 6.41 The search space for automated feature engineering

```
import keras_tuner as kt
                                                       Preprocessing
                                                       pipeline for
def build_model(hp):                                   numerical features
    numerical_transformer = Pipeline(steps=[    ◄──┘
        ('imputer', SimpleImputer(strategy='median')),
        ('normalizer', StandardScaler())
    ])                                              Preprocessing pipeline
                                                    for categorical features
                                                    to be one-hot encoded
    one_hot_transformer = Pipeline(steps=[   ◄──┘
        ('imputer', SimpleImputer(strategy='constant', fill_value='None')),
        ('one_hot_encoder', OneHotEncoder(handle_unknown='ignore'))
    ])
```

Preprocessing pipeline for categorical features to be ordinally encoded

```
int_transformer = Pipeline(steps=[
    ('imputer', SimpleImputer(strategy='constant', fill_value='None')),
    ('label_encoder', OrdinalEncoder(
        handle_unknown='use_encoded_value', unknown_value=-1))
])
```

Puts the preprocessing pipelines into a list to be used by the ColumnTransformer later

```
transformers = [
    ('numerical', numerical_transformer, numerical_columns),
    ('one_hot', one_hot_transformer, one_hot_columns),
    ('int', int_transformer, int_columns),
]
for index, (col1, col2) in enumerate(
    cat_column_pairs):
    if not hp.Boolean('combine_{i}'.format(i=index)):
        continue
    col1 = str(col1)
    col2 = str(col2)
    transformers.append((
        col1 + col2,
        CategoricalCombination(col1, col2),
        [col1, col2]))
```

Enumerates the categorical feature pairs to define the Boolean hyperparameters to generate new features

Enumerates the categorical and numerical feature pairs to define the Boolean hyperparameters to generate new features

```
for index, (col1, col2) in enumerate(
    mean_column_pairs):
    if not hp.Boolean('mean_{i}'.format(i=index)):
        continue
    col1 = str(col1)
    col2 = str(col2)
    transformers.append((
        col1 + col2,
        MeanEncoder(col1, col2),
        [col1, col2]))
print(transformers)
pipeline = Pipeline(steps=[
    ('preprocessing', ColumnTransformer(
        transformers=transformers)),
    ('impute', SimpleImputer(strategy='median')),
    ('model_selection', SelectKBest(
        mutual_info_classif,
        k=hp.Int('best_k',
            5,
            13 + len(transformers) - 3))),
    ('model', SVC()),
])

return pipeline
```

Initializes the ColumnTransformer as the first step of the pipeline to preprocess the data and generate new features

Initializes the overall pipeline

Initializes the feature selector for selecting the top k features

Imputes the data again to avoid any missing values during feature generation

Uses mutual information as the metric for feature selection

Defines a hyperparameter for the value of k

Selects all the features at most (13 features after preprocessing and encoding plus the newly generated features, which is the same as the number of transformers in the transformer list except for the three preprocessing pipelines)

Selects five features at least

To make sure the search space can build a model correctly, we can use the following code in listing 6.42 as a quick unit test.

Listing 6.42 A quick unit test for the search space

```
build_model(kt.HyperParameters()).fit(x_train, y_train)
```

Finally, we can start to search for the best model as shown here.

Listing 6.43 Searching for the best automated feature engineering model

```
from sklearn import metrics
import sklearn

tuner = kt.SklearnTuner(
    kt.oracles.RandomSearchOracle(          ◁─── Uses the random
        objective=kt.Objective('score', 'max'),        search algorithm
        max_trials=10,                                 for searching
    ),
    build_model,                                            Uses
    scoring=metrics.make_scorer(metrics.accuracy_score),  ◁─── accuracy as
    overwrite=True,                                         the metrics
)
tuner.search(x_train, y_train)
```

With automated feature engineering, we achieved a better accuracy score of 0.81.

6.4 *Controlling the AutoML process by customizing tuners*

In this section, let's delve into the tuner object and learn how to customize it to control the AutoML process and enable the tuning of models implemented with different libraries. Controlling the AutoML process means controlling the AutoML loop of several steps: instantiating an ML pipeline in each trial based on the hyperparameters selected by the search method (oracle), training and evaluating the performance of the pipeline, recording the evaluation results, and providing the results to update the oracle if needed (see figure 6.6). You've seen two types of tuners in the previous sections corresponding to the tuning of different models: a RandomSearch tuner for tuning the deep learning models (specifically implemented with TensorFlow Keras) with

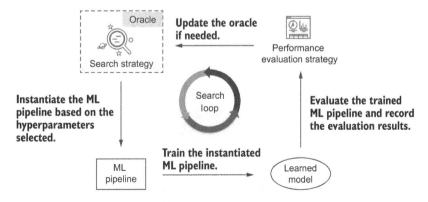

Figure 6.6 The search loop in the AutoML process

the random search method and the `SklearnTuner` for tuning the shallow models implemented with the scikit-learn library, in which you can select different search methods. The reason we choose different tuners is mainly because of the implementation difference of training and evaluating the deep learning and shallow models. This is quite a practical problem for doing AutoML because it's hard to find a package that contains all the possible ML models you might want to use. Although Keras-Tuner provides a universal way of customizing the search space by defining the `build()` function with the help of the `hp` container, training, evaluating, saving, and loading these models may still require different treatments. This can be addressed by defining your own tuners.

In the rest of the section, we introduce how to customize the tuners for tuning scikit-learn models and TensorFlow Keras models, respectively, to get you familiar with basic tuner design. Following the two examples, you'll learn how to design a tuner for jointly selecting and tuning deep learning and shallow models. You'll also learn to tune models beyond the scikit-learn models and Keras models with an additional example: tuning a *gradient-boosted decision tree* (GBDT) model implemented with the LightGBM library.

6.4.1   *Creating a tuner for tuning scikit-learn models*

Let's first learn to design a tuner to tune shallow models implemented with the scikit-learn library. We will work on the digit classification problem we used in section 6.2.1 and will use the same code for creating the search space and conducting the model selection and tuning. The only difference is that we customize our tuner rather than using the build-in scikit-learn model tuner (`kt.tuners.SklearnTuner`). The tuner, which we name `ShallowTuner`, should extend the tuner class (`Tuner`) in KerasTuner.

Overriding the `Tuner` class gives us full control over the search space, model building, training, saving, and evaluation process. Before getting into a real example, let's first see a barebones example to get an idea of how it works. In listing 6.44, we try to find the value of x, which minimizes `y=x*x+1`, by defining x as a hyperparameter. Yes, by subclassing `Tuner`, or any subclass of `Tuner`, like `RandomSearch`, you can use Keras-Tuner as a black-box optimization tool for anything. To do this, we only need to override `Tuner.run_trial()`, define the hyperparameter, and return the objective function value. The returned value will be minimized by default. `Tuner.run_trial()` is just running the experiment once and returning the evaluation results.

Listing 6.44   A barebones example for subclassing `Tuner`

```
import keras_tuner as kt

class MyTuner(kt.RandomSearch):          ←── Extends the
    def run_trial(self, trial, *args, **kwargs):       RandomSearch class
        hp = trial.hyperparameters       ←─┐ Gets the
        x = hp.Float('x', -1.0, 1.0)        │ HyperParameters
        return x * x + 1                    │ object from trial
```

```
tuner = MyTuner(max_trials=20)
tuner.search()
tuner.results_summary()
```

In this example, we did not use `hypermodel`. We did not specify an `objective`, either. These are all used by `Tuner.run_trial()`. If you don't use them, there is no need to specify them. For the return value of `Tuner.run_trial()`, it supports different formats. It is more common to use a dictionary, which we will show in the next example.

However, when we implement the `ShallowTuner`, we have more functions to override because we want to save the models along the way and load the best model after the search. In general, the following five functions need to be implemented for customizing a tuner:

- *An initialization function* (`__init__()`)—Initializes the tuner by providing the search method (`oracle`) and the defined model-building function or class (`hypermodel`), which we've learned in the previous sections, to characterize the search space and build up the model in each trial. The `oracle` and `hypermodel` will be saved as the attributes of the tuner (`self.oracle` and `self.hypermodel`).
- *A search function* (`search()`)—Starts the whole iterative AutoML search process when called. In each search iteration, it will first initiatiate an object named `trial`, which stores all the meta information in the current trial such as the hyperparameters selected by the search method and the status of the current trial to help track whether a trial is started or completed. Then the search function will call the core function introduced next to pursue the search process.
- *A core function* (`run_trial()`)—Implements the single search loop we described in figure 6.6.
- *A save function* (`save_model()`)—Saves the generated models.
- *A load function* (`load_model()`)—Loads the models for retraining if needed after the search process is done.

The code of our `ShallowTuner` is shown in listing 6.45. The initialization function and the search function can be ignored here because they only call the corresponding functions extended from the `Tuner` and do not have any specialized operations.

Listing 6.45 **Customizing a tuner for tuning scikit-learn models**

```
import os
import pickle
import tensorflow as tf
import keras_tuner as kt

class ShallowTuner(kt.Tuner):
    def __init__(self, oracle, hypermodel, **kwargs):
        super(ShallowTuner, self).__init__(            Initializes
            oracle=oracle, hypermodel=hypermodel, **kwargs)   ◁──  the tuner

    def search(self, X, y, validation_data):
        return super(ShallowTuner, self).search(     Performs the AutoML
            X, y, validation_data)            ◁────  search process
```

```
def run_trial(self, trial, X, y, validation_data):
    model = self.hypermodel.build(trial.hyperparameters)
    model.fit(X, y)
    X_val, y_val = validation_data
    eval_score = model.score(X_val, y_val)
    self.save_model(trial.trial_id, model)
    return {'score': eval_score}

def save_model(self, trial_id, model):
    fname = os.path.join(self.get_trial_dir(trial_id), 'model.pickle')
    with tf.io.gfile.GFile(fname, 'wb') as f:
        pickle.dump(model, f)

def load_model(self, trial):
    fname = os.path.join(
        self.get_trial_dir(trial.trial_id), 'model.pickle')
    with tf.io.gfile.GFile(fname, 'rb') as f:
        return pickle.load(f)
```

Builds, trains, and evaluates the model in the current trial

Saves the model to disk

Returns the evaluation result

Model-saving function with pickle package

Model-loading function with pickle package

Because the AutoML process is a loop process, the core function (run_trial()) in the custom tuner is called repeatedly in the search function (implemented in the based Tuner). Its inputs contain the data for training and evaluating the models instantiated in it (X for training features, y for training responses, validation_data for testing data). A trial object contains all the hyperparameters returned by the oracle in the current trial and some metadata to help summarize the results, such as a randomly generated ID of this trial (trial.trial_id).

Digging into the run_trial() function, we can see that it first builds up the model based on the hyperparameters selected by the oracle. trial.hyperparameters is a hyperparameter container that helps create the current model. Then, the model is trained and evaluated. The model.score() function adopts the default evaluation criterion of the scikit-learn model. You can also implement your own evaluation method here, such as cross-validation. In this case, the validation data can also be removed from the arguments because the cross-validation will automatically split part of the training data (X and y) as validation data. The evaluation result (a dictionary with the metric names as the keys) is returned to update the oracle.

The model is saved to disk for future usage by calling the save_model() function. This process strictly follows the search loop described in figure 6.6. To help save and load the models discovered in the search process, we also need to implement the save_model() and load_model() functions. The save_model() function, called in the run_trial() function, takes the unique ID of a trial and the trained scikit-learn model as inputs and saves the model using the pickle package. The load_model() function is used after the search process is finished. It helps retrieve the best model in the disk. It takes a trial object as input (containing all the meta information of this trial such as the trial ID, hyperparameters, model accuracy) and returns the trained model selected in the corresponding trial.

We follow the same process introduced in section 6.2.1 to load the data and create the search space. Notably, we do an extra split on the training data to get the validation dataset because our custom tuner requires the input of validation data. We didn't do this for the build-in scikit-learn tuner because it implements the cross-validation in the `run_trial()` function to evaluate each selected model. The search space here is still for joint model selection and hyperparameter tuning of the SVM model and random forest model. Code for conducting this AutoML task is shown in the following listing.

Listing 6.46 Tuning scikit-learn models for digits classification

```
from sklearn.datasets import load_digits
from sklearn.model_selection import train_test_split

digits = load_digits()

images, labels = digits.images, digits.target

X = images.reshape((n_samples, -1))

X_train, X_test, y_train, y_test = train_test_split(
    X, labels, test_size=0.2, shuffle=False)

X_train, X_val, y_train, y_val = train_test_split(
    X_train, y_train, test_size=0.2, shuffle=False)


from sklearn.svm import SVC
from sklearn.ensemble import RandomForestClassifier
from keras_tuner.engine import hyperparameters as hp


def build_model(hp):
    model_type = hp.Choice('model_type', ['svm', 'random_forest'])
    if model_type == 'svm':
        with hp.conditional_scope('model_type', 'svm'):
            model = SVC(
                C=hp.Float('C', 1e-3, 10, sampling='linear', default=1),
                kernel=hp.Choice('kernel_type',
                                 ['linear', 'rbf'],
                                 default='linear'),
                random_state=42)
    elif model_type == 'random_forest':
        with hp.conditional_scope('model_type', 'random_forest'):
            model = RandomForestClassifier(
                n_estimators=hp.Int('n_estimators', 10, 200, step=10),
                max_depth=hp.Int('max_depth', 3, 10))
    else:
        raise ValueError('Unrecognized model_type')
    return model

my_sklearn_tuner = ShallowTuner(
    oracle=kt.oracles.RandomSearch(
        objective=kt.Objective('score', 'max'),
        max_trials=10,
        seed=42),
```

Annotations:
- Loads the digits dataset
- Splits the dataset into training, validation, and test sets
- Creates a search space for model selection and hyperparameter tuning
- Initializes the custom tuner

```
        hypermodel=build_model,
        overwrite=True,
        project_name='my_sklearn_tuner')

my_sklearn_tuner.search(
        X_train, y_train, validation_data=(X_val, y_val))
```

Conducts the search process by feeding the training and validation datasets

You can also use the custom tuner to tune the scikit-learn pipelines, like we did in section 6.2.2. We won't further elaborate on it here and leave it for you as an exercise.

6.4.2 Creating a tuner for tuning Keras models

In the second example, let's create a custom tuner for tuning the deep learning models implemented with TensorFlow Keras. We've used a built-in tuner for tuning Keras models: the RandomSearch tuner, which is hardcoded with the random search method (oracle is the random search oracle and is not changeable). Now we create a custom tuner that can select between different search methods. Following the same steps we performed in the previous example, we create a tuner called DeepTuner by extending the base tuner class. As we've mentioned before, if the initialization function and the search function do not have any specialized operations compared to the base tuner ones, we can ignore them. Thus, we implement only three functions for the Deep-Tuner here: the run_trial(), save_model(), and load_model() functions.

Compared to the previous example, the major differences are how we evaluated the models in the run_trial() function and how we save and load these Keras models (see listing 6.47). Zooming into the run_trial() function, we can still build up the Keras model by calling the build() function of the hypermodel, the same as we did in the previous example. Then we call the fit() function of the instantiated Keras model to train it. Notably, training the deep learning models may require extra hyperparameters such as the batch size and number of epochs to help control the optimization algorithm. We can pass these hyperparameters in the **fit_kwargs arguments (as we will see later when calling the search() function of the tuner). Or, to be more automated, set the search space of it using the hyperparameter container (as we do for the batch_size in listing 6.47) to tune it along with other hyperparameters. After the model is trained, we can evaluate it with the validation data and use the evaluation results to update the oracle. Specifically, you may question how to update the oracle when we have multiple evaluation metrics. For example, by default, the evaluate() function of Keras will return the evaluation loss value and the classification accuracy in this example (assume that we've already created a search space of models for classifying the digits). A straightforward way of addressing this is to save the evaluation on all the metrics in a dictionary with the metric names as the keys and feed all of them to the oracle. When initializing the tuner, we can inform the tuner which specific metric we want to use to compare the models and update the oracle. As TensorFlow Keras provides methods for saving and loading the models, we can adopt these methods to implement the save_model() and load_model() functions.

Listing 6.47 Customizing a tuner for tuning Keras models

```
class DeepTuner(kt.Tuner):

    def run_trial(self, trial, X, y, validation_data, **fit_kwargs):
        model = self.hypermodel.build(trial.hyperparameters)

        model.fit(X, y, batch_size=trial.hyperparameters.Choice(
            'batch_size', [16, 32]), **fit_kwargs)          ◁─── Trains model with a
                                                                 tunable batch size
        X_val, y_val = validation_data
        eval_scores = model.evaluate(X_val, y_val)
        self.save_model(trial.trial_id, model)
        return {name: value for name, value in zip(
            model.metrics_names,                      Returns the
            eval_scores)}          ◁──────────────── evaluation results

    def save_model(self, trial_id, model, step=0):
        fname = os.path.join(self.get_trial_dir(trial_id), 'model')
        model.save(fname)

    def load_model(self, trial):
        fname = os.path.join(self.get_trial_dir(
            trial.trial_id), 'model')
        model = tf.keras.models.load_model(fname)
        return model
```

Next, we use the custom tuner to tune the MLPs for the digit classification. As shown in listing 6.48, we create a search space of MLPs in a `build_model()` function and use it to initialize a `DeepTuner` object. As we can see, we select the oracle ourselves, which the `RandomSearch` tuner cannot do. The objective is specified as the classification accuracy, which will be the metric to compare the models and used in the `run_trial()` function to update the oracle. By calling the `search` function, we can execute the search process. The number of epochs will be passed from the `search` function to the `run_trial()` function (via the `**fit_kwargs`) to control the training epochs of each selected MLP.

Listing 6.48 Tuning MLPs with the custom tuner for digits classification

```
import keras_tuner as kt
                                     Creates a search space
                                     for tuning MLPs
def build_model(hp):          ◁──┘
    model = tf.keras.Sequential()
    model.add(tf.keras.Input(shape=(64,)))
    for i in range(hp.Int('num_layers', min_value=1, max_value=4)):
        model.add(tf.keras.layers.Dense(hp.Int(
            'units_{i}'.format(i=i), min_value=32, max_value=128, step=32),
                activation='relu'))
    model.add(tf.keras.layers.Dense(10, activation='softmax'))
    model.compile(loss='sparse_categorical_crossentropy',
        metrics=['accuracy'])
    return model
```

```
my_keras_tuner = DeepTuner(
    oracle=kt.oracles.RandomSearch(
        objective=kt.Objective('accuracy', 'max'),          ◁──
        max_trials=10,
        seed=42),
    hypermodel=build_model,
    overwrite=True,
    project_name='my_keras_tuner')

my_keras_tuner.search(
    X_train, y_train, validation_data=(X_val, y_val), epochs=10)    ◁──
```

Uses the classification accuracy as the objective for model comparison and oracle update

Executes the search process

From the two examples of tuner design, we can find that as long as we know how to train, evaluate, save, and load the models implemented with any ML library, we should be able to write a tuner that can control, select, and tune these models. By customizing the tuner, we can fully control the AutoML process and enable a broader search space, such as tuning the batch size and tuning models from different libraries. In the next two examples, we will further show the benefit of tuner design on enlarging the search space for tuning models in different libraries.

6.4.3 Jointly tuning and selection among deep learning and shallow models

Although deep learning models have shown their prominence in many ML tasks recently, they're not universally optimal solutions. In many cases, we don't know in advance whether using deep learning models would beat the shallow models, especially when the dataset is small. You may face this situation at some point. The next example will show how to do joint model selection and tuning among the shallow models and deep learning models. We combine the search space used in the previous two examples into a unified search space. The search space contains three types of model structures—SVM, random forest, and MLP—each with their specified space of hyperparameters. To further clarify the search space hierarchy, we set up the conditional scope for the hyperparameters under each type of model as shown in the following listing.

Listing 6.49 **Creating a search space both deep and shallow models**

```
from sklearn.svm import SVC                                  Sets up the conditional
from sklearn.ensemble import RandomForestClassifier          hyperparameter scope for
                                                             each type of model
def build_model(hp):
    model_type = hp.Choice('model_type', ['svm', 'random_forest', 'mlp'],
        default='mlp')
    if model_type == 'svm':
        with hp.conditional_scope('model_type', 'svm'):      ◁──
            model = SVC(
                C=hp.Float('C', 1e-3, 10, sampling='linear', default=1),
                kernel=hp.Choice('kernel_type', ['linear', 'rbf'],
                    default='linear'),
                random_state=42)
```

Selects whether to use shallow models or MLP

```
        elif model_type == 'random_forest':
            with hp.conditional_scope('model_type', 'random_forest'):
                model = RandomForestClassifier(
                    n_estimators=hp.Int('n_estimators', 10, 200, step=10),
                    max_depth=hp.Int('max_depth', 3, 10))
        elif model_type == 'mlp':
            with hp.conditional_scope('model_type', 'mlp'):
                model = tf.keras.Sequential()
                model.add(tf.keras.Input(shape=(64,)))
                for i in range(hp.Int('num_layers', min_value=1, max_value=4)):
                    model.add(tf.keras.layers.Dense(hp.Int(
                        f'units_{i}', min_value=32, max_value=128,
                            step=32), activation='relu'))
                model.add(tf.keras.layers.Dense(10, activation='softmax'))
                model.compile(
                    loss='sparse_categorical_crossentropy', metrics=['accuracy'])
        else:
            raise ValueError('Unrecognized model_type')
        return model
```

Sets up the conditional hyperparameter scope for each type of model

Now it's time to create the tuner. Following the previous two examples, a feasible idea is to merge the two tuners into one. Because the creation of deep learning models and shallow models is the same (by calling the `build()` function with the hyperparameters in each trial), we can set a model discriminator to judge whether a model created in each trial is a shallow model or deep model. Whenever we got a deep learning model (Keras model), we train, evaluate, and save it in the `DeepTuner`. On the contrary, if a shallow model (scikit-learn) is created, we'll follow the steps implemented in the `ShallowTuner`. We implement the tuner in listing 6.50.

As you can see, the `run_trial()`, `save_model()`, and `load_model()` functions all can decide whether or not the model is a Keras model. To ensure the oracle will receive the same type of evaluation for different models, we keep the classification accuracy of only the deep learning models. A tricky point here is that different models are saved and loaded in different ways. During training, we can directly save a model with its tailored saving method based on the model type. However, when loading a model, we do not have the model in advance to select the corresponding loading method. To address this problem, we predefine an attribute in the initialization function (`trial_id_to_type`) to record the model type in each trial. It is a dictionary to map the trial ID to the corresponding model type (`Keras` or scikit-learn), so when loading the model, we can select the corresponding loading method based on the trial ID.

Listing 6.50 Customizing a tuner for tuning both deep and shallow models

```
import pickle
import os
import tensorflow as tf
import keras_tuner as kt

class ShallowDeepTuner(kt.Tuner):
```

```
def __init__(self, *args, **kwargs):
    super().__init__(*args, **kwargs)
    self.trial_id_to_type = {}
```

Adds an attribute to record the type of model selected in each trial

```
def run_trial(
    self, trial, x, y, validation_data, epochs=None, **fit_kwargs):
    model = self.hypermodel.build(trial.hyperparameters)
    x_val, y_val = validation_data
    if isinstance(model, tf.keras.Model):
        model.fit(
            x, y, validation_data=validation_data,
            batch_size=trial.hyperparameters.Choice(
                'batch_size', [16, 32]),
            epochs=epochs,
            **fit_kwargs)
        accuracy = {name: value for name, value in zip(
            model.metrics_names,
            model.evaluate(x_val, y_val))}['accuracy']
        self.trial_id_to_type[trial.trial_id] = 'keras'
    else:
        model = self.hypermodel.build(trial.hyperparameters)
        model.fit(x, y)
        accuracy = model.score(x_val, y_val)
        self.trial_id_to_type[trial.trial_id] = 'sklearn'
    self.save_model(trial.trial_id, model)
    return {'accuracy': accuracy}
```

Checks the model type for model training

Retrieves the accuracy of only the Keras model

Records the model type

```
def save_model(self, trial_id, model):
    fname = os.path.join(self.get_trial_dir(trial_id), 'model')
    if isinstance(model, tf.keras.Model):
        model.save(fname)
    else:
        with tf.io.gfile.GFile(fname, 'wb') as f:
            pickle.dump(model, f)
```

```
def load_model(self, trial):
    fname = os.path.join(self.get_trial_dir(trial.trial_id), 'model')
    if self.trial_id_to_type[trial.trial_id] == 'keras':
        model = tf.keras.models.load_model(fname)
    else:
        with tf.io.gfile.GFile(fname, 'rb') as f:
            model = pickle.load(f)
    return model
```

Checks the model type of model loading

The rest of the work is to instantiate the tuner and use it to explore the mixed search space of deep and shallow models (see listing 6.51). We select the random search method here and set the objective for comparing the models as accuracy, which aligns the one we specified in the run_trial() function of the tuner. We search for 30 trials, and the best model explored so far is an SVM classifier.

Listing 6.51 Exploring the mixed search space with the custom tuner

```
>>> random_tuner = ShallowDeepTuner(
...     oracle=kt.oracles.RandomSearch(
...         objective=kt.Objective('accuracy', 'max'),
...         max_trials=30,
...         seed=42),
...     hypermodel=build_model,
...     overwrite=True,
...     project_name='random_tuner')

>>> random_tuner.search(
...     x_train, y_train, validation_data=(x_val, y_val), epochs=10)

>>> best_model = random_tuner.get_best_models(1)[0]
>>> print(type(best_model))

<class 'sklearn.svm._classes.SVC'>
```

Sets the objective as the classification accuracy

Retrieves the best model

In the last example, we will work on tuning the models that are not implemented with TensorFlow Keras and scikit-learn APIs. This can help you generalize the AutoML techniques you've learned to a broader range of models and libraries you may want to use in practice.

6.4.4 *Hyperparameter tuning beyond Keras and scikit-learn models*

As an example, we use the LightGBM library (https://lightgbm.readthedocs.io/en/latest/), which is a gradient-boosting framework for tree-based learning algorithms. It contains several representative tree-based learning algorithms such as the GBDT algorithm and the random forest algorithm, which you may have seen before (see appendix B for more details on these algorithms). Learning how to tune these algorithms requires us to know how to apply them in advance. Specifically, you need to know how to instantiate the algorithm and use it to train a model. You should also know how to evaluate the learned model, save it, and load it back to make predictions when needed. We work on the California housing price-prediction task here and train a regression model with the GBDT algorithm (specified by the boosting_type argument) as shown in listing 6.52. The algorithm will create and add decision trees to the final GBDT model sequentially. We train a GBDT model with an ensemble of at most 10 trees and 31 leaves in each tree. The learning rate here is a weighting factor for the corrections of the predictions given by new trees when added to the ensemble model. The best iteration here means the number of trees in the ensemble that achieves the best performance. We refer you to check the details of using this library from the official website: http://mng.bz/q2jJ. We evaluate the trained model, save it, and reload it to check whether the model is saved correctly.

Listing 6.52 Applying the GBDT model in the LightGBM library for regression

```
import pandas as pd
from sklearn.datasets import fetch_california_housing
```

```
house_dataset = fetch_california_housing()
data = pd.DataFrame(house_dataset.data, columns=house_dataset.feature_names)
target = pd.Series(house_dataset.target, name = 'MEDV')

from sklearn.model_selection import train_test_split
X_train, X_test, y_train, y_test = train_test_split(
    data, target, test_size=0.2, random_state=42)
X_train, X_val, y_train, y_val = train_test_split(
    X_train, y_train, test_size=0.2, shuffle=False)

!pip install lightgbm -q
import lightgbm as lgb
from sklearn.metrics import mean_squared_error

gbdt_model = lgb.LGBMRegressor(
    boosting_type='gbdt',
    num_leaves=31,
    learning_rate=0.05,
    n_estimators=10
)

validation_data = (X_val, y_val)
gbdt_model.fit(X_train, y_train,
        eval_set=[validation_data],
        eval_metric='mse',
        early_stopping_rounds=5)

y_pred_gbdt = gbdt_model.predict(
    X_test, num_iteration=gbdt_model.best_iteration_)
test_mse_1 = mean_squared_error(y_test, y_pred_gbdt)
print('The GBDT prediction MSE on test set: {}'.format(test_mse_1))


fname = 'gbdt_model.txt'
gbdt_model.booster_.save_model(
    fname, num_iteration=gbdt_model.best_iteration_)
gbdt_model_2 = lgb.Booster(model_file=fname)
gbdt_model_2.predict(X_test)
test_mse_2 = mean_squared_error(y_test, y_pred_gbdt)
print('The reloaded GBDT prediction MSE on test set: {}'.format(test_mse_2))
```

- **Installs and imports the LightGBM package**
- **Creates and fits a GBDT model**
- **Evaluates the learned GBDT model**
- **Saves, loads, and reevaluates the model**

As shown next, the MSE of the GBDT model is around 0.75, and the model-saving and -loading methods could save the learned model in a .txt file successfully:

```
>>> The GBDT prediction MSE on test set: 0.7514642734431766
>>> The reloaded GBDT prediction MSE on test set: 0.7514642734431766
```

In listing 6.53, we try to tune the GBDT algorithm implemented with LightGBM with the AutoML technique we learned in the previous sections. Suppose we want to tune the maximum number of trees, the maximum number of leaves in each tree, and the learning rate of the GBDT algorithm. Because we know how to instantiate a single

GBDT regressor, we can leverage the `hp` container and specify the search space of these concerned hyperparameters in a model-building function, the same as we've done for tuning the scikit-learn and Keras models.

Listing 6.53 Creating a search space for selecting and tuning LightGBM models

```
def build_model(hp):
    model = lgb.LGBMRegressor(
        boosting_type='gbdt',
        num_leaves=hp.Choice('num_leaves', [15, 31, 63], default=31),
        learning_rate=hp.Float(
            'learning_rate', 1e-3, 10, sampling='log', default=1),
        n_estimators=hp.Int('n_estimators', 10, 200, step=10)
    )

    return model
```

Characterizes the search space of the concerned hyperparameters — (annotation pointing to the `num_leaves`...`n_estimators` lines)

Following the method for customizing the tuner introduced in the previous examples, we create a `LightGBMTuner`, extending the base tuner in KerasTuner, and implement the three core functions for executing a search trial, saving the trained model, and loading the model from disk, respectively. From the code shown in listing 6.54, we can see that except for several AutoML steps, including the model building with the selected hyperparameters and the oracle update, the code combining the three functions is the same as the code we implement a single GBDT algorithm with LightGBM for conducting the regression task.

Listing 6.54 Customizing a tuner for tuning LightGBM models

```
import os
import pickle
import tensorflow as tf
import keras_tuner as kt
import lightgbm as lgb
from sklearn.metrics import mean_squared_error

class LightGBMTuner(kt.Tuner):

    def run_trial(self, trial, X, y, validation_data):
        model = self.hypermodel.build(
            trial.hyperparameters)
        model.fit(
            X_train, y_train,
            eval_set=[validation_data],
            eval_metric='mse',
            early_stopping_rounds=5)
        X_val, y_val = validation_data
        y_pred = model.predict(X_val, num_iteration=model.best_iteration_)
        eval_mse = mean_squared_error(y_val, y_pred)
        self.save_model(trial.trial_id, model)
        return {'mse': eval_mse}
```

Builds and fits a GBDT model — (annotation pointing to `model.fit(...early_stopping_rounds=5)`)

Evaluates the learned GBDT model — (annotation pointing to `X_val, y_val = validation_data` ... `eval_mse = mean_squared_error(y_val, y_pred)`)

Returns the model evaluation MSE — (annotation pointing to `return {'mse': eval_mse}`)

Saves the learned GBDT model to disk — (annotation pointing to `self.save_model(trial.trial_id, model)`)

```
def save_model(self, trial_id, model, step=0):
    fname = os.path.join(self.get_trial_dir(trial_id), 'model.txt')
    model.booster_.save_model(fname, num_iteration=model.best_iteration_)

def load_model(self, trial):
    fname = os.path.join(self.get_trial_dir(trial.trial_id), 'model.txt')
    model = lgb.Booster(model_file=fname)
    return model
```

We use the created model-building function and the custom tuner to tune the three hyperparameters in the GBDT algorithm implemented with the LightGBM library. By exploring the search space for 10 trials, the test MSE of the best-discovered model is largely reduced compared to the one from our initial model, which demonstrates the effectiveness of our tuning strategy (see listing 6.55). The hyperparameters of the best model can be printed out by calling the result_summary() function of the tuner, which is inherited from the base tuner.

Listing 6.55 Executing the hyperparameter tuning and evaluating the best model

```
>>> my_lightgbm_tuner = LightGBMTuner(
...     oracle=kt.oracles.RandomSearch(
...         objective=kt.Objective('mse', 'min'),
...         max_trials=10,
...         seed=42),
...     hypermodel=build_model,
...     overwrite=True,
...     project_name='my_lightgbm_tuner')
>>> my_lightgbm_tuner.search(X_train, y_train, validation_data=(X_val, y_val))

>>> from sklearn.metrics import mean_squared_error
>>> best_model = my_lightgbm_tuner.get_best_models(1)[0]
>>> y_pred_test = best_model.predict(X_test)
>>> test_mse = mean_squared_error(y_test, y_pred_test)
>>> print('The prediction MSE on test set: {}'.format(test_mse))

The prediction MSE on test set: 0.20391543433512713


>>> my_lightgbm_tuner.results_summary(1)      ◁──┐  Prints the hyperparameter
Results summary                                  │  and evaluation information
Results in ./my_lightgbm_tuner                   │  of the best trial
Showing 1 best trials
Objective(name='mse', direction='min')
Trial summary
Hyperparameters:
num_leaves: 31
learning_rate: 0.09504947970741313
n_estimators: 190
Score: 0.2202899505068673
```

You've now learned how to design the tuner to extend the search space to a broader range of models implemented with different libraries. Before ending this chapter, we want to point out several notes.

NOTE

- Adopting KerasTuner requires you to know the implementation of creating the model. You also have to know how to train, evaluate, save, and load the model if you want to customize a tuner for tuning models not implemented with Keras or the scikit-learn library.

- We separate the model instantiation part in the `build_model()` function and the model-training part in the tuners. This separation is doable because of the support for the APIs of Keras and scikit-learn. However, some libraries may not allow the separation of model instantiation and training. In other words, you have to instantiate the model with the hyperparameters and fit the model with the training data in one sentence, such as the default training API of LightGBM (http://mng.bz/7Wve). To accommodate this case, a straightforward way is to use the `build_model()` function to return the hyperparameters rather than the create model, and use these hyperparameters to instantiate the model in the `run_trial()` function of the tuner simultaneously, with the model training leveraging the API of the library covering the model you want to tune.

- KerasTuner requires us to define the performance evaluation of each selected model in the tuner. Some AutoML toolkits define the model-training and -evaluation (objective) function outside the tuner and feed it into the tuner during the search process, such as Ray Tune (https://docs.ray.io/en/latest/tune/index.html) or Hyperopt (https://github.com/hyperopt/hyperopt). The general APIs are quite similar to the KerasTuner implementation, and you can learn more details from their official websites.

- Though we often have to design a tailored tuner for tuning the models implemented with different libraries, the oracle is often universal and can be used in different tuners because the inputs and outputs of the oracle are always the numerical representations of the hyperparameters extracted in the `hp` container. We will introduce more details in the next chapter.

Summary

- To achieve extra flexibility of search space design for tuning and selecting deep learning models, you can create the entire search space in one `build()` function in a layerwise fashion. This way of model building is similar to creating a Keras model, except you should change the relevant hyperparameters to a space of feasible values.

- You can create the search space for tuning shallow models in the same way as deep learning models with KerasTuner. Multiple preprocessing methods and shallow models can be jointly selected and tuned by creating a scikit-learn pipeline.

- A tuner contains a search method and organizes the training and evaluation of the selected pipelines during the search process. Different search methods can be chosen by changing the oracle in KerasTuner.

- For models with different training and evaluation strategies or implemented with different libraries, you may have to select a tuner with a suitable training and evaluation strategy or customize your own tuner.
- A typical case for customizing a tuner requires you to specify three functions: a `run_trial()` function to process a single AutoML loop (including the model instantiation, training, evaluation, and saving; and the oracle update), a model-saving function, and a model-loading function.

Part 3

Advanced topics
in AutoML

The last part of the book leads you to explore some advanced AutoML design and setup in practice. You'll learn how to customize your own search method to explore the hyperparameter search space and discover better hyperparameters in chapter 7 and how to adopt different strategies to accelerate the search process, even with limited computing resources in chapter 8. A quick recap of what you should take away from this book is provided in chapter 9, along with a short list of resources and strategies for learning more about AutoML and staying up-to-date with the latest developments in the field.

Customizing the search method of AutoML

7

This chapter covers

- Understanding sequential search methods
- Customizing a random search method
- Vectorizing hyperparameters for the model-based search method
- Understanding and implementing a Bayesian optimization search method
- Understanding and implementing an evolutionary search method

In this chapter, we will explore how to customize a sequential search method to iteratively explore the hyperparameter search space and discover better hyperparameters. You will learn how to implement different sequential search methods for selecting pipelines from the search space in each trial. These search methods fall into the following two categories:

- *History-independent* sequential search methods cannot be updated during the search process. For example, grid search, which we looked at in chapter 2, traverses all the possible combinations of values in the candidate hyperparameter sets, and in chapter 6, we used the random search method to select hyperparameter combinations from the search space randomly. These are the two most representative history-independent methods. Some other advanced random search methods make use of history, such as the quasi-random search method using Sobol sequences (http://mng.bz/6Z7A), but here we'll consider only the vanilla uniform random search method.

- *History-dependent* sequential search methods, such as Bayesian optimization, are able to improve the effectiveness of the search by leveraging the previous results.

7.1   *Sequential search methods*

In chapter 6, you learned how to customize a tuner to control the AutoML search loop (see figure 7.1). ML pipelines are generated by iteratively calling the oracle (search method). Models learned from the ML pipeline are evaluated, and the results are fed back to the oracle to update it so it can better explore the search space. Because the oracle generates ML pipelines in a sequential manner, we call it a *sequential search method*. It generally consists of the following two steps:

- *Hyperparameter sampling*—Sampling hyperparameters from the search space to create the ML pipelines.
- *Oracle update* (optional)—Updating the search method, leveraging the history of existing models and evaluations. The goal is to increase the speed at which better ML pipelines are identified in the search space. This step differs across search methods, and it takes place only in history-dependent methods. For example, grid search and random search do not take history into account, so with these methods, the oracle does not need to be updated during the search process.

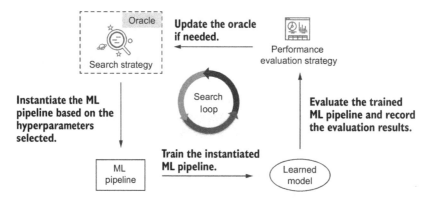

Figure 7.1   A single search loop when using a sequential search method

As mentioned previously, if the oracle can leverage historical evaluations to update itself and guide its sampling of new hyperparameters from the search space, we can divide the sequential search methods into two categories: history-dependent methods and history-independent methods. The history-dependent methods can be further classified into the following two main categories based on how the updating is done:

- *Heuristic methods*—Often inspired by biological behavior. A representative example is the *evolutionary method*, which generates new samples by simulating the evolution of an animal population across generations. We will introduce how to create an evolutionary search method in the last section of this chapter.
- *Model-based methods*—Leverages certain ML models, such as the decision tree model, to predict which hyperparameters in the search space will be good choices. The historical evaluations of the previous hyperparameter sets are used as training data to train the ML model. A representative method is the Bayesian optimization method that we used in the previous chapter. You'll learn how to implement this method in section 7.3.

Together, these are probably the most widely used sequential search methods in the existing literature. We'll begin, however, with a history-independent method: random search. We'll continue here with the example of tuning LightGBM models for the California housing price-prediction problem used in chapter 6. The code will mainly focus on the oracle. The code for loading data and the implementation of the tuner class are unchanged, and won't be repeated here. The complete code can be found in the book's GitHub repository: http://mng.bz/oaep.

7.2 Getting started with a random search method

In this section, we will introduce how to create a random search method with Keras-Tuner to explore the search space and find better hyperparameters. The random search method is one of the simplest and most traditional ways of doing hyperparameter tuning in AutoML. The vanilla random search method randomly explores the hyperparameter combinations in the search space. This approach has been empirically shown to be more powerful than the grid search method in most cases.

Why is random search often better than grid search?

We'll use an example to describe this. You can find more details in the paper "Random Search for Hyper-Parameter Optimization" by James Bergstra and Yoshua Bengio (www.jmlr.org/papers/v13/bergstra12a.html). Suppose we have two continuous hyperparameters, x and y, forming a two-dimensional search space. Assume the model performance is a function related to these hyperparameters. More specifically, it's an additive function of two functions, each dependent on one of the hyperparameters: $f(x, y) = h(x) + g(y)$.

Different hyperparameters have different effects on the final model's performance, so some will have less of an effect than others. Let's assume the hyperparameter y has marginal effects compared to x, indicating that $f(x, y) \sim h(x)$. Along the two boundaries (left and upper) of the space, we provide two function curves forming a

(continued)

one-dimensional subspace of each hyperparameter and its function. The height of each function curve can also be understood as indicating the importance of the hyperparameter to the evaluation of the final models. If we use the grid search method to explore the search space with nine trials, it will bucketize the search space and sample a grid of points (see figure a), which gives an even coverage of the space. In this case, even though the hyperparameters are of different importance, the grid search provides equal coverage of the subspace of each one, whereas random search provides more thorough coverage of the subspace of hyperparameter *y* (the important one) as shown in figure b.

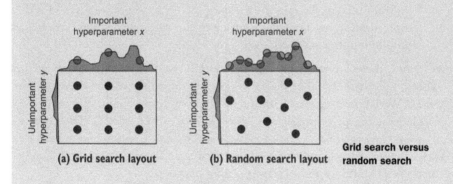

(a) Grid search layout   (b) Random search layout   **Grid search versus random search**

The search method in KerasTuner is implemented as an `Oracle` object that can be called by the tuners. Before implementing the oracle, we need to understand the relationship (reference logic) between the functions of the oracle and those of the tuner.

The main functions called during the search process are shown in listing 7.1. The `search()` function of the tuner will call two main functions in a loop. The first one, `create_trial()`, is a function of the oracle. It creates a `trial` object containing the hyperparameters selected by the oracle in the current trial and sets the status of the trial to `RUNNING`, meaning that the trial is executing. The sampling of the hyperparameters is done in a private method called `populate_space()`, which is the main function of the oracle we need to implement. If the search method is history-dependent, we will need to update it before sampling, based on the evaluations. After the `trial` object is created, it will carry the hyperparameters to the main function of the tuner (`run_trial()`), which as we learned in chapter 6, is used to instantiate, train, evaluate, and save the ML model in the current trial.

Listing 7.1   The reference logic between the functions of the tuner and the oracle

```
search (tuner)
    |-- create_trial (oracle)
        |-- populate_space (oracle)
    |-- run_trial (tuner)
```

```
|-- instantiate, fit, evaluate model
|-- save_model (tuner)
|-- return the evaluation results
```

Because KerasTuner has already helped us encapsulate some functions in the base Oracle class (such as the create_trial function), we can extend the base class and implement only one core function—populate_space()—which conducts hyperparameter sampling and updates the oracle.

Note the Oracle class contains an update_trial() function, which uses the returned value from Tuner.run_trial() to update the oracle. However, it is not required to use this function to update the search method. If the search method needs to be updated based on the historical evaluations, we can take care of this with the populate_space() function before doing hyperparameter sampling. You'll learn how to do this in section 7.3, when implementing a history-dependent search method.

Because the random search method is history-independent, all the populate_space() function needs to do is uniformly random-sample the hyperparameters. We use a private utility method of the base Tuner class, _random_values, to generate random samples from the search space. The output of the populate_space() function should be a dictionary containing the status of the trial and the sampled hyperparameter values of this trial. If the search space is empty or all the hyperparameters are fixed, we should set the trial status to STOPPED to end this trial.

Listing 7.2 shows how the random search oracle is implemented. Though it's negligible, we include the initialization function here for reference. You may use some hyperparameters to help control the search algorithm, such as the random seed, so you can add attributes for these hyperparameters. It is worth pointing out that the hyperparameters of the search method are not contained in the search space, and we need to tune these ourselves. They're considered *hyper-hyperparameters*, which are the hyperparameters used to control the hyperparameter tuning process. We will see some examples in the following sections.

Listing 7.2 The random search oracle

```
class RandomSearchOracle(Oracle):

    def __init__(self, *args, **kwargs):        ⟵┘ The initialization
        super().__init__(*args, **kwargs)          function of the oracle

    def populate_space(self, trial_id):            Randomly sampled
        values = self._random_values()   ⟵┘       hyperparameter values
        if values is None:                          from the search space
            return {'status': <4> trial_lib.TrialStatus.STOPPED,
                    'values': None}
        return {'status': trial_lib.TrialStatus.RUNNING,   ⟵─┐
                'values': values}
```

Checks whether the sampled hyperparameter values are valid

Returns the selected hyperparameter values and the correct trial status

Listing 7.3 shows how we can apply the random search oracle to tune a gradient-boosted decision tree (GBDT) model implemented with the LightGBM library to address the California housing price-prediction task. A GBDT model builds up multiple trees sequentially and orients each newly constructed tree to address the erroneous classifications or weak predictions of the previous tree ensemble. More details can be found in appendix B, if you're not familiar with this model. The code for loading the dataset and implementing the tuner is the same as in the previous chapter, so we won't show that again. Here, we tune three hyperparameters of the GBDT model: the number of leaves in each tree, the number of trees (n_estimators), and the learning rate. After searching for 100 trials, the best discovered model achieves an MSE of 0.2204 on the test set.

Listing 7.3   Using the customized random search oracle to tune a GBDT model

```
def build_model(hp):
    model = lgb.LGBMRegressor(
        boosting_type='gbdt',
        num_leaves=hp.Int('num_leaves', 5, 50, step=1),
        learning_rate=hp.Float(
            'learning_rate', 1e-3, 1, sampling='log', default=0.01),
        n_estimators=hp.Int('n_estimators', 5, 50, step=1)
    )

    return model

>>> random_tuner = LightGBMTuner(
...     oracle=RandomSearchOracle(          ◁———  Provides the customized random search oracle to the tuner
...         objective=kt.Objective('mse', 'min'),
...         max_trials=100,
...         seed=42),
...     hypermodel=build_model,
...     overwrite=True,
...     project_name='random_tuner')

>>> random_tuner.search(X_train, y_train, validation_data=(X_val, y_val))

>>> from sklearn.metrics import mean_squared_error         Retrieves and
>>> best_model = random_tuner.get_best_models(1)[0]        evaluates the best
>>> y_pred_test = best_model.predict(X_test)               discovered model
>>> test_mse = mean_squared_error(y_test, y_pred_test)
>>> print(f'The prediction MSE on test set: {test_mse} ')

The prediction MSE on test set: 0.22039670222190072
```

To show what the search process looks like, we extract the evaluation performance of all the searched models and plot them in order. The models are recorded in the order the trials finished as a list in the end_order attribute of the oracle, which is random_tuner.oracle.end_order in our example. The finishing order of the trials is the same as the starting order because we're not doing parallel trials in this case. Code for plotting the search curve is shown in listing 7.4.

Listing 7.4   Plotting the search process

```
import matplotlib.pyplot as plt

def plot_curve(x, y, xlabel, ylabel, title):
    plt.plot(x, y)
    plt.xlabel(xlabel)
    plt.ylabel(ylabel)
    plt.title(title)
    plt.show()

mse = [random_tuner.oracle.get_trial(trial_id).score for trial_id
➥ in random_tuner.oracle.end_order]
ids = list(range(len(mse)))
plot_curve(ids, mse, 'Trials in finishing order',
    'Validation MSE', 'Searched results')
```

In figure 7.2, we can see that the evaluation results of models discovered during the random search process fluctuate considerably. Because the random search cannot take historical evaluations into account, the models discovered later do not benefit from previous results and do not tend to be better than the earlier ones.

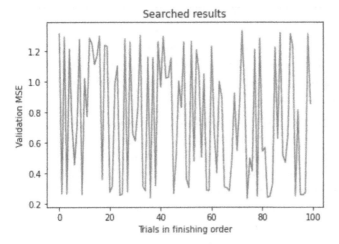

Figure 7.2   The model evaluation results during the random search process

In the next section, we will introduce a history-dependent sequential search method that can leverage the historical evaluations to boost search efficiency.

7.3   *Customizing a Bayesian optimization search method*

In this section, we introduce a model-based sequential search method called *Bayesian optimization*. It was designed to optimize *black-box functions*, which are functions that do not have the analytical form of solutions. This is frequently the case in the context of AutoML, where the function to be optimized is the model evaluation performance. Black-box functions are often expensive to evaluate, making it impractical to find the global optimal solution via brute-force random sampling and evaluation. Due to the cost of model training and evaluation, it may not be possible to conduct numerous hyperparameter search trials. The key idea of the Bayesian optimization method for solving this challenge is correlated with the following two functions:

- We train a function (or model) called the *surrogate function* (or *surrogate model*) to approximate the model evaluation performance. Statistically, this surrogate function is a probability model that approximates the objective function. We estimate its prior distribution ourselves, based on our belief of what we think the objective function will look like (e.g., later we'll use the Gaussian process prior, which is the most commonly used prior). The surrogate model is trained with the historical evaluations of the ML models and serves as a much cheaper way to get the performance of previously unseen models, albeit approximated. This process is very similar to solving regression tasks, in which each model is an instance. The hyperparameters are the features of the instances, and the model performance is the target. Theoretically, with a good enough surrogate model, we wouldn't have to conduct real training and evaluations of the ML models. But because we have only limited training data (the model evaluations), this is often practically impossible in an AutoML problem.
- Once we have a surrogate model, we can sample a new hyperparameter combination to create a model for evaluation. To proceed with the sampling, we need to design another function, called the *acquisition function*, based on the surrogate function. This function specifies the criteria for comparing the ML models (determined by the hyperparameters) so that we can pick the most promising one to train and evaluate.

As you can see, the two functions correspond to the two steps in the search loop of the sequential AutoML process. In the update step, we train the surrogate model based on the historical evaluations. In the sampling step, we use the acquisition function to sample the next model to be evaluated. Iterating the two steps will provide us with additional historical samples to help train a more accurate surrogate model. In the remainder of this section, we will provide a step-by-step implementation of a Bayesian optimization search method. Along the way, you will learn the following:

- How to vectorize hyperparameters for training the surrogate model
- The kind of surrogate model you should select
- How to initialize the process for training the initial surrogate model
- How to design an acquisition function and sample the hyperparameters to be evaluated based on it

7.3.1 *Vectorizing the hyperparameters*

Because a Bayesian optimization search method, like other model-based search methods, trains a model based on the visited samples, a natural question is how to convert the hyperparameters into model-acceptable features. The most common way to do this is to encode the hyperparameters selected in each trial as a numerical vector, representing the features of an ML pipeline chosen in this trial. An inverse conversion will be applied to decode a vector selected in the sampling step into the original hyperparameters for instantiating an ML pipeline.

Let's first implement the function for vectorizing the hyperparameters. We'll make this a private method of the `Oracle` class named `_vectorize_trials`. The key idea is to extract all the hyperparameters one by one and concatenate them into a vector. During the search process, all the trials are saved in a dictionary attribute of the `Oracle` class named `self.trials`. The values and keys represent the `trial` objects and their unique IDs, respectively. The hyperparameters are saved in an attribute of the `trial` object (`trial.hyperparameters`). This is a hyperparameter container that contains the selected hyperparameters of the trial as well as the whole search space structure. We can retrieve the selected hyperparameters in each trial into a dictionary using `trial.hyperparameters.values`. Then, converting the hyperparameters selected in a trial becomes a matter of converting the values of a dictionary into a vector. If all our hyperparameter values are originally numerical, such as learning rate, number of units, and number of layers, we can directly concatenate them one by one. However, you need to pay attention to the following issues:

- *Handling hyperparameters with fixed values*—Because these hyperparameters do not affect the comparison between models, we can explicitly remove them so that the search method will not consider them. This can reduce the burden on the search method and avoid introducing extra noise into the update of the search method.

- *Dealing with inactive conditional hyperparameters*—Some conditional hyperparameters may not be selected in every trial. For example, suppose we have a hyperparameter called `'model_type'` to select between MLPs and CNNs. The hyperparameters of a CNN, such as the number of filters, will not be selected and used if the model selected for a trial is an MLP. This will cause the converted vectors to be of different lengths, so the elements in the same position in two vectors may not correspond to the same hyperparameter. A naive way of solving this problem is to use the default values of any inactive (not selected) hyperparameters in the vector. The hyperparameter container provides a method called `is_active()` to check whether a hyperparameter has been selected. You can append the selected value of the hyperparameter if it's active or extract the default value saved in `hyperparameters.default` and append that instead if it isn't.

- *Dealing with hyperparameters with different scales*—Hyperparameters are often on different scales. For example, the learning rate is often smaller than 1, and the number of trees in a GBDT model could be larger than 100. To normalize the hyperparameters, we can use the cumulative probability to transform them to values between 0 and 1. Figure 7.3 shows two examples for converting the discrete search spacc and the continuous search space into the corresponding

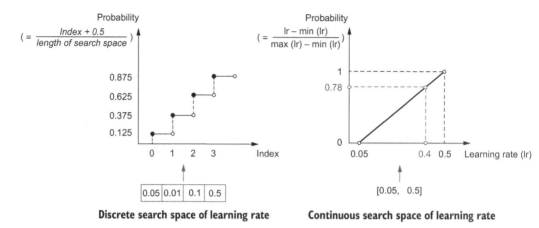

Figure 7.3   **Normalizing hyperparameter values based on cumulative probabilities**

cumulative distributions. For the continuous search space, we directly map it into the intervals of 0 and 1. It will apply a log transformation if the hyperparameter is sampled in the logarithmic scale. For the discrete search space, we assume each value is uniformly distributed, and the probability unit will be equally bucketized based on the number of value choices in the space. We use the center value in each probability bucket to represent each value choice.

- *Dealing with categorical hyperparameters such as the model type*—To convert categorical hyperparameters to numerical features, we can use the index of the features in the list. For example, if we have four models to be selected, [MLP, CNN, RNN, GBDT], the list can be converted to [0, 1, 2, 3], where the models are represented by 0, 1, 2, and 3, respectively. The vector is then further normalized into 0 and 1 based on the mechanism for converting the discrete search space into the cumulative probabilities.

The code in listing 7.5 describes the details of the vectorization process. We loop through all the existing trials to convert all the hyperparameters into feature vectors and the evaluation score of the corresponding model into one response vector. For each trial, we ignore the fixed hyperparameters and loop through the rest. If a hyperparameter is detected as active (used in the pipeline selected in the current trial), we will directly use the value selected by the search method. Otherwise, the default value is used to pad the vector to the same length as the others. Values in the vector are further substituted by the cumulative probabilities for normalization purposes. If a trial is completed, the evaluation result is appended in the response vector y. Because for some metrics, smaller values are better (such as the MSE), and for others, larger values are better (such as classification accuracy), we unify them such that larger values are better in all cases by multiplying the values of the first type of metric by −1.

Listing 7.5   The private method to encode the hyperparameters as vectors

```
from keras_tuner.engine import hyperparameters as hp_module

class BayesianOptimizationOracle(oracle_module.Oracle):
    def _vectorize_trials(self):
        x, y = [], []
        for trial in self.trials.values():
            trial_hps = trial.hyperparameters
            vector = []
            nonfixed_hp_space = [hp for hp in self.hyperparameters.space
                if not isinstance(hp, hp_module.Fixed)]
            for hp in nonfixed_hp_space:
                if trial_hps.is_active(hp):
                    trial_value = trial_hps.values[hp.name]
                else:
                    trial_value = hp.default
                prob = hp_module.value_to_cumulative_prob(trial_value, hp)
                vector.append(prob)

            if trial.status == 'COMPLETED':
                score = trial.score
                if self.objective.direction == 'min':
                    score = -1 * score
            else:
                continue

            x.append(vector)
            y.append(score)

        x = np.array(x)
        y = np.array(y)
        return x, y
```

Annotations:
- **Loops through all the trials** → `for trial in self.trials.values():`
- **Records the hyperparameters that are not fixed** → `nonfixed_hp_space = [hp for hp in self.hyperparameters.space if not isinstance(hp, hp_module.Fixed)]`
- **Detects if a hyperparameter is selected in the current trial** → `if trial_hps.is_active(hp):`
- **Uses the default value for the unused hyperparameter** → `trial_value = hp.default`
- **Unifies the evaluation score so that larger values are always better** → `score = -1 * score`

Once we have a new set of hyperparameters represented in a vector format sampled based on the acquisition function, which will be introduced later, we need to feed the vector into the hyperparameter container as the values. The inverse transformation is straightforward and involves the following steps:

1 Convert the cumulative probabilities in the vector to the real values of each hyperparameter.

2 Feed the values of each hyperparameter into the hyperparameter container.

By looping through all the hyperparameters in the search space, we convert each value in the vector in order using these two steps. For each fixed hyperparameter, the default value (`hp.value` in the following listing) is put into the container. All the values are saved in a dictionary of the hyperparameter container (`hps.values`) and returned to help create the next trial. The implementation of the inverse transformation function is introduced in listing 7.6. We will use this in the `populate_space()` function to help convert the vectors selected by the acquisition function.

Listing 7.6   The private method to decode vectors into hyperparameters

```
class BayesianOptimizationOracle(oracle_module.Oracle):
    def _vector_to_values(self, vector):
        hps = hp_module.HyperParameters()
        vector_index = 0
        for hp in self.hyperparameters.space:
            hps.merge([hp])
            if isinstance(hp, hp_module.Fixed):
                value = hp.value
            else:
                prob = vector[vector_index]
                vector_index += 1
                value = hp_module.
cumulative_prob_to_value(prob, hp)

            if hps.is_active(hp):
                hps.values[hp.name] = value
        return hps.values
```

Creates an empty hyperparameter container

Merges the hyperparameter into the container

Uses the default value if the hyperparameter is fixed

Converts the cumulative probability back to the hyperparameter value

Puts the original value of the hyperparameter into the container

The encoding of hyperparameters should match the surrogate model adopted in the search method. We'll use the Gaussian process as our surrogate model in the next stage, which takes vector inputs, so we adopt the vector representation here.

NOTE   Some recent work in the research community instead represents the hyperparameters as trees or graphs, where each node in the tree or graph represents a hyperparameter, and its leaves denote its conditional hyperparameters. These structures are good at representing the conditional hierarchy among the hyperparameters, and we can use some advanced tree-based or graph-based search methods to directly traverse the trees or graphs for sampling new combinations of hyperparameters. You can find more of them in the survey paper "Techniques for Automated Machine Learning," by Yi-Wei Chen et al. (ACM SIGKDD Explorations Newsletter, 2020).

7.3.2   Updating the surrogate function based on historical model evaluations

In the context of AutoML, before it's given any data, the surrogate function is only a prior denoting our subjective belief of what we think the real hyperparameter evaluation function will look like. For example, a common selection is a Gaussian process prior, shown in figure 7.4(a), which can be understood as a distribution function composed of infinitely many Gaussian random variables depicting the evaluation performance of all the models in our search space. The Gaussian process is fully specified by a mean function and a covariance function of all the Gaussian variables. The curve in the middle is the mean function presenting the mean values of all the Gaussian random variables, which we can denote by $\mu(x)$. x denotes vectorized hyperparameters in AutoML (here, we have only one hyperparameter for illustrative purposes). The gray ranges indicate the standard deviation (STD) of the Gaussian variables, which can be

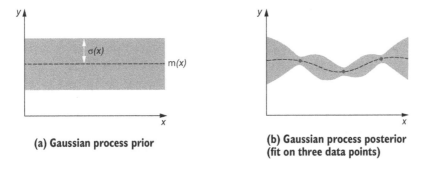

(a) Gaussian process prior

(b) Gaussian process posterior
(fit on three data points)

Figure 7.4   The update of the Gaussian process surrogate model

denoted by $\sigma(x)$. In this case, each longitudinal section represents a Gaussian distribution. The mean value approximates the evaluation performance of an ML pipeline given the selected hyperparameters, x. The variance (or STD) indicates the uncertainty of the approximation. Because the variables have correlations, to fully describe the Gaussian process we need to define a covariance function, $\kappa(x, x')$ (often called the *kernel function*), to model the covariance between any two of the Gaussian variables, specifically, $\kappa(x, x) = (\sigma(x))^2$. The covariance between variables is quite important to help predict the distribution given unseen hyperparameters. For example, if all the variables are independent, it means there are no conditional correlations in the performance of any two ML pipelines given their hyperparameters.

In this case, the noise we have is white noise (corresponding to the *white kernel* in the Gaussian process). The only way to measure the performance of the ML pipelines is to evaluate them one by one on the real data, and the noise of each model is estimated by evaluating it multiple times. This is often not what we want because we expect to reduce the number of model evaluations, and it is often not the case in practice because similar hyperparameter settings tend to generate ML pipelines that have closer performance. As more and more data is collected (models are evaluated), the predicted mean function will pass through the new points, and the uncertainty (STD) will decrease, as shown in figure 7.4(b).

The selection of the kernel function depends on our assumption of the smoothness of the objective function. It is a hyper-hyperparameter that is not included in the search space and should be manually selected or tuned. A common kernel selection is the *Matérn kernel*. It has a parameter (ν) to set the degree of smoothness of the function. We often set ν to 0.5, 1.5, or 2.5, corresponding to our assumption that the function should be one, two, or three times differentiable, respectively. When ν approaches infinity, the Matérn kernel becomes closer to a kernel called the *squared exponential kernel* (also known as the *RBF kernel*, which you may recall from the SVM model in the previous chapter), reflecting that the objective function is infinitely differentiable. There are also some kernels for modeling periodic functions, such as the *Exp-Sine-Squared kernel*. You can learn more about different kernels in the book

Gaussian Processes for Machine Learning by Carl Edward Rasmussen and Christopher K. I. Williams (MIT Press, 2006).

To implement a Gaussian process model for Bayesian optimization, we can use the gaussian_process module in the scikit-learn library. When initializing the oracle, we can create a Gaussian process model with the Matérn kernel. The alpha parameter is used to specify the amount of random noise introduced during the evaluation of the models. We often set it to be a small number, and empirically, this is enough and good for taking environmental noise into account. We implement the initial training and sequential update of the Gaussian process model in the populate_space() function. The Gaussian process model is updated once we have the evaluation of the new models searched in each round. In the beginning, we randomly sample several models for evaluation, then conduct the initial training of the Gaussian process model. The number of random samples is defined as two, if not provided in the num_initial_points attribute, to make sure the kernel function can feasibly be applied. (Empirically, the square root of the number of hyperparameters in the search space is a good number of random points to use to initialize the Gaussian process model.)

Once we have enough random samples, we vectorize the hyperparameters and the evaluations and fit the Gaussian process model by calling the fit() function, as shown in listing 7.7. Later, whenever a new model is evaluated during the sequential search process, we will fit the model again based on all the completed trials. Here we describe only the update of the Gaussian process model and do not show the sampling process based on the acquisition function. You'll see the full implementation of the populate_space() function in the next step.

> **Listing 7.7   Creating and updating the Gaussian process model in the oracle**

```
from sklearn import exceptions
from sklearn import gaussian_process

class BayesianOptimizationOracle(oracle_module.Oracle):
    def __init__(self,
                 objective,
                 max_trials,
                 num_initial_points=None,
                 seed=None,
                 hyperparameters=None,
                 *args, **kwargs):
        super(BayesianOptimizationOracle, self).__init__(
            objective=objective,
            max_trials=max_trials,
            hyperparameters=hyperparameters,
            seed=seed,
            *args, **kwargs)
        self.num_initial_points = num_initial_points
            or 2
        self.seed = seed or random.randint(1, 1e4)
        self.gpr = self._make_gpr()
```

Uses 2 as the initial number of random points if not specified ⟶

Initializes the Gaussian process model ←

```
def _make_gpr(self):
    return gaussian_process.GaussianProcessRegressor(
        kernel=gaussian_process.kernels.Matern(nu=2.5),
        alpha=1e-4,
        normalize_y=True,
        random_state=self.seed)


def populate_space(self, trial_id):

    if self._num_completed_trials() < self.num_initial_points:
        return self._random_populate_space()

    x, y = self._vectorize_trials()
    try:
        self.gpr.fit(x, y)
    except exceptions.ConvergenceWarning:
        raise e
```

Vectorizes all the trials → `x, y = self._vectorize_trials()`

Conducts random sampling for initializing the Gaussian process model → `return self._random_populate_space()`

Fits the Gaussian process model based on the completed trials → `self.gpr.fit(x, y)`

The complexity for fitting n data points would be $O(n^3)$, which is quite time-consuming. This is the major drawback of the Gaussian process for the model-based search method. Different methods use other surrogate models, such as tree-based models (e.g., random forests) and neural networks, to overcome this. You can learn more about surrogate models used for Bayesian optimization in AutoML from the book *Automated Machine Learning: Methods, Systems, Challenges* by Frank Hutter, Lars Kotthoff, and Joaquin Vanschoren (Springer Nature, 2019).

7.3.3   *Designing the acquisition function*

Once we have a surrogate model, we need an acquisition function to help sample the next ML pipeline for evaluation and create a closed sequential search loop. Let's first introduce the design criteria of an acquisition function and then discuss how to sample a point based on that function.

DESIGN CRITERIA OF AN ACQUISITION FUNCTION

A good acquisition function should measure how desirable a point is for sampling. Desirability is a tradeoff between two aspects: *exploitation* and *exploration*. Exploitation means we want to discover the points that the surrogate model predicts to be good. This would take into account the promising regions we have already explored but lack the power of exploring unknown regions. For example, in figure 7.5, suppose our real objective function curve is $f(x)$, and given five points, we fit a Gaussian process with mean function $\mu(x)$ running through three of the points. The region around the hyperparameter x_a has been explored more than the region around point x_b, leading the STD around x_b to be much larger than the one around x_a. If we consider only the predicted mean function, which takes full advantage of the exploitation power, x_a is better than x_b. However, x_a is worse than x_b on the objective function. This requires an acquisition function to balance both exploitation (mean) and exploration (variance).

Let's now look at three commonly used acquisition functions and their implementations.

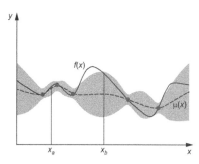

Figure 7.5   Updating the Gaussian process surrogate model

UPPER CONFIDENCE BOUND

Assuming larger values for y are better, the *upper confidence bound* (UCB) balances exploitation and exploration in a straightforward way by adding the mean and STD functions together: $UCB(x) = \mu(x) + \beta\sigma(x)$, where β is a user-specified positive parameter for balancing the tradeoff between the two terms. As shown in figure 7.6, the curve $g(x)$ is the UCB acquisition function when $\beta = 1$. If smaller values are preferable, we can use $UCB(x) = \mu(x) - \beta\sigma(x)$.

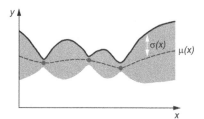

Figure 7.6   Upper confidence bound

Example code for implementing the function is shown in the following listing. Here, self.gpr denotes the fitted Gaussian process regressor, and x denotes the vectorized hyperparameters of an ML pipeline.

Listing 7.8   Calculating the upper confidence bound

```
def upper_confidence_bound(x):
    x = x.reshape(1, -1)
    mu, sigma = self.gpr.predict(x, return_std=True)
    return mu + self.beta * sigma
```

PROBABILITY OF IMPROVEMENT

Probability of improvement (PI) measures the probability of a sample achieving better performance than the best sample found so far. As shown in figure 7.7, given the best point, $x^\star$, and the corresponding objective value, $y^\star$, the probability that the point x would achieve better performance than $x^\star$ equals the shaded region of the Gaussian distribution defined by $\mu(x)$ and $\sigma(x)$. We can calculate this with the help of the cumulative distribution function of the normal distribution.

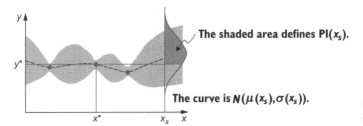

The shaded area defines PI(x_s).

The curve is $N(\mu(x_s), \sigma(x_s))$.

Figure 7.7   Probability of improvement

The code implementation of PI is shown in listing 7.9. We can directly use the evaluation objective if we assume no environmental noise will exist, or we can set a noise value (alpha!=0 when creating the regressor with scikit-learn) and select the best point using the predicted value given by the noise-based Gaussian process regressor. A problem with PI is that it tends to query the points that are close to the ones we've already evaluated, especially the best point, leading to a high tendency of exploitation and low exploration power of underexplored regions.

Listing 7.9   Calculating the probability of improvement

```
def _probability_of_improvement(x):
    x_history, _ = self._vectorize_trials()
    y_pred = self.gpr.predict(
        x_history, return_std=False)
    y_best = max(yhat)
    mu, sigma = self.gpr.predict(x, return_std=True)
    z = (mu - y_best) / (sigma+1E-9)
    prob = norm.cdf(z)
    return prob
```

Vectorizes all the trials →

Calculates the best surrogate score found so far ←

Calculates mean and standard deviation via surrogate function ←

Calculates the probability of improvement

EXPECTED IMPROVEMENT

Expected improvement (EI) mitigates the problem of PI by weighting the calculation of the probability of improvement using the magnitude of improvement (see figure 7.8). This is equivalent to calculating the expectation of the improvement over the optimal value found so far: $EI(x) = \mathbb{E}\,max(\mu(x) - y^\star, 0)$.

Listing 7.10 provides an explicit equation to calculate EI leveraging the probability density function (norm.pdf) and cumulative distribution function (norm.pdf) of the

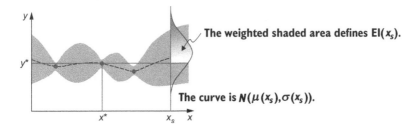

The weighted shaded area defines EI(x_s).

The curve is $N(\mu(x_s), \sigma(x_s))$.

Figure 7.8   Expected improvement of a point

normal distribution. The detailed derivation of the equation can be found in the paper "Efficient Global Optimization of Expensive Black-Box Functions," by Donald R. Jones, Matthias Schonlau, and William J. Welch (http://mng.bz/5KlO).

Listing 7.10   Calculating the expected improvement

```
def _expected_improvement(x):
    x_history, _ = self._vectorize_trials()
    y_pred = self.gpr.predict(x_history, return_std=False)
    y_best = max(yhat)
    mu, sigma = self.gpr.predict(x, return_std=True)
    z = (mu - y_best) / (sigma+1E-9)
    ei = (mu - y_best) * norm.cdf(z) + sigma * norm.pdf(z)
    return ei
```

To enhance the exploration power of PI and EI, we can also add a positive parameter to the optimal objective value: $(y^\star + \theta)$. A larger value for the parameter θ will lead to a greater amount of exploration. In practice, UCB and EI are the most commonly used types of acquisition functions in existing AutoML libraries. UCB is comparably more straightforward in balancing exploration and exploitation.

7.3.4   *Sampling the new hyperparameters via the acquisition function*

Now that you know how to create an acquisition function, it is time to leverage the function to sample the hyperparameter values evaluated in the next trial. The goal is to find the hyperparameter vector that achieves the maximum value of the acquisition function. This is a constraint optimization problem, because each hyperparameter is bounded by the defined search space. A popular optimization method for minimizing functions with bound constraints is the *L-BFGS-B algorithm*.

> **NOTE** BFGS is an optimization algorithm that starts with an initial vector and iteratively refines it toward the local optimum based on an estimate of the inverse Hessian matrix. We can optimize multiple times with different initialization vectors to achieve a better local optimum. L-BFGS optimizes it with approximation so that the amount of memory used during the optimization can be limited. L-BFGS-B further extends the algorithm to handle bounding box constraints of the search space. More details can be found in the article by D. C. Liu and J. Nocedal, "On the Limited Memory Method for Large Scale Optimization," *Mathematical Programming* 45, no. 3 (1989): 503–528 (doi:10.1007/BF01589116).

The method is implemented with the `optimize` module in the `scipy` Python toolkit, as shown in listing 7.11. We first implement a function called `get_hp_bounds()` to collect the bounds of the hyperparameters. Because we've normalized the hyperparameters based on the cumulative probabilities, the bounds are set to be 0 to 1 for each hyperparameter. We optimize the acquisition function 50 times with 50 different initialization vectors uniformly generated in the x_seeds. The optimization is done in a continuous vector space, and the optimal vector can be transformed back to the original hyperparameter values using the function self._vector_to_values defined in the Oracle base class.

Listing 7.11 Sample based on the UCB acquisition function

```python
from scipy import optimize as scipy_optimize

class BayesianOptimizationOracle(oracle_module.Oracle):
    def __init__(self,
                 objective,
                 max_trials,
                 beta=2.6,
                 num_initial_points=None,
                 seed=None,
                 hyperparameters=None,
                 *args, **kwargs):
        super(BayesianOptimizationOracle, self).__init__(
            objective=objective,
            max_trials=max_trials,
            hyperparameters=hyperparameters,
            seed=seed,
            *args, **kwargs)

        self.num_initial_points = num_initial_points or 2
        self.beta = beta
        self.seed = seed or random.randint(1, 1e4)
        self._random_state = np.random.RandomState(self.seed)
        self.gpr = self._make_gpr()

    def _make_gpr(self):
        return gaussian_process.GaussianProcessRegressor(
            kernel=gaussian_process.kernels.Matern(nu=2.5),
            alpha=1e-4,
            normalize_y=True,
            random_state=self.seed)

    def _get_hp_bounds(self):
        nonfixed_hp_space = [hp for hp in self.hyperparameters.space
            if not isinstance(hp, hp_module.Fixed)]
        bounds = []
        for hp in nonfixed_hp_space:
            bounds.append([0, 1])            # Appends the
        return np.array(bounds)              # normalized bound
                                             # for a hyperparameter

    def populate_space(self, trial_id):

        if self._num_completed_trials() < self.num_initial_points:
            return self._random_populate_space()   # Does random search
                                                    # for training the initial
        x, y = self._vectorize_trials()             # Gaussian process
        try:                                        # regressor
            self.gpr.fit(x, y)
        except exceptions.ConvergenceWarning:
            raise e
```

```
def _upper_confidence_bound(x):
    x = x.reshape(1, -1)
    mu, sigma = self.gpr.predict(x, return_std=True)
    return -1 * (mu + self.beta * sigma)
```
> The sign of the UCB score is flipped for minimization purposes.

```
optimal_val = float('inf')
optimal_x = None
num_restarts = 50
bounds = self._get_hp_bounds()
x_seeds = self._random_state.uniform(bounds[:, 0], bounds[:, 1],
                           size=(num_restarts, bounds.shape[0]))
for x_try in x_seeds:
    result = scipy_optimize.minimize(_upper_confidence_bound,
                          x0=x_try,
                          bounds=bounds,
                          method='L-BFGS-B')
    if result.fun[0] < optimal_val:
        optimal_val = result.fun[0]
        optimal_x = result.x

values = self._vector_to_values(optimal_x)
return {'status': trial_lib.TrialStatus.RUNNING,
        'values': values}
```

Uniformly generates 50 random vectors within the boundaries

Minimizes the flipped acquisition function

Maps the optimal vector to the original hyperparameter values

By combining the vectorization function, the sampling function, and the function for creating the Gaussian process regressor, we can create a complete Bayesian optimization oracle for conducting AutoML tasks. Next, we'll use it to tune the GBDT model for the housing price-prediction task.

7.3.5   *Tuning the GBDT model with the Bayesian optimization method*

We load and split the data the same way we did in the random search section and use the customized tuner for tuning the GBDT model. The only difference is that we change the random search oracle to the Bayesian optimization oracle, as shown in the following listing. The best model achieves an MSE of 0.2202 on the final test set.

Listing 7.12   Sampling based on the UCB acquisition function

```
>>> bo_tuner = LightGBMTuner(
...     oracle=BayesianOptimizationOracle(
...         objective=kt.Objective('mse', 'min'),
...         max_trials=100,
...         seed=42),
...     hypermodel=build_model,
...     overwrite=True,
...     project_name='bo_tuner')
```
> **Uses the customized Bayesian optimization search oracle**

```
>>> bo_tuner.search(X_train, y_train, validation_data=(X_val, y_val))

>>> from sklearn.metrics import mean_squared_error
>>> best_model = bo_tuner.get_best_models(1)[0]
>>> y_pred_test = best_model.predict(X_test)
```

```
>>> test_mse = mean_squared_error(y_test, y_pred_test)
>>> print('The prediction MSE on test set: {}'.format(test_mse))

The prediction MSE on test set: 0.2181461078854755
```

Let's compare the results of Bayesian optimization search with random search to understand the two methods better. We extract the evaluation performance of all the models discovered in order. Figure 7.9(a) directly displays the MSE of the discovered models evaluated on the validation set during the search process. Unlike with the random search method, the performance of models searched by Bayesian optimization gradually stabilizes as the search process continues. This is because Bayesian optimization takes the historical information into account and can leverage exploitation for searching, so the models discovered later are likely to achieve comparable or even better performance than the ones discovered earlier. Figure 7.9(b) plots the performance of the best model found so far as the search process proceeds. We can see that the random search performs a bit better at the beginning but becomes worse in the later stages. This is because random search can provide a better exploration of the search space than Bayesian optimization search at the beginning, but as the amount of historical data collected increases, that information can be exploited to benefit the search process.

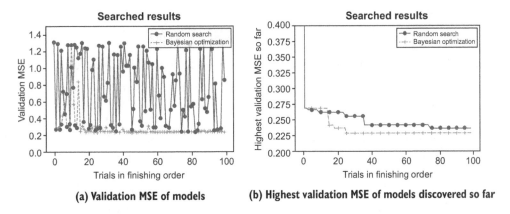

(a) Validation MSE of models   (b) Highest validation MSE of models discovered so far

Figure 7.9 Comparing the results of Bayesian optimization and random search

Although the Bayesian optimization method outperforms random search in this example, this is not always the case in practice, especially when the search space is small and there are a lot of categorical and conditional hyperparameters. We should select and tune different search methods, taking into account the size of the search space, the number of search iterations, and the time and resource constraints (the vanilla Bayesian optimization method runs much slower than random search, as you may have experienced). If no specific constraints are specified, Bayesian optimization search is a good place to start.

In addition to the increased complexity, another problem that you may face when applying Bayesian optimization is the local optimum issue. Though we've tried to explore multiple initialization points when optimizing the acquisition function for sampling, it is still likely to always sample from a local region if the surrogate model is not fit well based on the historical samples or if the acquisition function favors exploitation too much. Doing this will lead to concentrated exploitation of a local region while ignoring exploring other areas if the evaluation performance surface is not convex. Besides increasing the exploration preference of the acquisition function, such as by reducing the β parameter in the UCB acquisition function, we have the following two commonly used tricks to prevent Bayesian optimization from converging to a local optimum:

- Conduct Bayesian optimization search multiple times, and use different random seeds to sample different random points to fit the initial surrogate model.
- Combine Bayesian optimization and random search in a dynamic way: conduct a random search iteration after every several iterations (say, five) of Bayesian optimization search, alternating the two.

In addition, if the number of search iterations is large and you have the time, it's a good habit to use cross-validation for each discovered model rather than to simply evaluate each model on a fixed validation set. This can help prevent the search method from overfitting on the validation set and is often practically useful for any search algorithm.

7.3.6   *Resuming the search process and recovering the search method*

Because the AutoML process is often quite long and may be unexpectedly interrupted, we can add two auxiliary functions to help resume the search process and recover the oracle (see listing 7.13). The base `Oracle` class of KerasTuner provides two functions that can be extended to memorize and reload the historical trials and metadata to recover the oracle. First, we can extend the `get_state()` function, which memorizes the state of the historical trials and parameters of the oracle during the search process. This function will be called in every search loop to save the current state of the trials and the oracle. To implement it, we first need to call the `get_state()` function of the base class to get the state dictionary of the current trial, then update it with the unique hyperparameters of the search method. For example, we can save the random seeds, the number of random initialization trials, and the exploitation-exploration tradeoff parameter in the UCB acquisition function in the state object. Second, to reload the state of the oracle, we can extend the `set_state()` function. The function will access the previous state reloaded from the disk and retrieve information on all the historical trials and the oracle's parameters. For example, in a Bayesian optimization oracle, we can call the `set_state()` function to retrieve all the model evaluation information and recover the attributes of the oracle one by one using the loaded state dictionary.

Listing 7.13   Resuming the oracle

```
class BayesianOptimizationOracle(oracle_module.Oracle):

    def get_state(self):
        state = super().get_state()
        state.update({
            'num_initial_points': self.num_initial_points,
            'beta': self.beta,
            'seed': self.seed,
        })
        return state

    def set_state(self, state):
        super().set_state(state)
        self.num_initial_points = state[
    'num_initial_points']
        self.beta = state['beta']
        self.seed = state['seed']
        self._random_state = np.random.RandomState(
            self.seed)
        self.gpr = self._make_gpr()
```

Saves the oracle-specific configurations in the state →

Reloads the historical state ←

Resumes the Bayesian optimization oracle

When resuming the search process, we can initialize the tuner with the name of the project we want it to resume from and conduct the search in the same way as before. The only difference is that we set the `overwrite` argument to `False` during the initialization so that the tuner will automatically resume the search process if there is an existing project with the same name (bo_tuner in the following listing) in the working directory. The `set_state()` function we've implemented will then be called to help recover the oracle.

Listing 7.14   Resuming the oracle

```
bo_tuner = LightGBMTuner(
    oracle=BayesianOptimizationOracle(
        objective=kt.Objective('mse', 'min'),
        max_trials=100,
        seed=42),
    hypermodel=build_model,
    overwrite=False,
    project_name='bo_tuner')

bo_tuner.search(X_train, y_train, validation_data=(X_val, y_val))
```

Does not overwrite the project that's named, if it already exists

Provides the project name to resume and/or to save the search process

The next section will introduce another commonly used history-dependent method, which does not require the selection of a surrogate model or acquisition function.

7.4   *Customizing an evolutionary search method*

An *evolutionary search method* is a heuristic search method inspired by biological behaviors. One of the most popular methods that has been used in AutoML is the *population-based* evolutionary search method, which simulates the evolution of a biological population by following these four steps:

1   *Initial population generation*—Randomly generate a set of initial ML pipelines and evaluate them to form the initial population. We should predefine the size of the population before starting.

2   *Parent selection*—Select the fittest pipelines, called parents, for breeding the new child pipeline (offspring) to be evaluated in the next trial.

3   *Crossover and mutation*—These operations can be used to breed new offspring based on the parents. *Crossover* means we swap some of the hyperparameters of two parental pipelines to form two new pipelines. *Mutation* means we randomly change some of the hyperparameters of the parents or the offspring generated from the crossover operation to introduce some variation. This operation imitates the "tweak in the chromosome" of genetic mutation, to enhance the exploration power during the search process. Both the crossover and mutation operations do not have to be carried out. We can use just one of them to generate the new offspring. For example, rather than combining two pipelines, we can select one parent ML pipeline from the population in each trial and mutate one or more of its hyperparameters to generate the next pipeline to be evaluated.

4   *Survivor selection (population regeneration)*—After the new offspring have been evaluated, this step recreates a new population set of ML pipelines by replacing the least-fit pipelines with the new offspring.

Steps 2 to 4 are carried out iteratively during the search process to incorporate the new evaluations, as shown in figure 7.10.

7.4.1   *Selection strategies in the evolutionary search method*

Although the crossover and mutation step determines how we create new offspring from the existing pipelines, the chosen strategies in the two selection steps, parent selection and survivor selection, can be more important in designing a good evolutionary method. The selection steps should balance exploitation and exploration during the search process. Exploitation here represents how intensively we want to select a pipeline with good evaluation performance as the parent. Exploration means introducing more randomness to try out unexplored regions, rather than focusing only on the fittest pipelines. The tradeoff between exploitation and exploration is also called the balance between *selection intensity* and *selection diversity* in the literature of the evolutionary method. Let's look at three popular selection methods.

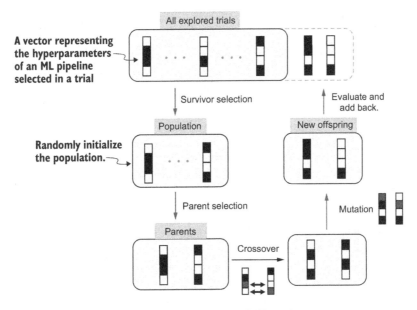

Figure 7.10 Population-based evolutionary search life cycle

PROPORTIONAL SELECTION

In *proportional selection* (or *roulette wheel selection*), we select an individual based on a probability distribution. The probability of selecting an individual is proportional to its fitness. For example, if we want to select an ML pipeline for classification, we can use the accuracy to measure the fitness of each pipeline. The higher the pipeline's accuracy, the larger the probability we should assign to it. A pipeline i could be selected as a parent with probability $\frac{f_i}{\sum_i f_i}$, where f_i denotes the non-negative accuracy of pipeline i, and the denominator sums up the accuracy of all the pipelines in the population. In the survivor selection step, we can use the accuracy summation of all the pipelines explored so far and sample multiple individuals without duplicates to form the population for the next search loop. Although this is a popular method, it suffers from a few problems. Notably, there's a risk of premature convergence because if certain pipelines have a much higher accuracy than others, they will tend to be selected repeatedly.

RANKING SELECTION

Ranking selection adopts a strategy similar to proportional selection but uses the fitness ranks of the pipelines to calculate the probability. For example, suppose we have three pipelines in the population whose accuracies are ranked 1, 2, and 3. We can assign them the probabilities $\frac{1}{2}$, $\frac{1}{3}$, and $\frac{1}{6}$, respectively, to select a parent from them. The design of the probability balances the selection intensity and diversity. The example here is a linear ranking selection strategy, in which the probability is proportional to the rank of the individual. We can also use nonlinear probability to enhance exploitation or exploration. For instance, by assigning a higher proportional probability to the pipelines with higher ranks, we favor exploitation more than exploration during the selection.

Ranking selection often performs better than proportional selection because it avoids the scale issue in proportional selection by mapping all the individuals into a uniform scale. For example, if all pipelines have close accuracy scores, ranking selection will still be able to distinguish them based on their ranks. Also, if an individual pipeline is better than all the rest of the pipelines, no matter how fit it is relative to the others, the probability of it being selected as the parent or survivor will not be changed. This sacrifices some selection intensity compared to proportional search but provides a more robust balance of selection intensity and diversity in general situations.

TOURNAMENT SELECTION

Tournament selection is a two-step selection process. It first randomly selects a certain number of candidates and then picks the best one among them as the parent to conduct crossover and mutation. It can be converted to a special type of ranking selection if we assign 0 probability to the bottom k individuals, where k is the number of candidate individuals to be selected for comparison in the tournament selection. The probability assigned to the rest of the individuals is $\frac{\binom{r_i + k - 1}{k}}{\binom{p+k}{1+k}}$, where r_i denotes the rank of pipeline i among the pipelines, p is the population size, and $\binom{a}{b}$ is the binomial coefficients ($\binom{n}{m} = \frac{n!}{m!(n-m)!}$). By increasing the number of candidates in the tournament selection, we can increase the selection intensity (exploitation) and reduce the selection diversity (exploration) because only the best one among the candidates will be selected as the parent. Considering two extra situations, if the candidate size (k) is 1, it is equivalent to selecting an individual from the population randomly. If the candidate size equals the population size, the selection intensity is maximized, so the best individual in the population will be selected as the parent.

In addition to the model evaluation performance, we can specify other objectives during the selection based on our desire for the optimal model. For example, we can create a function to consider both the accuracy and the complexity measure (such as floating-point operations per second, or FLOPS) of the pipelines and use the function value to assign a probability to each pipeline. For those who are interested in more details and other selection strategies, please refer to the book *Evolutionary Optimization Algorithms* by Dan Simon (Wiley, 2013).

7.4.2   *The aging evolutionary search method*

In this section, we will implement an evolutionary search method called *aging evolutionary search*, proposed by researchers from Google Brain in "Regularized Evolution for Image Classifier Architecture Search" (https://arxiv.org/abs/1802.01548). It was originally proposed for searching for the best neural network architectures but can be generalized to various AutoML tasks. The method uses tournament selection for selecting the parent pipeline from which to breed the pipeline and uses a heuristic aging selection strategy for survivor selection. The "age" of a pipeline (or a trial) means the number of iterations during a search process. When the trial is born (started), we define it as 0. The age becomes N when N more trials are selected and executed afterward. Coupling this with the four core steps of the population-based evolutionary search method, we elaborate the aging evolutionary search method as follows:

1 *Initial population generation*—Randomly sample a set of ML pipelines and evaluate them to form the initial population.

2 *Parent selection*—In each search iteration, a parent is selected from the population based on the tournament selection method.

3 *Mutation*—Randomly select a hyperparameter of the parent, and randomly change its value to a different one. If the generated offspring has been explored before, we will treat it as a collision and will retry the mutation step until a valid offspring is selected or the maximum number of collisions has been reached. We use a hashing string to represent the hyperparameters in a trial to check whether an offspring has been explored already.

4 *Survivor selection*—After a new offspring is generated, we keep the latest sampled trials as the new population. For example, suppose our population size is 100. When trial 101 is finished, the first (oldest) trial will be removed from the population, and the new (youngest) trial will be added to it. This is why the method is called the *aging* evolutionary method. Selecting the latest trials as survivors should enhance the exploitation power, because we assume the older ones will have performed worse than the latest ones.

The process is visualized in figure 7.11. We can see that the crossover operation is not used in this method; only the mutation operation is used to generate the new offspring.

We need to predefine two main hyper-hyperparameters to control the algorithm: the population size and the candidate size for the tournament selection strategy. They

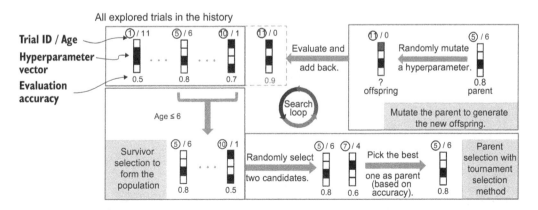

Figure 7.11 The aging evolutionary search life cycle

help balance exploration and exploitation. If we use a large population size, more old trials would be kept as a survivor and might be selected as the parent to breed the offspring. This will increase the exploration power because older trials are often worse than the younger ones, and the diversity in the population would be increased. If we select the larger candidate size, the selection intensity would be increased, as we've mentioned earlier, which increases the exploitation power of the method.

Listing 7.15 shows how the aging evolutionary oracle is implemented. We create a list to save the IDs of the population trials. The number of random initialization trials should be larger than the population size so that the population list can be filled. Look at the core function, `populate_space()`. In the beginning, trials are randomly sampled to form the population. After the population has been created, in each search loop we conduct survivor selection based on the ending order of the trials to maintain a fixed population size. Then we perform tournament selection by randomly selecting a set of candidates and picking the best one among them as the parent (`best_candidate_trial`). We mutate a randomly selected hyperparameter of the parent trial using the `_mutate` function, and the hyperparameter values of the offspring are returned and put into a dictionary along with the status of the offspring trial. The status is set as `RUNNING`, meaning the trial is ready for evaluation.

Listing 7.15   Evolutionary search oracle

```
import random
import numpy as np
from keras_tuner.engine import hyperparameters as hp_module
from keras_tuner.engine import oracle as oracle_module
from keras_tuner.engine import trial as trial_lib


class EvolutionaryOracle(oracle_module.Oracle):
    def __init__(self,
                 objective,
                 max_trials,
                 num_initial_points=None,
                 population_size=20,
                 candidate_size=5,
                 seed=None,
                 hyperparameters=None,
                 *args, **kwargs):
        super().__init__(
            objective=objective,
            max_trials=max_trials,
            hyperparameters=hyperparameters,
            seed=seed,
            *args, **kwargs)
        self.population_size = population_size
        self.candidate_size = candidate_size
        self.num_initial_points = num_initial_points or self.population_size
        self.num_initial_points = max(self.num_initial_points, population_size)
        self.population_trial_ids = []
```

Makes sure the random
initialization trials can
fill the population

A list to keep
the IDs of the
population
trials

```
                self.seed = seed or random.randint(1, 1e4)
                self._seed_state = self.seed
                self._max_collisions = 100

            def _random_populate_space(self):
                values = self._random_values()
                if values is None:
                    return {'status': trial_lib.TrialStatus.STOPPED,
                            'values': None}
                return {'status': trial_lib.TrialStatus.RUNNING,
                        'values': values}

            def _num_completed_trials(self):
                return len([t for t in self.trials.values() if t.status == 'COMPLETED'])

            def populate_space(self, trial_id):

                if self._num_completed_trials()
            < self.num_initial_points:
                    return self._random_populate_space()

                self.population_trial_ids = self.end_order[
            -self.population_size:]

                candidate_indices = np.random.choice(
                    self.population_size, self.candidate_size, replace=False
                )
                self.candidate_indices = candidate_indices
                candidate_trial_ids = list(
                    map(self.population_trial_ids.__getitem__, candidate_indices)
                )

                candidate_scores = [self.trials[trial_id].score
            for trial_id in candidate_trial_ids]
                best_candidate_trial_id =
            candidate_trial_ids[np.argmin(candidate_scores)]
                best_candidate_trial = self.trials[best_candidate_trial_id]

                values = self._mutate(best_candidate_trial)

                if values is None:
                    return {'status': trial_lib.TrialStatus.STOPPED, 'values': None}

                return {'status': trial_lib.TrialStatus.RUNNING,
                        'values': values}
```

Random selection for initializing the population

Survivor selection based on the age of trials

Selects candidate trials from the population

Gets the best candidate for parent based on the performance

Mutates a random selected hyperparameter of the parent

Stops the trial if the offspring is invalid (has already been evaluated)

Now let's see how to implement the mutation operation.

7.4.3 Implementing a simple mutation operation

Ideally, as long as a hyperparameter is not fixed, we can mutate it into other values. However, if the selected hyperparameter is a conditional hyperparameter, changing it may affect other hyperparameters. For example, if we selected the model type hyperparameter to mutate and its value is changed from MLP to decision tree, the tree depth hyperparameter, which was not active originally, will become active, and we will need to assign it a specific value (see figure 7.12). Thus, we need to check whether the mutation hyperparameter is a conditional hyperparameter. If it is, we need to assign its *descendant hyperparameters* (hyperparameters represented by the child nodes in the figure) randomly selected values.

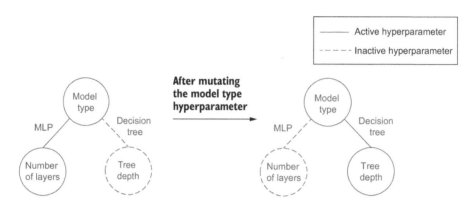

Figure 7.12   **A nonactive hyperparameter may become active due to the mutation**

So, we first collect the nonfixed and active hyperparameters in the parent trial (`best_trial`) and randomly select a hyperparameter to mutate from among them. Then we create a hyperparameter container instance named `hps` to save the hyperparameter values of the new offspring into. By looping through all the hyperparameters in the search space, we generate their values one by one and feed them into the container. Note that we need to loop through all the active hyperparameters in the search space rather than just processing the active hyperparameters in the parent trial, because some of the nonactive hyperparameters could become active if a conditional hyperparameter is mutated (see figure 7.12).

For any hyperparameter that is active in the parent trial but is not the selected mutation hyperparameter, we assign its original value to it and continue the mutation operation. For the selected mutation hyperparameter, we randomly select a new value. Suppose the selected mutation hyperparameter is a conditional hyperparameter. After its value is mutated, its descendant hyperparameters, which are changed to be active in the offspring, will also be assigned randomly selected values. Whether a descendant hyperparameter is active is determined by the statement `hps.is_active(hp)`, shown in listing 7.16. After the new offspring is generated, we check whether it has been evaluated before with the help of a hashing function (`_compute_values_hash`) inherited from the base `Oracle` class. If the offspring collides with a previous trial, we repeat the mutation process. We continue doing this until a valid offspring is generated or the maximum number of collisions is reached. The hashing values of the final offspring are collected in a Python set (`self._tried_so_far`) for checking the future trials.

Listing 7.16 Mutating the hyperparameters in the parent trial

```
def _mutate(self, best_trial):

    best_hps = best_trial.hyperparameters        ◁─┐ Extracts the
                                                    hyperparameters
                                                    in the best trial

    nonfixed_active_hps = [hp for hp in self.hyperparameters.space
        if not isinstance(hp, hp_module.Fixed) and
➡ best_hps.is_active(hp)]            ◁──┐ Collects the
                                         nonfixed and active
                                         hyperparameters

        hp_to_mutate = np.random.choice(
            nonfixed_active_hps, 1)[0]   ◁──┐ Randomly selects a
                                             hyperparameter to
        collisions = 0                       mutate
        while True:
            hps = hp_module.HyperParameters()
                                                    ┌ Loops through
                                                      all the active
            for hp in self.hyperparameters.space:  ◁ hyperparameters in
                hps.merge([hp])                       the search space

            if hps.is_active(hp):

                if best_hps.is_active(hp.name) and hp.name !=
➡ hp_to_mutate.name:
                    hps.values[hp.name] = best_hps.values[hp.name]
                        continue
                    hps.values[hp.name] =    ┐ Conducts a
➡ hp.random_sample(self._seed_state)         random mutation
                        self._seed_state += 1
                    values = hps.values

            values_hash = self._compute_values_hash(   ┐ Generates the
                values)                                   hashing string for
            if values_hash in self._tried_so_far:    ◁  the new offspring
                collisions += 1                       ◁─┐ Checks whether the
                if collisions <= self._max_collisions:   offspring has been
                    continue                             evaluated already
                return None
            self._tried_so_far.add(values_hash)
            break
        return values
```

Checks whether the current hyperparameter needs to be mutated

The following two points are worth noting:

- The determination of whether a hyperparameter is a descendant of a conditional hyperparameter leverages a property of KerasTuner: the descendant hyperparameters will always appear after the conditional hyperparameter in the hyperparameter list (`self.hyperparameters.space`). In fact, the hyperparameter search space can be treated as a graph, where each node represents a hyperparameter, and the links indicate their order of appearance in an ML pipeline or their conditional correlations. KerasTuner uses the topological order of the graph to save the hyperparameter search space in a list.

- To make sure the algorithm is aware of the conditional correlations between hyperparameters and detects whether a conditional hyperparameter's descendants are active when it is mutated, we need to explicitly define the conditional scope in the search space, as described in chapter 5. An illustrative definition of a synthetic search space is shown in the following listing, where `conditional_choice` is a conditional hyperparameter, whose descendant hyperparameters are `child1_choice` and `child2_choice`. During the search process, one of its two children will be active, depending on its value.

Listing 7.17 A conditional search space

```
def build_model(hp):
    hp.Choice('conditional_choice', [1, 2, 3], default=2)
    with hp.conditional_scope(
        'conditional_choice', [1, 3]):                      The conditional
        child1 = hp.Choice('child1_choice', [4, 5, 6])      scope of the
    with hp.conditional_scope(                              hyperparameters
        'conditional_choice', 2):
        child2 = hp.Choice('child2_choice', [7, 8, 9])
```

Combining the mutation function with the sampling function of the oracle learned previously, we finish the core implementation of the oracle. We can also add the functions to help save and resume the oracle. The hyper-hyperparameters used to control the oracle are saved in the state dictionary, and the population list should be reinitialized along with these hyper-hyperparameters when resuming the oracle in the `set_state()` function, as shown in the next listing.

Listing 7.18 Helping to resume an evolutionary search oracle

```
class EvolutionaryOracle(oracle_module.Oracle):

    def get_state(self):
        state = super(EvolutionaryOracle, self).get_state()
        state.update({
            'num_initial_points': self.num_initial_points,
            'population_size': self.population_size,        Saves the population
            'candidate_size': self.candidate_size,         size and candidate size
        })
        return state

    def set_state(self, state):                            Reinitializes
        super(EvolutionaryOracle, self).set_state(state)   the population
        self.num_initial_points = state['num_initial_points']   list during the
        self.population_size = state['population_size']     oracle's resuming
        self.candidate_size = state['candidate_size']
        self.population_trial_ids = self.end_order[-self.population_size:]
```

Finally, let's evaluate the aging evolutionary search method on the same regression task used in the previous sections (California housing price prediction) and compare it with the random search and Bayesian optimization search methods.

7.4.4 *Evaluating the aging evolutionary search method*

To evaluate the aging evolutionary search method, we search for 100 trials and set the population size and candidate size to be 20 and 5, respectively. These two hyperparameters are often set subjectively based on your sense of the search space and the empirical tuning results. Usually, if the search space is large, we use a large population size to cumulate enough diversified trials to breed the offspring. A population size of around 100 should be large enough to handle most situations. Here we've used a conservative choice (20) because the search space contains only three hyperparameters. Using half of or a quarter of the population size as the candidate size, as we've done here, often provides good performance empirically.

We list only the code for calling different search methods in the next code listing. The rest of the implementation for data loading, search space creation, and tuner customization is the same as we've used before and is available in a Jupyter notebook at https://github.com/datamllab/automl-in-action-notebooks.

Listing 7.19 Calling different search methods

```
evo_tuner_p20c5 = LightGBMTuner(
    oracle=EvolutionaryOracle(
        objective=kt.Objective('mse', 'min'),
        max_trials=100,
        population_size=20,          Uses the aging
        candidate_size=5,            evolutionary method
        seed=42),                    for searching
    hypermodel=build_model,
    overwrite=True,
    project_name='evo_tuner_p20c5')


evo_tuner_p20c5.search(X_train, y_train, validation_data=(X_val, y_val))



random_tuner = LightGBMTuner(
    oracle=kt.oracles.RandomSearch(
        objective=kt.Objective('mse', 'min'),
        max_trials=100,
        seed=42),                         Uses the built-in
    hypermodel=build_model,               random search method
    overwrite=True,                       of KerasTuner
    project_name='random_tuner')


random_tuner.search(X_train, y_train, validation_data=(X_val, y_val))



bo_tuner = LightGBMTuner(
    oracle=kt.oracles.BayesianOptimization(
        objective=kt.Objective('mse', 'min'),
```

```
    max_trials=100,
      seed=42),
  hypermodel=build_model,
  overwrite=True,
  project_name='bo_tuner')
```

Uses the built-in Bayesian
optimization search method
of KerasTuner

```
bo_tuner.search(X_train, y_train, validation_data=(X_val, y_val))
```

Figure 7.13 shows the evaluation performance of the best model found by each of the three methods as the search process progressed. We can see that the Bayesian optimization method performs the best among the three methods. Although the evolutionary method achieves more steps of improvement during the search process, it distinguishes less compared to random search. Each step of improvement is small because we let the mutation happen on only one hyperparameter at each stage, and improvements continue until late in the search process. This means the selection intensity (exploitation power) could be improved in the early stages.

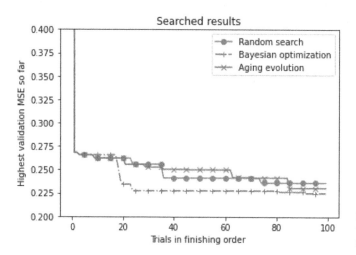

Figure 7.13   Comparing the search results of three search methods

Now let's increase the candidate size to 20 (which is an extreme choice because our population size is also 20) to enhance the exploitation power and see what happens. In figure 7.14, we can see that more improvement happens in the early stages, which confirms that the selection intensity (exploitation ability) can be enhanced at the beginning by increasing the candidate size. Although in this example, the final result is not improved much (and may even become worse than the result obtained using a smaller candidate size if we try further trials, due to the lack of exploration ability), this suggests that a larger candidate size could help us achieve comparable results with fewer trials if we consider only 100 trials. In practice, you can adjust these sizes based on your tolerance and available time. If you don't mind taking more time to explore the search space more thoroughly, you can select a smaller candidate size (and larger

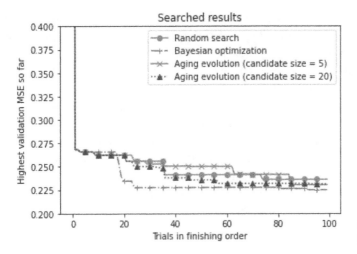

Figure 7.14 Comparison of different search methods

population size). If you expect to achieve a moderately good model within fewer trials, you could use a larger candidate size (and smaller population size).

In this example, Bayesian optimization performs the best of all the search algorithms. This is because the hyperparameters we're trying to tune are either continuous hyperparameters or have ordinal values. Generally, if our search space is dominated by hyperparameters with continuous or ordinal values, we prefer to use the Bayesian optimization algorithm. If the hyperparameters are mostly categorical or there are many conditional hyperparameters, the evolutionary method would be a good choice. Random mutation is not a good choice for exploring continuous hyperparameters. Some feasible solutions to improve this include using a logarithmic scale for some hyperparameters (such as learning rate) or combining the evolutionary method with the model-based method by adding a surrogate model to help guide the mutation— that is, conduct mutations randomly multiple times and select the best trial as the off-spring based on the surrogate model. The random search method can provide a strong baseline when the number of trials you want to explore is too few compared to the size of the search space. This is a common case in tasks that involve designing and tuning deep neural networks (neural architecture search).

Summary

- A sequential search method iteratively samples and evaluates hyperparameters from the search space. It generally consists of two steps: hyperparameter sampling and an optional update step to incorporate historical evaluations.
- History-dependent search methods can leverage the evaluated hyperparameters to better sample from the search space. Heuristic and model-based methods are the two main categories of history-dependent methods.
- The Bayesian optimization method is the most widely used model-based method in AutoML. It uses a surrogate model to approximate the model evaluation

performance and an acquisition function to balance exploration and exploitation when sampling new hyperparameters from the search space. The most commonly used surrogate model is the Gaussian process model, and some popular acquisition functions include the upper confidence bound (UCB), probability of improvement, and expected improvement.

- The evolutionary method is a heuristic search method that generates new samples by simulating the evolution of an animal population in new generations. It involves four steps: initial population generation, parent selection, crossover and mutation, and survivor selection. The aging evolutionary search method is a popular evolutionary search method originally proposed for neural architecture search. It utilizes the existing ages of trials for survivor selection and tournament selection for parent selection.

Scaling up AutoML

This chapter covers

- Loading large datasets into memory batch by batch
- Using multiple GPUs to speed up search and training
- Using Hyperband to efficiently schedule model training to make the best use of the available computing resources
- Using pretrained models and warm-start to accelerate the search process

This chapter introduces various techniques for large-scale training—for example, using large datasets to train large models on multiple GPUs. For datasets that are too big to fit into memory all at once, we'll show you how to load them batch by batch during the training. We'll also introduce different parallelization strategies to distribute the training and search processes onto multiple GPUs. In addition, we'll show you some strategies to accelerate the search process with limited computing resources, using advanced search algorithms and search spaces.

8.1   *Handling large-scale datasets*

One of the most important factors behind the power of deep learning is the availability of large amounts of data to train the models. Usually, the larger and more diverse the dataset is, the better the performance of the trained model is. All the datasets we have used in the earlier examples in this book were small enough to fit into the main memory of the machine on which the training was done. However, you may not have— or need—enough memory to hold the entire dataset. If you use GPUs, the dataset will be chopped into small batches, which are loaded into the GPU batch by batch. This means you need only one slot in the GPU's memory for a single batch of data, which will be overwritten when you load a new batch.

So, if you want to use a larger dataset that doesn't fit into the main memory of the machine you're using, instead of attempting to load the entire dataset at once, you can load one or more batches at a time, overwriting the previous batches. The batches can then be loaded into GPU memory during training as usual.

In summary, we have two ways of loading data. In both cases, the GPU holds a buffer for batches of data to be consumed by the machine learning model. In the first case, we load the entire dataset into the main memory and then load the data into the GPU's memory batch by batch. In the second case, the main memory is also used as a buffer to load the data in batches from the hard drive, where the entire dataset is held. The comparison between the two ways of loading data is shown in figure 8.1.

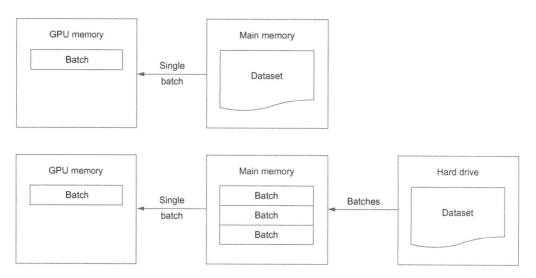

Figure 8.1   Different ways of loading data

In this section, we'll show you how to use the second option to load large datasets that do not fit into the main memory to search for a good model. We will first introduce loading image- and text-classification data, which is easy to do with existing data-loading APIs in AutoKeras. Then, we will show you how to load any dataset from the disk in batches.

8.1.1 Loading an image-classification dataset

There is a convenient function in AutoKeras that can help you load image-classification data from the disk. Here, we'll use the MNIST dataset as an example. To download and extract the dataset, you'll need to run the commands in the next code sample. You can run them directly in a Python notebook, or run them in your local Linux or Unix command-line terminal without the ! symbol. First, we download the compressed file of the MNIST dataset with the wget command, which stores the file at the given URL into the current directory. Then, we extract the files from the compressed file with the tar command. xzf is the most commonly used configuration for extracting files, where x means extract, z means to filter the archive content through gzip, and f means to read the content from a file:

```
!wget https://github.com/datamllab/automl-in-action-notebooks/raw/master/
    data/mnist.tar.gz
!tar xzf mnist.tar.gz
```

After extraction, we can see the images are grouped by their classes into different folders. The train and test directories each contain 10 subdirectories, named 0 to 9, which are the labels of the images, as shown here:

```
train/
├─0/
│  ├─1.png
│  └─21.png
│   ...
├─1/
├─2/
└─3/
   ...
test/
├─0/
└─1/
   ...
```

We can now use the built-in AutoKeras function image_dataset_from_directory() to load the image dataset. This function returns a tf.data.Dataset object containing the data. The first argument to the function is the path to the data directory, which is 'test' or 'train' in our case. Use image_size to specify the image size as a tuple of two integers, (height, width), and use batch_size to specify the batch size of the dataset. These are the required arguments for the function.

Calling this function yields a batch of tuples of images and labels. The first element in each tuple is the shape (batch_size, image_height, image_width, number_of_channels). We set the number of channels using the color_mode argument, which can be one of 'grayscale', 'rgb', or 'rgba'. The corresponding numbers of channels are 1, 3, and 4; the MNIST dataset consists of grayscale images, so the number of channels is 1.

The second element of the tuple is the label. The labels are strings, which are the same as the directory names in the test or train directory. In our case, they are numbers from '0' to '9'. The image_dataset_from_directory() function also takes a shuffle argument, which is True by default, meaning it will shuffle the images from different classes in different directories. To set the random seed for shuffling, you can use the seed argument.

We'll start by loading the testing data, as shown in the following listing. This doesn't require splitting the data, which means it's easier than loading the training data. We'll also print out some specs about the first batch of the loaded data—this is a useful debugging method when loading datasets.

Listing 8.1   Loading testing data from disk

```
import os
import autokeras as ak

batch_size = 32
img_height = 28
img_width = 28

parent_dir = 'data'
test_data = ak.image_dataset_from_directory(
    os.path.join(parent_dir, 'test'),      ←┐  Path to the
    seed=123,                               │  testing dataset
    color_mode='grayscale',
    image_size=(img_height, img_width),
    batch_size=batch_size,

for images, labels in test_data.take(1):   ←┐  Returns a new dataset
    print(images.shape, images.dtype)       │  with only the first batch
    print(labels.shape, labels.dtype))
```

As the output shows, this lists 10,000 images with 10 different class labels. The shape of one batch of loaded images is (32, 28, 28, 1), with a type of float32. The shape of the corresponding labels is (32,), with a type of string, as shown next:

```
Found 10000 files belonging to 10 classes.
(32, 28, 28, 1) <dtype: 'float32'>
(32,) <dtype: 'string'>
```

The dataset has been successfully loaded from the disk into a tf.data.Dataset object. However, it is not directly usable for AutoML because we will need at least two tf.data.Dataset objects for training and validation, respectively. Therefore, we need an efficient way to split the dataset into different subsets.

8.1.2   Splitting the loaded dataset

We have multiple ways to split a dataset. Listing 8.2 shows a simple but inefficient solution: it loads the entire set of training data and splits it with the take() and skip() functions. If you call dataset.take(n), it will return a dataset consisting of the first n

batches. If you call `dataset.skip(n)`, it will return a dataset consisting of the rest of the batches after the first *n* batches.

Listing 8.2 Loading and splitting the training data

```
all_train_data = ak.image_dataset_from_directory(
    os.path.join(parent_dir, 'train'),
    seed=123,
    color_mode='grayscale',
    image_size=(img_height, img_width),
    batch_size=batch_size,
)
train_data = all_train_data.take(int(60000 / batch_size * 0.8))
validation_data = all_train_data.skip(int(60000 / batch_size * 0.8))
```

This is inefficient because the `skip()` function has to go through the first *n* batches before it can start to iterate. We propose a more efficient solution in listing 8.3. Here, we call the `image_dataset_from_directory()` function twice, to get the training and validation sets separately. In each call, everything remains the same as when we loaded the testing set except for two new arguments, `validation_split` and `subset`, that control the splitting of the dataset. The `validation_split` argument specifies the percentage of the batches to include in the validation set, which should be between 0 and 1. The rest of the batches will be included in the training set. The `subset` argument should be either `'training'` or `'validation'`, to indicate which set the function should return. Notably, the `seed` argument has to be set manually here to ensure that in the two calls to the function, there is no difference in how the data is split.

Listing 8.3 Loading training and validation data from disk

```
train_data = ak.image_dataset_from_directory(       ◁──┐ Loads the
    os.path.join(parent_dir, 'train'),       ◁──────────┤ training split
    validation_split=0.2,
    subset='training',                                   Path to the training
    seed=123,                                            data directory
    color_mode='grayscale',
    image_size=(img_height, img_width),
    batch_size=batch_size,
)
                                                       ┐ Loads the
validation_data = ak.image_dataset_from_directory(  ◁──┘ validation split
    os.path.join(parent_dir, 'train'),       ◁──
    validation_split=0.2,                         Path to the training
    subset='validation',                          data directory
    seed=123,
    color_mode='grayscale',
    image_size=(img_height, img_width),
    batch_size=batch_size,
```

We've finished the data-loading specification part: all the data is wrapped into the format of a `tf.data.Dataset`. Next, we'll look at an easy technique that we can use to further improve the efficiency of using the loaded dataset, called *prefetching*.

IMPROVING DATA LOADING EFFICIENCY WITH PREFETCHING

Due to read inefficiency, loading data from the disk can take some time. Without prefetching, the program would start loading the next batch of data from the disk into memory only when all the batches currently in memory have been used up by the machine learning model. The model training or inference process would then be suspended to wait for the next batch of data to load. Clearly, this approach is not an efficient one.

Prefetching loads additional batches of data from the disk into memory in advance, in parallel with training or inference, so this process is not suspended. The difference between the two approaches is shown with sequence diagrams in figure 8.2. There are two tasks involved, training and loading. The lines from the top to the bottom show which task is running at a given time during the execution. As you can see, without prefetching, the loading and training tasks never run together; the training process needs to wait for the loading process to finish. With prefetching, on the other hand, they can run in parallel to save some time, so the program runs more efficiently.

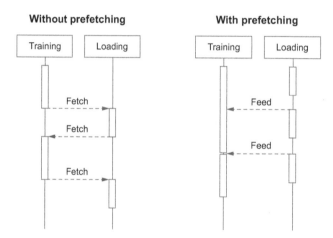

Figure 8.2 Prefetching sequence diagram

To enable prefetching for a `tf.data.Dataset`, you can call its member function `prefetch()`. The only required argument is the number of batches you want it to prefetch into memory: for example, calling `dataset.prefetch(5)` loads five batches into memory in advance. If you are not sure how many batches would be ideal for prefetching, you can use `dataset.prefetch(tf.data.AUTOTUNE)`, which will tune this number for you automatically.

The code for using prefetching for training, validation, and testing is shown in listing 8.4. Here, we prefetch five batches for the training and validation sets and automatically tune the number of batches for the testing data.

Listing 8.4 Improving loading efficiency with prefetching

```
import tensorflow as tf

train_data = train_data.prefetch(5)
validation_data = validation_data.prefetch(5)
test_data = test_data.prefetch(tf.data.AUTOTUNE)
```

Now let's try to train a simple image-classification model with this data. The code is shown in the next listing. As you can see, there's no difference from using a smaller dataset that we're able to load into memory all at once: we pass the training and validation sets directly to the fit() function.

Listing 8.5 Fitting an image classifier with data loaded from disk

```
clf = ak.ImageClassifier(overwrite=True, max_trials=1)
clf.fit(train_data, epochs=1, validation_data=validation_data)
print(clf.evaluate(test_data))
```

You now know how to load a large image dataset from the disk. However, we could encounter other types of large dataset, such as text datasets, which are also too big to fit into the main memory in many cases. We'll look at how to load a large text dataset from the disk next.

8.1.3 Loading a text-classification dataset

Loading a large text-classification dataset is not much different from loading a large image-classification dataset. Again, you can use a built-in function from AutoKeras named text_dataset_from_directory(); the only difference in usage is the arguments.

The text_dataset_from_directory() function doesn't have image_size and color_mode arguments, because those are related only to image data. Instead, it takes a new argument named max_length, which is the maximum number of characters in the string to keep for each text instance. If you leave max_length unspecified, the strings are preserved at their original length before being fed into the model.

Let's use the IMDb movie review dataset as an example to show how to load text data from the disk. First, we download the raw text files using the following commands. These two commands will download the dataset as a compressed file and extract the files into the current directory. As with downloading the image dataset, we can run the commands directly in a notebook, or we can run them locally in a Linux or Unix terminal without the ! symbol:

```
!wget https://github.com/datamllab/automl-in-action-notebooks/raw/master/
    data/imdb.tar.gz
!tar xzf imdb.tar.gz
```

After extraction, you'll have a directory named imdb with the following content. As you can see, the reviews are divided into training and testing datasets, each of which is organized by the two classes of reviews, positive and negative:

```
train/
├─pos/
│  ├─0_9.txt
│  └─10000_8.txt
│  ...
└─neg/
test/
├─pos/
└─neg/
```

Next, we can load the text data in the same way we loaded the image data. We load the data from the train directory and split it into a training set and a validation set with text_dataset_from_directory(). We also use prefetching to speed up the iteration process, with max_length=1000 to limit the maximum length of the loaded strings. Any characters over the 1,000-character limit will be discarded. As you can see in the following listing, when loading the testing data, we can omit several of the arguments because they are important only for training data.

Listing 8.6   Loading training, validation, and testing data from disk

```
train_data = ak.text_dataset_from_directory(          ◁──┐  Loads the
    'imdb/train',                                        │  training set
    validation_split=0.2,
    subset='training',
    seed=123,
    max_length=1000,
    batch_size=32,
).prefetch(1000)

validation_data = ak.text_dataset_from_directory(     ◁──┐  Loads the
    'imdb/train',                                        │  validation set
    validation_split=0.2,
    subset='validation',
    seed=123,
    max_length=1000,
    batch_size=32,
).prefetch(1000)

test_data = ak.text_dataset_from_directory(           ◁──┐  Loads the
    'imdb/test',                                         │  testing set
    max_length=1000,
).prefetch(1000)
```

After loading the data, we can now use a simple text classifier to test if the loaded data works as intended, as shown next.

Listing 8.7   Fittting a text classifier with data loaded from disk

```
clf = ak.TextClassifier(overwrite=True, max_trials=1)
clf.fit(train_data, epochs=2, validation_data=validation_data)
print(clf.evaluate(test_data))
```

So far, we have shown you how to load image- and text-classification data from the disk with AutoKeras's built-in functions and how to speed up the iteration of the dataset with prefetching. However, we need a more general way to load datasets of any data type, not just images and text.

8.1.4 Handling large datasets in general

In this section, we will introduce a way to load arbitrary datasets that are too large to fit into the main memory using an inner mechanism of tf.data.Dataset. We will continue to use this format to load the dataset to solve the memory issue. However, to enable more flexibility in the data types, we will use a *Python generator* to iterate through the data and convert the generator to a tf.data.Dataset.

First, what is a Python generator? Conceptually, it's an iterator for a sequence of data. For implementation purposes, it's a Python function that uses yield to provide the data to be iterated through. You can use a for loop to iterate over the function to get all the data, as shown in the following listing. Here, we define a Python generator called generator(). It's just a Python function that calls yield to provide all the elements in data.

Listing 8.8 Python generator example

```
data = [5, 8, 9, 3, 6]

def generator():          ◁——— Defines the generator
    for i in data:
        yield i

for x in generator():     ◁——|  Iterates over the generator using
    print(x)                   |  a for loop and prints its elements
```

The output of the generator, which follows, is the elements in the data list in listing 8.8:

```
5
8
9
3
6
```

The tf.data.Dataset class has a function named from_generator that constructs a new instance using a Python generator. To use this, we just provide the generator function and specify the data type with the output_types argument. Let's try to convert the Python generator we just built to a tf.data.Dataset instance. The code is shown in the next listing. The output will be the same as in the previous example.

Listing 8.9 Converting the Python generator to a tf.data.Dataset

```
dataset = tf.data.Dataset.from_generator(
    generator,                          ◁——— Specifies the generator function
```

```
    output_types=tf.int32)                   Specifies the output
for x in dataset:                            type as integer
    print(x.numpy())
```

Now that you know what a Python generator is and how to use one to build a `tf.data.Dataset` instance, let's try to load a real dataset with this method.

LOADING A DATASET WITH A PYTHON GENERATOR

Now we'll load the IMDb dataset using a Python generator using the following steps:

1 Load all the filepaths and labels into a NumPy array. Shuffle the array to mix the data from different directories.
2 Build a generator from the shuffled NumPy array to convert the filepaths to the actual text data by reading the contents of the files.
3 Create the `tf.data.Dataset` instance from the generator.

In the first step, we iterate over all the files in the different classes (directories). We create tuples of two elements: the path to the file and the label of the file. The path to the file is needed to load its contents later, during training. The label information is indicated by the directory containing the file, so we need to record this information during the iteration of the directories.

However, because we iterated through all the files directory by directory, all the files in the same directory (i.e., with the same class label) are next to each other in the array. So, we need to shuffle them to mix the data from different classes before using the files for training.

The reason we create a NumPy array first instead of creating the generator directly to iterate the files is that it's easier to do the shuffling and the split once the filepaths and labels have been loaded into memory. In addition, the filepaths won't take up much space in memory.

The code to perform this process is shown in the following listing. The `load_data()` function loads, shuffles, and returns the data as a NumPy array.

Listing 8.10   Loading IMDb dataset filenames

```
import numpy as np

path = os.path.join(parent_dir, 'train')          Enumerates
                                                  the class labels
def load_data(path):
    data = []                                              Iterates all the
    for class_label in ['pos', 'neg']:                     filenames in each
        for file_name in os.listdir(                       of the classes
            os.path.join(path, class_label)):
            data.append((os.path.join(                              Creates tuples
                path, class_label, file_name), class_label))        of (file_path,
    data = np.array(data)                                           class_label)
    np.random.shuffle(data)              Shuffles the data
    return data
                                                               Loads the
                                                               training data
all_train_np = load_data(os.path.join(parent_dir, 'train'))
```

With this NumPy array, we can create an iterator to convert each element in the array to the actual text data. Instead of directly implementing the generator, we implemented a function named get_generator(data) to return a generator because we may need different generators for the training, validation, and testing sets. With get_generator(data) we can pass the corresponding NumPy array to the function to dynamically create a generator for that NumPy array. Then, we can create the generator function as an inner function and return this function as the return value.

In the generator function, we'll use a for loop to iterate the filepaths, read the contents of each file, and yield the text and label together. In this way, the generator will generate the actual text data with the labels ready to be used for training. The code for get_generator() is shown in the following listing. The data_generator() function will be returned as the generator function.

Listing 8.11 Loading the IMDb dataset with a Python generator

```
def get_generator(data):          The generator
    def data_generator():         function           Iterates the
        for file_path, class_label in data:          NumPy array
            text_file = open(file_path, 'r')   Reads the file contents
            text = text_file.read()            using the filepaths
            text_file.close()
            yield text, class_label      Yields the text
    return data_generator            and class labels
```

Returns the generator function

The next step is to create a tf.data.Dataset instance. For the convenience of splitting the data, let's write a function, np_to_dataset(), to convert a NumPy array to a tf.data.Dataset. This function will call the get_generator() function to get the generator function and use tf.data.Dataset.from_generator() to get the tf.data .Dataset instance.

We split the NumPy array and call the np_to_dataset() function twice, for the training and validation sets. These contain 20,000 and 5,000 instances, respectively.

Several things need attention while creating the dataset. In the from_generator() function, we need to specify the output_types. Because both the text and the label are of type string, we can just specify the type as tf.string.

Using the dataset with AutoKeras requires it to have a concrete shape. Therefore, we specify the shape of the dataset with the output_shapes argument. The value of this argument needs to be an instance of tf.TensorShape. We can create it easily by passing the shape as a list to its initializer.

The created dataset is not directly usable because each instance in it is one tensor with shape (2,). However, the dataset used by AutoKeras should be tuples of two tensors, (x, y). Therefore, we need to call the map() function of the dataset to change its format.

The map() function accepts as its argument a lambda function, which takes the old instance as an argument and returns the new instance. We can then return the first and second dimensions of the original tensor as a tuple of two elements. The code for these steps follows.

Listing 8.12 **Creating a dataset from a generator**

```
def np_to_dataset(data_np):              ◄──────┐  The function to convert the
    return tf.data.Dataset.from_generator(      │  NumPy array to a tf.data.Dataset
        get_generator(data_np),          ◄───┐
        output_types=tf.string,              │  The generator function
        output_shapes=tf.TensorShape([2]),   │  for the array
    ).map(                               └──►
        lambda x: (x[0], x[1])               ┌─  Batches and sets      ┌─ Loads the
    ).batch(32).prefetch(5)          ◄───────┤   prefetching for       │  training set
                                             └─  the dataset           │
train_data = np_to_dataset(all_train_np[:20000])       ◄───────────────┘  ┌─ Loads the
validation_data = np_to_dataset(all_train_np[20000:])  ◄──────────────────┘  validation set
```

Converts the data from tensor to tuple

With all these procedures implemented as functions, we can load the testing set in the same way, as shown in the next code listing.

Listing 8.13 **Loading the testing set of the IMDb dataset with a Python generator**

```
test_np = load_data(os.path.join(parent_dir, 'test'))
test_data = np_to_dataset(test_np)
```

With the training set, validation set, and testing set ready in `tf.data.Dataset` format, we can then test whether it runs as intended with the AutoKeras text classifier, as shown next.

Listing 8.14 **Fitting the text classifier with data from the Python generator**

```
clf = ak.TextClassifier(overwrite=True, max_trials=1)
clf.fit(train_data, epochs=2, validation_data=validation_data)
print(clf.evaluate(test_data))
```

The primary purpose of this example was to show how to construct a dataset using a Python generator. Now you know how to use this method to load any dataset in any format into a `tf.data.Dataset`, which greatly improves your flexibility for loading a large dataset.

Furthermore, this approach isn't limited to loading data from the disk: if your data comes from a remote machine over the network or is dynamically generated with some Python code, you can also use a Python generator to wrap it into a dataset.

8.2 *Parallelization on multiple GPUs*

To scale up machine learning and AutoML for large models and large datasets, we can run our programs on multiple GPUs and multiple machines in parallel. Paralleliza-tion is typically used either to accelerate training and inference (*data parallelism*) or to load a very large model that does not fit into the memory of a single GPU (*model parallelism*). It's also sometimes used to accelerate the hyperparameter tuning process (*parallel tuning*). Figure 8.3 illustrates these three different types of parallelization and how the memory allocation for the datasets and models differs in each.

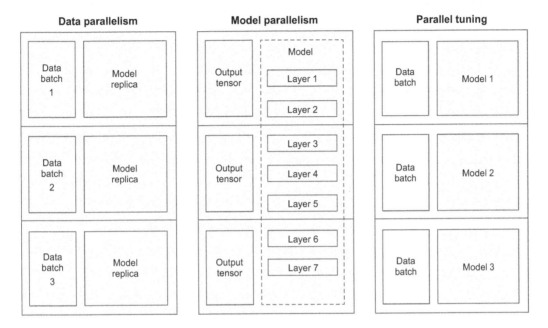

Figure 8.3   Three types of parallelism

This figure shows what each of the strategies looks like with three GPUs. On the left is the data parallelism approach, which accelerates the training process for large datasets. Each of the three GPUs has a copy of the same model but works on different data batches. The weight updates on the different GPUs are synchronized periodically.

In the middle of the figure is an example of the model parallelism strategy, which is mainly used for large models that cannot be contained in a single GPU's memory or for accelerating models whose inference processes can be parallelized. It breaks the model into pieces and allocates them to different GPUs. In figure 8.3, the first GPU holds the first two layers of the model and the training data. The second and the third GPUs hold the rest of the layers and the intermediate outputs of the layers. During the inference process, some pieces of the model may run in parallel to save time.

The parallel tuning strategy, which is used to accelerate the AutoML process, is depicted on the right. With this approach, models with different hyperparameter settings are placed on different GPUs, and the same dataset is used to train them. Therefore, the hyperparameter tuning process runs in parallel.

Let's look at each of these strategies a little more closely.

8.2.1   Data parallelism

With TensorFlow, data parallelism is managed using `tf.distribute.Strategy`, whose subclasses, such as `tf.distribute.MirroredStrategy`, implement different parallelism strategies. You can use these subclasses directly with AutoKeras and KerasTuner.

In AutoKeras, the `AutoModel` class and all the task API classes (like `ImageClassifier` and `TextClassifier`) have an argument in the initializer called `distribution_ strategy`. You can pass an instance of `tf.distribute.MirroredStrategy` (or one of the other subclasses) to it to have all the model training processes during the search use data parallelism. An example with the MNIST dataset is shown in the next listing. The code will run in a distributed manner on all the GPUs that are visible to the program.

Listing 8.15   Data parallelism with AutoKeras

```
import tensorflow as tf
from tensorflow.keras.datasets import mnist
import autokeras as ak

(x_train, y_train), (x_test, y_test) = mnist.load_data()
clf = ak.ImageClassifier(
    overwrite=True,                                                         Uses data
    max_trials=1,                                                          parallelism
    distribution_strategy=tf.distribute.MirroredStrategy())   ◁──┘        for training
clf.fit(x_train, y_train, epochs=1)
```

For KerasTuner, all the tuners, which are subclasses of the `Tuner` class (`Bayesian-Optimization`, `Hyperband`, and `RandomSearch`), also have this `distribution_strategy` argument in their initializers, and it works the same way as in AutoKeras. You can pass an instance of a TensorFlow distribution strategy, like `tf.distribute.Mirrored-Strategy`, to the argument. The models will use the distribution strategy for training.

AutoKeras uses this KerasTuner feature under the hood. A simple example of using data parallelism with KerasTuner is shown in the following listing. Here, we've designed a very basic search space for the MNIST dataset.

Listing 8.16   Data parallelism with KerasTuner

```
import keras_tuner as kt

def build_model(hp):
    model = tf.keras.Sequential()
    model.add(tf.keras.layers.Flatten())
    model.add(tf.keras.layers.Dense(
        units=hp.Int('units', min_value=32, max_value=512, step=32),
        activation='relu'))
    model.add(tf.keras.layers.Dense(10, activation='softmax'))
    model.compile(optimizer='adam', loss='sparse_categorical_crossentropy')
    return model

tuner = kt.RandomSearch(
    build_model,
```

```
        objective='val_loss',
        max_trials=1,
        directory='my_dir',
        distribution_strategy=tf.distribute.
➡   MirroredStrategy(),                        ◁─────┐  Uses data parallelism
        project_name='helloworld')                   │  for training

tuner.search(x_train, y_train,
                epochs=1,
                validation_data=(x_test, y_test))
```

The program can use all the GPUs available to split the data and aggregate the gradients to update the model. Besides data parallelism, let's see how other types of distributed strategies can help accelerate the training process.

8.2.2 *Model parallelism*

As mentioned previously, model parallelism is used mainly when working with large models. For models that are too large to be contained in one GPU's memory, it offers a way to ensure that all the computations are still done efficiently on GPUs by breaking the model into pieces and distributing them across the available processing units. It also enables you to offload some computations to different GPUs to run in parallel during inference.

A typical example is a model with multiple branches. An intermediate output is the input of two independent layers, which do not rely in any way on each other's output. An example of such a case is shown in figure 8.4. Four GPUs in total are shown in this figure: the two convolutional layers on GPU 2, and GPU 3 can run in parallel during inference because their inputs do not rely on each other's output.

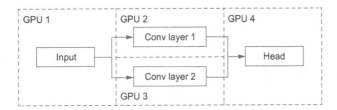

Figure 8.4   A model with multiple branches on multiple GPUs

Another not-so-common example is one layer that can be split into multiple parts to run in parallel. For example, in a convolutional layer, each filter works independently. Therefore, they can be split to run on multiple GPUs. The outputs can then be aggregated to form the output tensor of the entire convolutional layer.

The model parallelism is not well wrapped into simple APIs by the popular open source deep learning frameworks nowadays. In most of the cases, the model would be small enough to fit into the memory of a single GPU. To implement a model with model parallelism, one need to learn to use Mesh TensorFlow, which we will not go into detail in this book. If you are interested, you can check out Mesh TensorFlow on GitHub at https://github.com/tensorflow/mesh.

8.2.3   *Parallel tuning*

Parallel tuning means training models with different hyperparameters on different devices. For example, suppose you have four GPUs on a single machine, and you want to try eight different sets of hyperparameters in the search space. If you run four models in parallel, you only need the time it takes to train two models to finish the search.

Notably, parallel tuning also requires the tuning algorithm to be capable of receiving the evaluation results asynchronously. If not run in parallel, the tuning algorithm would start to train one model and wait for the evaluation result before starting to train another model. However, when run in parallel, the search algorithm needs to start the training of multiple models before receiving any evaluation results, and the evaluation results may not be received in the same order as the training processes started. The search algorithm will generate a new model to train whenever there is an available device to use.

Let's take a look at how to run parallel tuning with KerasTuner. It implements a *chief/worker* model for this purpose: at any given time, only one chief process is running, but there are multiple worker processes running. The chief process runs the search algorithm. It manages the workers to start the training process and collects the evaluation results from them.

One problem we encounter when tuning in parallel is where to store the models. When not running in parallel, the searched models and their trained weights are saved on the disk, so that we can load the best models after the search. When running in parallel, to save the models for loading them later, we need to have shared storage for all the workers and the chief. If we're using multiple GPUs on a single machine, this isn't a problem, because they use the same storage. If we're using multiple GPUs on multiple machines, we can mount the shared storage to the machines or use network storage that all the machines have access to, for example, a Google Cloud Storage bucket.

The communication pattern of the chief and the workers in parallel tuning is shown in figure 8.5. The solid lines are the control flows. The chief node sends the different hyperparameter sets to different workers, which build and train the models using the given hyperparameters. When finished, the workers send the evaluation results back to the chief node. The dashed lines in the figure are the data flows. The trained models and results are written to centralized storage, which all the workers and the chief can access. When the user calls the chief to load the best models, the chief should load the models from the centralized storage. The training and validation data should also be stored in centralized storage that all the workers can access.

Now, let's see how to spin up this parallel training in KerasTuner. To start the chief and the worker processes, we run the same Python script. KerasTuner will use environment variables to define whether the current process should be the chief or a worker.

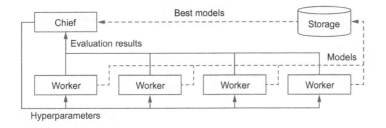

Figure 8.5 Communication pattern of parallel tuning

The `KERASTUNER_TUNER_ID` environment variable is used to specify the IDs of different processes. You can set it to `'chief'` for the chief process, and `'tuner0'`, `'tuner1'`, and so on for the workers.

We need to set two more environment variables for the workers to find the address of the chief, so they can report the evaluation results: `KERASTUNER_ORACLE_IP` and `KERASTUNER_ORACLE_PORT`. These specify the IP address and the port that the chief service runs on; they need to be set for both the chief and the workers.

In summary, we need to set three environment variables before running the script (run_tuning.py, which we'll look at shortly). Here, we provide two shell scripts to start the chief and worker processes. First we need to start the chief process. The following listing shows the commands to specify the environment variables and start the process. You can open a terminal to run these commands; the terminal will hang there and wait for the workers to start.

Listing 8.17 Starting the chief process

```
export KERASTUNER_TUNER_ID='chief'         ◁── Marks the process as the chief
export KERASTUNER_ORACLE_IP='127.0.0.1'                      ◁── The IP address of the chief
export KERASTUNER_ORACLE_PORT='8000'       ◁── The port of the chief
python run_tuning.py
```

Starts the chief process ↳

Now, open another terminal to start a worker process. You can do this with the script in the following listing. It's very similar to the previous one; the only difference is the `KERASTUNER_ TUNER_ID` to specify it as a worker.

Listing 8.18 Starting a worker process

```
export KERASTUNER_TUNER_ID='tuner0'        ◁── Marks the process as a worker
export KERASTUNER_ORACLE_IP='127.0.0.1'                      ◁── The IP address of the chief
export KERASTUNER_ORACLE_PORT='8000'       ◁── The port of the chief
python run_tuning.py
```

Starts the worker process ↳

As soon as you start a worker process, the tuning starts. To start the rest of the worker processes, use the same commands but specify a different `KERASTUNER_TUNER_ID` for each: for example, `'tuner1'`, `'tuner2'`, and so on.

The Python code in run_tuning.py starts the processes. Let's take a look at what's in this script. A simple KerasTuner example is shown in the following listing. No specific configuration is needed except for the directory argument, which must point to a directory accessible to all the workers and the chief.

Listing 8.19 Parallel tuning with KerasTuner

```python
import tensorflow as tf
from tensorflow.keras.datasets import mnist
import autokeras as ak
import keras_tuner as kt

(x_train, y_train), (x_test, y_test) = mnist.load_data()

def build_model(hp):
    model = tf.keras.Sequential()
    model.add(tf.keras.layers.Flatten())
    model.add(tf.keras.layers.Dense(
        units=hp.Int('units', min_value=32, max_value=512, step=32),
        activation='relu'))
    model.add(tf.keras.layers.Dense(10, activation='softmax'))
    model.compile(optimizer='adam', loss='sparse_categorical_crossentropy')
    return model

tuner = kt.RandomSearch(
    build_model,
    objective='val_loss',
    max_trials=1,
    directory='result_dir',          ◄──┤  A directory that is accessible
    project_name='helloworld')          │  to all workers and the chief

tuner.search(x_train, y_train,
             epochs=1,
             validation_data=(x_test, y_test))
```

So far, we've been talking about how to speed up tuning by running on more GPUs. However, we have other strategies to speed up tuning on the algorithmic level.

8.3   Search speedup strategies

In this section, we will introduce some speedup strategies for the search process. First, we will introduce a model-scheduling technique named *Hyperband*. Given a certain amount of computational resources, this technique can allocate them to train different models to different extents. Instead of fully training every model, it saves time by terminating some less promising models at an early stage.

Next, we'll look at how to use models with pretrained weights to speed up the training process. Finally, we'll introduce a widely used technique in AutoML, which is to *warm-start* the search space with some good models. This gives the tuner some guidance, requiring it to do less exploration to find a model with relatively good performance.

8.3.1 *Model scheduling with Hyperband*

Hyperband[1] is a widely used model-scheduling algorithm in AutoML. Instead of trying to model the relationship between the performance and the hyperparameters of the models, the core idea of Hyperband is to not fully train all of the possible models in the search space but to focus on the more promising ones, saving computation resources and time for those.

Here's a concrete example. Suppose we have four different hyperparameter sets to try, each of which will be instantiated into a deep learning model and each of which needs to be trained for 40 epochs. We can first train all four models for 20 epochs and then discard the two models that are performing the poorest at this stage. Now we have two good models left. We then train these models for another 20 epochs, so they're fully trained, and select the best one. We therefore save the time and resources required to train the two not-so-good models for 20 more epochs each.

To understand the process of using Hyperband, we first need to understand its subprocess, called *successive halving*. Successive halving involves a loop of two alternating steps: the first step is to reduce the number of remaining models by deleting the less promising ones, and the second step is to further train the remaining models. You need to provide the following four arguments to the successive halving algorithm:

- `models`—A list of all the models to be trained.
- `max_epochs`—The total number of epochs needed to fully train a model.
- `start_epochs`—The number of epochs to train all the models in the first round.
- `factor`—A measure of how fast we want to reduce the number of models and increase the number of epochs to train the remaining models; it defaults to 3. For example, with `factor=3`, every time through the loop, we'll reduce the number of remaining models to one-third of the current count and further train the remaining models to three times the number of already trained epochs.

This process repeats until all the remaining models are fully trained. It returns the best model and the validation loss of the best model.

At the start of the algorithm, we're given a list of models. We save them in `remaining_models`, and we remove some models in every round. We use `n_models` to record the total number of models at the beginning. We use `trained_epochs` to record the number of epochs already trained for the remaining models, which will be updated in each round of further training. `target_epochs` represents the target number of epochs to reach for the current round, which is also updated at the end of each round. We record the evaluation results in a dictionary, `eval_results`, whose keys are the models and whose values are the validation loss for each model.

---

[1] Li, Lisha, et al., "Hyperband: A Novel Bandit-Based Approach to Hyperparameter Optimization," *The Journal of Machine Learning Research* 18, no. 1 (2017): 6765–6816.

With these variables initialized, we are ready to start the outer loop, which repeats until all the remaining models are fully trained—in other words, until trained_epochs is equal to or greater than max_epochs. The first step in the loop is an inner loop to train and evaluate all the models in remaining_models and record the results in eval_results.

Then we discard the worst-performing models, reducing the number of remaining models by the specified factor. At the end of the round, we update the variables keeping track of the epochs.

Once the outer loop completes (when the models are fully trained), we can get the best model and return that model and its validation loss. The pseudocode of the successive halving process is shown in the following listing.

Listing 8.20   Successive halving pseudocode

```
import copy

def successive_halving(models, max_epochs, start_epochs, factor=3):
    remaining_models = copy.copy(models)
    n_models = len(models)
    trained_epochs = 0
    target_epochs = start_epochs
    eval_results = {}
    i = 0
    while trained_epochs < max_epochs:
        for model in remaining_models:
            model.fit(x_train, y_train,
                      epochs=target_epochs - trained_epochs)
            eval_results[model] = model.evaluate(x_val, y_val)
        remaining_models = sorted(remaining_models, key=lambda x:
    eval_results[x])[int(n_models / pow(factor, i))]
        trained_epochs = target_epochs
        target_epochs = trained_epochs * factor
        i += 1
    best_model = min(remaining_models, key=lambda x: eval_results[x])
    return best_model, eval_results[best_model]
```

Annotations:
- The round counter → (points to i = 0)
- The outer loop (continues until the remaining models are fully trained) → (points to while trained_epochs < max_epochs:)
- The inner loop → (points to for model in remaining_models:)
- Reduces the number of models → (points to eval_results[x])[int(n_models / pow(factor, i))])
- Updates the variables for the next round → (points to trained_epochs = target_epochs / target_epochs = trained_epochs * factor)

For successive halving to be effective, we need to pick the right number of models to explore and the right number of epochs to start training them for. If we don't start with enough models, the algorithm won't be explorative enough. If we start with too many, the algorithm will discard a lot of models in the early stages without exploiting them. Therefore, Hyperband comes up with a method to avoid specifying a fixed number of models during successive halving.

To avoid these problems, Hyperband runs the successive halving process multiple times to balance exploration and exploitation, trying out different factor values.

To run Hyperband, we need to specify two arguments, max_epochs and factor, which are the same as the ones passed to the successive halving algorithm.

Hyperband runs the successive halving algorithm multiple times. Each iteration is called a *bracket*. We use s_max to specify the number of brackets to run, whose value is close to log(max_epochs, factor).

For an intuitive understanding of how many models to generate in a bracket, in the first bracket, the number of models generated is equal to max_epochs. After that, in each bracket, the initial number of models is 1/factor of the number in the previous call (actually, in the implementation, the number of models is around pow(factor, s), but it's adjusted to be larger in the later brackets). Hyperband also can prevent having too few models in a bracket; for example, a bracket won't start with only one model. Different brackets do not share the models passed to them but randomly generate new models at the start of each bracket. The start_ epochs value for the bracket is strictly increased by factor times per bracket.

Now that you understand all the required arguments, let's take a look at the pseudocode for Hyperband, shown here.

Listing 8.21 Hyperband pseudocode

```
import math

def hyperband(max_epochs, factor=3):
    best_model = None
    best_model_loss = math.inf
    s_max = int(math.log(max_epochs, factor))          ←  Specifies the number of brackets
    for s in (s_max, -1, -1):                          ←  Loops through the brackets
        models = generate_models(math.ceil(pow(factor, s) * (s_max + 1) / (s + 1)))   ←  Generates new models
        start_epochs = max_epochs / pow(factor, s)
        model, loss = successive_halving(models, max_epochs, start_epochs, factor)    ←  Calls successive_halving
        if loss < best_model_loss:                     ←  Updates the best model
            best_model_loss = loss
            best_model = model
    return model
```

To better understand the code, let's walk through an example with concrete numbers. If we let max_epochs be 81 and let factor be 3, s will iterate from 4 to 0. The number of models for the brackets will be [81, 34, 15, 8, 5]. This is roughly pow(factor, s) but is adjusted to a larger number as pow(factor, s) becomes smaller.

Hyperband is already implemented in KerasTuner as one of the tuners, named Hyperband, which you can use directly. You can use it either on a single GPU or on multiple GPUs for parallel tuning. You can specify factor and max_epochs in the initializer of the Hyperband class. In addition, you can specify the number of brackets with hyperband_iterations, which corresponds to the s_max argument in listing 8.21, to control the time of the search. The following listing shows an example.

Listing 8.22 Running Hyperband with KerasTuner

```
import tensorflow as tf
from tensorflow.keras.datasets import mnist
```

```
import autokeras as ak
import keras_tuner as kt

(x_train, y_train), (x_test, y_test) = mnist.load_data()

def build_model(hp):
    model = tf.keras.Sequential()
    model.add(tf.keras.layers.Flatten())
    model.add(tf.keras.layers.Dense(
        units=hp.Int('units', min_value=32, max_value=512, step=32),
        activation='relu'))
    model.add(tf.keras.layers.Dense(10, activation='softmax'))
    model.compile(optimizer='adam', loss='sparse_categorical_crossentropy')
    return model

tuner = kt.Hyperband(
    build_model,
    objective='val_loss',
    max_epochs=10,
    factor=3,
    hyperband_iterations=2,
    directory='result_dir',
    project_name='helloworld')

tuner.search(x_train, y_train,
             epochs=1,
             validation_data=(x_test, y_test))
```

Specifies the maximum number of epochs as 10

Specifies the factor by which to decrease the number of remaining models as 3

Specifies the number of brackets as 2

The code is just a normal usage of KerasTuner but with a different tuner class.

8.3.2 *Faster convergence with pretrained weights in the search space*

Training a deep learning model usually takes a long time. We can use *pretrained weights* to accelerate the training, which makes the model converge in fewer epochs.

> **NOTE** Pretrained weights are the weights of a trained model.

In some cases, you may find your dataset is not large enough to train a good model that generalizes well. Pretrained weights can also help with this case: you can download and use a model with the weights trained using other (larger and more comprehensive) datasets. The features learned by the model should be generalizable to the new dataset. When using pretrained weights, you will need to further train the pretrained model with your dataset. This process is often referred to as a kind of transfer learning.

We can use pretrained weights in two ways. The first is fairly simple: just train the model with the new dataset directly. Usually, a smaller learning rate is preferred, because a large learning rate may change the original weights very quickly. The second approach you can take is to freeze most parts of the model and train only the output layers.

For example, suppose we're using a convolutional neural network with pretrained weights for a classification task. The output layer is a fully connected layer with the same number of neurons as the number of classes. We can keep just the convolutional part of the model and discard any fully connected layers. We then append our fully connected layer with newly initialized weights to the convolutional layers and start training the model with the convolutional layers frozen, so we update only the fully connected layer we added to the model (see figure 8.6). If the model is a different type of neural network, it usually can still be divided into the feature learning part (the convolutional layers, recurrent layers, and transformers) and the head (usually fully connected layers). Therefore, we can still apply the same methods for using pretrained weights.

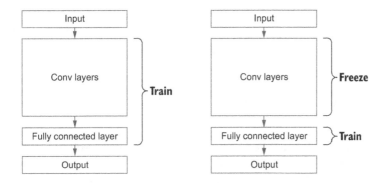

Figure 8.6 Two methods of using pretrained weights

Besides the two methods just mentioned, you can be more flexible in choosing which part of the model to freeze, which part of the model to keep, and how many layers to add to the model. For example, you can freeze some of the convolutional layers and leave others unfrozen. You can also keep one or more fully connected layers and append more than one layer to the model.

One requirement when using pretrained weights is that the training data and the dataset used to create the pretrained model must be of the same type. For example, if your dataset consists of English sentences, the pretrained model would also need to be a natural language model trained on sentences in English. If your dataset instead consisted of Chinese characters, the performance boost gained by using the pretrained weights from such a model would not be that significant, and in fact it might even have a negative effect.

AutoKeras already uses some pretrained weights in the search space. For some image- or text-related blocks, there's a Boolean hyperparameter named `pretrained` that you can specify in the initializer to indicate whether to use pretrained weights for the model. For image data, these include `ResNetBlock`, `XceptionBlock`, and

EfficientNetBlock, which use the ImageNet dataset for pretraining. For text data, BertBlock uses text extracted from Wikipedia for pretraining.

To use pretrained weights in AutoKeras, we can directly connect these blocks to form a search space using AutoModel, as shown in the following listing. This is a simple example of using a pretrained ResNet for image classification with the CIFAR-10 dataset. In the code, we specify the pretrained argument of ResNetBlock as True so that it will search for only ResNet models with pretrained weights.

Listing 8.23   Using pretrained ResNets in AutoKeras for image classification

```
import tensorflow as tf
import autokeras as ak

(x_train, y_train), (x_test, y_test) = tf.keras.datasets.cifar10.load_data()
input_node = ak.ImageInput()
output_node = ak.Normalization()(input_node)              Uses pretrained
output_node = ak.ImageAugmentation()(output_node)      weights for the block
output_node = ak.ResNetBlock(pretrained=True)(output_node)   ◁
output_node = ak.ClassificationHead()(output_node)
model = ak.AutoModel(
    inputs=input_node, outputs=output_node, max_trials=2, overwrite=True)
model.fit(x_train, y_train, epochs=10)
model.evaluate(x_test, y_test)
```

To build your own search space with models with pretrained weights, you can use Keras Applications, which has a collection of pretrained models to use. They can be imported under tf.keras.applications; for example, you can import a ResNet model from tf.keras.applications.ResNet50. Refer to https://keras.io/api/applications/ for a complete list of models.

To initialize the pretrained model object, you usually need to specify two arguments, include_top and weights. include_top is a Boolean argument specifying whether to include the classification head of the pretrained model. weights can be 'imagenet' or None, specifying whether to use the ImageNet pretrained weights or randomly initialized weights. An example using ResNet is shown in the following listing. Here, we create a ResNet without the fully connected layers and use the ImageNet pretrained weights.

Listing 8.24   Keras Applications example

```
import tensorflow as tf
resnet = tf.keras.applications.ResNet50(
    include_top=False,
    weights='imagenet')
```

You can use Keras Applications with KerasTuner to build a search space of pretrained models. For example, here we build a search space with two hyperparameters: the first one indicates whether to use pretrained weights, and the second indicates whether to freeze the model.

Listing 8.25   Using a pretrained ResNet with KerasTuner

Specifies whether to use ImageNet
pretrained weights or random weights

```
import tensorflow as tf
import keras_tuner as kt


def build_model(hp):
    if hp.Boolean('pretrained'):        ◁─┐  The hyperparameter
        weights = 'imagenet'              │  indicating whether to
    else:                                 │  use pretrained weights
        weights = None
    resnet = tf.keras.applications.ResNet50(    Does not include
        include_top=False,              ◁──┘   the classification
        weights=weights)                       head
    if hp.Boolean('freeze'):        ◁──┐  The hyperparameter indicating
        resnet.trainable = False       │  whether to freeze the model
    input_node = tf.keras.Input(shape=(32, 32, 3))
    output_node = resnet(input_node)
    output_node = tf.keras.layers.Dense(10, activation='softmax')(output_node)
    model = tf.keras.Model(inputs=input_node, outputs=output_node)
    model.compile(loss='sparse_categorical_crossentropy')
    return model


(x_train, y_train), (x_test, y_test) = tf.keras.datasets.cifar10.load_data()


tuner = kt.RandomSearch(
    build_model,
    objective='val_loss',
    max_trials=4,
    overwrite=True,
    directory='result_dir',
    project_name='pretrained')


tuner.search(x_train, y_train,
             epochs=1,
             validation_data=(x_test, y_test))
```

Builds and
returns
the Keras
model

Building such a search space to determine whether to use the pretrained weights and whether to freeze the model can help you select the best solution. Using pretrained weights and pretrained models is usually a good way to accelerate training and make your model generalize well if you have only limited training data. However, only through experimentation can you tell whether the pretrained weights are appropriate for your problem and dataset.

8.3.3   *Warm-starting the search space*

In AutoML and hyperparameter tuning, without warm-start, the search algorithm doesn't have any prior knowledge about the search space. It doesn't know the meaning of the different hyperparameters and has no idea about which models might perform well or poorly. Therefore, it has to explore a large, unknown search space gradually, sample by sample, which is not very efficient.

Warm-starting the search space means we hand-pick some good models and hyperparameters for the search algorithm to evaluate before the search starts. This is a good way to inject human knowledge of the performance of different models into the search process. Otherwise, the search algorithm may spend a lot of time on bad models and bad hyperparameter combinations before finding the good ones, which are far fewer in number than the bad ones!

With warm-start, the search algorithm can quickly find a good model with limited computational resources by exploiting the startup models. Based on this idea, we can use a greedy strategy to search the space. We start by evaluating the startup models. We then pick the best model and randomly modify its hyperparameter values a little bit to produce the model to be evaluated next.

This greedy strategy is already implemented in AutoKeras as the `Greedy` tuner. Some task-specific tuners, like `ImageClassifierTuner` and `TextClassifierTuner`, are subclasses of the `Greedy` tuner. These are the default tuners when using the task APIs, like `ImageClassifier` and `TextClassifier`. They offer a list of predefined hyperparameter values to be tried first before exploring the search space. Therefore, when you run these tasks in AutoKeras, these tuners are more efficient than tuners without warm-start.

Summary

- When the training dataset is too large to fit into the main memory, we can load the dataset into memory batch by batch for training and prediction.
- Data parallelism speeds up model training by keeping synchronized copies of the model on different devices and splitting the dataset to train them in parallel.
- Model parallelism divides a large model, putting different layers on different devices and allowing them to run in parallel (using the same data). This can also speed up training.
- Parallel tuning involves running models with different hyperparameter settings on different devices in parallel to speed up the tuning process.
- Hyperband can speed up the search process by allocating limited resources to unpromising models and using the saved resources for more promising models.
- Using pretrained weights learned on large datasets can allow for faster convergence on a new dataset and make the model generalize better when the new dataset is small.
- Warm-starting the search space gives the tuner a better overview of the space, thus speeding up the search process.

Wrapping up

9

This chapter covers

- Important takeaways from this book
- Open source toolkits and commercial platforms for AutoML
- The challenges and future of AutoML
- Resources for learning more and working in the field

We've almost reached the end of the book. This last chapter reviews the core concepts we've covered, while also aiming to expand your horizons. We'll start with a quick recap of what you should take away from this book. Next, we'll present an overview of some popular AutoML tools (both open source and commercial) outside the Keras ecosystem. An awareness of other emblematic toolkits in the current AutoML community will enable you to explore further based on your interests after reading the book. Finally, we offer some speculative thoughts about the core challenges and future evolution in the AutoML domain, which will be of particular interest if you'd like to delve into more fundamental research in this area. Understanding AutoML is a journey, and finishing this book is merely the first step. At the end of the chapter, we'll provide you with a short list of resources and strategies for learning more about AutoML and staying up-to-date with the latest developments in the field.

9.1   *Key concepts in review*

This section briefly summarizes the key takeaways from this book, to refresh your memory of what you've learned so far.

9.1.1   *The AutoML process and its key components*

AutoML allows a machine to mimic how humans design, tune, and apply ML algorithms so that we can adopt ML more easily. It aims to discover optimal machine learning solutions automatically when given an ML problem, thereby releasing data scientists from the burden of manual tuning and giving practitioners without extensive experience access to off-the-shelf machine learning techniques (see figure 9.1).

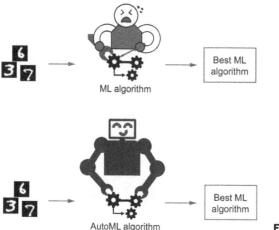

Figure 9.1   ML versus AutoML

The process of AutoML is an iterative one, typically consisting of three steps (figure 9.2):

1 Select an ML pipeline from the search space for observation based on the search strategy. The search space defines the set of hyperparameters we want to tune and the ranges of each hyperparameter from which to select. The search strategy explores the search space and selects a combination of hyperparameters in each iteration to instantiate a complete ML pipeline to be evaluated.
2 Train the selected ML pipeline on the training dataset and retrieve its performance evaluated on the validation set.
3 Update the search strategy if it is able to leverage the historical evaluations to accelerate the process of discovering better pipelines.

The three core components of AutoML are, therefore, the search space, the search strategy, and the validation process to evaluate and compare the selected pipelines. The search space is the part requiring most of your implementation work, whereas implementations of the other two are often built-in modules that you can select from an AutoML toolkit.

1. Generating
Select the next ML pipeline from
the search space for observation
based on the search algorithm.

3. Updating (optional)
Update the search algorithm based on the
evaluations if needed (e.g., updating the
Gaussian process surrogate model in the
Bayesian optimization search method).

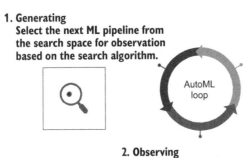

2. Observing
Train and evaluate the selected ML
pipeline on the dataset.

Figure 9.2   The search loop of a classic sequential AutoML process

9.1.2   *The machine learning pipeline*

As we described in chapter 2, a typical machine learning workflow can be summarized as follows:

- *Problem framing and data collection*—Define the goal of the problem, such as what kinds of things you want to predict or what kinds of patterns you want to extract from the data. Specify what kind of paradigm the problem belongs to, such as supervised learning, unsupervised learning, and so on. Identify a way to reliably measure the success of your final model, such as the prediction accuracy in an image-classification problem. You may need domain-specific metrics in many cases. Collect data to help train and evaluate your model.

- *Data preprocessing and feature engineering*—Process the data into a format suitable for feeding into an ML algorithm. Remove redundant features, and select or generate useful features, if needed, to help improve the performance of the algorithm. Think about how you will evaluate your model, and split the data into training, validation, and test sets to help with the evaluation process later.

- *ML algorithm selection*—Select the proper ML algorithm based on your experience and prior knowledge of the problem. You may want to try out different ML algorithms iteratively and select the best one before applying it on the final test set and deploying it.

- *Model training and evaluation*—Apply the ML algorithm to train an ML model, and evaluate it on the validation dataset based on your predefined measure.

- *Hyperparameter tuning*—Improve the pipeline to achieve better performance by iteratively tuning its hyperparameters. To avoid overfitting, make sure not to use the test set to select the ML algorithm and tune the hyperparameters.

- *Service deployment and model monitoring*—Deploy the final ML solution, and monitor its performance to continuously maintain and improve the pipeline.

9.1.3   The taxonomy of AutoML

Echoing the ML workflow, we can classify AutoML into the following three categories:

- *Automated feature engineering* often follows an iterative process of feature generation and selection. It intends to automatically discover informative and discriminative features for learning the best ML models based on predefined selection criteria.
- *Automated hyperparameter tuning* aims to select the optimal hyperparameters for one or several components in the ML pipeline. Generally, the tunable hyperparameters can include any hyperparameter in the ML pipeline, such as the model type, different data preprocessing methods, the hyperparameters of the optimization algorithm, and so on.
- *Automated pipeline search* aims to generate the entire ML pipeline based on the input data and tasks we tell the AutoML system to perform, such as classification or regression.

In the context of deep learning, we often focus on the last two of these, but automated feature engineering is also of great importance (especially for improving the performance and learning speed of shallow models).

9.1.4   Applications of AutoML

AutoML has been applied to the task of designing and tuning ML pipelines for a vast array of ML tasks. The main differences in applying AutoML in different situations lie in the design of the search space and the evaluation strategy. The search space should consist of all the ML pipelines that are applicable to the task at hand, such as CNNs for image classification, RNNs for time-series data, and so on. Designing a suitable search space for your ML task requires preliminary knowledge of task-specific ML models, and such knowledge can help narrow down the search scope to obtain better search results. The evaluation strategy should be tailored to the application so that it can provide useful measurements to compare the ML pipelines. For example, in classification tasks we can use classification accuracy as a measure, in recommendation tasks we can use the area under the curve (AUC) or normalized discounted cumulative gain (NDCG), and so on. The search methods are often applicable without modifications. Some representative AutoML applications that have been studied in literature include the following:

- *Automated object detection*—Object detection is a classic computer vision task that aims to detect objects of a certain class (such as humans, furniture, or cars) in images and videos. Automated object detection tries to generate a better fusion of multilevel object features and a better detection ML model structure to improve the object detection performance.
- *Automated semantic segmentation*—Semantic segmentation systems have two essential components: multiscale context modules and neural network architectures. The segmentation task is sensitive to spatial resolution changes. Thus, AutoML can be used to search different structures for every layer with appropriate spatial resolution.

- *Automated generative adversarial networks*—The backbone of a generative adversarial network has two components: a generator network and a discriminator network. AutoML can be used to search for the optimal network structures for the generator and the discriminator.

- *Automated network compression*—AutoML can search for the optimal combination of layer sparsity, number of channels, and bit width for network parameters to compress neural networks without a drop in accuracy or latency.

- *Automated graph neural networks*—AutoML can search for suitable graph convolution components for graph neural networks in node classification tasks, such as the number of hidden dimensions, the number of attention heads, and various types of attention, aggregate, and combine functions.

- *Automated loss function search*—The most common loss functions used in machine learning are cross-entropy and RMSE. Apart from these, AutoML can account for the intraclass/interclass distance and the levels of difficulty of samples in the loss functions for different computer vision tasks.

- *Automated activation function search*—Activation functions play an essential role in deep neural networks. Besides selecting the best existing activation function to use, AutoML can search a set of binary and unary math functions for a predefined function structure to design a new activation function.

- *Automated click-through rate* (CTR) *prediction*—CTR prediction is an important task in recommender systems. AutoML can design effective neural architectures to capture both the explicit and implicit feature interactions for better CTR predictions.

Other tasks include automated person re-identification, automated super-resolution, and automated video tasks in the computer vision domain; automated translation, automated language modeling, and automated keyword spotting in the natural language processing domain; and some model/algorithm/learning paradigm-specific and task-agnostic applications, such as automated unsupervised learning, automated reinforcement learning, automated federated learning, and so on. Generally speaking, the possible application domains of AutoML coincide with the ML space of possibilities. Wherever you can apply ML, you can apply AutoML to either generate the ML pipelines or improve a pipeline by changing its components or tuning its hyperparameters.

9.1.5 Automated deep learning with AutoKeras

Deep learning is a subfield of ML that has become a hot topic in the AI community and beyond. It shows promising performance and possibilities in a vast space of applications. Automated deep learning aims to design and tune deep learning pipelines automatically. Supported by the most popular open source deep learning library, AutoKeras, we're able to conduct automated deep learning in the following scenarios based on our requirements and different AutoKeras APIs:

- The AutoKeras task APIs can help us generate an end-to-end deep learning solution for a target ML task, such as image classification, in as few as three lines of code. These are the most straightforward AutoKeras APIs because they enable us to achieve the desired ML solution in a single step—feeding in the data—without knowing how to implement deep learning models ourselves. Six different task APIs support six different tasks in the latest release of AutoKeras, including classification and regression for image, text, and structured data. Before getting started, you should know clearly which API to use based on the ML problem you want to solve and prepare the raw data into one of the acceptable formats for AutoKeras.

- The AutoKeras input/output (I/O) API is a more general solution for handling multimodal and multitask learning problems. It accepts different types and numbers of inputs and outputs and requires you to explicitly specify their formats during initialization.

- The functional API is AutoKeras's most sophisticated API, dedicated to advanced users who want to tailor the search space to their needs. It resembles the TensorFlow Keras functional API and requires you to implement the AutoML pipeline by wiring together some AutoKeras building blocks. Each block represents a specific deep learning model (or data preprocessing method) composed of multiple Keras layers, such as a CNN, as well as the search space of the hyperparameters for the model. You can also specify the search space in each building block (or your own AutoML blocks) and wire them together with the built-in blocks to select and tune your own personalized deep neural networks.

Figure 9.3 shows examples of the use of each of these.

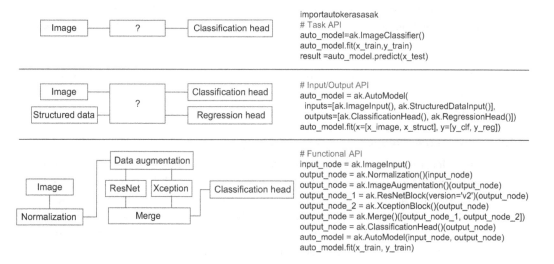

Figure 9.3   Automated deep learning with the AutoKeras APIs

AutoKeras supports your need for automated deep learning solutions for supervised learning problems, such as classification and regression. Its built-in blocks also save you effort in creating the search spaces. However, if none of the built-in blocks satisfies your needs, or you have a complex AutoML application that requires tuning the loss function, selecting shallow models, designing models for unsupervised learning problems, and so on, we suggest that you use the other AutoML toolkit in the Keras ecosystem: KerasTuner.

9.1.6 *Fully personalized AutoML with KerasTuner*

KerasTuner is a library for selecting and tuning both deep learning and shallow ML models. Besides the tasks that can be solved by AutoKeras, it tackles the following three scenarios that are difficult or introduce an extra burden for AutoKeras to handle:

- Pipelines in the search space have different training and evaluation strategies, such as shallow models implemented with scikit-learn and deep learning models implemented with TensorFlow Keras.
- You need to perform tasks other than supervised learning tasks.
- There are no built-in AutoML blocks in AutoKeras that are appropriate for use.

As stated in chapter 6, tuning a model with KerasTuner requires implementing a model-building function (or a class-extending `HyperModel`) that characterizes the search space and initializing a tuner object specifying the search method, as shown in the following listing.

Listing 9.1 Using random search to tune an MLP model with KerasTuner

```
import tensorflow as tf
from tensorflow import keras
from tensorflow.keras import layers
from keras_tuner import RandomSearch          Creates the model-
                                              building function, and
def build_model(hp):          ◄──────────────  specifies the search space
    input_node = keras.Input(shape=(20,))
    units = hp.Int('units', min_value=32, max_value=512, step=32)
    output_node = layers.Dense(units=units, activation='relu')(input_node)
    output_node = layers.Dense(units=1, activation='sigmoid')(output_node)
    model = keras.Model(input_node, output_node)

    optimizer = tf.keras.optimizers.Adam(learning_rate=1e-3)
    model.compile(
        optimizer=optimizer,
        loss='mse',
        metrics=['mae'])
    return model

tuner = RandomSearch(          ◄──────  Defines a random
    build_model,                        search tuner
    objective='val_mae',
    max_trials=5,
```

```
        executions_per_trial=3,
        directory='my_dir',
        project_name='helloworld')
```

A tuner contains a search method and organizes the training and evaluation of the
selected pipelines during the search process. Because KerasTuner is designed for tuning deep learning models, the built-in tuners (except the SklearnTuner) are dedicated to tuning deep learning pipelines. Each of them wraps up the training and
evaluation process of a deep learning pipeline, and the name denotes a specific
search method: for example, RandomSearch is a tuner that adopts the random search
method for tuning deep learning models.

We can create the search space for tuning shallow models implemented with the
scikit-learn library in the same way as for deep learning models by using the
SklearnTuner, which wraps up the training and evaluation process for scikit-learn
models or pipelines. In KerasTuner, the search method is called an oracle. So, we
can choose a different search method by changing the oracle in the tuner. We can
also customize a tuner to tune models implemented with other libraries (beyond
Keras and scikit-learn). Pseudocode for customizing a tuner is shown in the following listing; it requires the implementation of a run_trial() function for executing
the current trial and two auxiliary functions for saving and loading the evaluated
models.

Listing 9.2 Template for customizing a tuner

```
import tensorflow as tf
import keras_tuner as kt


class CustomTuner(kt.engine.base_tuner.BaseTuner):        ◁──┐ Builds and fits
                                                              a GBDT model

    def run_trial(self, trial, data):        ◁──────── Builds, trains, evaluates,
        ...                                             and saves the model
                                                        selected in the current
    def save_model(self, trial_id, model, step=0):  ◁─┐ trial, and updates the
        ...                                             oracle, if needed

    def load_model(self, trial):  ◁──┐ The model-       Saves the
        ...                            loading           model to disk
        return model                  function

my_custom_tuner = CustomTuner(
    oracle=kt.oracles.RandomSearch(
        objective=...,
        max_trials=...,
        seed=...),
    hypermodel=build_model,
    overwrite=True,
    project_name='my_custom_tuner')
>>> my_custom_tuner.search(data)
```

In addition to selecting different search methods for our custom tuner by changing the oracle, we can implement our own search techniques by customizing an oracle class, as shown in the next section.

9.1.7 *Implementing search techniques*

Existing AutoML search methods can be classified as either history-independent or history-dependent, depending on whether they can take historical search results into account to improve their performance.

Random search and grid search are two representative history-independent methods. Heuristic methods such as evolutionary methods and model-based methods, such as the Bayesian optimization method, are the two most widely used types of history-dependent methods. An evolutionary method simulates the evolution of a biological population. It randomly initializes a population of trials, and samples several parent trials from the population to generate offspring based on mutation and crossover operations of hyperparameters. After the new offspring trial is evaluated, the population is updated based on certain selection strategies, such as ranking selection. Bayesian optimization adopts a surrogate model trained with the historical evaluations of the ML pipelines as a much cheaper way to approximate the performance of unseen models. An acquisition function will leverage the approximation of the surrogate model to help sample the next available trial.

Designing a history-dependent search method requires balancing exploitation and exploration. *Exploitation* means we want to take advantage of past experience, selecting the next hyperparameter based on its proximity to the best-performing ones at present because we're confident about these points. *Exploration* means we want to explore more of the undeveloped regions in the search space to avoid getting trapped in local optima and missing the global optimum.

Implementing a history-dependent search method requires implementing two steps: hyperparameter sampling and algorithm update. The sampling and updating of a search method are implemented in the populate_space() function, as shown in the following listing.

> Listing 9.3 Template for customizing an oracle (search method)

```
class CustomOracle(Oracle):

    def __init__(self, *args, **kwargs):        Extra initialization
        super().__init__(*args, **kwargs)       steps of search method
        ...                                 ◁── can be put here

    def populate_space(self, trial_id):
        values = ...                 ◁──┐ Samples the hyperparameter
        ...                             │ values in the current trial
        if values is None:
            return {'status': trial_lib.TrialStatus.STOPPED,
                    'values': None}
        return {'status': trial_lib.TrialStatus.RUNNING,
                'values': values}
```

Updates the search method based on the search history

NOTE   In the research community, some recent advances focus on *reinforcement learning* and *gradient-based methods*, especially in the area of automated deep learning. We'll provide references to some useful learning materials at the end of this chapter so that, after reading this book, you can do some further exploration to catch up with these advances.

9.1.8   Scaling up the AutoML process

The biggest challenges of applying AutoML in practice are data scalability and time and space complexities. A typical way to tackle these challenges is to adopt parallelization techniques. As we discussed in chapter 8, the following three types of parallelization strategies exist (see figure 9.4):

- *Data parallelism* makes it possible to work with large datasets by making use of multiple machines (or CPUs/GPUs/TPUs). With this approach, you train multiple copies of the same model on different machines with different batches of data and synchronize these machines periodically to update the model weights.

- *Model parallelism* is mainly used for large models that cannot be contained in a single GPU's memory or for accelerating models whose inference processes can be parallelized. It breaks the model into different pieces and allocates them to different GPUs so that the entire model can fit in the available memory. During inference, some pieces of the model may run in parallel to save time.

- *Parallel tuning* is used to accelerate the AutoML process. With this approach, you put models with different hyperparameter settings on different GPUs and use the same dataset to train them, so the hyperparameter tuning process runs in parallel.

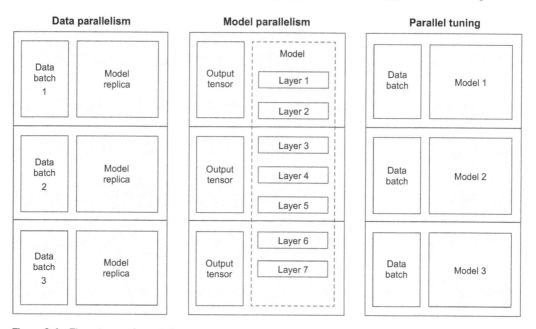

Figure 9.4   Three types of parallelism

Besides leveraging more hardware resources, we can also accelerate the search process from the algorithm's perspective in the following ways:

- *Using fidelity-based techniques*—We can use low-fidelity estimations to approximately compare the performance of different ML pipelines. Some typical methods include early stopping, subsampling data for training and evaluating the models discovered in the search process, and directly adopting an advanced scheduler method, such as Hyperband.
- *Using pretrained weights and models*—We can use pretrained weights and share them (partially) across the discovered ML models to accelerate the training of these models. This is especially useful in automated deep learning.
- *Warm-starting the search space*—We can inject some human prior knowledge into the search algorithm by hand-picking some good models and hyperparameters to evaluate before the search starts and letting the search algorithm build off of these.

9.2 AutoML tools and platforms

The development of tools and platforms has spurred the growth in the AutoML field. We introduce a selection of these here. Although the environment configurations for different tools are quite different, and some of them also provide GUIs for better visualization and easier human interaction, their APIs are often quite similar to those of AutoKeras and KerasTuner. They are all built around the three components of AutoML: the search space, the search algorithm, and the evaluation criteria. With the previous chapters as background, you should be able to adapt to any of these tools without a steep learning curve by exploring their repositories and tutorials.

9.2.1 Open source AutoML tools

The available open source AutoML toolkits can be divided into a few categories based on their core focus. These include the following:

- Tools for automated feature engineering
- Tools for automated hyperparameter tuning, model selection, and end-to-end automated pipeline search
- Tools for automated deep learning

Let's take a look at a few representative examples of each.

FeatureTools is probably the most popular open source Python library for automated feature engineering at the time of writing. It abstracts the feature engineering operations as primitives and applies them to generate features from relational datasets and temporal datasets.

Most of the existing AutoML projects focus on hyperparameter tuning or generating end-to-end ML pipelines. One of the earliest projects in this area is Auto-WEKA, which was built on top of a data analysis package named Weka (Waikato Environment for Knowledge Analysis). It conducts hyperparameter tuning and generates ML pipelines leveraging the Bayesian optimization approach, mainly for supervised learning tasks. A similar attempt that's built on top of the scikit-learn library, named Auto-Sklearn, has shown promising performance in many AutoML competitions. It also searches with the Bayesian optimization method and discovers ensemble models to boost performance. The latest version of Auto-Sklearn has a succinct API that is similar to the task API of AutoKeras, as you can see in the following listing. Some other popular libraries include TPOT, Hyperopt, Microsoft NNI, and the open source version of the H2O AutoML toolkit.

Listing 9.4   Comparing Auto-Sklearn and the AutoKeras task API

```
from autosklearn.classification import AutoSklearnClassifier
automl = AutoSklearnClassifier()
automl.fit(X_train, y_train)              ◁─── Initializes the automated
predictions = automl.predict(X_test)           classification learner of
                                               Auto-Sklearn


clf = ak.StructuredDataClassifier()       ◁─── Initializes the automated
clf.fit(x_train, y_train, epochs=10)           classification learner of
predicted_y = clf.predict(x_test)              AutoKeras
```

In recent years, most of the development effort has focused on automated deep learning. Besides AutoKeras, researchers from Amazon have proposed a package named AutoGluon, which is built on top of the Gluon deep learning API. It targets MXNet and PyTorch users and is designed to be easy to use on AWS cloud infrastructure. Other libraries, such as Auto-PyTorch, also provide neural architecture search capabilities with a similar API to AutoKeras.

In additon to the tools mentioned here, many others offer AutoML components. For example, a famous distribution execution framework for ML named Ray has a module called Ray Tune, which collects a set of open source AutoML search algorithms and utilizes the Ray framework to enable distributed tuning. The Ludwig toolbox, which allows you to train and evaluate deep learning models without writing any code, also includes an AutoML module for hyperparameter tuning and model selection. A summary of these tools is presented in table 9.1.

Table 9.1   Selected open source AutoML tools

Core task	Framework	URL
Automated feature engineering	FeatureTools	https://www.featuretools.com
Automated hyperparameter tuning or pipeline search	Hyperopt	http://hyperopt.github.io/hyperopt/
	Auto-WEKA	https://www.cs.ubc.ca/labs/beta/Projects/autoweka/
	Auto-Sklearn	https://automl.github.io/auto-sklearn/master/
	Ray Tune	https://docs.ray.io/en/master/tune/index.html

Table 9.1 **Selected open source AutoML tools** *(continued)*

Core task	Framework	URL
	KerasTuner	https://keras.io/keras_tuner/
	TPOT	http://epistasislab.github.io/tpot/
	Microsoft NNI	https://nni.readthedocs.io
	H2O AutoML toolkit	https://www.h2o.ai/products/h2o-automl/
	Ludwig	https://github.com/ludwig-ai/ludwig
Automated deep learning	AutoKeras	https://autokeras.com
	Auto-Gluon	https://auto.gluon.ai/stable/index.html

9.2.2 *Commercial AutoML platforms*

Besides the open source projects, many companies, especially those providing cloud services, are also exploring the commercial opportunity of AutoML. Some examples follow:

- Google Cloud AutoML (https://cloud.google.com/automl) provides a graphical interface for customizing ML models based on their application domain and data structures. Google's AutoML products include AutoML Vision for computer vision tasks, AutoML Natural Language for natural language processing tasks, Vertex AI for easy model building and deployment, and more.

- Amazon SageMaker Autopilot (https://aws.amazon.com/sagemaker/autopilot/) mainly focuses on the generation of end-to-end ML pipelines for tabular data classification or regression. It helps you automatically build, train, and tune the best ML model by simply feeding in the raw tabular data and the targets, and it can take advantage of the power of AWS for large-scale tasks. You can also deploy the model to production with a single click and iteratively improve it by leveraging Amazon SageMaker Studio.

- Microsoft Azure AutoML (http://mng.bz/aDEm) offers experiences tailored to two different user groups. For users who are experienced with ML and know how to implement ML models with Python code, the Azure Machine Learning Python SDK can be a good choice, enabling you to build ML models with speed and scale. For users who do not have coding experience with ML, Azure Machine Learning Studio (https://ml.azure.com) is a good match; it provides a graphical interface to perform AutoML with a few simple clicks.

- IBM Watson Studio AutoAI (https://www.ibm.com/cloud/watson-studio/autoai) automates all four steps of the AI life cycle: data preparation, feature engineering, model development, and hyperparameter optimization. You can use the tool to manage the entire life cycle and deploy your model with one click.

As well as the previously mentioned platforms, efforts are also being made by many startups, including DataRobot, 4Paradigm, H2O.ai, Feature Labs, DarwinML, and more (see table 9.2). We believe that AutoML will continue to be used and show its benefits in more and more products in the future and will help democratize ML techniques so that they can be used by more companies for different industrial applications.

Table 9.2 **Selected commercial AutoML platforms**

Company	Product	Examples of users
Google	Google Cloud AutoML	Disney, ZSL, URBN
Amazon	Amazon SageMaker Autopilot	Amazon AWS
Microsoft	Microsoft Azure AutoML	Azure Machine Learning, Power BI, and other Microsoft products
IBM	IBM Watson Studio AutoAI	IBM Cloud
DataRobot	DataRobot enterprise AI platform	Snowflake, Reltio, Alteryx, AWS, Databricks
4Paradigm	4Paradigm AutoML platform	Bank of China, PICC, Zhihu
H2O.ai	H2O AutoML platform	AWS, Databricks, IBM, NVIDIA
Feature Labs	Feature Labs AutoML platform	NASA, Monsanto, Kohl's
DarwinML	DarwinML AutoML platform	Intelligence Qubic

9.3 *The challenges and future of AutoML*

AutoML is still in its early stages, with a huge range of possibilities to be discovered and limitations to be addressed. In this section, we share our thoughts on the main challenges in the AutoML field today and provide a look forward to how these challenges may be tackled.

9.3.1 *Measuring the performance of AutoML*

Before doing AutoML, we need to clarify the objective we want to use to measure its performance. Although in most of this book we used an accuracy metric, such as image classification accuracy, to decide whether a model discovered by the AutoML algorithm is good, AutoML is not just about improving model accuracy. In practice, we may want or need to consider many objectives when applying AutoML. For example, we may want to select a deep learning model with a small model size (limiting memory consumption) or lower training/inference speed so that we can deploy it on edge devices. In this case, we might need to consider complexity measures, such as floating-point operations per second (FLOPS) during the search process. As another example, we may want a model that's able to generate results that are highly interpretable and convincing, rather than just providing accurate predictions. This is quite common in medical applications, where interpretability and transparency are of great importance. Morality and ethics also point to the importance of data privacy and prediction fairness of ML models, leading to some new research directions such as AutoML with federated learning to enhance these objectives. Because the exact objectives vary on a case-by-case basis, an ideal AutoML system should be able to take into account these task-specific requirements, and different AutoML algorithms should be better benchmarked to help users without much ML background easily select the best one to use.

9.3.2 Resource complexity

Resource consumption is one of the dominant challenges in the AutoML domain today. As datasets and ML models are becoming increasingly larger, it is often prohibitive for end users to adopt AutoML to design or tune their own ML models. We often have to settle for less due to resource constraints. Though some recent advances in the research community have aimed to propose *one-shot methods* to avoid the iterative tuning process, there is still a lot of exploration to do to reduce the time and space complexity of AutoML, from both an ML algorithm perspective and a hardware design perspective.

9.3.3 Interpretability and transparency

AutoML should ultimately facilitate convenient usage for its users and lighten their burden. This requires the AutoML system to be human-centric, meaning that users should be involved in the search process in several ways. First, the results provided by the AutoML system should be interpretable to convince users of its efficacy and foster trust in the adoption of AutoML solutions for domain-specific applications, such as medical applications. Second, users should be able to adjust the search space or the objective to accelerate the search process, which requires visibility. Third, the search method should be transparent to users to help them better understand the search process and ensure that data privacy is protected and predictions are fair. Ensuring the interpretability and transparency of AutoML also requires a deeper theoretical understanding of different ML pipelines and AutoML search techniques.

9.3.4 Reproducibility and robustness

The reproducibility of ML and the robustness of ML models are hot topics in the ML community. These issues are also important—and even more challenging—in the context of AutoML, because the AutoML system not only may control the training of multiple ML pipelines but also contains multiple "hyper-hyperparameters" that control the search algorithm. A difference in a single seed can lead to a huge difference in the training results of one ML pipeline and may also result in great variance in the hyperparameter sampling and the updating of the search algorithm. In addition, ML models, and especially deep learning models, are vulnerable to adversarial examples and human imperception perturbations. Ensuring the robustness of training and evaluating ML models and the robustness of hyperparameter sampling and search algorithm updates are indispensable for protecting the AutoML system.

9.3.5   *Generalizability and transferability*

In a real-world application, we might have multiple datasets and tasks. A human-designed model is often applicable to different datasets and can even be transferred across multiple tasks. We expect an AutoML solution to also be able to generalize to different ML applications. It is also expected to have lifelong learning ability, meaning that the meta-knowledge learned from the previous AutoML tasks can be memorized and applied to new tasks, just like how we humans accumulate knowledge and experience.

9.3.6   *Democratization and productionization*

AutoML plays an important role in democratizing advanced ML techniques, especially for users who do not have much ML expertise. Despite the open source community increasing their efforts in developing easy-to-use AutoML solutions, the learning curve of using most of these tools is still steep, requiring preliminary ML knowledge and understanding of the AutoML system. Also, because generating an AutoML solution from a universal search space is impractical, adopting AutoML methods to deal with ML tasks beyond the commonly-faced ones often requires extra manual data preprocessing work and domain-specific search space design. Commercializing and productionizing AutoML solutions also calls for more optimized system design. Deploying them can be even more complicated than embracing classic ML methods with manual design and tuning.

9.4   *Staying up-to-date in a fast-moving field*

To help you keep up with the fast-moving AutoML field, in this section we'll point you toward some useful resources that can help you keep track of and learn about recent developments in AutoML technologies. Several research groups and individual researchers survey and organize the latest advances in AutoML toolkits and papers on their websites or GitHub pages, so we'll start with a few of these (which are, at present, regularly updated). You can refer to the following resources for fast search and retrieval of materials from the AutoML literature:

- The website of the AutoML research group from the University of Freiburg, led by Professor Frank Hutter and Marius Lindauer: https://www.automl.org. In addition to hosting the project led by the research group, the site presents curated lists of AutoML papers and other resources based on categorizations such as neural architecture search (NAS).
- The GitHub web page initiated by Dr. Mark Lin, which provides a curated list of AutoML papers and other resources: https://github.com/hibayesian/awesome-automl-papers.
- The GitHub web page started by Wayne Wei, which curates a list of AutoML-related literature and toolkits: https://github.com/windmaple/awesome-AutoML

Besides these reference websites, we also recommend the following three sites where you can search for and stay up to date with the latest AutoML research papers or practice with some of the code and implementations on real-world applications:

- arXiv (https://arxiv.org) is an open-access preprint server for scientific research papers. Researchers in the ML community often post their findings or research ideas here, before their papers are even published. Though monitoring the vast numbers of papers on the site may be overwhelming, it's still a good channel, allowing you to keep track of new findings in AutoML.
- Papers with Code (https://paperswithcode.com/) curates papers with free open source code for ML. You can browse cutting-edge AutoML papers as well as explore example code and datasets for learning and practicing.
- Kaggle (https://kaggle.com) is an online community for data science and ML practitioners where participants can publish datasets, organize competitions, and solve data challenges with ML models. By participating in these competitions and learning about other practitioners' ML or AutoML solutions for different tasks, you'll gain a deeper understanding of ML models and AutoML techniques.

AutoML hasn't been on the horizon for long, but without a doubt, it's an important step toward general AI. Full automation of all ML problems is possible in the long term, but it's unlikely to happen in the near future. We may be at the peak of the inflated expectations for AutoML, and the path to general AI still holds many challenges. Its development heavily relies on the participation of researchers, developers, and practitioners from many different domains. We encourage you to continue on your way toward learning about, using, questioning, and developing AutoML, which can be a lifelong journey. Although many people think that democratizing AI may render human experts useless, to be substituted by AI agents, we believe that the wisdom of machines will never completely transcend that of human beings, and instead we will grow and learn together. All in all, we can only imagine what the future will bring, based on what we know today— but when we look back to the past and how people imagined their futures then, we often find today's reality is beyond their wildest dreams.

Summary

- This chapter summarized the core concepts you've learned in this book. We hope you've learned a thing or two about AutoML and how to apply it with the help of AutoKeras and KerasTuner, as well as caught a tempting glimpse of machine learning from the AutoML perspective.
- An increasing number of open source and commercial AutoML toolkits have been proposed, and research in this area is active. These tools help democratize ML techniques to diverse research areas and industrial applications.
- AutoML is still in its early stages, with a huge space of possibilities to be discovered and limitations to be addressed. We encourage you to learn from the provided resources to continue your exploration in this field and never stop moving toward understanding the mysteries of AutoML.

appendix A
Setting up an environment for running code

This appendix provides instructions for setting up an environment to run the code examples in this book. All the code snippets in the book are provided in the form of Jupyter Notebook scripts, or *notebooks.* Jupyter Notebook (https://jupyter.org/) is an open source web application that's popular in the machine learning and data science communities; it offers support for interactive code design, data processing and visualization, narrative text, and more for various languages, including Python. It has a flatter learning curve than running standalone Python at the command line or in an IDE such as PyCharm, facilitating learning and development.

All the code snippets shown in this book can be downloaded from https://github.com/datamllab/automl-in-action-notebooks. To run the scripts, you have the following two options:

- Use an online service or platform such as Google Colaboratory (Colab), AWS EC2, and so on.
- Install Jupyter Notebook on your local workstation.

I recommend using Google Colab, because it has a relatively flat learning curve and is easy to set up for running ML experiments. It also provides free hardware resources (CPUs and GPUs), making running experiments—especially for deep learning—much easier.

I'll begin by providing setup and configuration instructions for the Google Colab environment, then introduce some basic operations for creating and running notebooks. I'll also show you how to install the additional packages you need to run the notebooks in this book and how to configure the runtime. In the last section, I'll briefly describe how to set up the environment on your local machine so that you have more options for running the code.

A.1 Getting started with Google Colaboratory

Google Colab is a free Jupyter Notebook environment that you can use to run ML experiments. It runs entirely in the cloud and requires no installation. The default environment comes with most of the machine learning packages you'lll need, such as TensorFlow, and you have free (but limited) access to a GPU.

> **NOTE** A GPU, or graphics processing unit, is a single-chip processor used for extensive and efficient graphical and mathematic computations. GPUs are faster and more efficient than CPUs, so they're well suited to training ML models.

To get started with Colab, visit http://colab.research.google.com/ in a browser. You have the following choices:

- Create your own script by clicking New Notebook.
- Use existing scripts by uploading local files or loading them from GitHub.

If you click New Notebook (shown in figure A.1), a new Python 3 notebook environment is created for you.

Figure A.1 Click New Notebook if you want to create a new notebook in Google Colab.

All the code from this book is provided on GitHub, so you can load the notebooks directly from there by clicking the GitHub tab (see figure A.2).

Enter the URL for the book's repository, https://github.com/datamllab/automl-in-action-notebooks, and click the search button (see figure A.3).

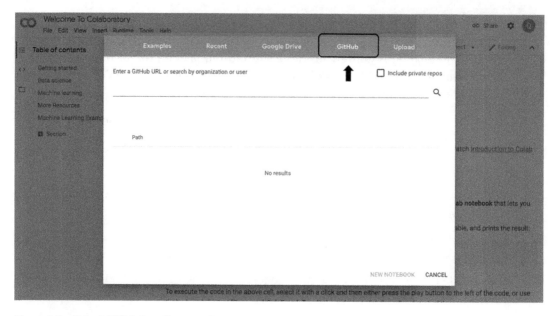

Figure A.2   Select GitHub from the menu bar to load a notebook from a GitHub repository.

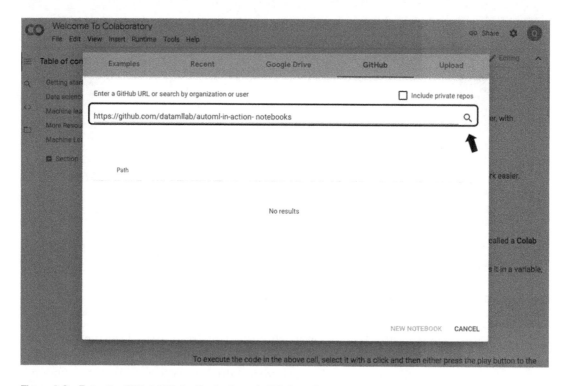

Figure A.3   Enter the GitHub URL for the book, and click Search.

The Repository menu should be set to datamllab/automl-in-action-notebooks and the Branch menu to master. Below these, you will see all the Jupyter notebooks from the book (see figure A.4).

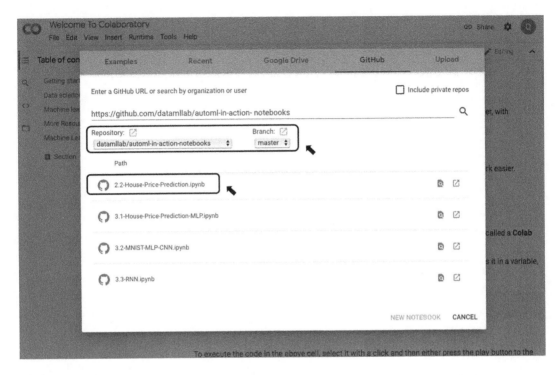

Figure A.4 Viewing the notebooks in the book's GitHub repository

If you choose the first Jupyter notebook (2.2-House-Price-Prediction.ipynb), high-lighted in the previous figure, Colab will automatically configure a Python 3 environment with CPUs that allows you to run the notebook (see figure A.5).

A.1.1 *Basic Google Colab notebook operations*

Each chunk of code or text in a notebook is called a *cell.* You can directly modify the code or text in an existing cell by clicking inside it. To run a cell, use the Shift+Enter keyboard shortcut or click the triangular Run Cell button at the left side of the cell (shown in figure A.6).

Figure A.5   The loaded 2.2-House-Price-Prediction.ipynb script

Figure A.6   Press the Run Cell button to run the code in a cell.

To add a new cell containing executable Python code, you can click + Code in the toolbar. For example, you can add a Python code cell to import the numpy package, create a numpy.ndarray object, and then run it, as shown in figure A.7.

You can also create a text cell, in which you can use Markdown syntax. To do this, click + Text in the toolbar (see figure A.8).

Figure A.7 Creating and running a code cell

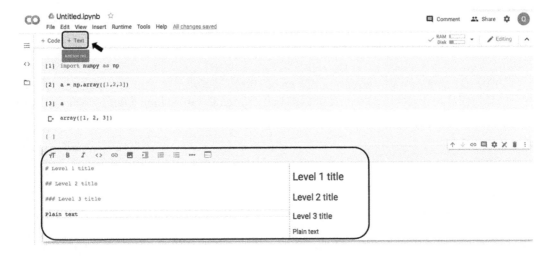

Figure A.8 Creating a new text cell

More operations, such as deleting, copying, and moving cells, can be performed by selecting a cell and using the toolbar at the upper-right corner of the selected cell (shown in figure A.9).

A.1.2 Packages and hardware configuration

The default environment of Google Colab includes most of the libraries required by this book (such as NumPy, pandas, and TensorFlow), so you don't have to install them after setting up a new environment. If you do need to install new Python packages, like AutoKeras or KerasTuner, you can use `pip`, as shown here:

```
!pip install $PACKAGE_NAME
```

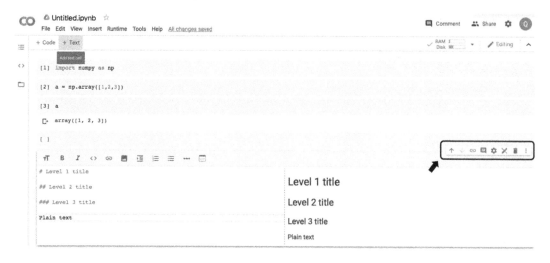

Figure A.9   The toolbar for other cell operations

For example, you can install AutoKeras as shown in figure A.10. The exclamation point (!) tells Colab to run a command as a shell command rather than a notebook command.

Figure A.10   Using `pip` to install the AutoKeras package in a Colab notebook

A list of all the packages you will need to install to run the code in this book is provided in the requirements.txt file in the book's repository (http://mng.bz/QWZ6). You can install all of them before running any of the scripts, or install them one at a time as needed.

To change the runtime or adjust the hardware, select Runtime > Change Runtime Type from the main menu (see figure A.11).

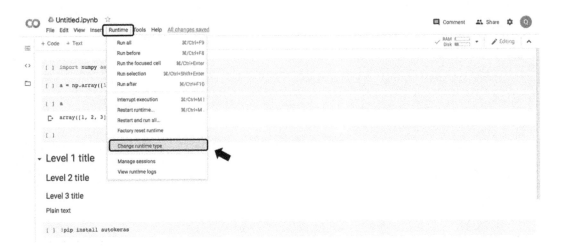

Figure A.11 Configuring the runtime and hardware

You can change the Python version from the default "book" to Python 3, and you can select the type of hardware accelerator to use: GPU, TPU, or None (the default CPU), as shown in figure A.12.

That's all you need to know to get up and running with Colab. Next, we'll show you how to install Jupyter Notebook on your local machine.

A.2 Setting up a Jupyter Notebook environment on a local Ubuntu system

This section describes how to set up a Jupyter environment to run the scripts in this book locally, on an Ubuntu/Debian system. The four basic steps follow:

- Install Python 3. It's recommended that you use Python 3 because Python 2 is deprecated and no longer supported by the Python Software Foundation.
- Create a Python 3 virtual environment, using the venv command to allow you to better manage the environment.
- Clone the book's repository, and install all the required Python packages, such as jupyter and autokeras.
- Work on the provided Jupyter notebooks.

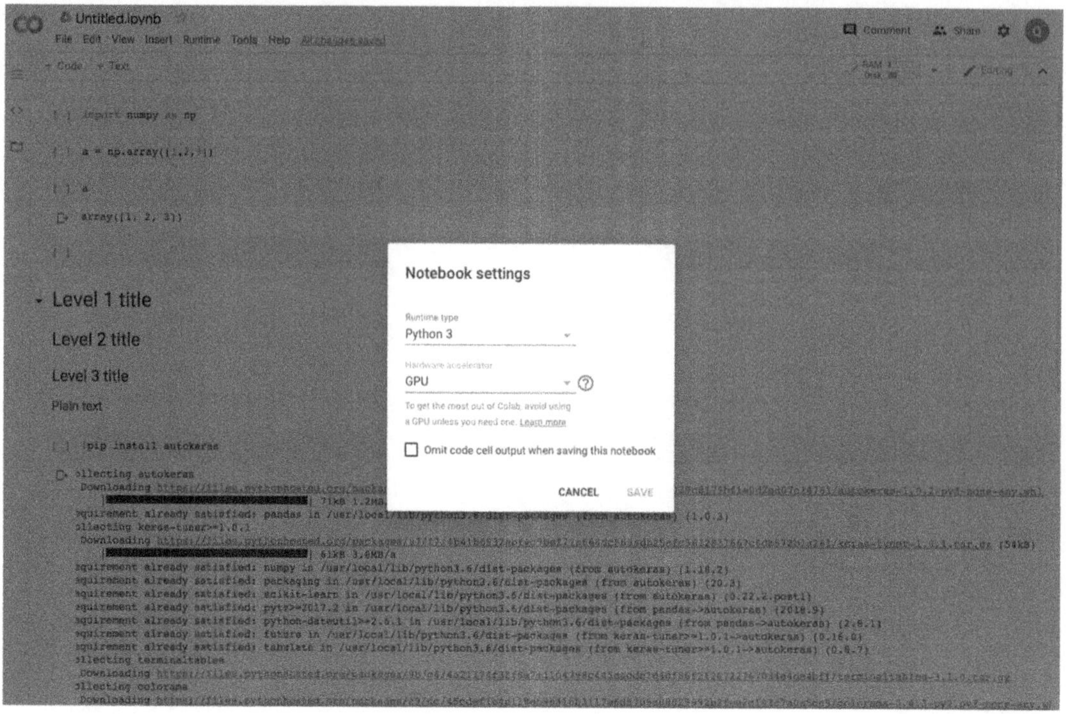

Figure A.12 Using a GPU with Google Colab

I assume you have experience installing and working in a Python 3 environment if you're choosing this option, so I'll walk through only setting up the virtual environment for running the Jupyter notebooks and the following steps in the remainder of this section. If you need details on setting up a GPU environment locally, please refer to the book *Deep Learning with Python* by François Chollet (Manning, 2021).

A.2.1 Creating a Python 3 virtual environment

I recommend using the venv to help you create a clean Python 3 environment. This will allow you to run a virtual Python environment, whose installed packages are separated from your system Python packages. First, install the venv command as follows:

```
$ sudo apt-get install python3-venv
```

Then, create a Python 3 environment named automl, as shown here:

```
$ python3 -m venv ~/automl
```

You need to activate the virtual environment before you run any Python related commands like so:

```
$ source ~/automl/bin/activate
(automl) ...$
```

When the setup is complete, you will see an (automl) prefix at the beginning of your command line, indicating the virtual environment has been launched, as shown in the previous code snippet. You can use the deactivate command to log out of the environment.

A.2.2   *Installing the required Python packages*

Once you've created your virtual environment, you'll need to install the required packages. A list of packages to install is provided in the requirements.txt file in the book's repository. You can clone the whole repository and install it with the following commands:

```
(automl) ...$ git clone https://github.com/datamllab/automl-in-
➥ action-notebooks.git

(automl) ...$ cd automl-in-action-notebooks

(automl) .../automl-in-action-notebooks$ pip install -r requirements.txt
```

The package for Jupyter Notebook is also contained in it, so you don't have to install it separately. If you have any other packages to install, you can simply use the pip command as follows:

```
(automl) .../automl-in-action-notebooks$ pip install $PACKAGE_NAME
```

A.2.3   *Setting up the IPython kernel*

You've now installed the Jupyter Notebook application and all the packages required for running the examples in this book in the virtual environment. Before working on the notebooks, you need to connect your virtual environment with Jupyter Notebook so that the code can execute in a specific Python environment. You do this by installing the virtual environment as a notebook kernel as shown here:

```
(automl) .../automl-in-action-notebooks$ ipython kernel install
➥ --user --name=automl
```

A kernel is a computational engine to help execute notebook code. An IPython kernel is used to execute Python code. You can switch between multiple kernels, which allows you to have different environments for running different code.

A.2.4   *Working on the Jupyter notebooks*

To work on a Jupyter notebook, first open the web application as follows:

```
(automl) .../automl-in-action-notebooks$ jupyter notebook
```

This will launch the application in a browser window. You can also run a Jupyter notebook on a remote server without a browser, optionally specifying the port (--port=XXXX, the default port number is 8888). It will allow you to launch the application in a local browser with the link http://localhost:XXXX as follows:

```
(automl) .../automl-in-action-notebooks$ jupyter notebook
➡ --no-browser --port=XXXX
```

This will give you a link, as shown in figure A.13, that you can use to open the Jupyter web application in your local browser.

```
(automl) qq@datalab3:~/test_book/automl-in-action-notebooks$ jupyter notebook
[I 09:23:09.955 NotebookApp] Serving notebooks from local directory: /home/qq/test_book/automl-in-action-notebooks
[I 09:23:09.955 NotebookApp] Jupyter Notebook 6.1.4 is running at:
[I 09:23:09.955 NotebookApp] http://localhost:8888/   ⬅
[I 09:23:09.956 NotebookApp] Use Control-C to stop this server and shut down all kernels (twice to skip confirmation).
[W 09:23:09.963 NotebookApp] No web browser found: could not locate runnable browser.
```

Figure A.13   Opening the Jupyter Notebook web application from the command line

After you open Jupyter Notebook and enter the folder of the downloaded repository, you'll see a list of all the notebooks for this book (as shown in figure A.14).

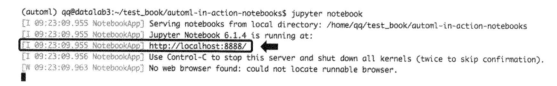

○	0 ▾	⬛ / automl-in-action-notebooks	Name ↓	Last Modified	File size
		🗀 ..		seconds ago	
○		2.2-House-Price-Prediction.ipynb		2 days ago	607 kB
○		3.1-Image-Hand-Written-Digits-Recognition.ipynb		3 days ago	309 kB
○		3.2-Text-20newsgroups.ipynb		3 days ago	164 kB
○		3.3-Tabular-Titanic.ipynb		3 days ago	98.2 kB
○		4.1-House-Price-Prediction-MLP.ipynb		3 days ago	255 kB
○		4.2-MNIST-MLP-CNN.ipynb		3 days ago	46.3 kB
○		4.3-RNN.ipynb		3 days ago	14.3 kB
○		5.2-Task-API-ImageClassifier-MNIST.ipynb		3 days ago	69.3 kB
○		5.3.1-Task-API-TextClassifier-20newsgroup.ipynb		3 days ago	69.5 kB
○		5.3.2-Task-API-StructuredDataClassifier-Titanic.ipynb		3 days ago	92.8 kB
○		5.3.3-Task-API-StructuredDataRegressor-California.ipynb		3 days ago	254 kB
○		5.3.4-Task-API-Multi-label.ipynb		3 days ago	35.7 kB
○		5.4.1-IO-API-Image-Classification.ipynb		3 days ago	56.4 kB

Figure A.14   Viewing the notebooks in the web application

You can open a notebook and then set the kernel to `automl`, as shown in figure A.15.

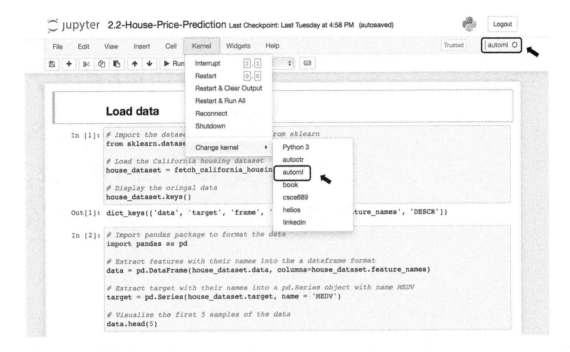

Figure A.15   Setting the kernel for a Jupyter notebook

The selected kernel will appear in the upper-right corner. You can now run or modify the notebook as desired. You can also see some useful shortcuts by pressing Cmd+Shift+P (on a Mac) or Ctrl+Shift+P (on Linux or Windows).

appendix B
Three examples: Classification of image, text, and tabular data

In chapter 2, we studied how to build an end-to-end ML pipeline to solve a regression problem with tabular (structured) data. This appendix provides three more examples aimed at getting you more familiar with the ML pipeline. The examples illustrate solving classification problems involving image, text, and tabular data with various classic ML models. If you're not experienced with ML, you'll learn how to prepare these different types of data for the models using tailored data-preprocessing methods. The problems presented here are also solved in the second part of the book with AutoML techniques. We'll begin with an image classification problem.

B.1 Image classification: Recognizing handwritten digits

Our first problem is to recognize handwritten digits in images. Following the workflow of building an ML pipeline introduced in chapter 2, we begin by framing the problem and assembling the dataset.

B.1.1 Problem framing and data assembly

This is a classification problem, because we assume the digit in each image can be only an integer in the range of 0 to 9. Recognizing the digits is, therefore, equivalent to classifying the images into the right digit classes. We can further specify the problem as a *multiclass classification problem* because we have more than two different types of digits. If there are only two target classes, we call it a *binary classification problem*.

The data we will work with is the digits dataset that comes with the scikit-learn library, consisting of 1,797 images of handwritten digits with size 8×8. We can load it with the `load_digits()` function, which we import from scikit-learn, as shown in the following listing. This returns the images and their corresponding labels (digits), which we store separately.

Listing B.1 Loading the digits dataset

```
from sklearn.datasets import load_digits

digits = load_digits()

images, labels = digits.images, digits.target
```

> **Loads the digits dataset**
>
> **Separately stores the images and corresponding targets**

The loaded data contains 1,797 images grouped into a three-dimensional array of shape 1797×8×8. Each element in the array is an integer value between 0 and 16, corresponding to a pixel in an image. The second and third dimensions are the height and width of the images, respectively, as shown next:

```
>>> images.shape, labels.shape
((1797, 8, 8), (1797,))
```

In practice, the images you're dealing with may have different sizes and resolutions, requiring crop and resize operations to align them. The dataset in this example is already in good shape, so we can move on to some exploratory data analysis (EDA) to prepare it for the ML model.

B.1.2 *Exploring and preparing the data*

We can visualize the first 20 samples using the code in listing B.2 to get a glimpse of what the data looks like. The first 20 images are shown in figure B.1.

Listing B.2 Visualizing the first 20 digit images and their labels

```
import matplotlib
import matplotlib.pyplot as plt

n = 20
_, axes = plt.subplots(2, 10, figsize=(10, 2))
plt.tight_layout()
for i in range(n):
    row, col = i // 10, i % 10
    axes[row, col].set_axis_off()
    axes[row, col].imshow(images[i,], cmap=plt.cm.gray_r,
        interpolation='nearest')
    axes[row, col].set_title('Label: %i' % labels[i])
```

> **Creates a figure and 20 subplots with layout 2×10**
>
> **Automatically adjusts the subplot parameters to give the specified padding**
>
> **Plots the first 20 digit images**

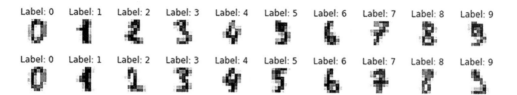

Figure B.1   Visualization of the first 20 digit images and their labels

Many classification algorithms cannot be directly applied to two-dimensional images, so next we reshape each image into a vector, as shown in the following code snippet. The reshaped data becomes a two-dimensional array of shape 1797×64. Each row vector in the array represents an image:

```
>>> n_samples = len(digits.images)
>>> X = digits.images.reshape((n_samples, -1))
>>> X.shape
(1797, 64)
```

The reshaped data has a similar format to the tabular data we worked with in chapter 2, but each image has 64 features (compared to 8 in the California housing example). More features usually translates to more computational resources and more time spent on model training. It may also make it harder to learn the ML model and extract useful classification patterns from the data. We have many feature engineering methods to deal with this issue, one of which is introduced in the next section.

B.1.3   *Using principal component analysis to condense the features*

Before performing the feature engineering, let's first hold out 20% of the data to use as the final testing set, as shown next. This will help prevent overfitting to the training data:

```
>>> from sklearn.model_selection import train_test_split
>>> X_train, X_test, y_train, y_test = train_test_split(
...     X, labels, test_size=0.2, shuffle=False)
>>> X_train.shape, X_test.shape
((1437, 64), (360, 64))
```

A natural solution to reduce the number of features in the data is to select a percentage of them. However, image features (pixels) often do not have practical meaning, which makes it hard to formulate assumptions about which ones to select. Naively selecting some of the features may spoil some images and affect the performance of the classification algorithm. For example, suppose the digits can appear either on the left or the right in any given image. Their labels will be the same, no matter which side they appear on. But if you remove the left half of all the images, some of the images will no longer contain a digit, leading to a loss of information that is useful for classification.

One classic method for reducing the number of features in images while retaining as much information as possible is *principal component analysis* (PCA). It tries to linearly transform the original features into fewer features by fitting an ellipsoid to the data (see figure B.2) and creating a low-dimensional space based on the axes of the ellipsoid. The axes are pointed out by a set of orthogonal vectors called *principal components*. Based on these components, we can redefine the coordinate space and represent each data point with the new axes. The coordinate values of each data point are its new features. We carry out the dimensionality reduction by selecting some of the principal components, using the axes they point out to form a subspace, and then projecting the data onto the new space. The selection of the subspace is based on the variances of the new features within the whole dataset. The variance is visualized by the lengths of the ellipsoid axes in the figure. To preserve more information in the dataset, we select the principal components corresponding to the largest variances. We can choose the number of principal components empirically, based on how much of the whole feature variance they can preserve.

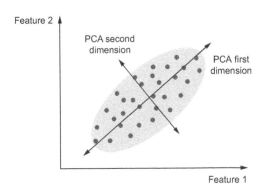

Figure B.2 Illustration of PCA: The two principal components of a cloud of data points with two features

In figure B.2, we can see that if the number of components we select is the same as the original number of features, doing the PCA transformation is the same as rotating the coordinates and mapping the data onto the new coordinate system spanned by the two principal components. If we choose to use one component, it will project the points onto the longer axis of the ellipse (the first PCA dimension in figure B.2).

For the digit images, we select 10 features here as an example, and implement PCA with scikit-learn as follows.

Listing B.3 Applying PCA on training data

```
from sklearn.decomposition import PCA

n_components = 10
pca = PCA(n_components=n_components).fit(X_train)

X_train_pca = pca.transform(X_train)
```

Imports the PCA model

Fits the model with the training data

Transforms the training data to the lower-dimensional space

For our training data, the shapes of the original feature matrix and the transformed feature matrix are (1437, 64) and (1437, 10), respectively, as shown here:

```
>>> X_train.shape, X_train_pca.shape
((1437, 64), (1437, 10))
```

To fit the PCA model, we need to input only X_train without providing the target labels. This is different from the supervised learning paradigm, where we need to provide some targets to train the ML models. This learning paradigm is called *unsupervised learning*. It aims to find undetected patterns or learn hidden transformations directly from the features without human supervision, such as labels. Unsupervised learning models such as PCA are very helpful for EDA, enabling us to uncover patterns in the data. For example, getting back to our problem, we can project the data into the two-dimensional space spanned by the first two principal components and color them with corresponding labels to visualize patterns in the training data like so (and as depicted in figure B.3):

```
plt.figure(figsize=(8, 6))
plt.scatter(X_train_pca[:, 0], X_train_pca[:, 1],
            c=y_train, edgecolor='none', alpha=0.5,
            cmap=plt.cm.get_cmap('Spectral', 10))
plt.xlabel('Component 1')
plt.ylabel('Component 2')
plt.title('PCA 2D Embedding')
plt.colorbar();
```

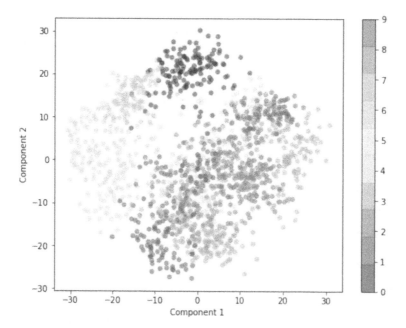

Figure B.3   Visualization of training data in 2-D space after the PCA transformation

The visualization shows a clustering pattern among the training images. That is, the images within the same digit class tend to be closer to each other in this projected two-dimensional space. Now that we've condensed the features, it's time to select an ML model to build up the classification algorithm.

B.1.4   *Classification with a support vector machine*

This section introduces one of the most popular classification models, the *support vector machine* (SVM), and two hyperparameters that we can tune to improve its performance. The simplest version of SVM is a *linear* SVM for two-class classification. We'll use binary classification as an example and assume the data has two features. The main idea of a linear SVM model is to find a line to separate the two classes of points and maximize the margin between them. The instances located on the boundaries of the margin (e.g., instances A and B in figure B.4(a)) are called *support vectors* because they "support" the two boundary lines of the margin. Suppose the two classes are directly separable, which means we can find a line that ensures all the training instances within the same class are located on the same side. In that case, we call the margin a *hard margin*. Otherwise, we can achieve only a *soft margin*, which is tolerant of some violations. A hyperparameter C can be used to decide the strength of this tolerance. Adjusting this hyperparameter is useful for a linear SVM, especially when the two classes are nearly linearly separable. For example, we can reduce C to increase the tolerance and achieve a larger margin, as shown in figure B.4(c).

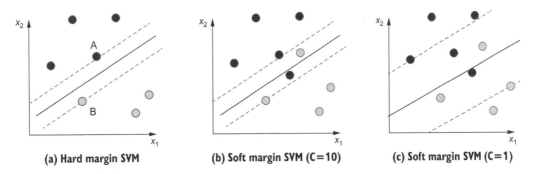

(a) Hard margin SVM   (b) Soft margin SVM (C=10)   (c) Soft margin SVM (C=1)

Figure B.4   An illustration of SVM for hard margin classification (a) and soft margin classification with different values for the hyperparameter C (b and c). The size of C here is only for illustration purposes.

Sometimes the dataset is not even close to being linearly separable (as shown in figure B.5(a)). In this case, we can use a *nonlinear* SVM. The main idea of a nonlinear SVM is to augment the number of features by mapping the original features into a higher-dimensional feature space so that the instances can become more linearly separable (see figure B.5(b)). We can make this transformation implicitly with the help of a mathematical technique called the *kernel trick*. It applies a function called a *kernel function* to directly compute the similarity between the instances in the new feature

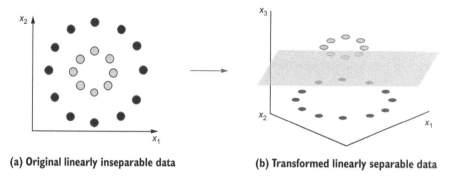

(a) Original linearly inseparable data   **(b) Transformed linearly separable data**

Figure B.5   Making linearly inseparable 2-D data linearly separable by transforming it into a 3-D space

space without explicitly creating the new features, thus greatly improving the efficiency of the SVM algorithm.

SVMs were originally designed for binary, or two-class, classification. To generalize this approach for multiclass classification, we can use the common approach of a *one-versus-one* (OvO) scheme. The scheme selects two classes from the full set of classes and builds a binary SVM classifier on this pair. Repeating this process for each pair of classes results in $\frac{c(c-1)}{2}$ classifiers, where c is the number of classes. During the testing phase, all the binary SVM classifiers are tested. Each one will classify the current example into one of the two classes with which it's trained, meaning every example will receive $\frac{c(c-1)}{2}$ votes across all the classes. The final class that a sample belongs to is the class receiving the most votes. The scikit-learn implementation of a multiclass linear SVM classifier is shown in the following example. The kernel parameter specifies the type of kernel to use.

Listing B.4   Building and training an SVM classifier

```
from sklearn.svm import SVC          ⟵——| Imports the SVM
                                          classifier module

clf = SVC(kernel='linear', random_state=42)    ⟵——┐ Creates a support vector
                                                     classifier with a linear kernel
clf.fit(X_train, y_train)
```

We use the accuracy score to evaluate our model. The prediction accuracy is defined as the number of correctly classified samples divided by the total number of test samples, as shown here:

```
>>> from sklearn.metrics import accuracy_score
>>> y_pred_test = clf.predict(X_test)

>>> acc = accuracy_score(y_test, y_pred_test)
>>> print('Prediction accuracy: {:.2f} %'.format(acc * 100))

Prediction accuracy: 93.06 %
```

The classification accuracy can be more comprehensively visualized with a *confusion matrix*, which displays the number of correct and incorrect predictions in each class like so:

```
>>> from sklearn.metrics import plot_confusion_matrix
>>> disp = plot_confusion_matrix(clf, X_test, y_test)
>>> disp.figure_.suptitle('Confusion Matrix (linear SVM classifier)')
>>> plt.show()
```

Each row in the confusion matrix corresponds to a true label, and each column is a predicted label. For example, the first row in figure B.6 corresponds to the true label 0, and the first column is the predicted label 0. The elements in a row indicate how many instances with that label were predicted to have each of the possible labels. The summation of each row equals the total number of instances in the test set with that label. The diagonal of the confusion matrix indicates the number of correct labels predicted for each class. In figure B.6, you can see that the created classifier performs worst when classifying test images with the label 3: it misclassifies six images with the true label 3 as 8s.

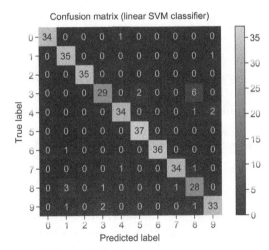

Figure B.6   Confusion matrix of linear SVM Classifier

For more details about the commonly used metrics for model evaluation, like F1-score, precision, and recall, you may refer to the book of *Deep Learning with Python* by François Chollet.

For greater convenience in data processing and hyperparameter tuning, we can combine the steps of applying PCA for feature engineering and an SVM for classification into an integrated pipeline.

B.1.5 *Building a data-processing pipeline with PCA and SVMPCA (principal component analysis)*

scikit-learn provides a simple pipeline module that we can use to assemble multiple data-processing components sequentially. The code for building up a sequential pipeline with two components (PCA followed by SVM) is shown in the following listing.

Listing B.5 Building a scikit-learn pipeline with PCA and SVM

```
from sklearn.pipeline import Pipeline
image_clf = Pipeline([                                    ⟵  Builds the image
    ('pca', PCA(n_components=10)),                             classification pipeline
    ('clf', SVC(kernel='linear', random_state=42)),])         and assigns a name
                                                              for each component

image_clf.fit(X_train, y_train)      ⟵——— Trains the pipeline

y_pred_test = image_clf.predict(X_test)      ⟵——— Tests the pipeline
```

If we check the test accuracy, as shown next, we see that it's lower than when we applied the SVM without PCA:

```
>>> acc = accuracy_score(y_test, y_pred_test)
>>> print(f'The prediction accuracy: {acc * 100:.2f} %')
The prediction accuracy: 89.44 %
```

As we saw earlier, although PCA reduces the number of features, it may also remove some discriminating information that is useful for classification. That's likely what has happened here. We shouldn't deny the usefulness of PCA in condensing the features in our data, but we should always consider the tradeoff between accuracy and simplicity when designing a pipeline.

Now, to improve the classification accuracy, let's try to tune both the PCA and SVM models in the pipeline.

B.1.6 *Jointly tuning multiple components in the pipeline*

In this example we have a scikit-learn pipeline with two different components, each of which may have multiple hyperparameters to tune. For example, we can tune both the C hyperparameter and the kernel type for the SVM classifier. Tuning a pipeline with scikit-learn is almost the same as tuning a single model. The only difference is how the names of hyperparameters in the search space are defined. To differentiate the hyperparameters in different pipeline components, we add a prefix to each one's name to indicate which component the hyperparameter belongs to (as in ComponentName_HyperparameterName). Then we can perform a grid search on all the hyperparameters by feeding in the whole pipeline.

Listing B.6 Jointly tuning three hyperparameters

```
>>> from sklearn.model_selection import GridSearchCV
>>> from sklearn.metrics import make_scorer
```

```
>>> hps = {
...     'pca__n_components': [2, 5, 10, 20],
...     'clf__C': [0.05, 0.1, 0.2, 0.5, 1, 2, 3, 4, 5, 6, 7, 8, 9, 10, 15],
... }

>>> scoring_fnc = make_scorer(accuracy_score)
```

Constructs a scoring function for performance estimation

```
>>> grid_search = GridSearchCV(estimator=image_clf,
...                            param_grid=hps,
...                            scoring=scoring_fnc,
...                            cv=3,
...                            verbose=5,
...                            n_jobs=-1)
```

Creates the grid search object for the whole pipeline with three-fold CV

Fits the grid search object to the training data to search for the optimal model

```
>>> grid_search = grid_search.fit(X_train, y_train)

Fitting 3 folds for each of 120 candidates, totalling 360 fits
[Parallel(n_jobs=-1)]: Using backend LokyBackend with 48 concurrent workers.
[Parallel(n_jobs=-1)]: Done  66 tasks      | elapsed:    1.5s
[Parallel(n_jobs=-1)]: Done 192 tasks      | elapsed:    2.1s
[Parallel(n_jobs=-1)]: Done 338 out of 360 | elapsed:    3.0s remaining:    0.2s
[Parallel(n_jobs=-1)]: Done 360 out of 360 | elapsed:    4.1s finished
```

Creates a dictionary as the hyperparameter search space

We can then print the best combination of hyperparameters and retrieve the corresponding pipeline for final testing. The final testing result is much better than we achieved with the previous pipeline, in line with our expectations, as shown here:

```
>>> grid_search.best_params_
>>> best_pipeline = grid_search.best_estimator_

>>> print('The best combination of hyperparameters is:')

>>> for hp_name in sorted(hps.keys()):
...     print('%s: %r' % (hp_name, grid_search.best_params_[hp_name]))

The best combination of hyperparameters is:
clf__C: 3
clf__kernel: 'rbf'
pca__n_components: 20

>>> y_pred_train = best_pipeline.predict(X_train)
>>> y_pred_test = best_pipeline.predict(X_test)

>>> train_acc = accuracy_score(y_train, y_pred_train)
>>> test_acc = accuracy_score(y_test, y_pred_test)
>>> print(f'Prediction accuracy on training set: {train_acc * 100:.2f} %')
>>> print(f'Prediction accuracy on test set: {test_acc * 100:.2f} %')

Prediction accuracy on training set: 99.93 %
Prediction accuracy on test set: 96.67 %
```

In this example, we explored a classic image-classification problem and learned how to stack together and jointly tune different components (models) in an ML pipeline. In the next section, we'll turn to another important data type in ML applications—text data.

B.2 Text classification: Classifying topics of newsgroup posts

In this section, we focus on a classification example with text data. In contrast with image data and tabular data, with text data we have consider semantic meaning and stronger dependencies between the features (words). We will use the 20 newsgroups dataset for our exploration here, which can be fetched with the scikit-learn library. It contains 18,846 newsgroup posts on 20 topics (http://qwone.com/~jason/20Newsgroups/). You'll learn how to preprocess text data for use with *probabilistic classification models,* which use statistical principles for classification.

B.2.1 Problem framing and data assembly

As usual, we start by framing the problem and assembling the dataset. As shown in the next listing, this is a multiclass classification problem, with 20 classes representing different newsgroup topics. Our goal is to predict the topic to which a previously unseen post belongs. The data is downloaded with the built-in data loader `fetch_20newsgroups` in scikit-learn. It has already been split into training and test sets for ease of use.

Listing B.7   Loading the 20 newsgroup dataset via the scikit-learn library

```
from sklearn.datasets import fetch_20newsgroups

news_train = fetch_20newsgroups(subset='train',
    shuffle=True, random_state=42)                    ◁─┐  Loads the training and test
news_test = fetch_20newsgroups(subset='test',            │  data separately and shuffles
    shuffle=True, random_state=42)                    ◁─┘  the data in each of them

doc_train, label_train = news_train.data,
    news_train.target                                 ◁─┐  Separately stores the
doc_test, label_test =  news_test.data,                  │  text documents and
    news_test.target                                  ◁─┘  corresponding targets
```

A quick inspection shows that `doc_train` and `doc_test` are lists of 11,314 and 7,532 documents, respectively, as shown here:

```
>>> len(doc_train), len(doc_test)
(11314, 7532)
```

Let's print a sample document to get a sense of what the raw text features look like. Each document is a string containing letters, numbers, punctuation, and some special characters, as shown in the following code sample:

```
>>> type(doc_train[0]), doc_train[0]
(str,
 'From: lerxst@wam.umd.edu (where's my thing)\nSubject: WHAT car is
     this!?\nNntp-Posting-Host: rac3.wam.umd.edu\nOrganization: University
     of Maryland, College Park\nLines: 15\n\n I was wondering if anyone out
     there could enlighten me on this car I saw\nthe other day. It was a 2-
     door sports car, looked to be from the late 60s/\nearly 70s. It was
     called a Bricklin. The doors were really small. In addition,\nthe front
     bumper was separate from the rest of the body. This is \nall I know.
     If anyone can tellme a model name, engine specs, years\nof production,
     where this car is made, history, or whatever info you\nhave on this
     funky looking car, please e-mail.\n\nThanks,\n- IL\n    ---- brought to
     you by your neighborhood Lerxst ----\n\n\n\n\n')
```

The raw text is not something we can input to an ML model directly, so let's do some data preparation to make it neater.

B.2.2 *Data preprocessing and feature engineering*

The current text documents are in a string format, so we'll start by converting the strings into numeric vectors that we can feed to our ML algorithms.

In general, all the words, special characters, and punctuation can be features of a text document. We can group multiple words and/or characters as one feature (called a "word" or "term") and deal with them jointly. An intuitive way to numerically encode the features of the dataset is to collect all the unique words appearing in all the documents of the corpus and convert each document into a numeric vector, where the length of the vector equals the number of unique words it contains. Each element in the vector denotes the occurrence of the corresponding word in this document. This transformation method is called the *bag of words* (BoW) approach (shown in figure B.7).

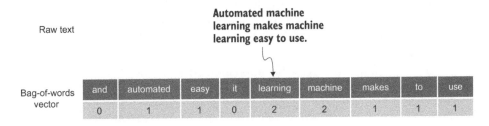

Figure B.7 Transforming a document into a BoW representation

To implement the approach, we need to first partition each document into a set of words (*tokens*). This process is called *tokenization*. The tokenization and BoW transformation can be done together with a single call of the built-in class CountVectorizer in scikit-learn, as follows.

> **Listing B.8   Transforming the training documents to a BoW representation**

```
from sklearn.feature_extraction.text import CountVectorizer

count_vec = CountVectorizer()

X_train_counts = count_vec.fit_transform(doc_train)
```

Constructs a CountVectorizer object ⟵ `count_vec = CountVectorizer()`

Converts the training text documents to a matrix of token counts ⟵ `X_train_counts = count_vec.fit_transform(doc_train)`

By printing the shape of the transformed training documents, as shown next, we can see that the transformed matrix has 130,107 columns representing the BoW extracted from the training documents:

```
>>> X_train_counts.shape
(11314, 130107)
```

The BoW approach helps us convert our collection of string documents into a matrix of token counts that can be fed into an ML algorithm. However, the number of the occurrence of words in the documents may not be good features to be used directly, due to the following two problems:

- Documents are of different lengths. A word that occurs the same number of times in two documents may not have the same importance in both of them.
- Some words may have a very high rate of occurrence in the whole text corpus, such as "the" and "a." They often carry little meaningful information for classification compared with some low-frequency words.

To address these problems, we often use a feature transformation technique named *Term Frequency-Inverse Document Frequency* (TF-IDF). The core idea is to evaluate how important a word is in a document by calculating its frequency (usually just a raw count) and dividing it by the number of documents in the corpus that contain this word. Terms that occur very frequently in a document but less frequently across the whole corpus are considered to be more important for that document than words that occur frequently, not only in that document but also in a large number of other documents.

The transformation can be implemented with the `TfidfTransformer` class in scikit-learn as follows:

```
from sklearn.feature_extraction.text import TfidfTransformer
tfidf_transformer = TfidfTransformer()
X_train_tfidf = tfidf_transformer.fit_transform(X_train_counts)
```

Despite the advantages of TF-IDF, it also suffers from some problems, such as high computational complexity and limited power to capture the semantic similarities between words. Further exploration is left as an exercise for the reader. Another approach, using *word embeddings*, is introduced in chapter 3.

Our next step is to build a text classifier and train it with the prepared dataset. The following two sections introduce two probabilistic classifiers that can be used to address this problem. Both of them are fundamental ML models that have been widely used in the areas of text classification and beyond.

B.2.3   *Building a text classifier with the logistic regression model*

The first model we will explore is the *logistic regression model*. From the name, you may think it is a regression model similar to the linear regression model introduced in chapter 2, but, in fact, it is designed for classification problems. The difference between the linear regression model and the logistic regression model is in their outputs. Whereas the linear regression model directly outputs a predicted target value based on a sample's features, the logistic regression model outputs the *logits* of the sample. A logit is defined as $logit(p) = log(\frac{p}{1-p})$, where p is the probability of a sample belonging to a specific class. We can estimate this probability by counting the frequency of labels of each class in the training set. During the testing phase, given an unseen example, we can calculate the probability of it belonging to each of the classes based on its features and assign it to the class with the highest probability.

For multiclass classification, we can use the OvO scheme (similar to the multiclass SVM model), or we can use another scheme called *one-versus-rest* (OvR). Unlike the OvO scheme, which needs to build a classifier for each pair of classes, the OvR scheme requires building n classifiers, where n is the number of classes. Each classifier corresponds to one of the classes. It then tries to discriminate the examples in each class from the remaining $n{-}1$ classes. In the testing phase, we apply all n classifiers to an unseen example to get the sample's probabilities for every class. The example is assigned to the class with the highest probability.

We can construct a multiclass logistic regression classifier and perform training with the preprocessed documents using the following code:

```
from sklearn.linear_model import LogisticRegression
lr_clf = LogisticRegression(multi_class='ovr', random_state=42)
lr_clf.fit(X_train_tfidf, label_train)
```

We then apply the same transformers on the test data and evaluate the learned logistic regression classifier as follows:

```
>>> from sklearn.metrics import accuracy_score

>>> X_test_counts = count_vec.transform(doc_test)
>>> X_test_tfidf = tfidf_transformer.transform(X_test_counts)
>>> label_pred_test = lr_clf.predict(X_test_tfidf)

>>> lr_acc = accuracy_score(label_test, label_pred_test)
>>> print(f'Test accuracy: {lr_acc * 100:.2f} %')

Test accuracy: 82.78 %
```

The test accuracy is 82.78%. You can also plot the confusion matrix if you're interested in more detailed classification results across different labels.

B.2.4   *Building a text classifier with the naive Bayes model*

Another well-known probabilistic model that is often used for text classification is the *naive Bayes model*. It applies Bayes' theorem to calculate the probability that a given data point belongs to each class. The "naive" here means we assume all the features are independent of each other. For example, in this news topic classification problem, we assume the probability of each term occurring in a specific topic class is independent of other terms. That assumption might sound unreasonable to you, especially for text data, but it often works quite well in practice.

When applying the naive Bayes model, we need to perform the following two operations during the training phase:

- Count the occurrences of each term that appears in each class in the training set, and divide it by the total number of terms in this class. This serves as the estimation of the probability $P(term_i|class_j)$.
- Count the frequency of each class that appears in the training set, which is the estimation of $P(class_j)$.

The naive Bayes model can also handle multiclass classification by assuming the probability distribution of $(term_i, class_j)$ to be a multinomial distribution. We will not get into the mathematical details but focus only on the scikit-learn implementation. Here's the code to train a naive Bayes model with the preprocessed text data:

```
from sklearn.naive_bayes import MultinomialNB
nb_clf = MultinomialNB().fit(X_train_tfidf, label_train)
```

During the testing phase, we can apply Bayes' theorem to calculate the probability of a document belonging to each class based on the features it contains. The final label of the document is predicted as the class with the largest probability. We apply the same transformers fit on the training data to the test data and evaluate the learned naive Bayes classifier as follows:

```
>>> X_test_counts = count_vec.transform(doc_test)
>>> X_test_tfidf = tfidf_transformer.transform(X_test_counts)

>>> label_pred_test = nb_clf.predict(X_test_tfidf)

>>> lr_acc = accuracy_score(label_test, label_pred_test)

>>> print(f'Test accuracy: {lr_acc * 100:.2f} %')
>>> Test accuracy: 77.39 %
```

The final test accuracy of the multinomial naive Bayes model with default hyperparameters in scikit-learn is 77.39%—a bit worse than 82.78% achieved by the previous logistic regression model. Let's try to improve it by tuning some of the key hyperparameters.

B.2.5 Tuning the text-classification pipeline with grid search

Up to now, we have introduced the following three data processing components into the text classification pipeline:

- BoW transformer
- TF-IDF transformer
- Classifier (logistic regression model/naive Bayes model)

We can use the same process introduced in section B.1.6 to construct a sequential pipeline combining all three components for joint hyperparameter tuning. We select the multinomial naive Bayes classifier here as an example to build up the scikit-learn pipeline, and choose the folllowing three hyperparameters to tune:

- `ngram_range` *in the* `CountVectorizer` *operation*—`CountVectorizer` counts the occurrences of each term in the document to perform the BoW transformation. It can also count the occurrences of *n* consecutively appearing terms, which is called a *ngram*. For example, in the sentence "I love machine learning," the 1-grams (unigrams) are "I," "love," "machine," and "learning"; the 2-grams (bigrams) are "I love," "love machine," and "machine learning."
- `use_idf`—Determines whether we want to use the TF-IDF transformation or the TF transformation.
- `alpha`—The smoothing hyperparameter in the multinomial naive Bayes classifier. One problem with the naive Bayes model is that if a term never occurs in any documents in a given topic class in the training set ($P(term_i|class_j) = 0$), we will never assign a document with this term to that class during testing. To mitigate this problem, we usually introduce a smoothing hyperparameter to assign a small probability to these terms in these classes so that each term has a chance to occur in each class.

We can set up the whole pipeline and customize the search spaces of the three hyperparameters with the following code.

> ### Listing B.9 Creating a pipeline for text classification

```
text_clf = Pipeline([
    ('vect', CountVectorizer()),
    ('tfidf', TfidfTransformer()),          Defines the
    ('clf', MultinomialNB()),])     ◁──┘   pipeline

hps = {
    'vect__ngram_range': [(1, 1), (1, 2)],
    'tfidf__use_idf': (True, False),              Declares the hyperparameters
    'clf__alpha': (1, 1e-1, 1e-2),                to be searched and defines
}                                    ◁────────    their search spaces
```

We apply grid search and use three-fold CV for model selection as follows:

```
>>> scoring_fnc = make_scorer(accuracy_score)

>>> grid_search = GridSearchCV(estimator=text_clf,
...                            param_grid=hps,
...                            scoring=scoring_fnc,
...                            cv=3,
...                            verbose=5,
...                            n_jobs=-1)

>>> grid_search = grid_search.fit(doc_train, label_train)

Fitting 3 folds for each of 12 candidates, totalling 36 fits
[Parallel(n_jobs=-1)]: Using backend LokyBackend with 48 concurrent workers.
[Parallel(n_jobs=-1)]: Done   5 out of  36 | elapsed:
➥ 7.1s remaining:   43.8s
[Parallel(n_jobs=-1)]: Done  13 out of  36 | elapsed:
➥ 10.0s remaining:   17.6s
[Parallel(n_jobs=-1)]: Done  21 out of  36 | elapsed:
➥ 18.2s remaining:   13.0s
[Parallel(n_jobs=-1)]: Done  29 out of  36 | elapsed:
➥ 20.2s remaining:    4.9s
[Parallel(n_jobs=-1)]: Done  36 out of  36 | elapsed:   21.6s finished
```

We then retrieve the search results of each pipeline represented by the three hyperparameters from `grid_search.cv_results_`. The best pipeline can be obtained as follows:

```
>>> grid_search.best_params_
>>> best_pipeline = grid_search.best_estimator_

>>> for hp_name in sorted(hps.keys()):
...     print('%s: %r' % (hp_name, grid_search.best_params_[hp_name]))

clf__alpha: 0.01
tfidf__use_idf: True
vect__ngram_range: (1, 2)
```

If we do not specify the `refit` hyperparameter in the `GridSearchCV` object, the best pipeline will be automatically trained on the whole training dataset after CV. Thus, we can directly evaluate the final results of the best pipeline on the test set. As shown next, the final accuracy is 83.44%, which is much better than the 77.39% achieved by the initial one:

```
>>> test_acc = accuracy_score(label_test, label_pred_test)
>>> print(f'Test accuracy: {test_acc * 100:.2f} %')

Test accuracy: 83.44 %
```

Now that you've seen how to approach classification tasks on image data and text data, let's come back to tabular data to work on a comparably more complex example.

B.3   *Tabular classification: Identifying Titanic survivors*

Our last example will use the famous Titanic Kaggle competition dataset, edited by Michael A. Findlay. It contains the personal information of 1,309 passengers on the *Titanic*, such as name and gender (891 in the training set and 418 in the test set). Our goal is to identify the survivors. Instead of having a well-prepared numeric feature matrix for the tabular data, you'll learn how to preprocess a more coarse dataset with mixed data types and missing values. The techniques described here are commonly seen in many Kaggle competitions that deal with tabular datasets and are also widely used in practical applications, even today with the prevalence of deep learning.

B.3.1   *Problem framing and data assembly*

The problem here is a binary classification problem, where the target label indicates whether the passenger survived (1) or not (0). We collect the data from the OpenML platform.[1] scikit-learn provides a built-in API to fetch the dataset. We can format the fetched data into a DataFrame by setting the as_frame option to True, as shown in the following listing.

Listing B.10   Fetching the Titanic dataset

```
from sklearn.datasets import fetch_openml

titanic = fetch_openml(
    name='titanic', version=1, as_frame=True)    ◁── Fetches the first version of
                                                    the Titanic dataset from
                                                    OpenML as a DataFrame

data, label = titanic.data.copy(), titanic.target.copy()    ◁── Deep copies the data
                                                                to avoid in-place
data.head(5)    ◁── Views the features of the                   data-processing
                    first five passengers                       operations later
```

The first five examples in the raw feature matrix are shown in figure B.8.

	pclass	name	sex	age	sibsp	parch	ticket	fare	cabin	embarked	boat	body	home.dest
0	1.0	Allen, Miss. Elisabeth Walton	female	29.0000	0.0	0.0	24160	211.3375	B5	S	2	NaN	St Louis, MO
1	1.0	Allison, Master. Hudson Trevor	male	0.9167	1.0	2.0	113781	151.5500	C22 C26	S	11	NaN	Montreal, PQ / Chesterville, ON
2	1.0	Allison, Miss. Helen Loraine	female	2.0000	1.0	2.0	113781	151.5500	C22 C26	S	None	NaN	Montreal, PQ / Chesterville, ON
3	1.0	Allison, Mr. Hudson Joshua Creighton	male	30.0000	1.0	2.0	113781	151.5500	C22 C26	S	None	135.0	Montreal, PQ / Chesterville, ON
4	1.0	Allison, Mrs. Hudson J C (Bessie Waldo Daniels)	female	25.0000	1.0	2.0	113781	151.5500	C22 C26	S	None	NaN	Montreal, PQ / Chesterville, ON

Figure B.8   Raw features of the first five samples of the Titanic data

---

[1] The OpenML platform (https://openml.org), founded by Joaquin Vanschoren, is an online platform for sharing data, code, models, and experiments to make ML and data analysis simple, open, accessible, and reproducible.

By viewing the first five samples, we can observe that the passengers have 13 features. The features are of different formats and data types. For example, the name feature is of type string, the sex feature is a categorical feature, and the age feature is a numerical feature. Let's do some further exploration of the dataset and prepare it for the ML algorithms.

B.3.2 Data preprocessing and feature engineering

We can consider the following three typical procedures to prepare the tabular data:

- Recover missing data.
- Extract features based on prior knowledge, such as extracting the gender feature based on the titles in passenger names (Mr., Ms., and so on).
- Encode categorical features to numerical ones.

First let's check for missing values. By counting the number of missing values in each feature, we can see that there are seven features with missing values, as shown here: age, fare, cabin, port of embarkation (embarked), boat, body, and passenger's home/destination (home.dest):

```
>>> data.isnull().sum()
pclass         0
name           0
sex            0
age          263
sibsp          0
parch          0
ticket         0
fare           1
cabin       1014
embarked       2
boat         823
body        1188
home.dest    564
dtype: int64
```

Considering that we only have 1,309 data points, the numbers of missing values in the cabin, boat, body, and home.dest features are quite large. Imputing these data points improperly could hurt the model's performance, so we'll drop these four features and consider imputing missing values only for the remaining three, as shown here:

```
data = data.drop(['cabin', 'boat', 'body', 'home.dest'], axis=1)
```

We can use many techniques to impute the missing data, of which the next three are quite common:

- *Manually extrapolate the features based on sensible feature correlations*—This often requires domain expertise and human effort but can be more accurate than the other options. For example, we can extract the two passengers whose embarked feature is missing a value and check their ticket fares to guess their embarkation ports.

- *Use statistical information*—For example, we can use the mean or median value to impute the missing `fare` value. This is often a convenient and efficient approach but may lose some discriminative information for classification.
- *Use ML models to estimate the values based on other features*—For example, we can treat the `age` feature as a target and use regression to estimate the missing values based on other features. This method can be powerful but may overfit the data by overusing the feature correlation. It also highly relies on and can be biased by the model used to impute the missing data.

Because the `fare` and `embarked` features are missing only a few values, let's first impute them with some sensible feature correlation. We begin by plotting a set of box plots of the passengers' fares, grouping them by their embarked port (`embarked`) and the class they were in (`pclass`), as shown in the next code sample.

Listing B.11   Box plots of fares grouped by `embarked` and `pclass`

```
import seaborn as sns
boxplot = sns.boxplot(
    x='embarked', y='fare', data=data,hue='pclass')
boxplot.axhline(80)
boxplot.set_title(
    'Boxplot of fare grouped by embarked and pclass')
boxplot.text(
    x=2.6, y=80, s='fare = $80', size='medium', color='blue', weight='bold')
```

Draws the box plots

Imports the package for drawing the box plots

Sets the $80 fare horizontal line

Adds a title

Adds a plot legend

From figure B.9, we can observe that passengers with the same port of embarkation have quite different distributions on the `fare` feature, highly related to the `pclass` feature.

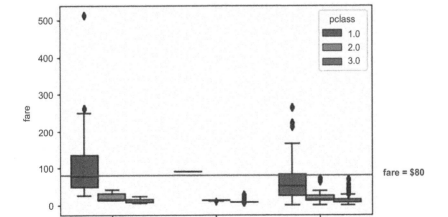

Box plots of fares grouped by `embarked` and `pclass`

Figure B.9   Box plots of passenger fares grouped by the `embarked` and `pclass` features

By checking the passengers who are missing the `embarked` feature, we can see that both of the passengers are in first class with an $80 fare paid for their tickets (see figure B.10), as shown here:

```
>>> data[data['embarked'].isnull()]
```

	pclass	name	sex	age	sibsp	parch	ticket	fare	embarked
168	1.0	Icard, Miss. Amelie	female	38.0	0.0	0.0	113572	80.0	NaN
284	1.0	Stone, Mrs. George Nelson (Martha Evelyn)	female	62.0	0.0	0.0	113572	80.0	NaN

Figure B.10   Passengers missing the `embarked` feature

The $80 reference line on the plot shows that passengers in first class who paid a fare of $80 are highly likely to have embarked at port C. Thus, we'll fill in the missing embarked feature for these two passengers with port C as follows:

```
>>> data['embarked'][[168, 284]] = 'C'
```

Similarly, we can check the passenger with the missing fare (see figure B.11) like so:

```
>>> data[data['fare'].isnull()]
```

	pclass	name	sex	age	sibsp	parch	ticket	fare	embarked
1225	3.0	Storey, Mr. Thomas	male	60.5	0.0	0.0	3701	NaN	S

Figure B.11   Passengers missing the `fare` feature

This passenger traveled in third class and embarked at port S. We can combine this with statistical information and impute the missing fare by supplying the median fare value of the passengers in the same class who also embarked at port S, as shown next:

```
>>> data['fare'][1225] = data.groupby(
...      ['embarked', 'pclass'])
...      .get_group(('S', 3))['fare']
...      .median()
```

For the last missing feature (age), we directly use the statistical median to impute the missing values as follows:

```
>>> data['age'].fillna(data['age'].median(skipna=True), inplace=True)
```

After dealing with all the missing data, the next step is to do some feature extraction based on common sense. We use the `name` feature as an example here. This feature seems to be quite chaotic and useless at first glance, but on examination we can see that the names include titles (Mr., Mrs., Master, and so on) that may reflect the passengers' marital status and potential social status. We first extract the titles and explore the frequency of each as follows:

```
>>> data['title'] = data['name'].str.extract(' ([A-Za-z]+)\.', expand=False)
>>> data['title'].value_counts()
Mr          757
Miss        260
Mrs         197
Master       61
Rev           8
Dr            8
Col           4
Major         2
Ms            2
Mlle          2
Capt          1
Don           1
Mme           1
Countess      1
Dona          1
Lady          1
Jonkheer      1
Sir           1
Name: title, dtype: int64
```

As some of the titles are similar from a machine learning perspective, such as "Ms" and "Miss," we can unify them first. And because several of the titles appear only rarely in the dataset, a common practice we can use here is to combine the rare titles into one category to aggregate the information. In the next listing, we consider titles that appear fewer than eight times as rare titles.

Listing B.12 Unifying synonymous titles and combining rare titles

```
data['title'] = data['title'].replace('Mlle', 'Miss')      Aggregates titles with
data['title'] = data['title'].replace('Ms', 'Miss')        same meaning by
data['title'] = data['title'].replace('Mme', 'Mrs')        reassigning

data['title'] = data['title'].replace(
    ['Lady', 'Countess','Capt', 'Col','Don', 'Dr',
     'Major', 'Rev', 'Sir', 'Jonkheer', 'Dona'], 'Rare')    ◄───   Combines the
                                                                    remaining rare
data = data.drop(['name'], axis=1)   ◄─┐                            titles into one

       Drops the original name column ─┘
```

After doing the title extraction, we display the current data again by viewing the first five examples (see figure B.12) as follows:

```
>>> data.head(5)
```

	pclass	sex	age	sibsp	parch	ticket	fare	embarked	title
0	1.0	female	29.0000	0.0	0.0	24160	211.3375	S	Miss
1	1.0	male	0.9167	1.0	2.0	113781	151.5500	S	Master
2	1.0	female	2.0000	1.0	2.0	113781	151.5500	S	Miss
3	1.0	male	30.0000	1.0	2.0	113781	151.5500	S	Mr
4	1.0	female	25.0000	1.0	2.0	113781	151.5500	S	Mrs

Figure B.12   The first five samples of the Titanic dataset after missing data imputation and name title extraction

The last step is to convert the categorical features, including sex, embarked, and title, into numerical ones. Although some ML libraries can directly accept string-valued categorical features, we'll do this preprocessing for the purposes of illustration. An intuitive way of transforming these features is to encode them as integers. This method can work well for categorical features with a low number of levels (in other words, few categories), such as sex, but it can affect the model's performance when the number of levels is high. This is because we introduce ordinal relationships in the transformed numerical values that do not necessarily exist originally. Another popular option is *one-hot encoding*, which does not have this problem but may harm efficiency by introducing too many new features. One-hot encoding is done by converting a categorical feature into N binary categorical features, where the N new features represent the N levels of the original categorical feature. For each instance, we will set only one of the N new features (the category it belongs to) to 1; the others will be set to 0. For example, the sex feature of a female and a male passenger will be transformed to $[1, 0]$ and $[0, 1]$, respectively, where the first element in the vector indicates that the passenger is female, and the second indicates that the passenger is male. We can do the transformation for all the categorical features in the same way as follows.

Listing B.13   One-hot encoding of categorical data

```
import pandas as pd
encode_col_list = ['sex', 'embarked', 'title']
for i in encode_col_list:
    data = pd.concat(
        [data, pd.get_dummies(data[i], prefix=i)],axis=1)    ← Performs the one-hot encoding
    data.drop(i, axis = 1, inplace=True)    ← Removes the original feature
data.drop('ticket', axis = 1, inplace=True)    ← Drops the ticket feature because it contains too many levels
```

Note that although the ticket feature is also a categorical feature, we directly drop it without encoding it. This is because it contains too many unique categories compared with the total number of examples, as shown in the next code snippet:

```
>>> data['ticket'].describe()
count            1309
unique            929
top          CA. 2343
freq               11
Name: ticket, dtype: object
```

The final data contains 15 features, as shown in figure B.13.

	pclass	age	sibsp	parch	fare	sex_female	sex_male	embarked_C	embarked_Q	embarked_S	title_Master	title_Miss	title_Mr	title_Mrs	title_Rare
0	1.0	29.0000	0.0	0.0	211.3375	1	0	0	0	1	0	1	0	0	0
1	1.0	0.9167	1.0	2.0	151.5500	0	1	0	0	1	1	0	0	0	0
2	1.0	2.0000	1.0	2.0	151.5500	1	0	0	0	1	0	1	0	0	0
3	1.0	30.0000	1.0	2.0	151.5500	0	1	0	0	1	0	0	1	0	0
4	1.0	25.0000	1.0	2.0	151.5500	1	0	0	0	1	0	0	0	1	0

Figure B.13   Final features of the first five samples of the Titanic dataset

Finally, we split the data into training and test sets, as shown next. The split number 891 is set based on the original split of the dataset in the Kaggle competition:

```
>>> X_train, X_test, y_train, y_test = data[:891], data[891:], label[:891],
        label[891:]
```

Now that we've finished our preprocessing, we are ready to apply ML algorithms on the Titanic dataset.

B.3.3   Building tree-based classifiers

Until the rise of deep learning, tree-based models were often considered the most powerful models for tabular data classification. This section introduces three types of tree-based classification models. The first one is a regular decision tree model, similar to the one we used in chapter 2. The others are *ensemble models*, which aim to leverage the collective power of multiple decision trees for better classification accuracy.

In the California housing price-prediction example in chapter 2, we created a decision tree model to perform the regression task. We can also build a decision tree model for a classification problem with a few minor modifications—we need to change the tree-split criterion from a regression performance measurement to a classification performance measurement during training, and we need to alter the way we make predictions as follows:

- In the regression example, we used MSE as the split criterion to measure the quality of each node split. Here we can use a criterion called *entropy*, which measures the useful information gain for classification achieved by a specific node split. The mathematical definition of entropy is beyond the scope of this book.

- In the regression example, we did the prediction using the mean value of the training samples in the same leaf node as the test sample. Here we use the mode value of the target labels of those training samples instead.

Implementing a decision tree classifier is straightforward with the help of scikit-learn, as shown in the next listing.

Listing B.14   Creating a tree a decision tree classifier on the Titanic dataset

```
from sklearn.tree import DecisionTreeClassifier
dt_clf = DecisionTreeClassifier(
    criterion='entropy', random_state=42)          ◁─┐  Creates a decision tree
                                                      │  classifier with entropy
dt_clf.fit(X_train, y_train)                          │  as the split criterion
```

The test accuracy is calculated as follows:

```
>>> from sklearn.metrics import accuracy_score
>>> y_pred_test = dt_clf.predict(X_test)
>>> acc = accuracy_score(y_test, y_pred_test)
>>> print('Test accuracy: {:.2f} %'.format(acc * 100))

Test accuracy: 71.05 %
```

Now let's create two more advanced decision tree–based models leveraging the technique of *ensemble learning*. As the proverb goes, two heads are better than one, and the idea of the wisdom of the crowd holds not only for humans but also for ML models in many cases. Ensemble learning is a process of aggregating multiple ML models to achieve better predictions. We'll look at the following two representative tree-based algorithms using ensemble learning, which are probably the most popular models in the Kaggle competitions:

- *Random forest*—This approach builds up multiple decision trees simultaneously and jointly considers their predictions by voting. We can select the number of trees to be assembled and control the hyperparameters for individual trees, such as the split criterion and the trees' maximum depth.
- *Gradient-boosted decision tree* (GBDT)—This approach builds up multiple trees sequentially and orients the newly constructed tree to address the erroneous classifications or weak predictions of the previous tree ensemble. We can control the number of trees to be assembled, the relative contribution of each tree to the final ensemble model (the learning_rate hyperparameter), and the hyperparameters for individual trees.

You can import both of the classifiers from the sklearn.ensemble module. The following listing shows how to apply them to the Titanic dataset.

Listing B.15 Applying random forest and GBDT algorithms to the Titanic dataset

```
from sklearn.ensemble import RandomForestClassifier,
    GradientBoostingClassifier

rf_clf = RandomForestClassifier(
    n_estimators=100, random_state=42)          Trains and tests
rf_clf.fit(X_train, y_train)                    the random forest
y_pred_test = rf_clf.predict(X_test)            algorithm
acc_rf = accuracy_score(y_test, y_pred_test)

gbdt_clf = GradientBoostingClassifier(n_estimators=100, random_state=42)
gbdt_clf.fit(X_train, y_train)
y_pred_test = gbdt_clf.predict(X_test)          Trains and tests the
acc_gbdt = accuracy_score(y_test, y_pred_test)  GBDT algorithm
```

The final performance shows that both models perform better than our previous decision tree model, which achieved an accuracy of 71.05%. The obtained GBDT model performs slightly better than the random forest model, as shown next:

```
>>> print(f'Random forest test accuracy: {acc_rf * 100:.2f} %')
>>> print(f'GBDT test accuracy: {acc_gbdt * 100:.2f} %')

Random forest test accuracy: 72.01 %
GBDT test accuracy: 72.97 %
```

We can also tune the hyperparameters for each of the three algorithms using grid search, similar to the previous examples. That exercise is left to the reader as a self-test.

index

Numerics

20 newsgroups dataset 83–85

A

accuracy measurement 8
acquisition function,
    designing 201–204
  design criteria of acquisition
    function 201
  expected improvement
    203–204
  probability of improvement
    202–203
  upper confidence bound 202
activation operation 46
adam optimizer 58
ak.ClassificationHead()
    function 91, 93
ak.ImageInput() function
    91–92
ak.RegressionHead()
    function 93
ak.TextInput() function 93
alpha parameter 200
annotations (targets) 19
ANNs (artificial neural
    networks) 42
applications of AutoML
    252–253
as_frame option 295
autoencoders 147
AutoKeras 73–76, 253–255
AutoKeras IO API 91–93
autokeras package 273

automated activation function
    search 253
automated CTR (click-through
    rate) prediction 253
automated data
    preprocessing 101
automated deep learning 102
automated feature
    engineering 101, 252
automated generation of end-to-
    end ML solutions
  addressing tasks with multiple
    inputs or outputs
    91–96
    automated image classifica-
      tion with AutoKeras IO
      API 91–93
    automated multi-input
      learning 93–94
    automated multi-output
      learning 94–96
  AutoKeras 73–76
  automated image
    classification 76–82
    attacking problem with
      five lines of code
      76–80
    configuring tuning
      process 81–82
    handling different data
      formats 80
  end-to-end AutoML solutions
    for four supervised learn-
    ing problems 83–91
    multilabel image
      classification 89–91

    structured data classifica-
      tion with Titanic
      dataset 85–88
    structured data regression
      with California housing
      dataset 88–89
    text classification with 20
      newsgroups dataset
      83–85
automated generative adversar-
    ial networks 253
automated graph neural
    networks 253
automated hyperparameter
    tuning 100–101, 252
automated image classification
    76–82
  attacking problem with five
    lines of code 76–80
  configuring tuning
    process 81–82
  handling different data
    formats 80
automated loss function
    search 253
automated machine learning
    4–6
Automated Machine Learning
    (Hutter, Kotthoff,
    Vanschoren) 201
automated model selection 101
automated network
    compression 253
automated object detection 252
automated pipeline search 101,
    252

automated pipeline tuning
102
automated semantic
segmentation 252
automation 6
AutoML 12–16
applications of 252–253
full automation, whether
achieveable 15–16
key components of 12–14
process and its key components 250
taxonomy of 252
tools and platforms 259–262
automl environment 274, 277
AutoModel class 91
AutoModel object 91, 94, 140
AveRooms feature 26

B

backpropagation 50
Barry, Ronald 19
batch size 47
Bayesian optimization search
method, customizing
193–209
designing acquisition
function 201–204
design criteria of acquisition function 201
expected improvement
203–204
probability of improvement
202–203
upper confidence bound
202
resuming search process and
recovering search
method 208–209
sampling new hyperparame-
ters via acquisition
function 204–206
tuning GBDT model with
Bayesian optimization
method 206–208
updating surrogate function
based on historical model
evaluations 198–201
vectorizing hyperparameters
194–198
Bayes model, naive 292
best_candidate_trial parent
214
best_trial parent trial 216

bias addition operation 46
binary classification problem
278
binary_crossentropy
function 69
black-box functions 193
Block class 126
block_type hyperparameter
115
border effect 61
build function 126–129, 131,
135, 139–140, 143, 170, 174,
177
build_model function 144, 146,
152, 175, 183

C

California housing price prediction with multilayer
perceptron 43–55
assembling and preparing
data 44–45
building up multilayer
perceptron 45–48
training and testing the neural
network 49–52
tuning number of epochs
52–55
call function 148, 152
challenges and future of
AutoML 262–264
democratization and productionization 264
generalizability and transferability 264
interpretability and transparency 263
measuring performance of
AutoML 262–263
reproducibility and robustness
263
resource complexity 263
Chollet, François 6, 74, 79, 113,
274, 285
classification. See image classification, tabular classification, text classification
classification problem 20
CNNs (convolutional neural
networks),
classifying handwritten digits with 55–64
addressing problem with
CNN 59–64

addressing problem with
MLP 57–58
assembling and preparing
dataset 55–56
coefficient 29
commercial AutoML
platforms 261–262
compile method 50
_compute_values_hash
function 216
conditional_choice
hyperparameter 218
conditional hyperparameter
135
confusion matrix 285
Conv2D layer 61
convolutional blocks 109
convolutional layer 59
core function 171–172
CountVectorizer class 289
create model 183
create_trial function 191
crossover 210
cross-validation 34
current hyperparameter value
container 128

D

data augmentation
methods 117
data collection 18, 251
data inputs component 7
data modalities 91
data parallelism 236–237, 258
data preprocessing 18, 251
*Data Science from Scratch 2nd Edi-
tion* (Grus) 45
data transformation 7
deactivate command 275
decision tree model 29
deck feature 86
decoder 147
deep learning
California housing price prediction with multilayer
perceptron 43–55
assembling and preparing
data 44–45
building up multilayer
perceptron 45–48
training and testing the
neural network 49–52
tuning number of
epochs 52–55

deep learning (continued)
  classifying handwritten digits
    with convolutional neu-
    ral networks 55–64
  addressing problem with
    CNN 59–64
  addressing problem with
    MLP 57–58
  assembling and preparing
    dataset 55–56
  IMDB review classification
    with recurrent neural
    networks 64–69
  building up the RNN
    67–69
  preparing the data 65–67
  training and validating the
    RNN 69
  Keras 43
  overview 42–43
  TensorFlow 43
Deep Learning with Python, 2nd
  edition (Chollet) 6, 74, 79,
  113, 274, 285
DeepTuner 174, 177
democratization 264
dense layers 46, 57
DenseNet
  selecting among different
    DenseNet models
    133–135
  selecting between ResNet
    and 135–137
depth, of deep learning
  models 42
descendant hyperparameters
  216
dimensionality reduction 147
dropout layer 79

E

EDA (exploratory data
  analysis) 22, 279
embarked feature 297–298,
  300
Embedding layer 66
embedding vector 66
encode function 150
encoder 147
end_order attribute 192
end-to-end ML solutions, automated generation of
  addressing tasks with multiple
    inputs or outputs 91–96

automated image classification with AutoKeras IO
  API 91–93
automated multi-input
  learning 93–94
automated multi-output
  learning 94–96
AutoKeras 73–76
automated image classification 76–82
attacking problem with five
  lines of code 76–80
configuring tuning
  process 81–82
handling different data
  formats 80
end-to-end AutoML solutions
  for four supervised learning problems 83–91
multilabel image classification 89–91
structured data classification with Titanic
  dataset 85–88
structured data regression
  with California housing
  dataset 88–89
text classification with 20
  newsgroups dataset
  83–85
end-to-end pipeline of ML project
  assembling dataset 19–22
  data preprocessing 22–25
  feature engineering 25–27
  framing problem 19–22
  grid search 34–39
  ML algorithm selection
    28–33
  building decision tree
    model 31–33
  building linear regression
    model 29–31
  overview 18–19
ensemble learning 302
ensemble models 301
entropy 301
environment for running code,
  setting up
  Google Colaboratory
    267–273
  notebook operations
    269–271
  packages and hardware
    configuration 271–273

Jupyter Notebook environ-
  ment, setting up on local
  Ubuntu system 273–277
  creating Python 3 virtual
    environment 274–275
  installing Python
    packages 275
  setting up IPython
    kernel 275
  working on Jupyter
    notebooks 275–277
evaluate function 174
evaluate method 77, 87
evolutionary search method,
  customizing 210–221
  aging evolutionary search
    method 212–215
  evaluating aging evolutionary
    search method 219–221
  implementing simple muta-
    tion operation 215–219
  selection strategies in evolu-
    tionary search
    method 210–212
  proportional selection 211
  ranking selection 211–212
  tournament selection 212
exhaustive cross-validation
  methods 34
exploitation 201, 257
exploration 201, 257
exploratory data analysis
  (EDA) 22, 279
exponential kernel (RBF
  kernal) 199
export_model method 85
Exp-Sine-Squared kernel 199

F

fare feature 297
Fashion MNIST dataset 148
feature engineering 25–27, 251
feature generation 25, 159
feature map 60
feature selection 25, 159
feature-wise normalization 44
fetch_20newsgroups data
  loader 288
fidelity-based techniques 259
filters 60
fit function 141, 162–163, 174,
  200
Flatten layer 57, 59
forward pass 48

fully connected layers 46
future of AutoML. *See* challenges and future of AutoML

G

Gaussian Processes for Machine Learning (Rasmussen/ Williams) 200
gaussian_process module 200
GBDT (gradient-boosted decision tree) model 170, 192, 302
gender feature 296
generalizability 264
generalization 6–7
get_file(…) function 86
get_hp_bounds function 204
get_state function 208
global optimum point 49
Google Colaboratory 267–273
notebook operations 269–271
packages and hardware configuration 271–273
gradient-based methods 258
gradient-boosted decision tree (GBDT) model 170, 192, 206–208, 302
gradient vanishing 112
graph-structured AutoML pipelines, designing 121–125
grid search 34–39, 293–294
GridSearchCV 36, 154, 294
Grus, Joel 45

H

handwritten digits, classifying with convolutional neural networks 55–64
addressing problem with CNN 59–64
addressing problem with MLP 57–58
assembling and preparing dataset 55–56
hard margin 283
Harrington, Peter 6
heuristic methods 189
hidden layers 46
history-dependent sequential search methods 188
history-independent sequential search methods 187
holdout method 35

hp (hyperparameters) module 108
hp.Choice function 127–129, 134–135, 143
hp.conditional_scope method 135
hp container 127–128, 131, 135, 140, 151, 153, 170, 183
hp.Int method 129
hps.values container 197
Hudgeon, Doug 18
Hutter, Frank 201
Hyperband, model scheduling with 241–244
hyperblocks, automated pipeline search with 111–121
automated model selection for image classification 112–117
automated selection of image preprocessing methods 117–121
HyperModel class 144, 171
HyperModel.fit() function 144, 146
Hyperopt 183
hyperparameters
tuning 9–11
vectorizing 194–198
hyperparameter sampling 188
hyperparameters module 139
hyperparameter tuning 18, 251

I

image classification 278–288
automated 76–82
attacking problem with five lines of code 76–80
configuring tuning process 81–82
handling different data formats 80
automated model selection for 112–117
joint model selection and hyperparameter tuning for image classification 115–117
ResNet 112–113
Xception 113–115
building data-processing pipeline with PCA and SVM 286

classification with support vector machine 283–285
exploring and preparing data 279–280
jointly tuning multiple components in pipeline 286–288
loading image-classification dataset 225–226
problem framing and data assembly 278–279
using principal component analysis to condense features 280–283
ImageClassifier object 77
ImageInput node 136
IMDB review classification with recurrent neural networks 64–69
building up RNNs 67–69
preparing the data 65–67
training and validating RNNs 69
imputation 24
init (initialization) function 148, 151–152, 171
initial population generation 210, 213
Input class 102
input node 102
intercept 29
interpretability 263
IPython kernel, setting up 275

J

Jupyter Notebook environment, setting up on local Ubuntu system 273–277
creating Python 3 virtual environment 274–275
installing Python packages 275
setting up IPython kernel 275
working on Jupyter notebooks 275–277
jupyter package 273

K

Keras 43
creating tuner for tuning Keras models 174–176
implementing autoencoder with 148–151

Keras Applications module 133
Keras library 43
KerasTuner 255–257
  tuning MLP for regression
      with 139–147
    jointly tuning optimization
        function 143–144
    tuning data preprocessing
        method 145–147
    tuning model-training
        process 144–145
keras_tuner.engine.hyperparam-
    eters.Choice class 128
keras_tuner.engine.hyperparam-
    eters module 127
kernel function 199, 283
kernel matrix 46
kernel parameter 284
kernel trick 283
k-fold cross-validation 35
KFold cross-validator 35
KFold module 156
Kotthoff, Lars 201

L

large-scale datasets,
      handling 224–234
  handling large datasets in
      general 231–234
  loading image-classification
      dataset 225–226
  loading text-classification
      dataset 229–231
  splitting loaded dataset
      226–229
latent_dim hyperparameter 149
layer.adapt function 145
layers 42
L-BFGS-B algorithm 204
learning algorithm
      component 7
Learning for Business
    (Hudgeon/Nichol) 18
learning rate 50
learning_rate hyperparameter
    302
leave-one-out cross-validation 35
LightGBM library 170
linear regression model 29
linear SVM (support vector
      machine) 283
load_digits function 154, 279
loaded dataset, splitting
      226–229

load function 171
load_model function 171–172,
    174, 177
local optimum point 49
logistic regression model, build-
    ing text classifier with 291
logits 57, 291
loss function (objective
    function) 8, 49

M

machine learning 6–12
  hyperparameter tuning 9–11
  obstacles to applying 11–12
  overview 6–7
  process of 7–9
Machine Learning in Action
    (Harrington) 6
Machine Learning Systems
    (Smith) 18
MAE (mean absolute error) 50,
    141
make_scorer function 36–37
Matérn kernel 199
max_depth
    hyperparameter 34–35
MaxPooling2D layers 63
max_words parameter 67
mean squared error (MSE) 29,
    50, 148
measuring performance 262–263
MedInc feature 26
metrics component 49
min-max rescaling method 56
ML algorithm selection 28–33
  building decision tree
      model 31–33
  building linear regression
      model 29–31
MLP (multilayer perceptron) 46
MLPs 57–58
  tuning with custom MLP
      block 125–132
    customizing block for tun-
        ing different types of
        hyperparameters
        129–130
    customizing block for tun-
        ing number of
        units 125–129
    using custom block to cre-
        ate AutoML pipeline
        131–132
MNIST dataset 55

model-based methods 189
Model class 148–149
model evaluation 18
model.fit() function 144
model monitoring 18, 251
model parallelism 237–238, 258
model.score function 172
model training 18
model_type hyperparameter
    135, 155
MSE (mean squared error) 29,
    50, 148
multiclass classification
    problem 278
multi-input learning, auto-
    mated 93–94
multilabel image classification
    89–91
multilayer perceptron, Califor-
    nia housing price predic-
    tion with 43–55
  assembling and preparing
      data 44–45
  building up multilayer
      perceptron 45–48
  training and testing the neural
      network 49–52
  tuning number of epochs
      52–55
multimodal learning 91
multi-output learning,
    automated 94–96
multitask learning 91
_mutate function 214
mutation 210, 213
mutual information 165

N

naive Bayes model, building text
    classifier with 292
name feature 298
NDCG (normalized discounted
    cumulative gain) 252
network block 103
neural architecture search 102
neural networks 42
neurons 46
ngrams 293
Nichol, Richard 18
nonexhaustive cross-validation
    methods 35
nonlinear SVM (support vector
    machine) 283
normalization layer 104

normalized discounted cumula-
    tive gain (NDCG) 252
norm.pdf function 203
notebooks 266
num_initial_points
    attribute 200
NumPy arrays (np.ndarray) 80
numpy library 271
numpy.ndarray object 270
numpy package 270

O

Objective class 82
objective function (loss
    function) 8, 49
one-hot encoding 300
one-shot methods 263
open source AutoML tools
    259–261
optimization method 8–9
optimize module 204
optimizer component 49
oracle 155
Oracle class 191, 195, 205, 208,
    216
Oracle object 190
oracle search method 171, 174
outliers 24
output head 103
output layer 46
overfitting 11
OvO (one-versus-one)
    scheme 284
OvR (one-versus-rest) 291

P

Pace, R. Kelley 19
padding 62
pandas library 271
parallel tuning 238–240, 258
parameters 7, 9
parent selection 210, 213
PCA (principal component
    analysis) 42, 281
pclass feature 297
pd.DataFrame DataFrame 80
Pearson's correlation
    coefficient 25
performance, measuring
    262–263
performance evaluation strategy
    component 14
pickle package 172

pipelines
    automated pipeline search
        with hyperblocks
        111–121
    automated model selection
        for image classification
        112–117
    automated selection of
        image preprocessing
        methods 117–121
    custom AutoML blocks,
        designing 125–137
    designing hyperblock for
        model selection
        132–137
    tuning MLPs with custom
        MLP block 125–132
    graph-structured, designing
        121–125
    sequential, creating for auto-
        mated hyperparameter
        tuning 102–111
    tuning CNNs for image
        classification 109–111
    tuning MLPs for structured
        data regression
        103–109
    sequential, working with
        100–102
platforms 261–262
pooling layer 59
populate_space function 190–
    191, 197, 200, 214, 257
population-based evolutionary
    search method 210
predict function 85, 87
prefetching 228–229
preprocessor block 102
pretrained models 259
pretrained weights 244–247,
    259
pretrained word embeddings
    66
principal component analysis
    (PCA) 42, 281, 286
principal components 281
probabilistic classification
    models 288
problem framing 18, 251
productionization 264
Python
    creating Python 3 virtual
        environment 274–275
    installing Python packages
        275

    loading dataset with Python
        generator 232–234
    setting up IPython kernel 275

R

random forest 302
RandomSearch 155, 169,
    174–175
random search method 189–193
random tuner 92
Rasmussen, Carl Edward 200
Ray Tune 183
read_csv(…) function 160
refit hyperparameter 294
regression problem 20
regularization 117
reinforcement learning 258
ReLU (rectified linear unit) 46
reproducibility 263
ResNet
    general discussion 112–113
    selecting between DenseNet
        and 135–137
resource complexity 263
results_summary function 105,
    142, 182
rmsprop optimizer 58
RNNs (recurrent neural net-
    works), IMDB review classi-
    fication with 64–69
    building up the RNN 67–69
    preparing the data 65–67
    training and validating the
        RNN 69
robustness 263
run_trial function 171–175,
    177–178, 183, 190, 256

S

save function 171
save_model function 171–172,
    174, 177
scaling up AutoML 258–259
    handling large-scale
        datasets 224–234
    handling large datasets in
        general 231–234
    loading image-classification
        dataset 225–226
    loading text-classification
        dataset 229–231
    splitting loaded
        dataset 226–229

scaling up AutoML *(continued)*
  parallelization on multiple
      GPUs 234–240
    data parallelism 236–237
    model parallelism 237–238
    parallel tuning 238–240
  search speedup
      strategies 240–248
    faster convergence with
        pretrained weights
        in search space
        244–247
    model scheduling with
        Hyperband 241–244
    warm-starting the search
        space 247–248
scikit-learn library 35, 44, 83, 89,
    154, 170, 200, 256, 260, 279,
    288
scikit-learn models 155, 170,
    172–174, 256
scikit-learn pipelines 174, 256,
    286, 293
scipy Python toolkit 204
search method, customizing
  Bayesian optimization search
      method, customizing
      193–209
    designing acquisition
        function 201–204
    resuming search process
        and recovering search
        method 208–209
    sampling new hyperparame-
        ters via acquisition
        function 204–206
    tuning GBDT model with
        Bayesian optimization
        method 206–208
    updating surrogate func-
        tion based on historical
        model evaluations
        198–201
    vectorizing hyperparame-
        ters 194–198
  evolutionary search method,
      customizing 210–221
    aging evolutionary search
        method 212–215
    evaluating aging evolution-
        ary search method
        219–221
    implementing simple
        mutation operation
        215–219

  selection strategies in evolu-
      tionary search method
      210–212
  random search method
      189–193
  sequential search methods
      188–189
search space, customizing. *See*
    pipelines
search space, fully customized
  controlling AutoML process
      by customizing tuners
      169–183
    creating tuner for tuning
        Keras models 174–176
    creating tuner for tuning
        scikit-learn models
        170–174
    hyperparameter tuning
        beyond Keras and scikit-
        learn models 179–183
    jointly tuning and selection
        among deep learning
        and shallow models
        176–179
  customizing search space in
      layerwise fashion
      139–151
    tuning autoencoder model
        for unsupervised
        learning 147–151
    tuning MLP for regression
        with KerasTuner
        139–147
  tuning autoencoder
      model 151–153
  tuning shallow models with
      different search
      methods 154–169
    automated feature
        engineering 159–169
    selecting and tuning shal-
        low models 154–157
    trying out different search
        methods 158–159
    tuning shallow model
        pipeline 157–158
search space component 13
search space container 128
search strategy component 14
search techniques 257–258
selection diversity 210
selection intensity 210
self.hypermodel attributes
    171

self.hyperparameters.space
    hyperparameter list 217
self.oracle attribute 171
self.trials attribute 195
self._vector_to_values
    function 205
separable convolutional
    layer 109
sequential AutoML pipelines
  creating for automated hyper-
      parameter tuning
      102–111
    tuning CNNs for image
        classification 109–111
    tuning MLPs for structured
        data regression 103–109
  working with 100–102
Sequential model 145
sequential search methods
    188–189
Series object 20
service deployment 18, 251
set_state function 208–209, 218
SGD (stochastic gradient
    descent) 49
sgd optimizer 58
shallow models, tuning with dif-
    ferent search methods
    154–169
  automated feature
      engineering 159–169
  selecting and tuning shallow
      models 154–157
  trying out different search
      methods 158–159
  tuning shallow model
      pipeline 157–158
ShallowTuner tuner 170, 177
SimpleRNN class 68
skip connection 112
sklearn.ensemble module 302
Sklearn tuner 170, 256
Smith, Jeff 18
soft margin 283
softmax function 57
softmax layer 57
Sparse Spatial Autoregressions
    (Pace/Barry) 19
state vector 67
step value 128
stop criterion 8–9
stride 60
structured data 39
structured data classification,
    with Titanic dataset 85–88

StructuredDataClassifier
    object 86
structured data regression,
    with California housing
    dataset 88–89
summarize_search_space
    method 141
summary function 48, 142
supervised learning problem 19
support vectors 283
surrogate function (surrogate
    model) 194
survivor selection 210, 213
SVM, building data-processing
    pipeline with 286
symbolic AI 6

T

tabular classification 295–303
    building tree-based
        classifiers 301–303
    data preprocessing and feature
        engineering 296–301
    problem framing and data
        assembly 295–296
tabular data 39
targets (annotations) 19
taxonomy of AutoML 252
TensorFlow 43
tensorflow.keras.Model class 125
tensorflow.keras.Sequential
    class 125
tensor-matrix dot product 46
tensor processing units
    (TPUs) 43
test set 10
text classification 288–294
    building text classifier with
        logistic regression
        model 291

building text classifier with
    naive Bayes model 292
data preprocessing and fea-
    ture engineering
    289–291
loading dataset 229–231
problem framing and data
    assembly 288–289
tuning text-classification
    pipeline with grid
    search 293–294
with 20 newsgroups
    dataset 83–85
tf.data.Dataset TensorFlow
    Datasets 80
TF-IDF (Term Frequency-
    Inverse Document
    Frequency) 290
TfidfTransformer class 290
tf.keras.Model class 148
tf.keras.Model.fit model 141
tf.keras.Sequential object
    149
tf.nest.flatten flatten
    operation 127
ticket feature 300
Titanic dataset 85–88
title feature 300
tokenization 289
tools 259
TPUs (tensor processing
    units) 43
transferability 264
Transformer instance 165
transform function 162, 164
transparency 263
tree-based classifiers, building
    301–303
trial_id_to_type function 177
trial object 171–172, 190
Tuner class 170, 191

Tuner.run_trial() function
    170–171, 191
tuners 92, 140
Tuner.search() function 144,
    146

U

UCB (upper confidence
    bound) 202
units hyperparameter 126–128,
    140–141
unsupervised learning 147–151,
    282
update_trial() function 191

V

validation set 10
vanilla CNN 112
Vanschoren, Joaquin 201
_vectorize_trials method 195
vectorizing hyperparameters
    194–198

W

warm-starting search
    spaces 247–248
weights 29
Weka (Waikato Environment
    for Knowledge Analysis)
    package 259
white kernel 199
Williams, Christopher K. I.
    200
word embeddings 66, 290

X

Xception 113–115